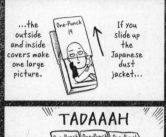

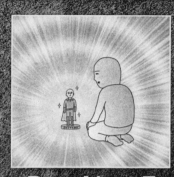

O N E

I'm glad Saitama got an action figure. Gazing at it soothes my soul.

—ONE

Manga creator ONE began *One-Punch Man* as a webcomic, which quickly went viral, garnering over 10 million hits. In addition to *One-Punch Man*, ONE writes and draws the series *Mob Psycho 100* and *Makai no Ossan*.

If you slide up the Japanese dust jacket...
...the outside and inside covers make one large picture.
One-Punch 19
TADAAAH
And three together make an even bigger picture!
One-Punch 19
One-Punch 20
One-Punch 21
Vol. 19
Vol. 20
Vol. 21

Y U S U K E M U R A T A

Starting with this volume, the Japanese covers are special, so be sure to check out each volume through volume 21!

—Yusuke Murata

A highly decorated and skilled artist best known for his work on *Eyeshield 21*, Yusuke Murata won the 122nd Hop Step Award (1995) for *Partner* and placed second in the 51st Akatsuka Award (1998) for *Samui Hanashi*.

ONE-PUNCH MAN 19

ONE + YUSUKE MURATA

★THE STORIES, CHARACTERS AND INCIDENTS MENTIONED IN THIS PUBLICATION ARE ENTIRELY FICTIONAL.

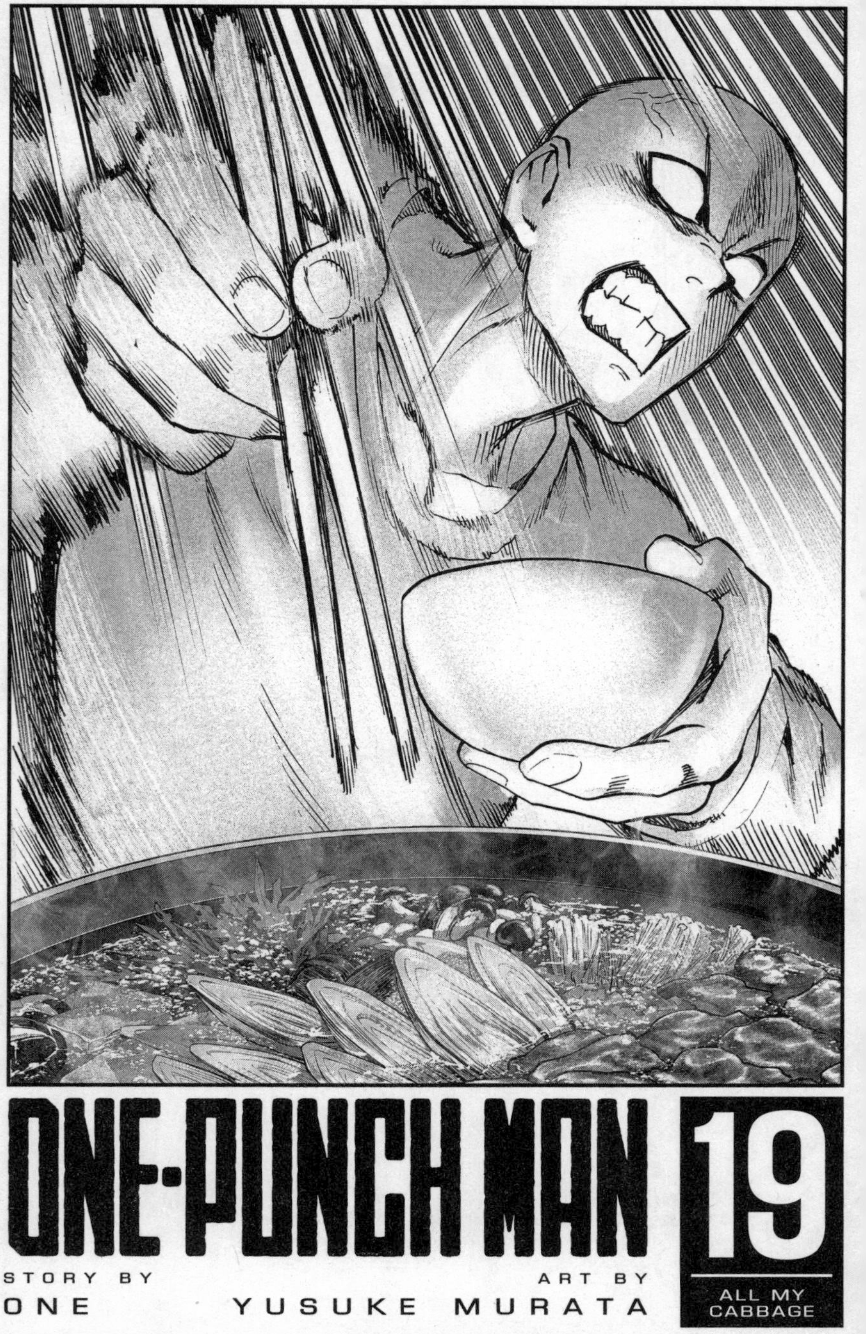

ONE-PUNCH MAN 19

ALL MY CABBAGE

STORY BY ONE
ART BY YUSUKE MURATA

CHARACTERS

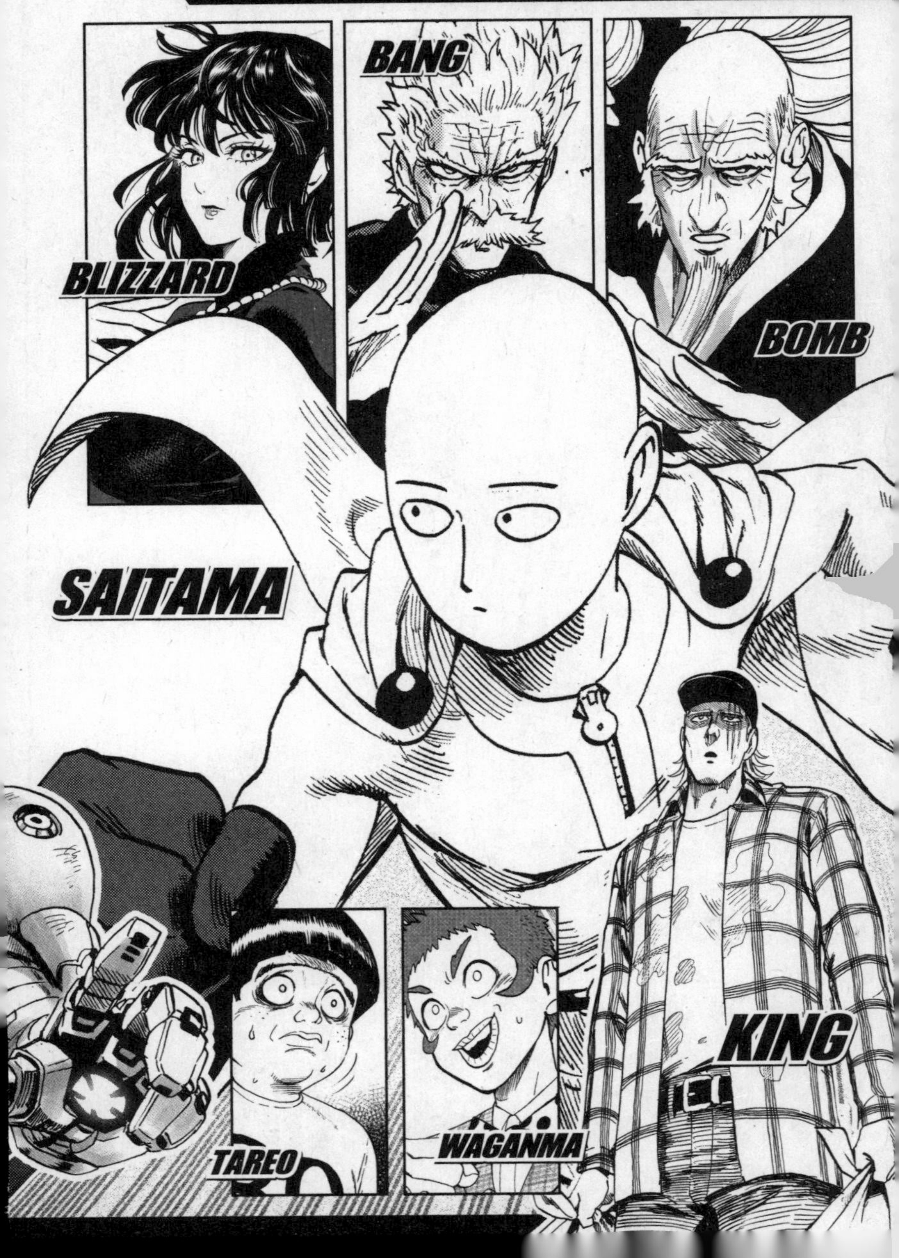
BANG
BLIZZARD
BOMB
SAITAMA
KING
WAGANMA
TAREO

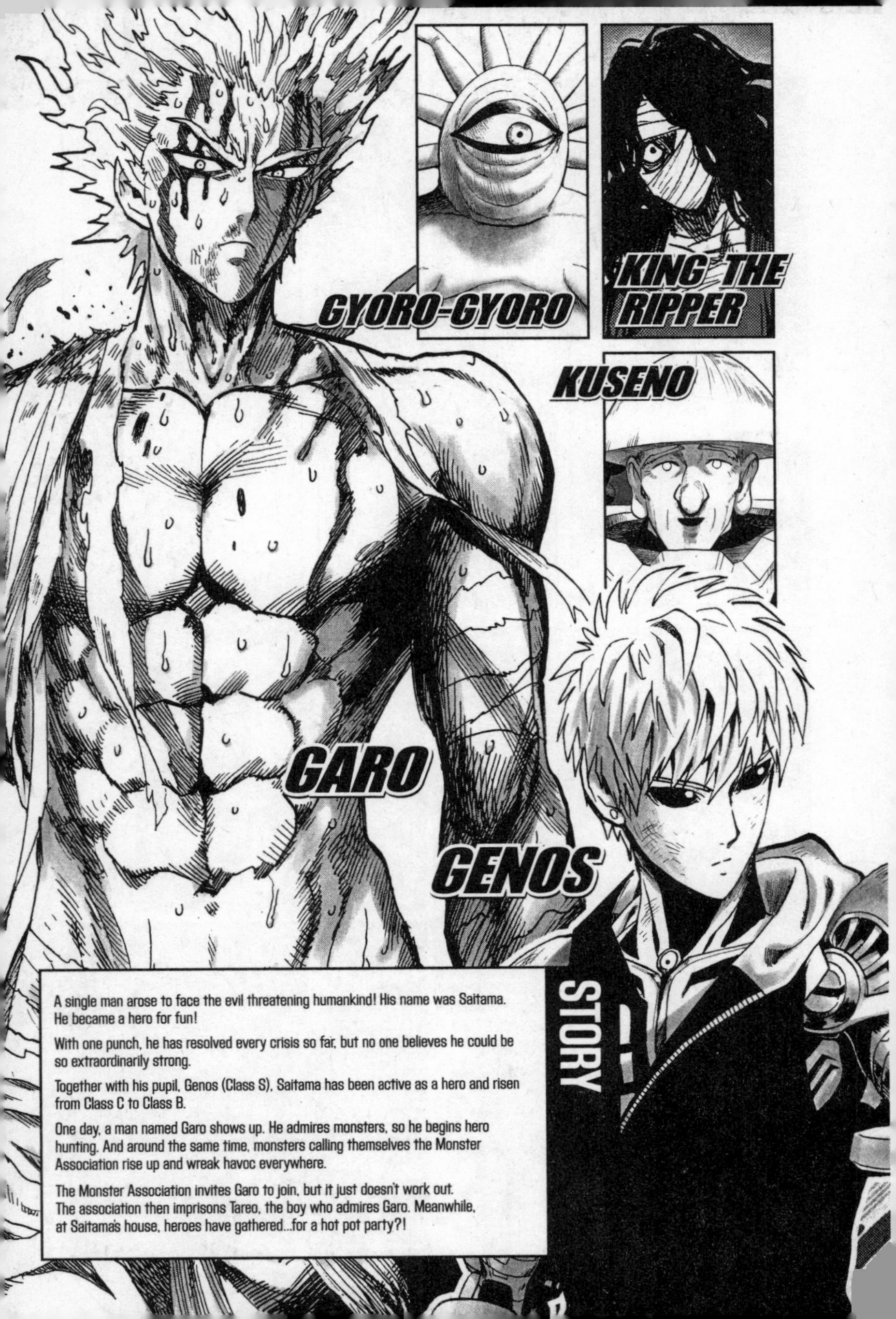
GYORO-GYORO
KING THE RIPPER
KUSENO
GARO
GENOS

STORY

A single man arose to face the evil threatening humankind! His name was Saitama. He became a hero for fun!

With one punch, he has resolved every crisis so far, but no one believes he could be so extraordinarily strong.

Together with his pupil, Genos (Class S), Saitama has been active as a hero and risen from Class C to Class B.

One day, a man named Garo shows up. He admires monsters, so he begins hero hunting. And around the same time, monsters calling themselves the Monster Association rise up and wreak havoc everywhere.

The Monster Association invites Garo to join, but it just doesn't work out. The association then imprisons Tareo, the boy who admires Garo. Meanwhile, at Saitama's house, heroes have gathered...for a hot pot party?!

SHWUF
GWUP
KACHAK

ONE-PUNCH MAN

19

[ALL MY CABBAGE]

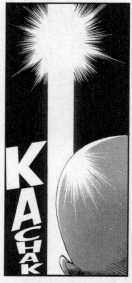

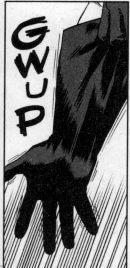

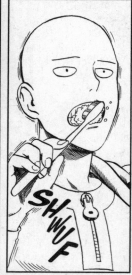

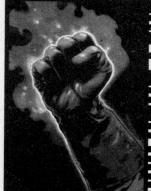

ONE-PUNCH MAN VOLUME NINETEEN

ONE + YUSUKE MURATA

My name is Saitama. I am a hero. My hobby is heroic exploits. I got too strong. And that makes me sad. I can defeat any enemy with one blow. I lost my hair. And I lost all feeling. I want to feel the rush of battle. I would like to meet an incredibly strong enemy. And I would like to defeat it with one blow. That's because I am One-Punch Man.

CONTENTS

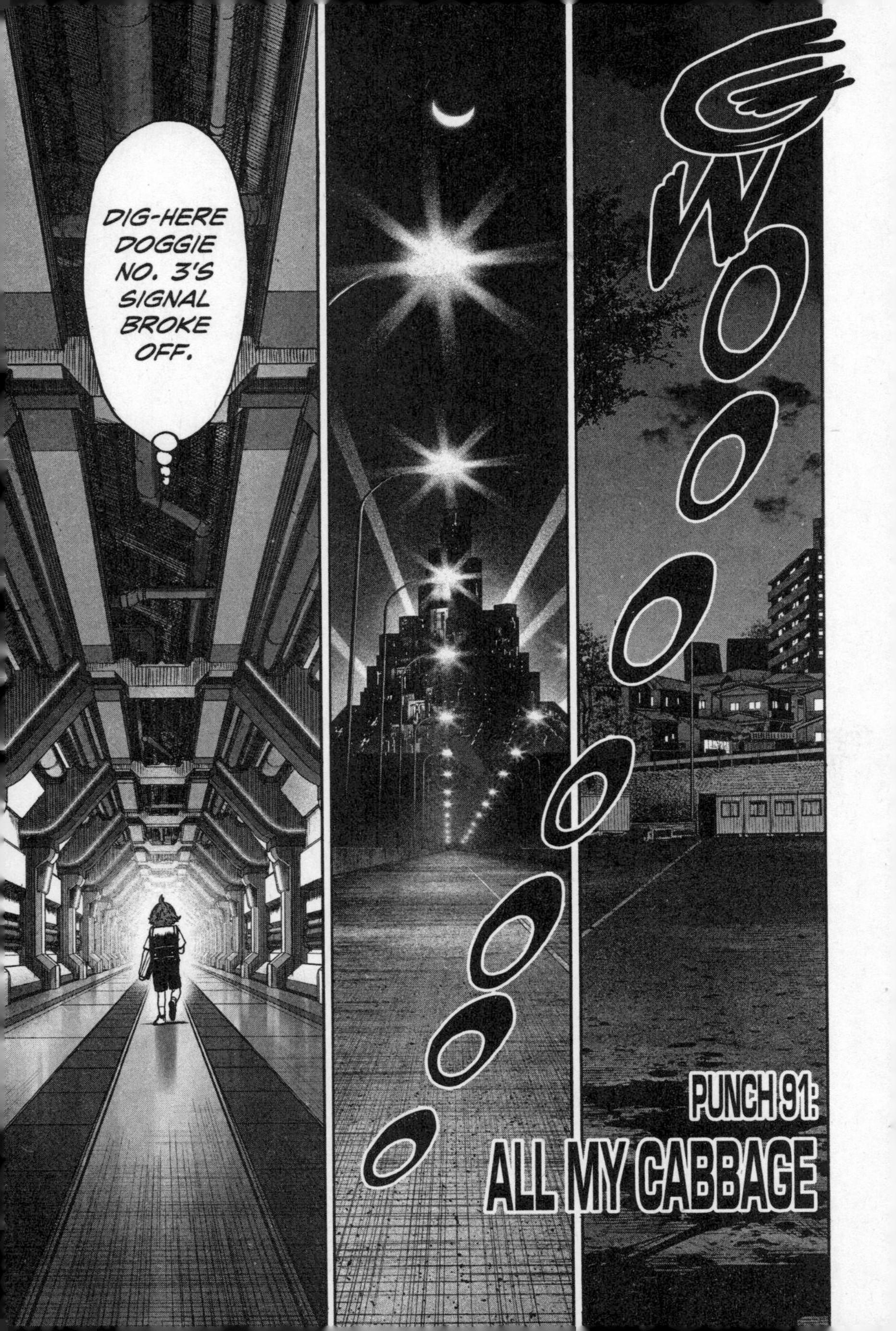
GWOOOO
PUNCH 91:
ALL MY CABBAGE
DIG-HERE DOGGIE NO. 3'S SIGNAL BROKE OFF.

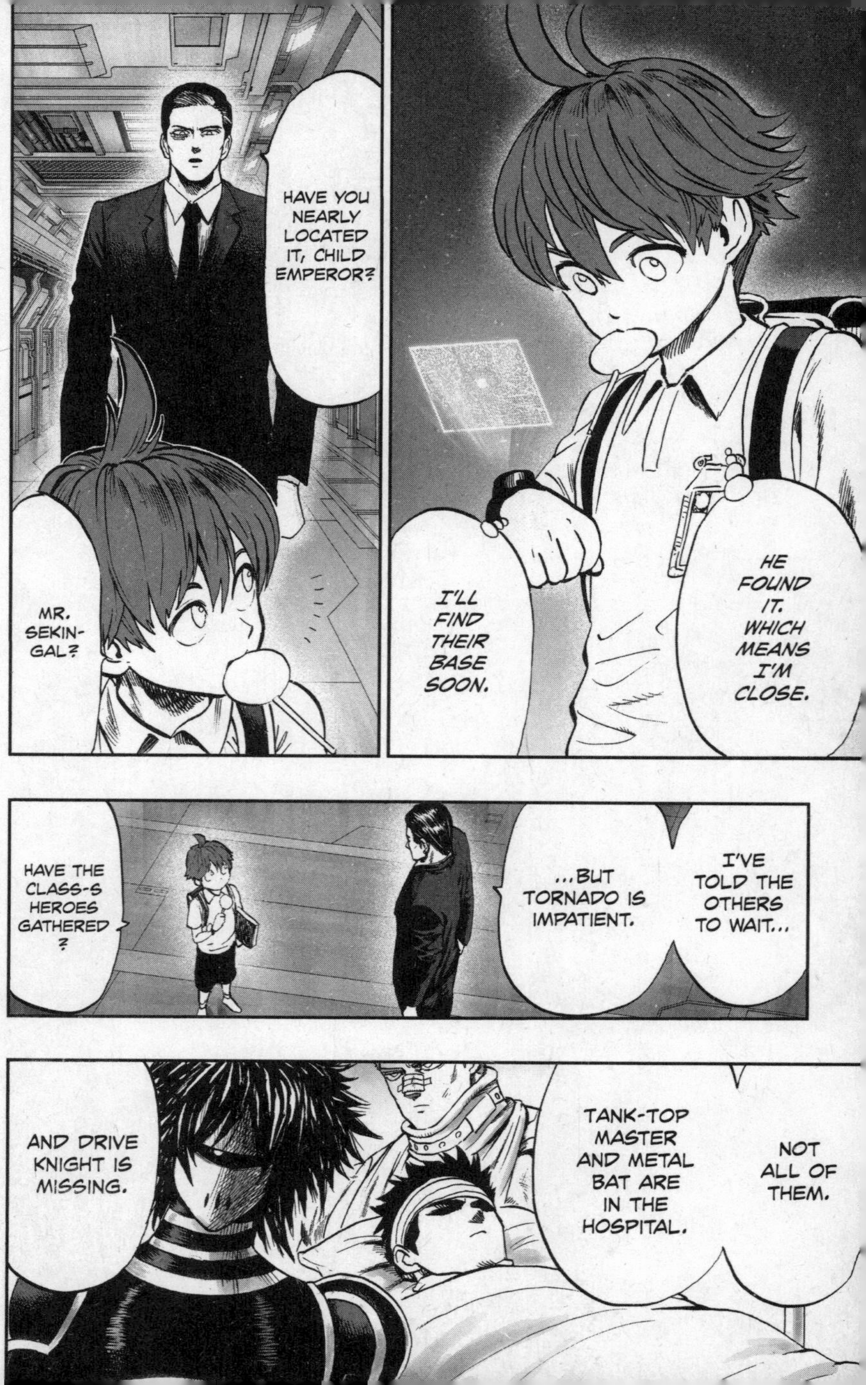

HE FOUND IT. WHICH MEANS I'M CLOSE.
I'LL FIND THEIR BASE SOON.
HAVE YOU NEARLY LOCATED IT, CHILD EMPEROR?
MR. SEKIN-GAL?
I'VE TOLD THE OTHERS TO WAIT...
...BUT TORNADO IS IMPATIENT.
HAVE THE CLASS-S HEROES GATHERED?
NOT ALL OF THEM.
TANK-TOP MASTER AND METAL BAT ARE IN THE HOSPITAL.
AND DRIVE KNIGHT IS MISSING.

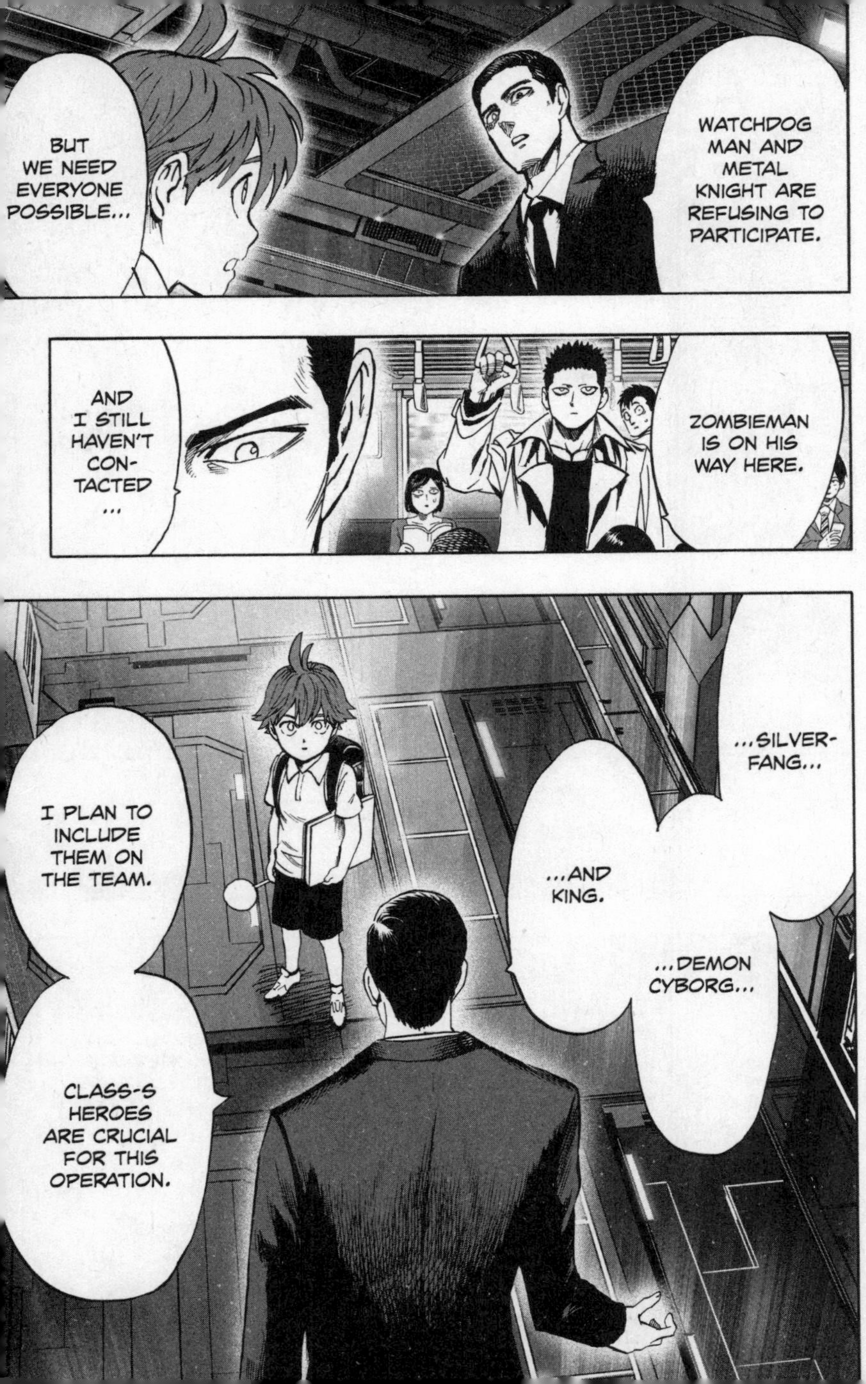
WATCHDOG MAN AND METAL KNIGHT ARE REFUSING TO PARTICIPATE.
BUT WE NEED EVERYONE POSSIBLE...
ZOMBIEMAN IS ON HIS WAY HERE.
AND I STILL HAVEN'T CON-TACTED ...
...SILVER-FANG...
...DEMON CYBORG...
...AND KING.
I PLAN TO INCLUDE THEM ON THE TEAM.
CLASS-S HEROES ARE CRUCIAL FOR THIS OPERATION.

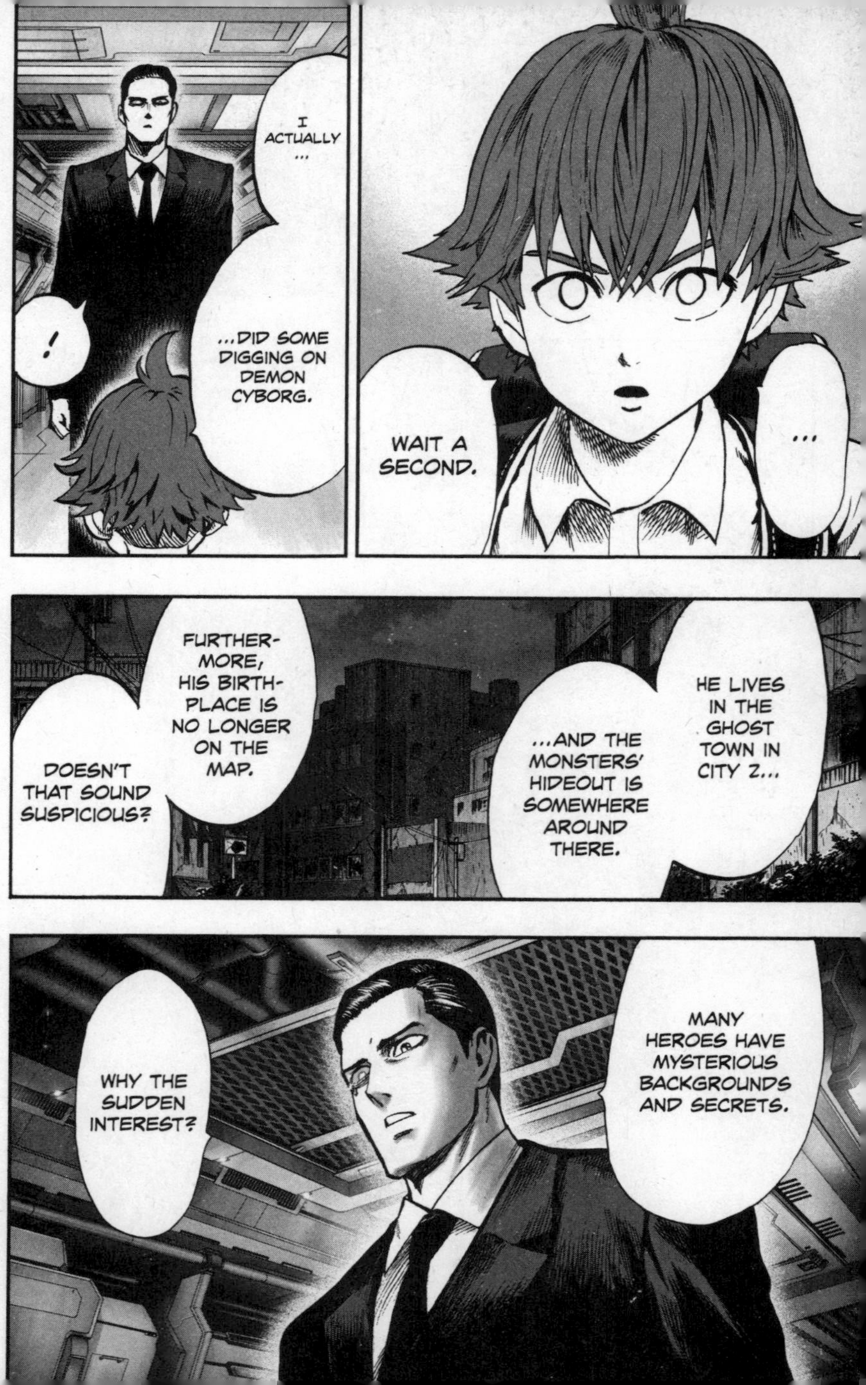
...
WAIT A SECOND.
I ACTUALLY ...
!
...DID SOME DIGGING ON DEMON CYBORG.
HE LIVES IN THE GHOST TOWN IN CITY Z...
...AND THE MONSTERS' HIDEOUT IS SOMEWHERE AROUND THERE.
FURTHER-MORE, HIS BIRTH-PLACE IS NO LONGER ON THE MAP.
DOESN'T THAT SOUND SUSPICIOUS?
MANY HEROES HAVE MYSTERIOUS BACKGROUNDS AND SECRETS.
WHY THE SUDDEN INTEREST?

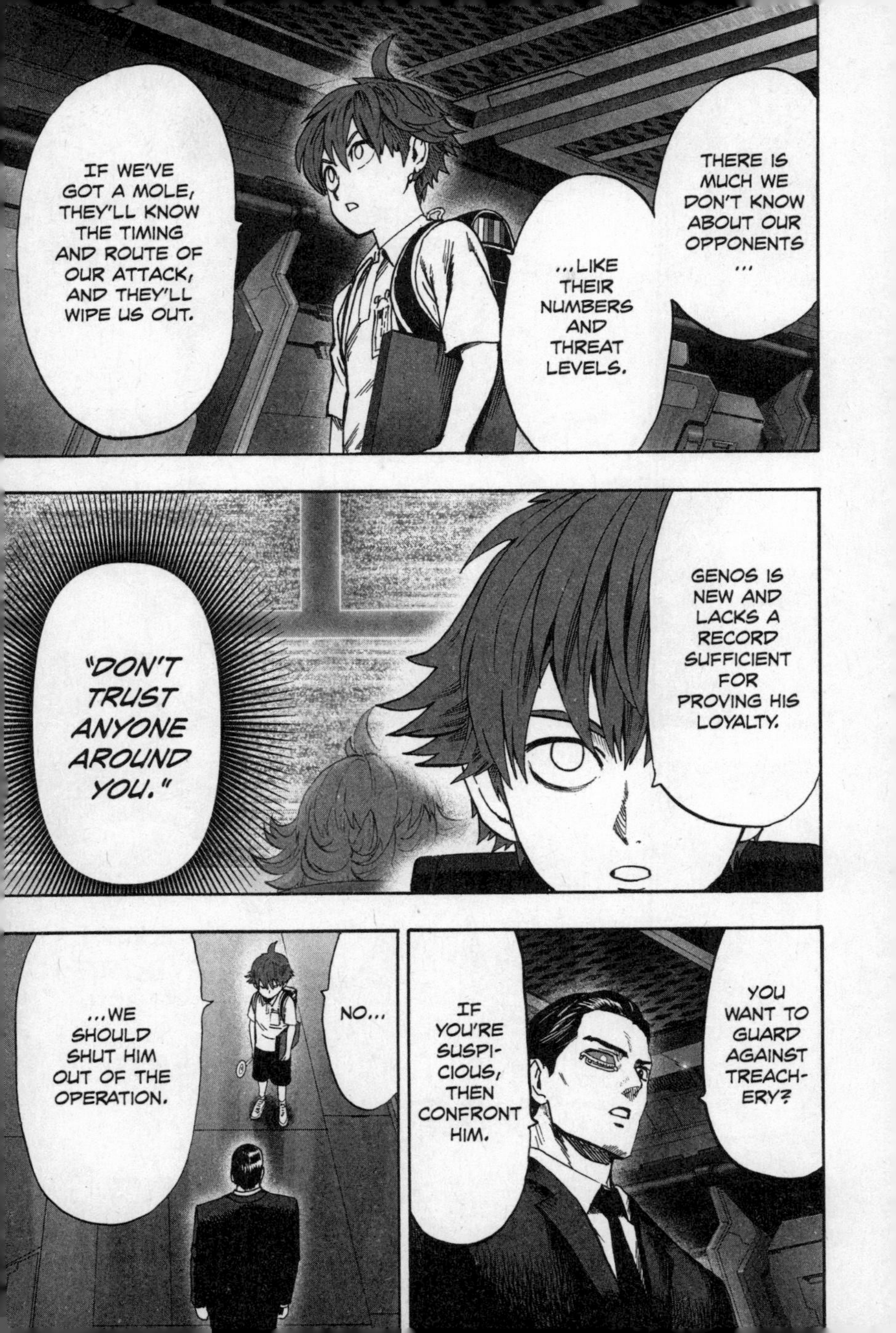
THERE IS MUCH WE DON'T KNOW ABOUT OUR OPPONENTS...
...LIKE THEIR NUMBERS AND THREAT LEVELS.
IF WE'VE GOT A MOLE, THEY'LL KNOW THE TIMING AND ROUTE OF OUR ATTACK, AND THEY'LL WIPE US OUT.
GENOS IS NEW AND LACKS A RECORD SUFFICIENT FOR PROVING HIS LOYALTY.
"DON'T TRUST ANYONE AROUND YOU."
YOU WANT TO GUARD AGAINST TREACH-ERY?
IF YOU'RE SUSPI-CIOUS, THEN CONFRONT HIM.
NO...
...WE SHOULD SHUT HIM OUT OF THE OPERATION.

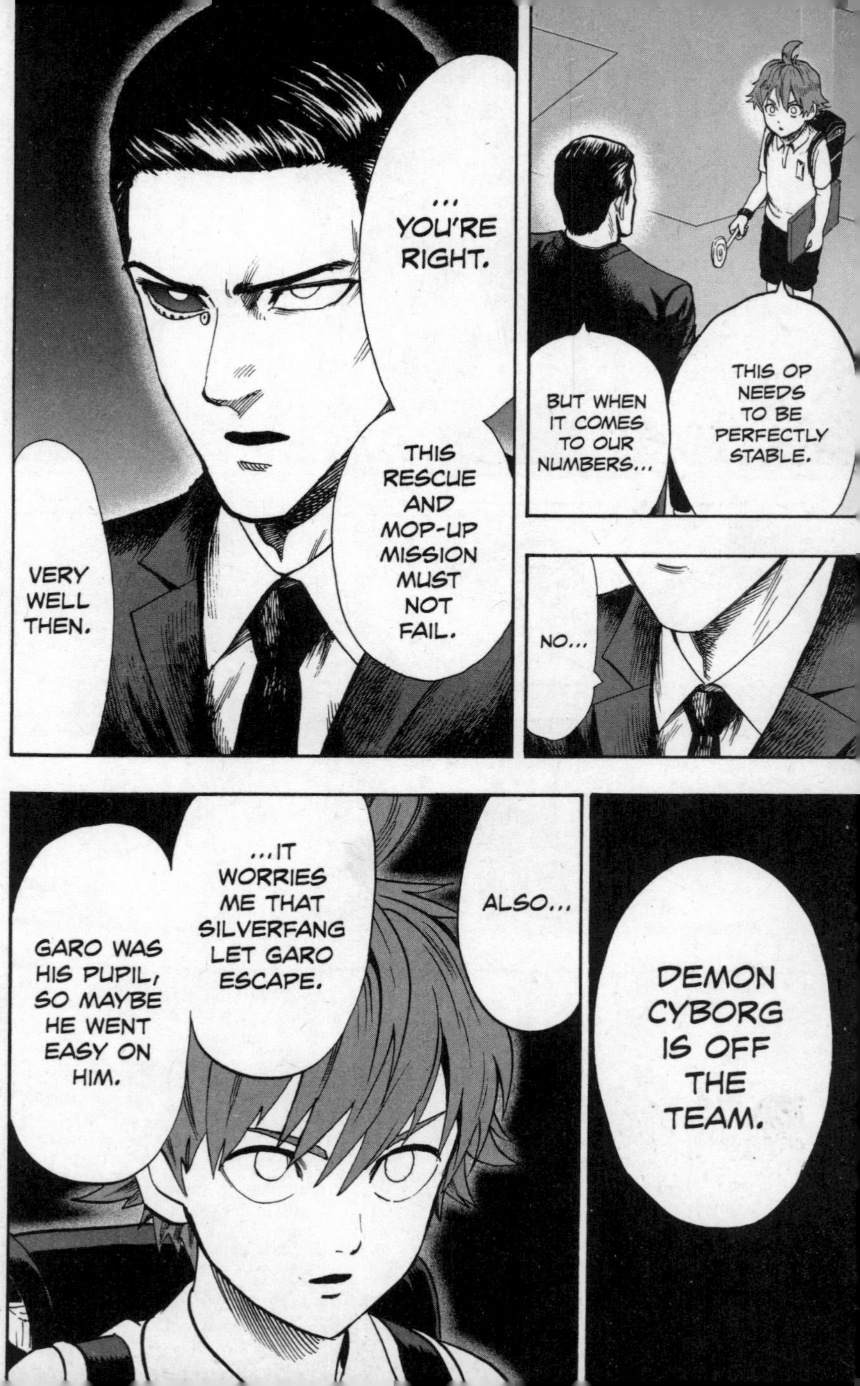
THIS OP NEEDS TO BE PERFECTLY STABLE.
BUT WHEN IT COMES TO OUR NUMBERS...
NO...
... YOU'RE RIGHT.
THIS RESCUE AND MOP-UP MISSION MUST NOT FAIL.
VERY WELL THEN.
DEMON CYBORG IS OFF THE TEAM.
ALSO...
...IT WORRIES ME THAT SILVERFANG LET GARO ESCAPE.
GARO WAS HIS PUPIL, SO MAYBE HE WENT EASY ON HIM.

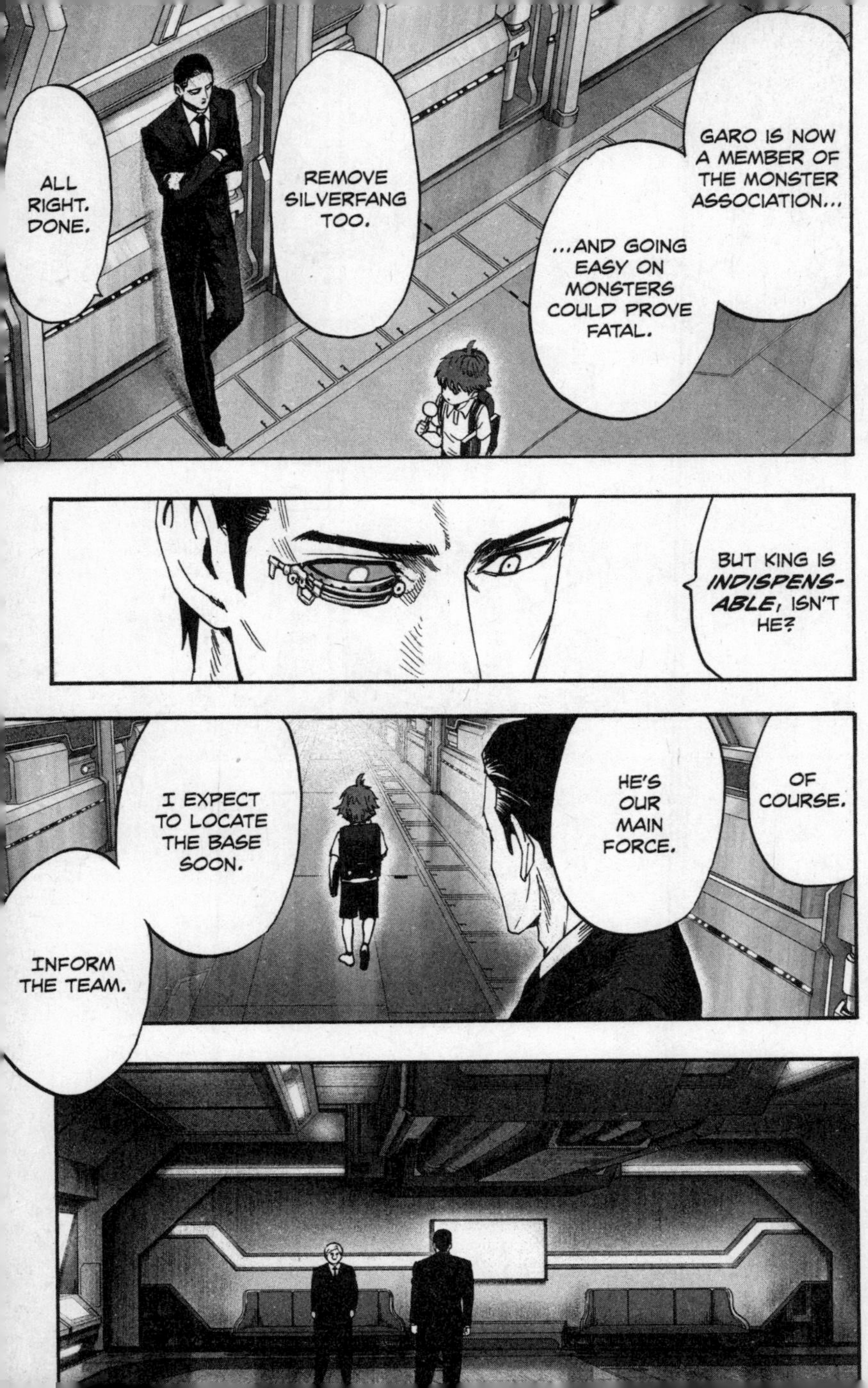
GARO IS NOW A MEMBER OF THE MONSTER ASSOCIATION...
...AND GOING EASY ON MONSTERS COULD PROVE FATAL.
REMOVE SILVERFANG TOO.
ALL RIGHT. DONE.
BUT KING IS *INDISPENSABLE*, ISN'T HE?
OF COURSE.
HE'S OUR MAIN FORCE.
I EXPECT TO LOCATE THE BASE SOON.
INFORM THE TEAM.

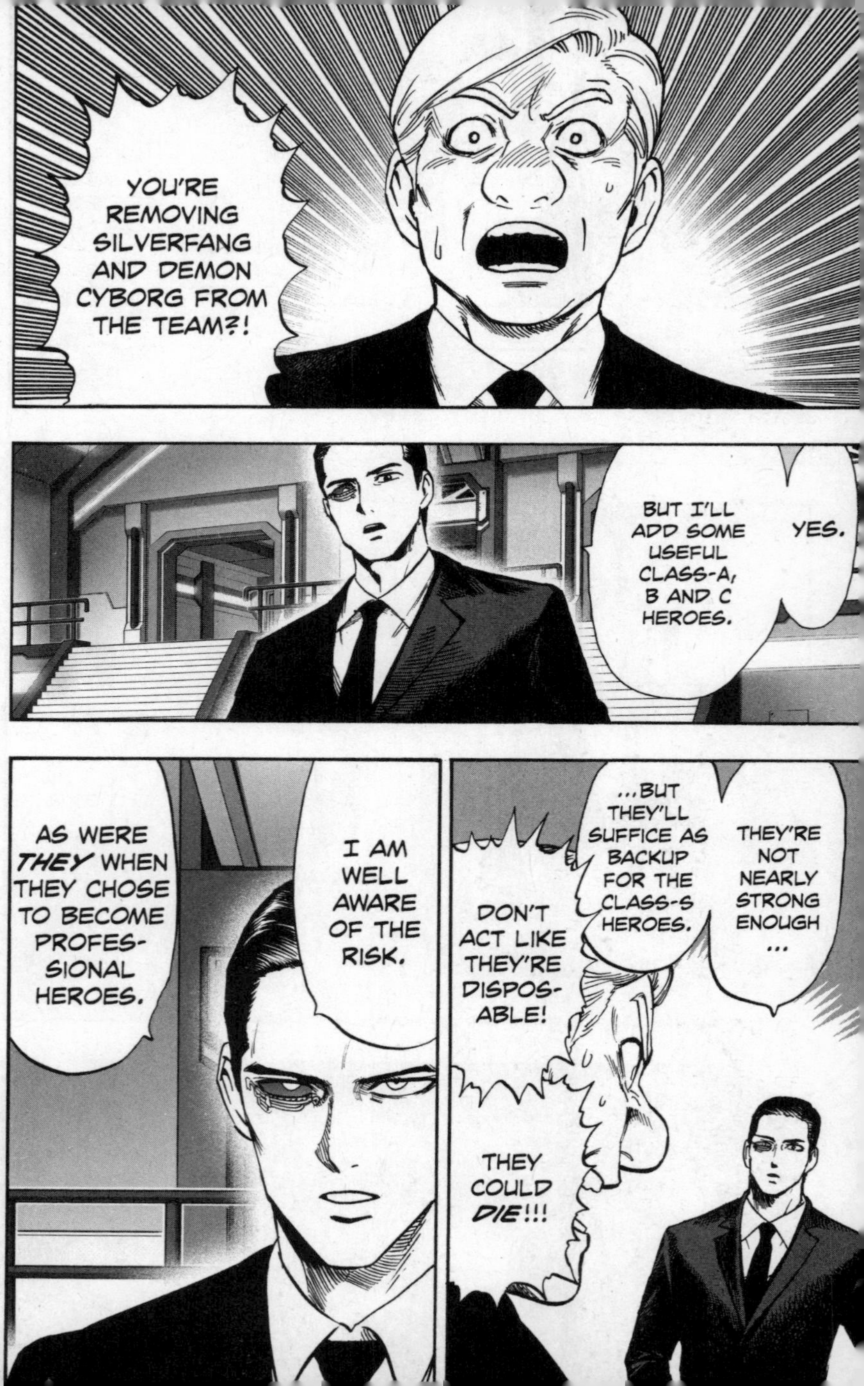

YOU'RE REMOVING SILVERFANG AND DEMON CYBORG FROM THE TEAM?!
YES.
BUT I'LL ADD SOME USEFUL CLASS-A, B AND C HEROES.
THEY'RE NOT NEARLY STRONG ENOUGH...
...BUT THEY'LL SUFFICE AS BACKUP FOR THE CLASS-S HEROES.
DON'T ACT LIKE THEY'RE DISPOSABLE!
THEY COULD *DIE*!!!
I AM WELL AWARE OF THE RISK.
AS WERE *THEY* WHEN THEY CHOSE TO BECOME PROFES-SIONAL HEROES.

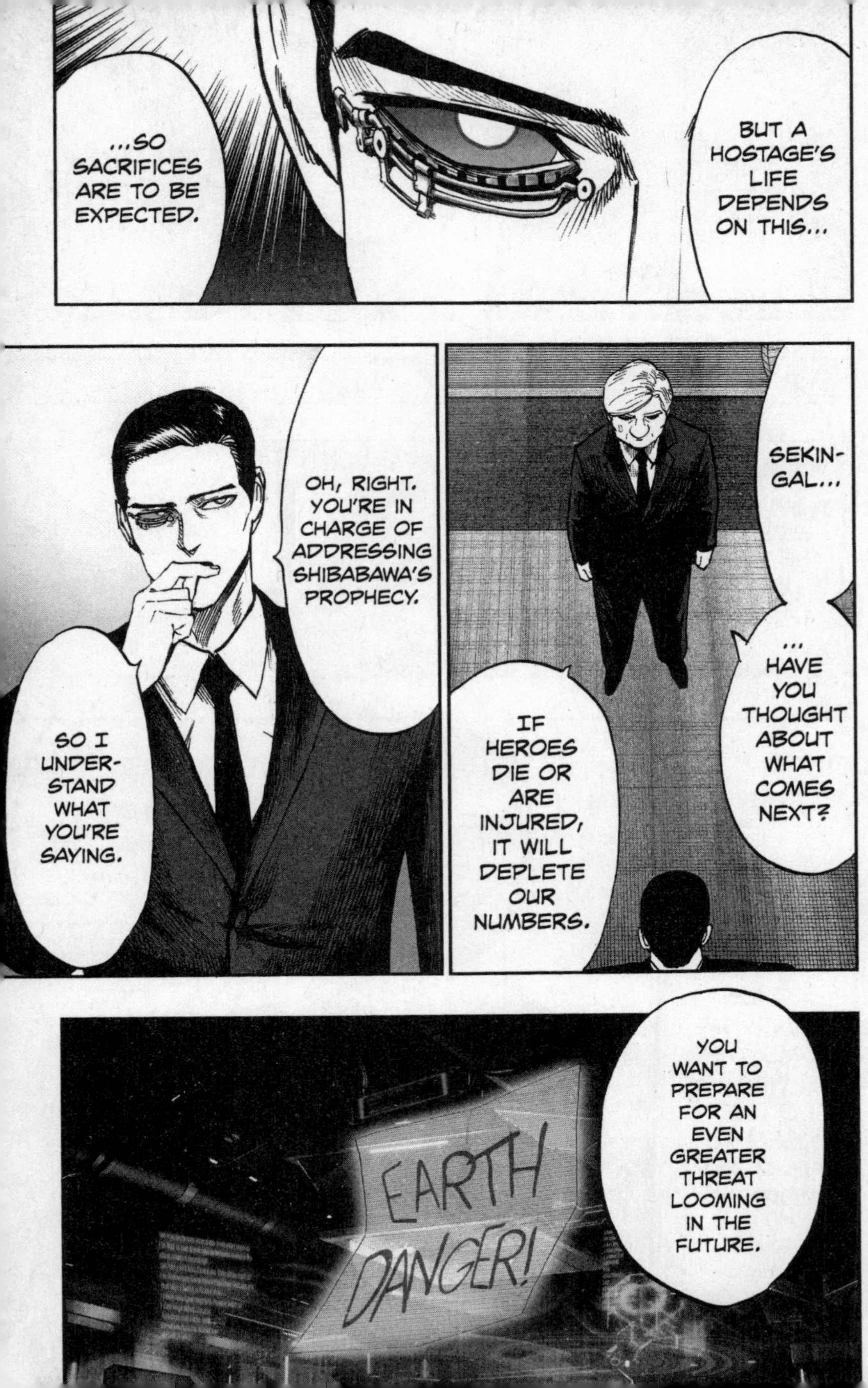
BUT A HOSTAGE'S LIFE DEPENDS ON THIS...
...SO SACRIFICES ARE TO BE EXPECTED.
SEKINGAL...
...HAVE YOU THOUGHT ABOUT WHAT COMES NEXT?
IF HEROES DIE OR ARE INJURED, IT WILL DEPLETE OUR NUMBERS.
OH, RIGHT. YOU'RE IN CHARGE OF ADDRESSING SHIBABAWA'S PROPHECY.
SO I UNDERSTAND WHAT YOU'RE SAYING.
YOU WANT TO PREPARE FOR AN EVEN GREATER THREAT LOOMING IN THE FUTURE.
EARTH DANGER!

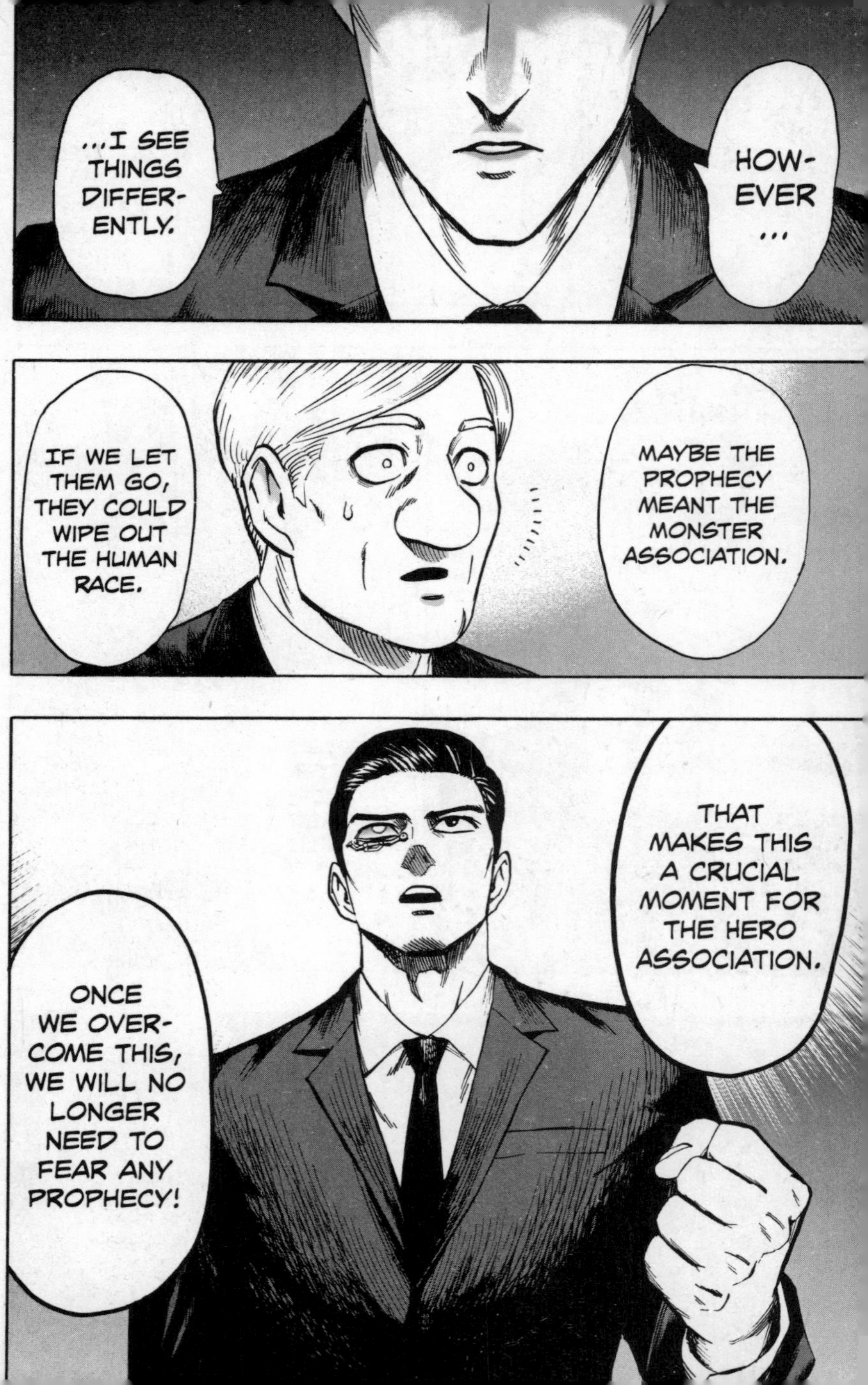
HOW-EVER ...
...I SEE THINGS DIFFER-ENTLY.
MAYBE THE PROPHECY MEANT THE MONSTER ASSOCIATION.
IF WE LET THEM GO, THEY COULD WIPE OUT THE HUMAN RACE.
THAT MAKES THIS A CRUCIAL MOMENT FOR THE HERO ASSOCIATION.
ONCE WE OVER-COME THIS, WE WILL NO LONGER NEED TO FEAR ANY PROPHECY!

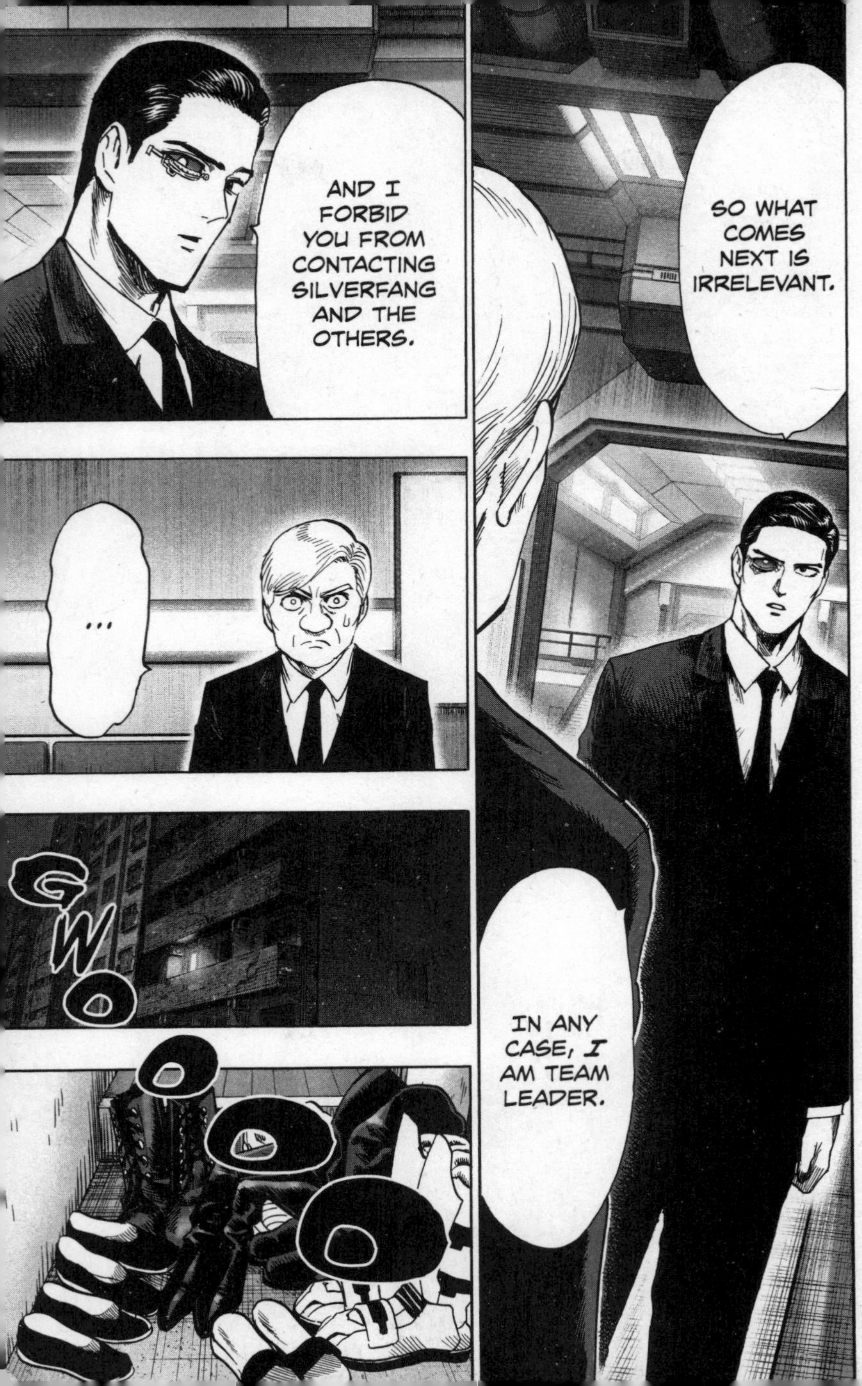
SO WHAT COMES NEXT IS IRRELEVANT.
IN ANY CASE, I AM TEAM LEADER.
AND I FORBID YOU FROM CONTACTING SILVERFANG AND THE OTHERS.
...
GWO
OOO

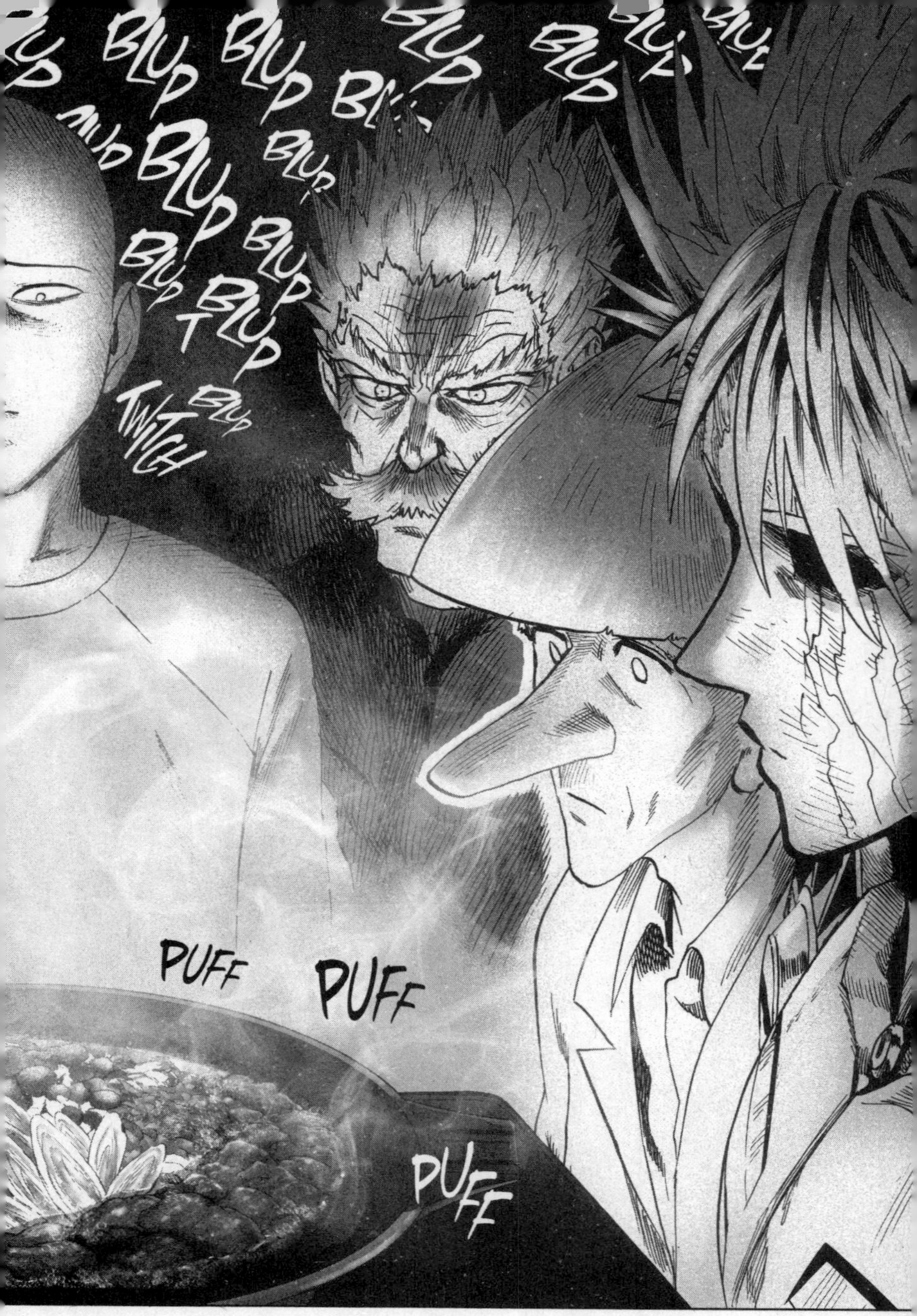
BLUP
BLUP
BLUP
BLUP
BLUP
BLUP
BLUP
BLUP
BLUP
BLUP
BLUP
BLUP
BLUP
BLUP
TWITCH
PUFF
PUFF
PUFF

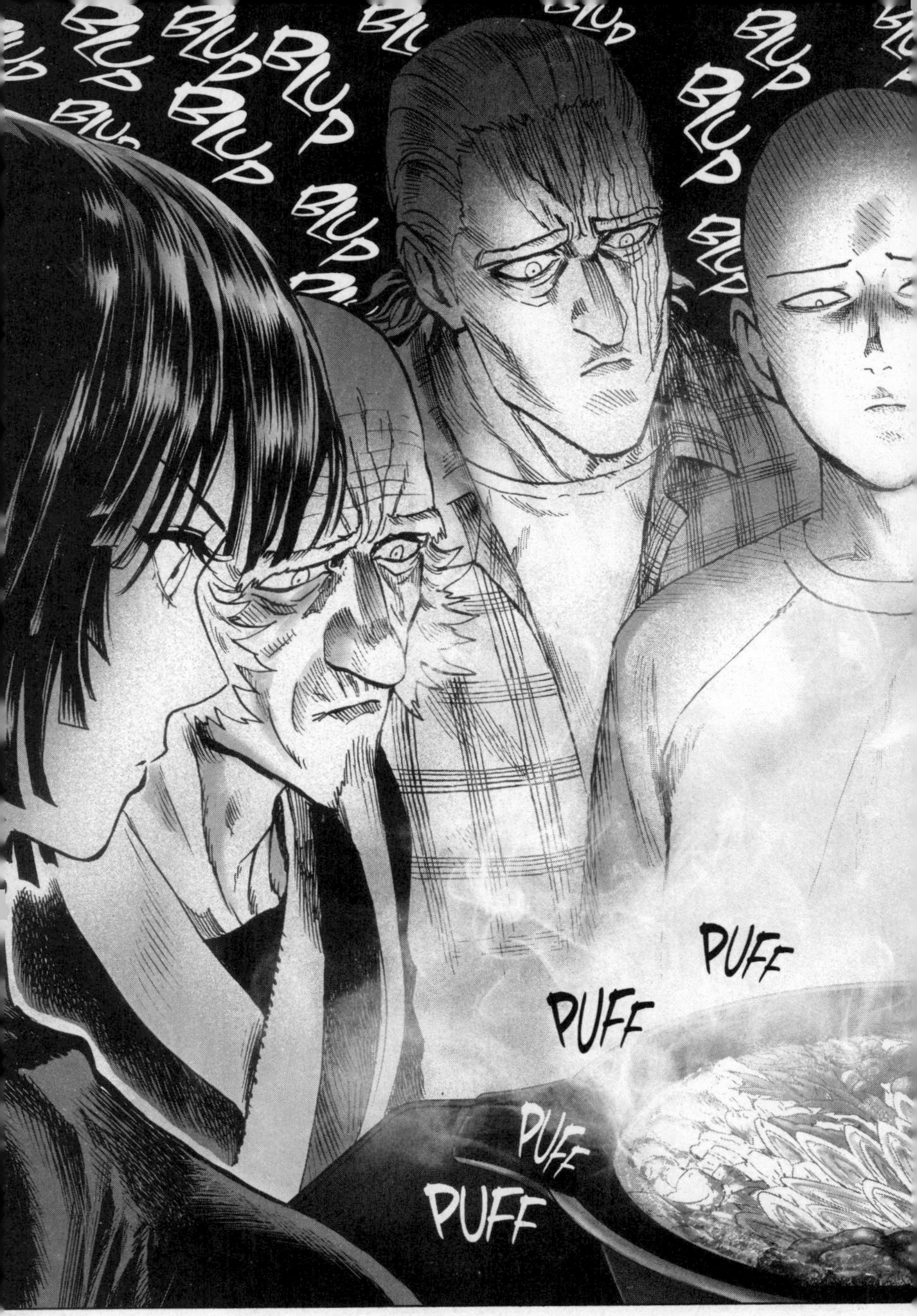
BLUP BLUP
BLUP BLUP
BLUP BLUP
BLUP BLUP
BLUP
PUFF
PUFF
PUFF
PUFF

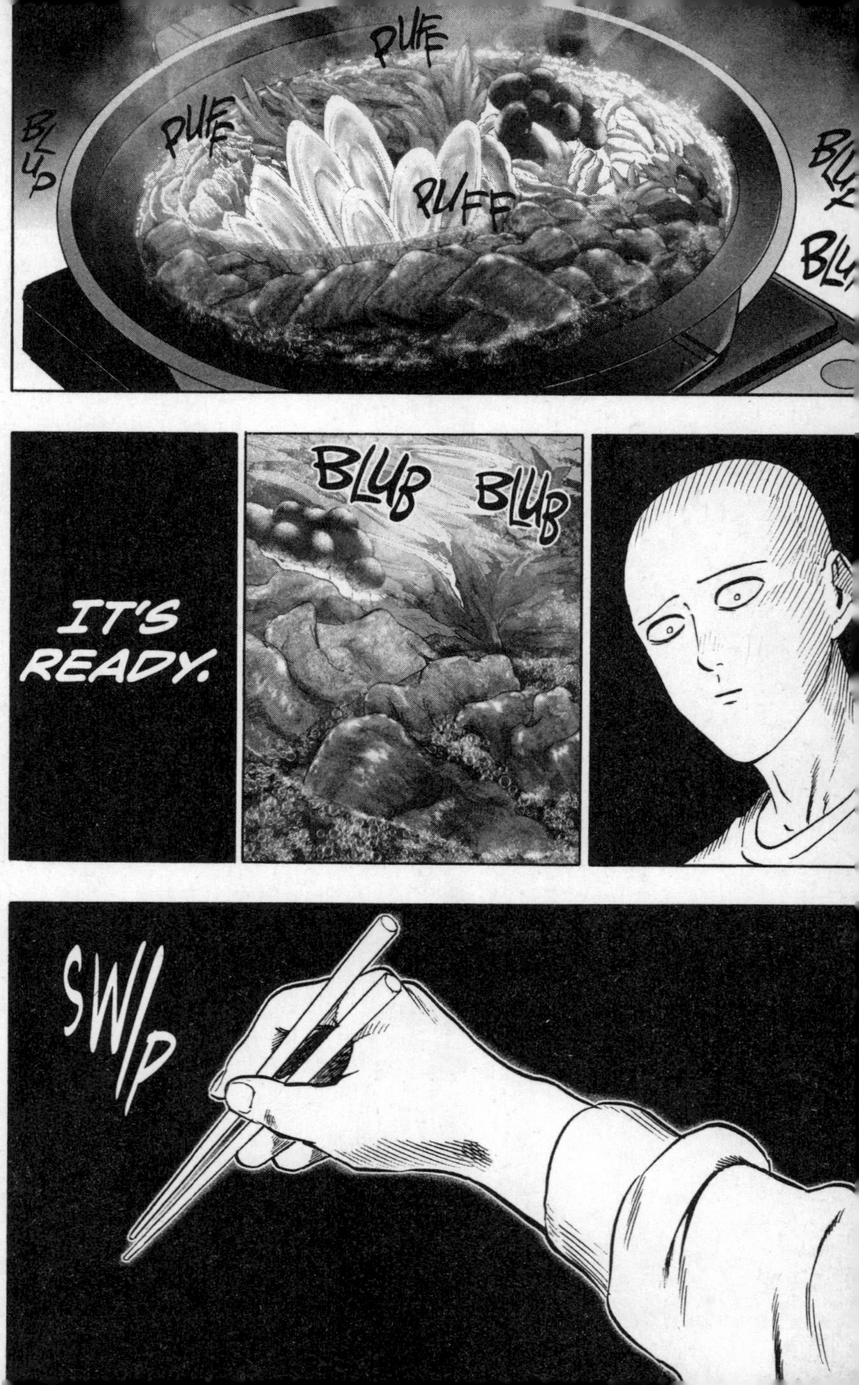
PUFF
PUFF
PUFF
BLUP
BLUB
BLUB
IT'S READY.
SWIP

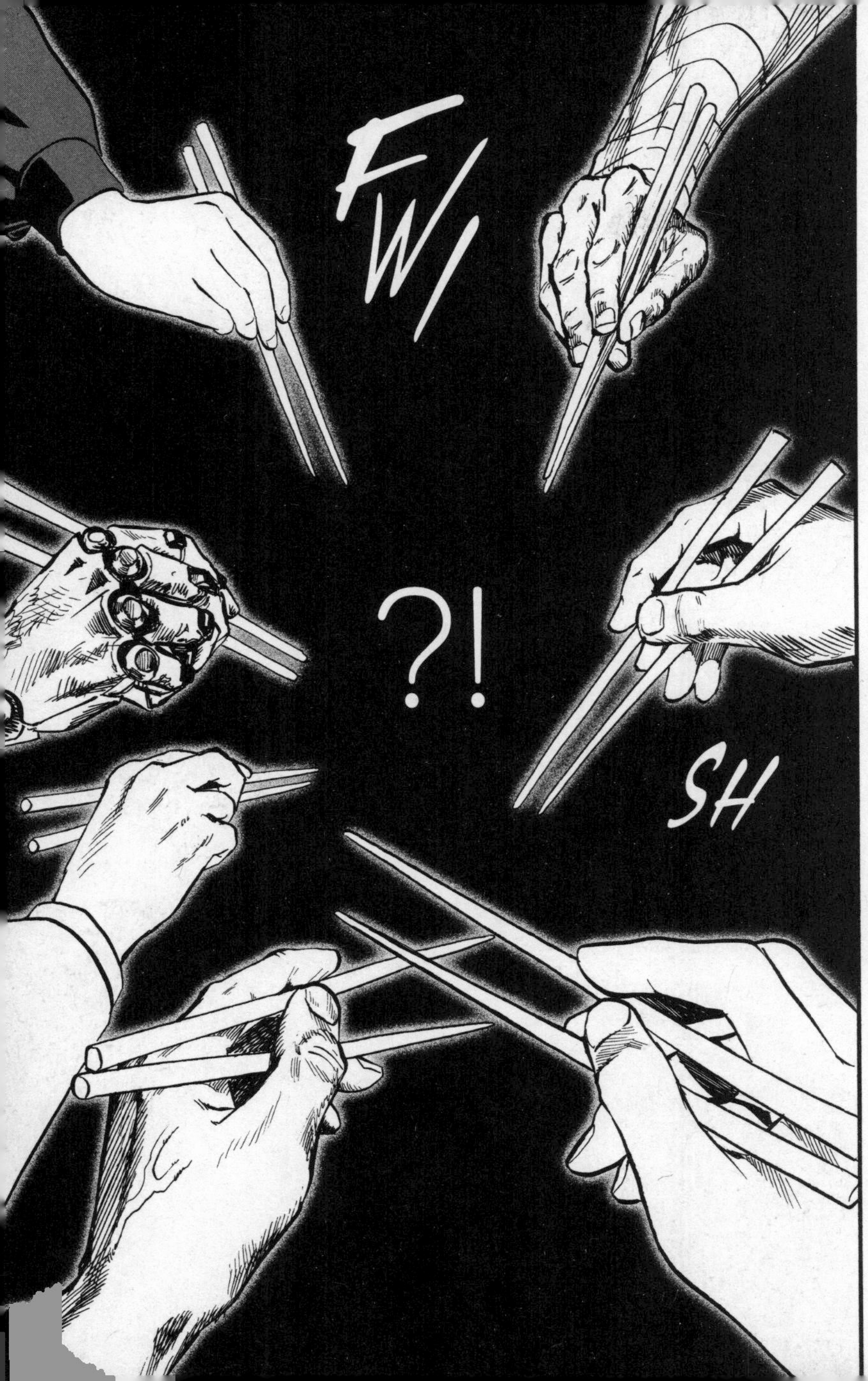
FWI
?!
SH

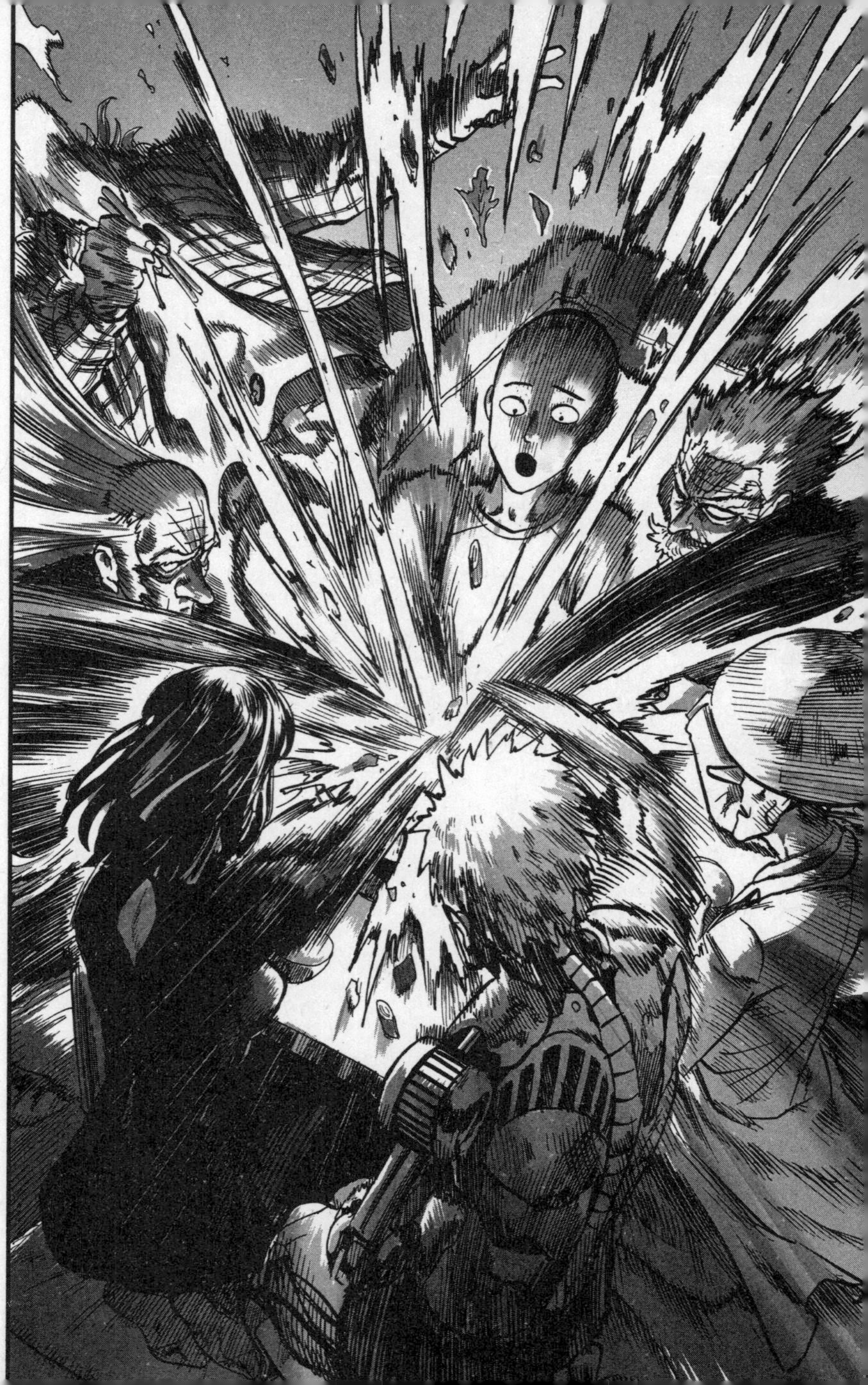

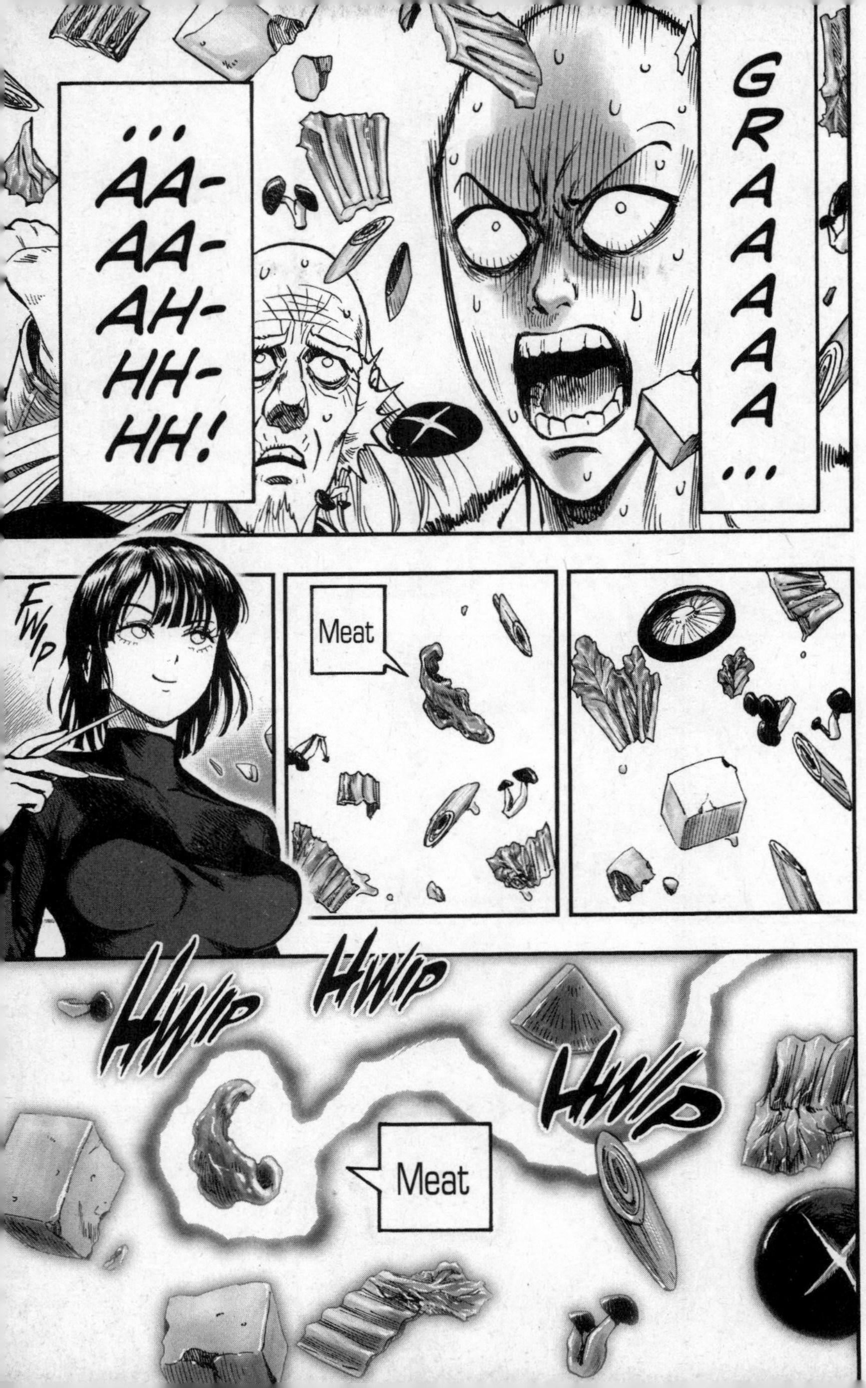
GRAAAAAA...
...AA-AA-AH-HH-HH!
Meat
FWIP
HWIP
HWIP
HWIP
Meat

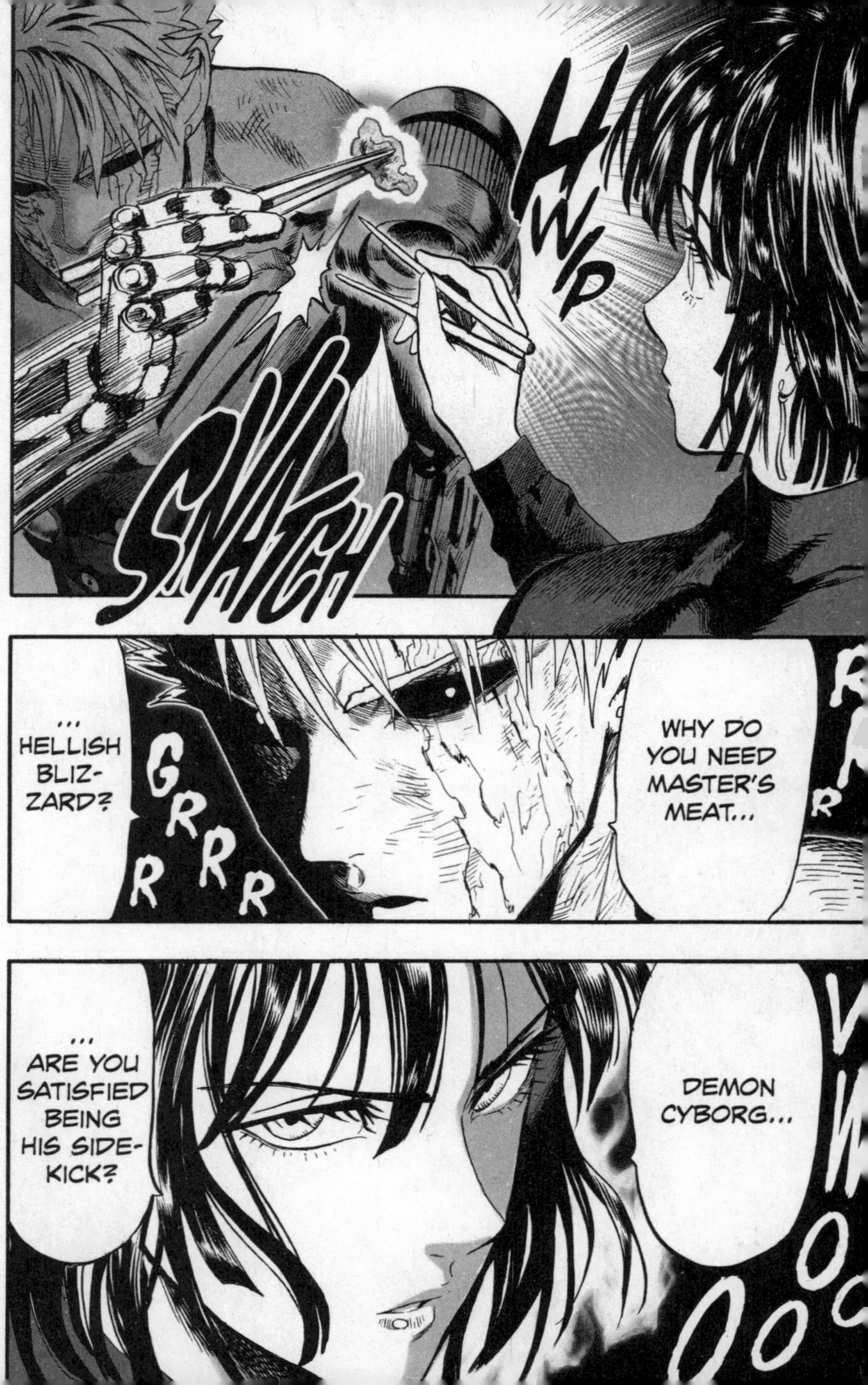
HWIP
SNATCH
WHY DO YOU NEED MASTER'S MEAT...
... HELLISH BLIZZARD?
GRRRR
DEMON CYBORG...
... ARE YOU SATISFIED BEING HIS SIDEKICK?

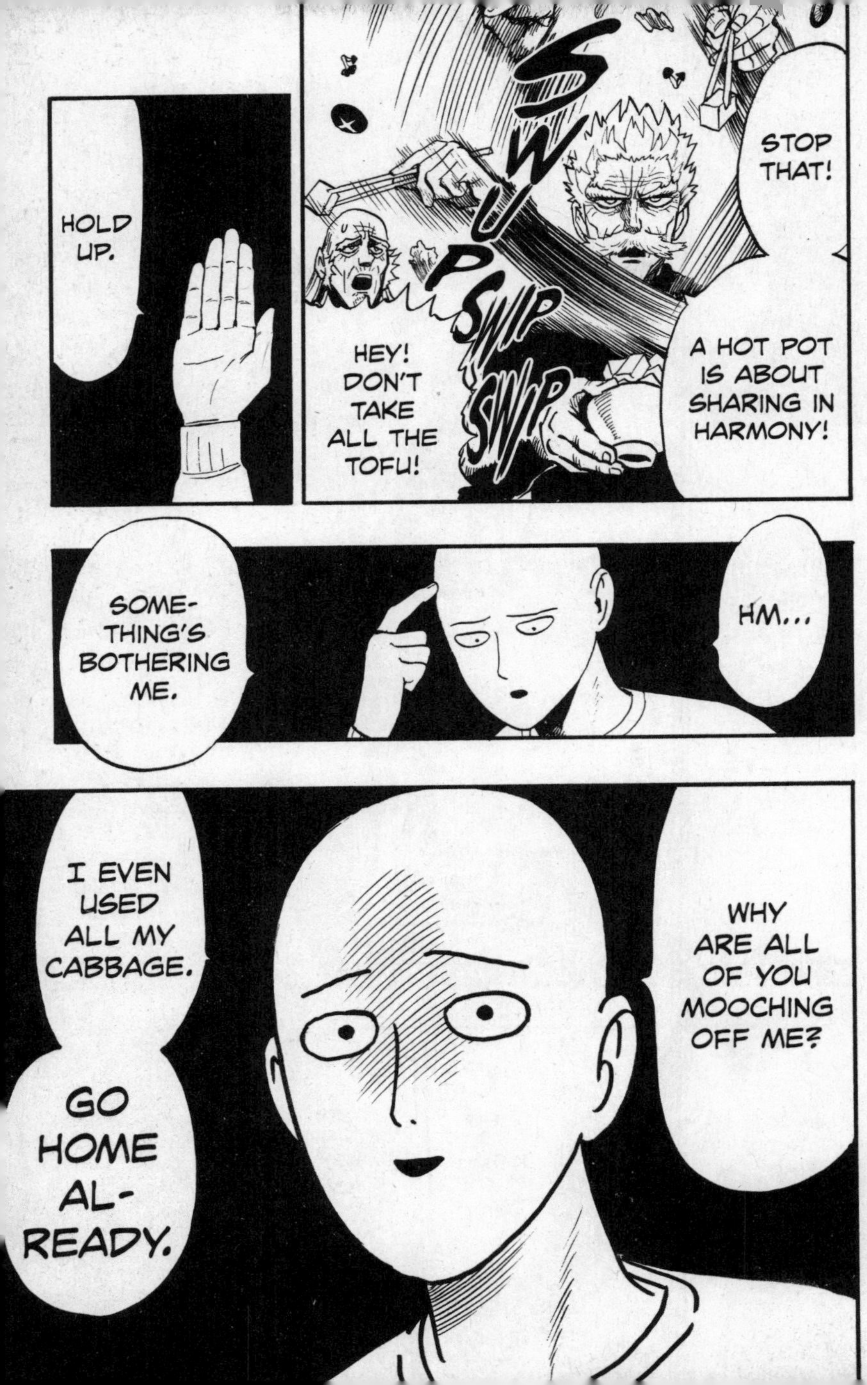
STOP THAT!
A HOT POT IS ABOUT SHARING IN HARMONY!
SWUP
SWIP
SWIP
HEY! DON'T TAKE ALL THE TOFU!
HOLD UP.
HM...
SOME-THING'S BOTHERING ME.
WHY ARE ALL OF YOU MOOCHING OFF ME?
I EVEN USED ALL MY CABBAGE.
GO HOME AL-READY.

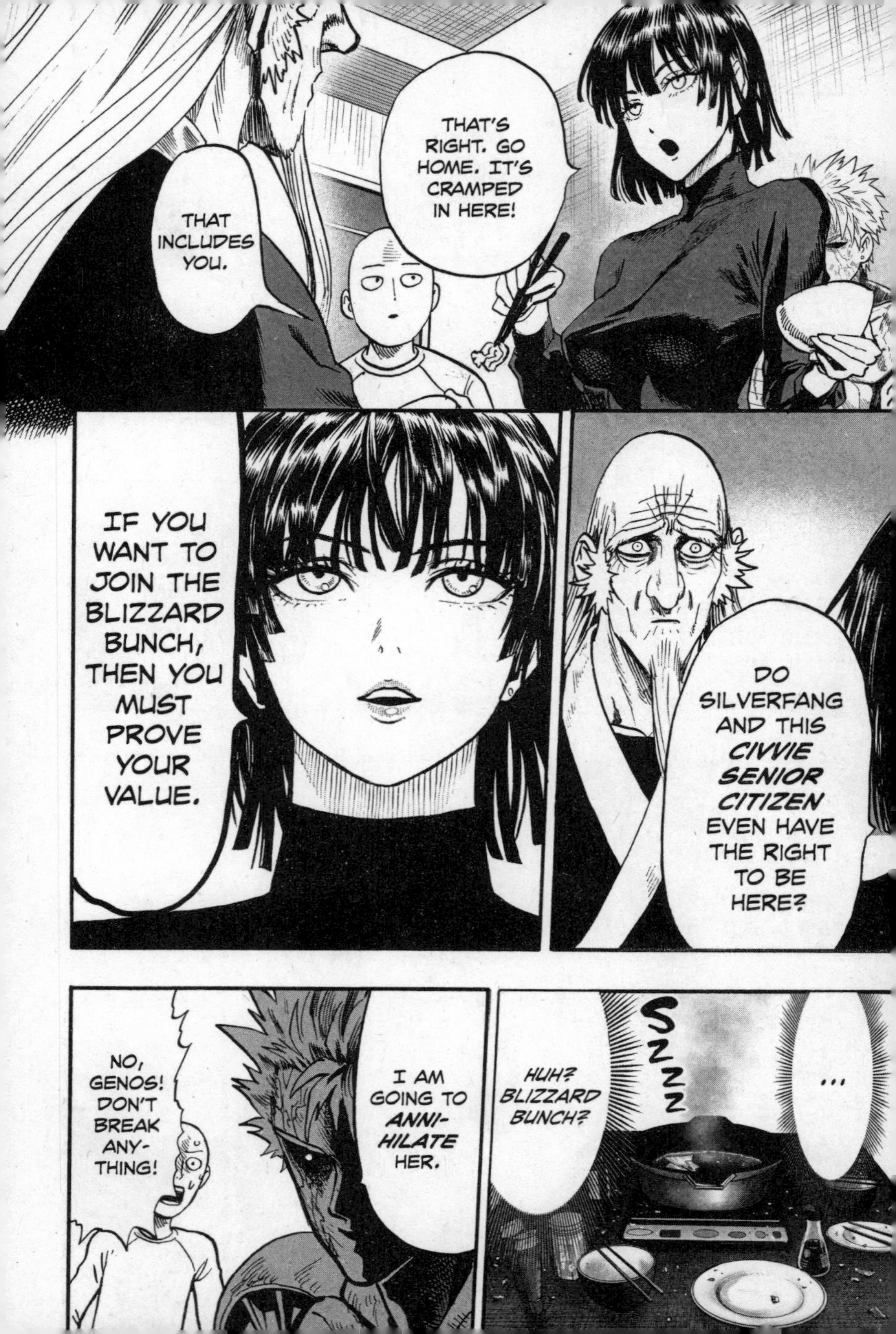
THAT'S RIGHT. GO HOME. IT'S CRAMPED IN HERE!
THAT INCLUDES YOU.
DO SILVERFANG AND THIS *CIVVIE SENIOR CITIZEN* EVEN HAVE THE RIGHT TO BE HERE?
IF YOU WANT TO JOIN THE BLIZZARD BUNCH, THEN YOU MUST PROVE YOUR VALUE.
...
SZZZ
HUH? BLIZZARD BUNCH?
I AM GOING TO *ANNIHILATE* HER.
NO, GENOS! DON'T BREAK ANYTHING!

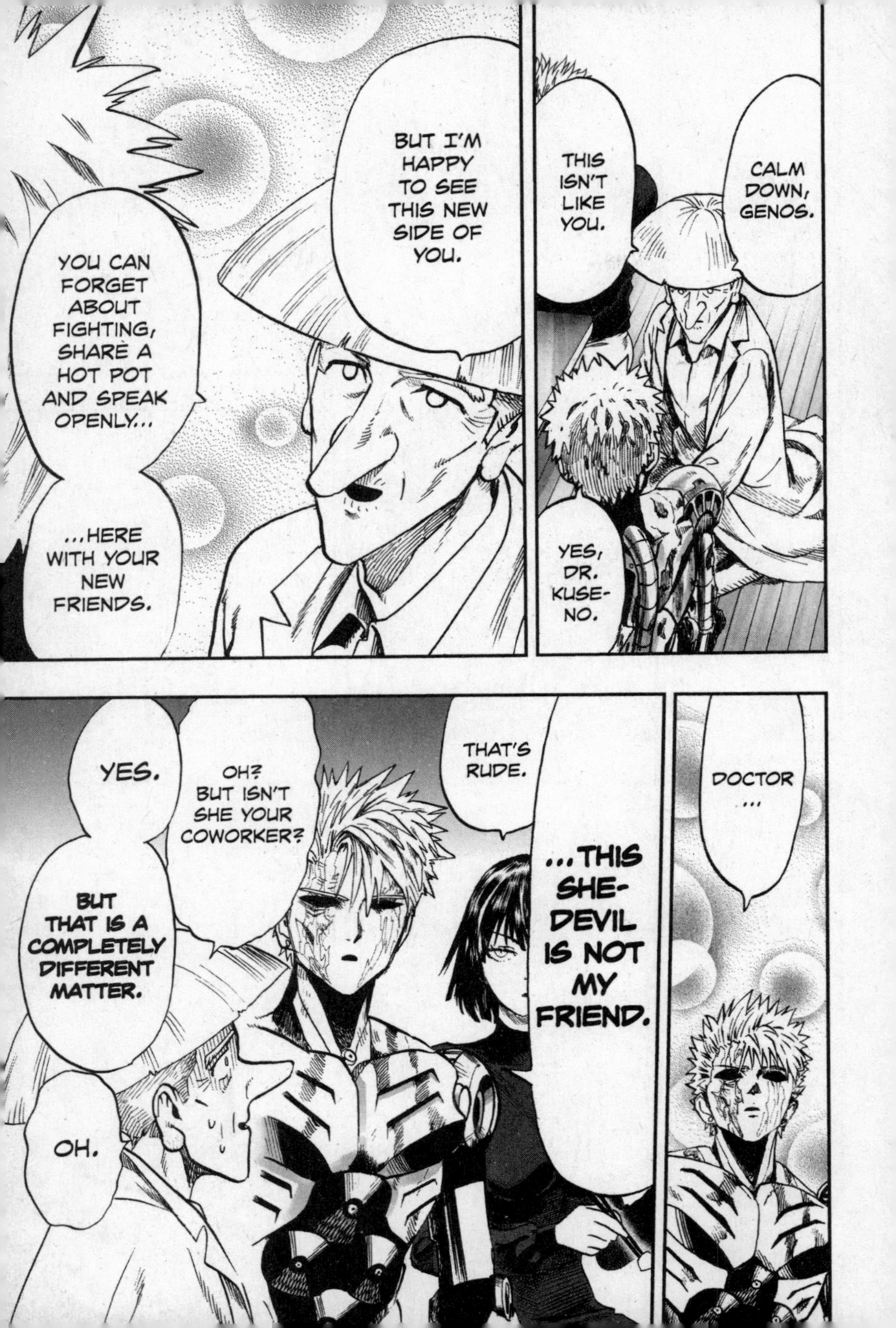

CALM DOWN, GENOS.
THIS ISN'T LIKE YOU.
YES, DR. KUSE-NO.
BUT I'M HAPPY TO SEE THIS NEW SIDE OF YOU.
YOU CAN FORGET ABOUT FIGHTING, SHARE A HOT POT AND SPEAK OPENLY...
...HERE WITH YOUR NEW FRIENDS.
DOCTOR ...
...THIS SHE-DEVIL IS NOT MY FRIEND.
THAT'S RUDE.
OH? BUT ISN'T SHE YOUR COWORKER?
YES.
BUT THAT IS A COMPLETELY DIFFERENT MATTER.
OH.

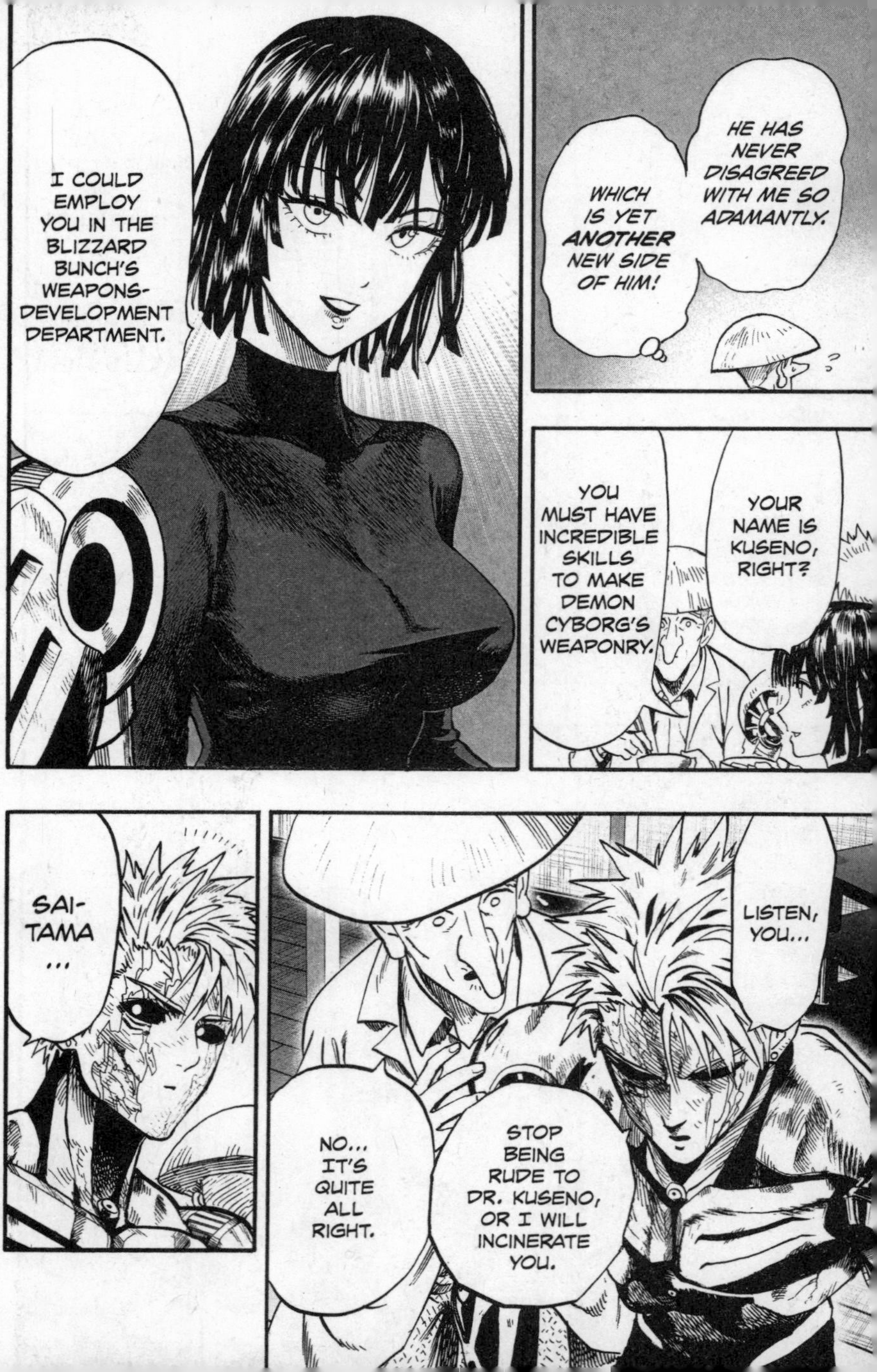
HE HAS NEVER DISAGREED WITH ME SO ADAMANTLY.
WHICH IS YET **ANOTHER** NEW SIDE OF HIM!
YOUR NAME IS KUSENO, RIGHT?
YOU MUST HAVE INCREDIBLE SKILLS TO MAKE DEMON CYBORG'S WEAPONRY.
I COULD EMPLOY YOU IN THE BLIZZARD BUNCH'S WEAPONS-DEVELOPMENT DEPARTMENT.
LISTEN, YOU...
STOP BEING RUDE TO DR. KUSENO, OR I WILL INCINERATE YOU.
NO... IT'S QUITE ALL RIGHT.
SAI-TAMA ...

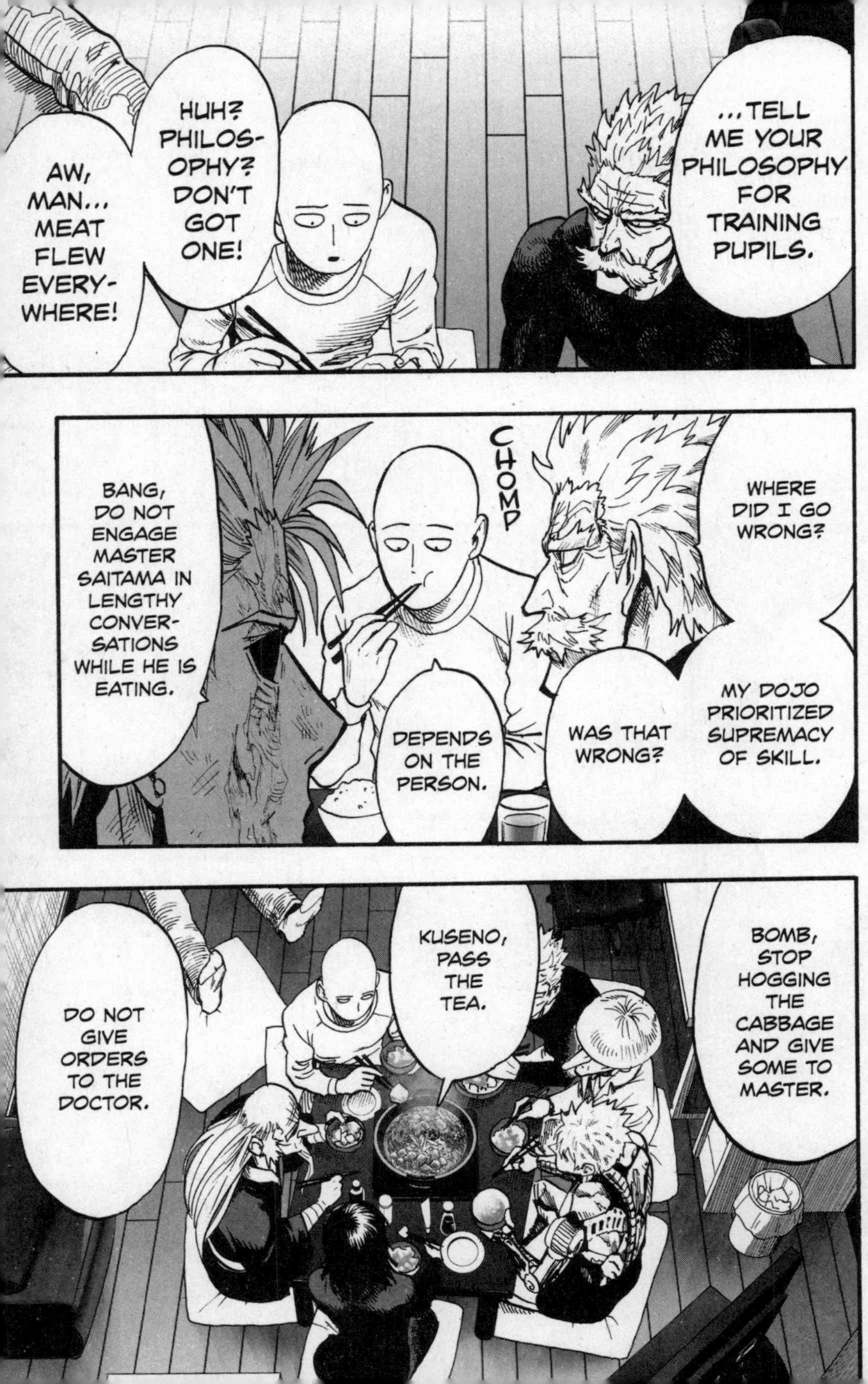
...TELL ME YOUR PHILOSOPHY FOR TRAINING PUPILS.
HUH? PHILOSOPHY? DON'T GOT ONE!
AW, MAN... MEAT FLEW EVERYWHERE!
WHERE DID I GO WRONG?
MY DOJO PRIORITIZED SUPREMACY OF SKILL.
WAS THAT WRONG?
CHOMP
DEPENDS ON THE PERSON.
BANG, DO NOT ENGAGE MASTER SAITAMA IN LENGTHY CONVERSATIONS WHILE HE IS EATING.
BOMB, STOP HOGGING THE CABBAGE AND GIVE SOME TO MASTER.
KUSENO, PASS THE TEA.
DO NOT GIVE ORDERS TO THE DOCTOR.

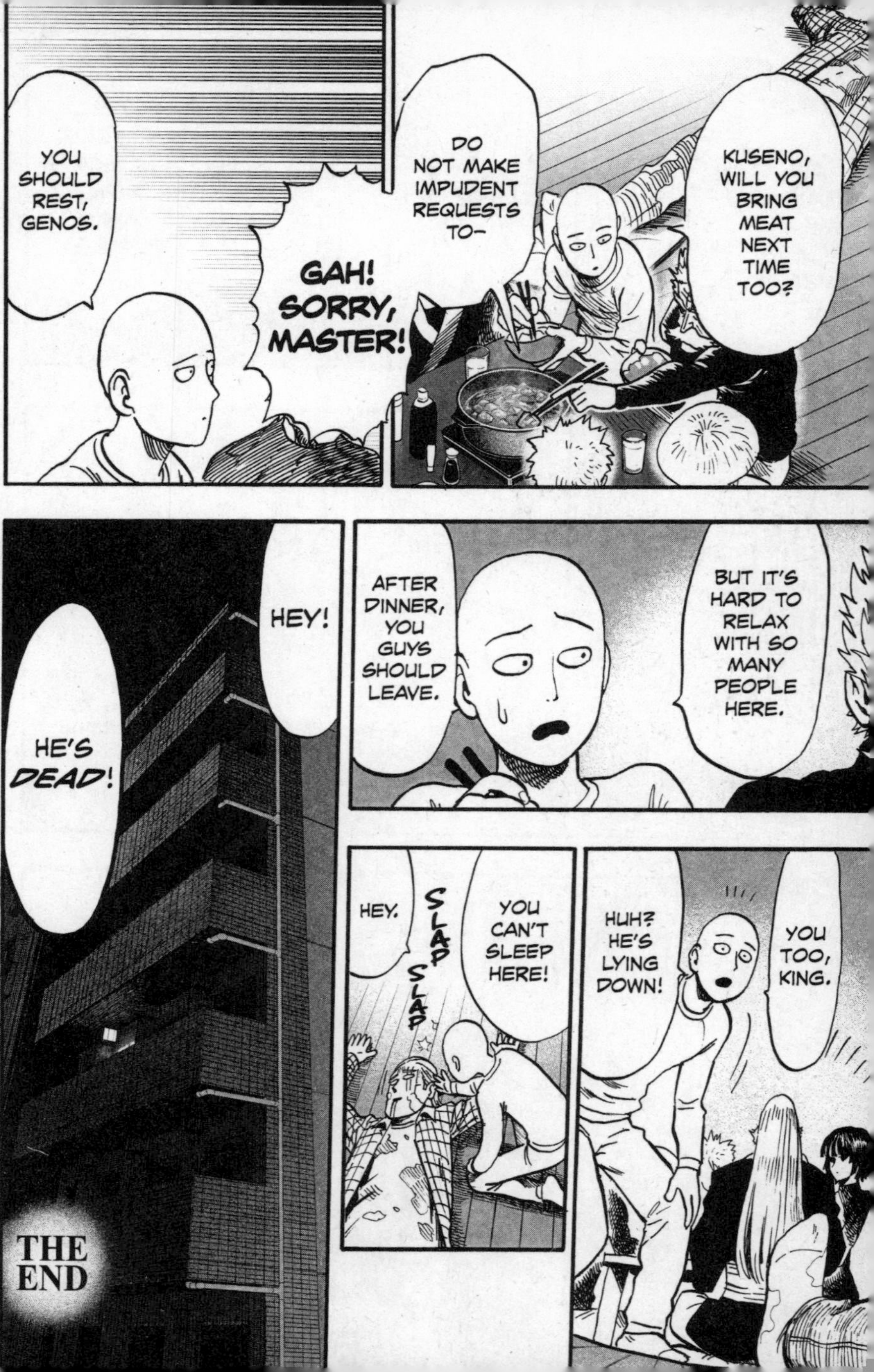
KUSENO, WILL YOU BRING MEAT NEXT TIME TOO?
DO NOT MAKE IMPUDENT REQUESTS TO-
GAH! SORRY, MASTER!
YOU SHOULD REST, GENOS.
BUT IT'S HARD TO RELAX WITH SO MANY PEOPLE HERE.
AFTER DINNER, YOU GUYS SHOULD LEAVE.
YOU TOO, KING.
HUH? HE'S LYING DOWN!
YOU CAN'T SLEEP HERE!
SLAP SLAP
HEY.
HEY!
HE'S DEAD!
THE END

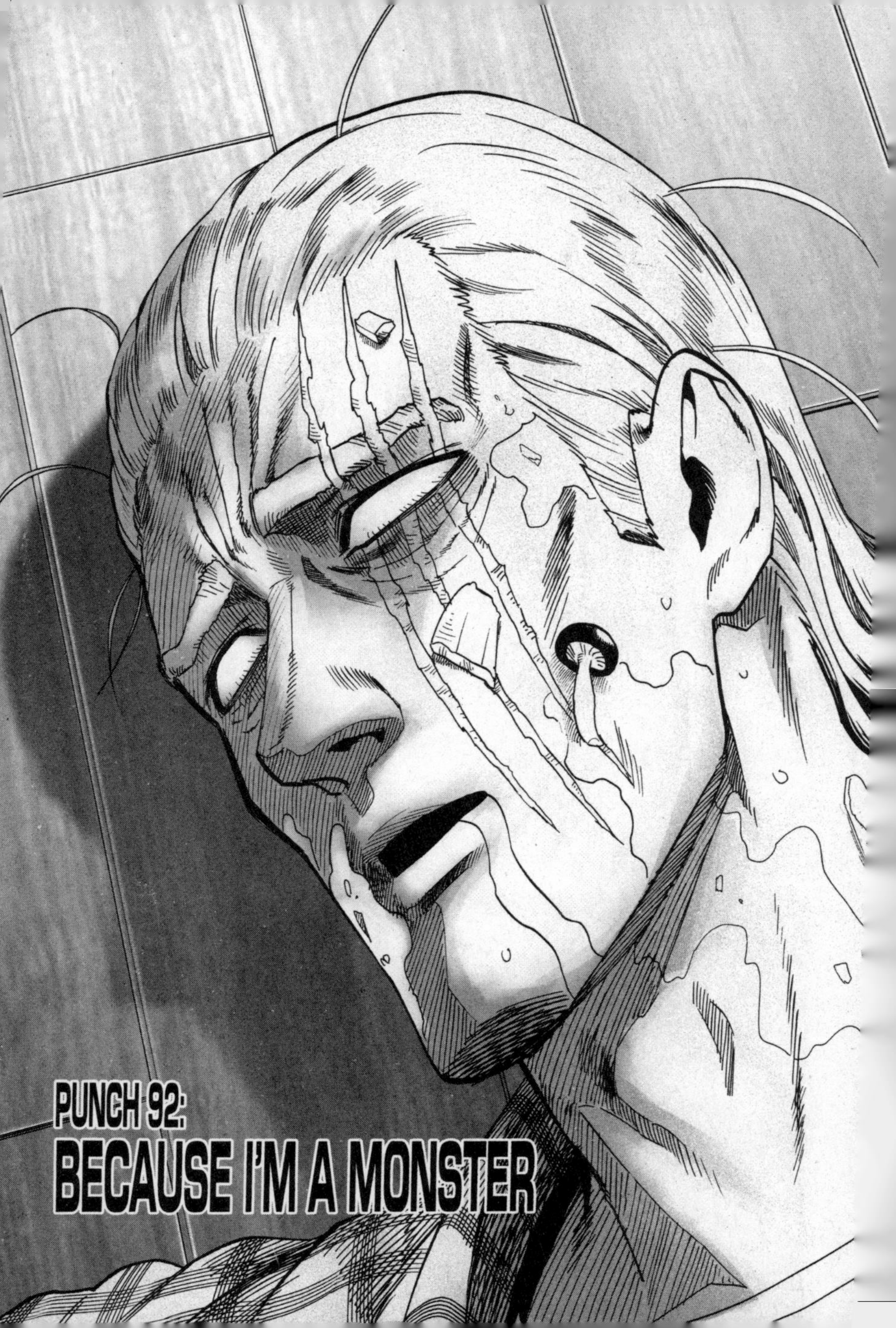
PUNCH 92:
BECAUSE I'M A MONSTER

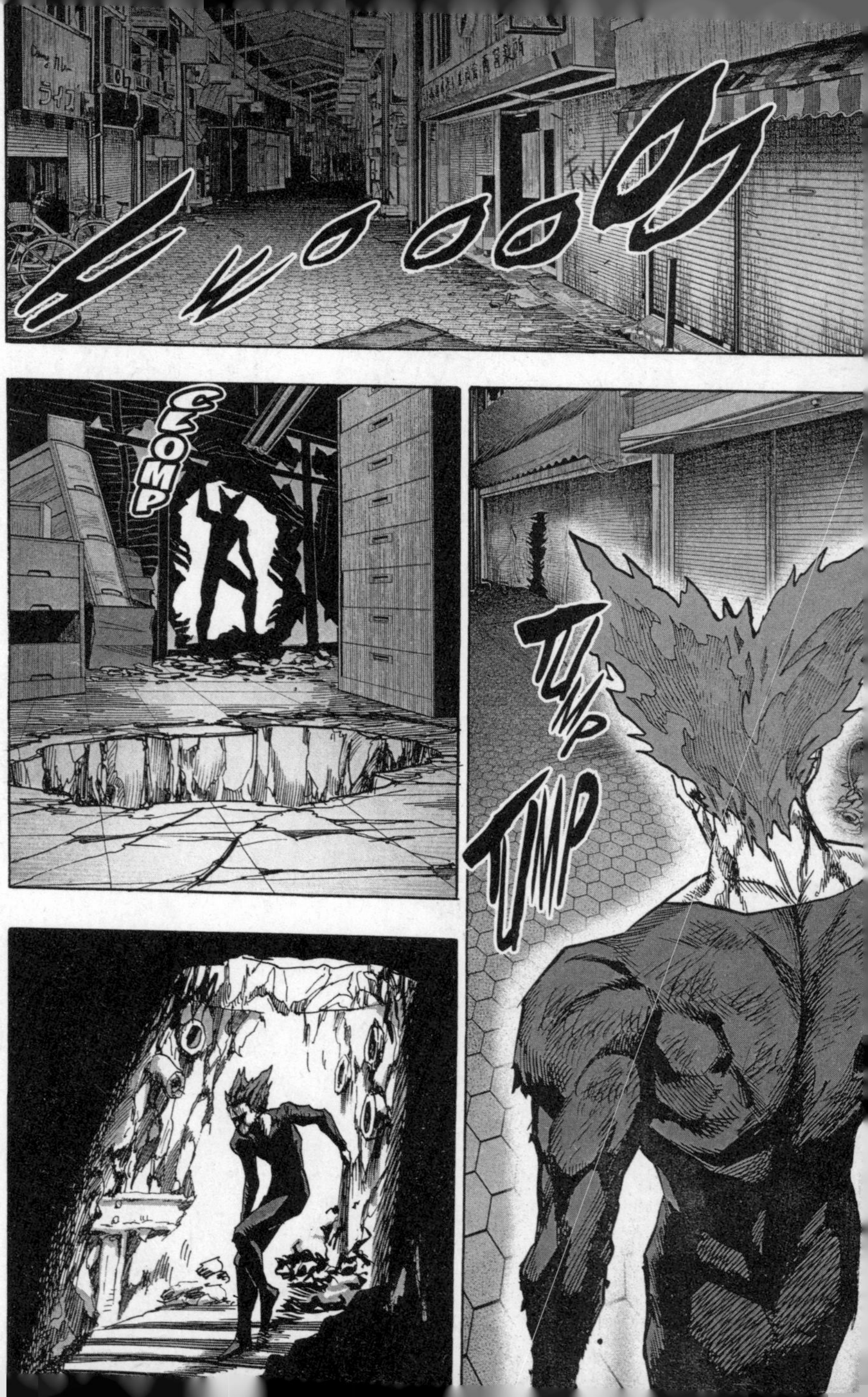
CLOMP
TUMP
TUMP

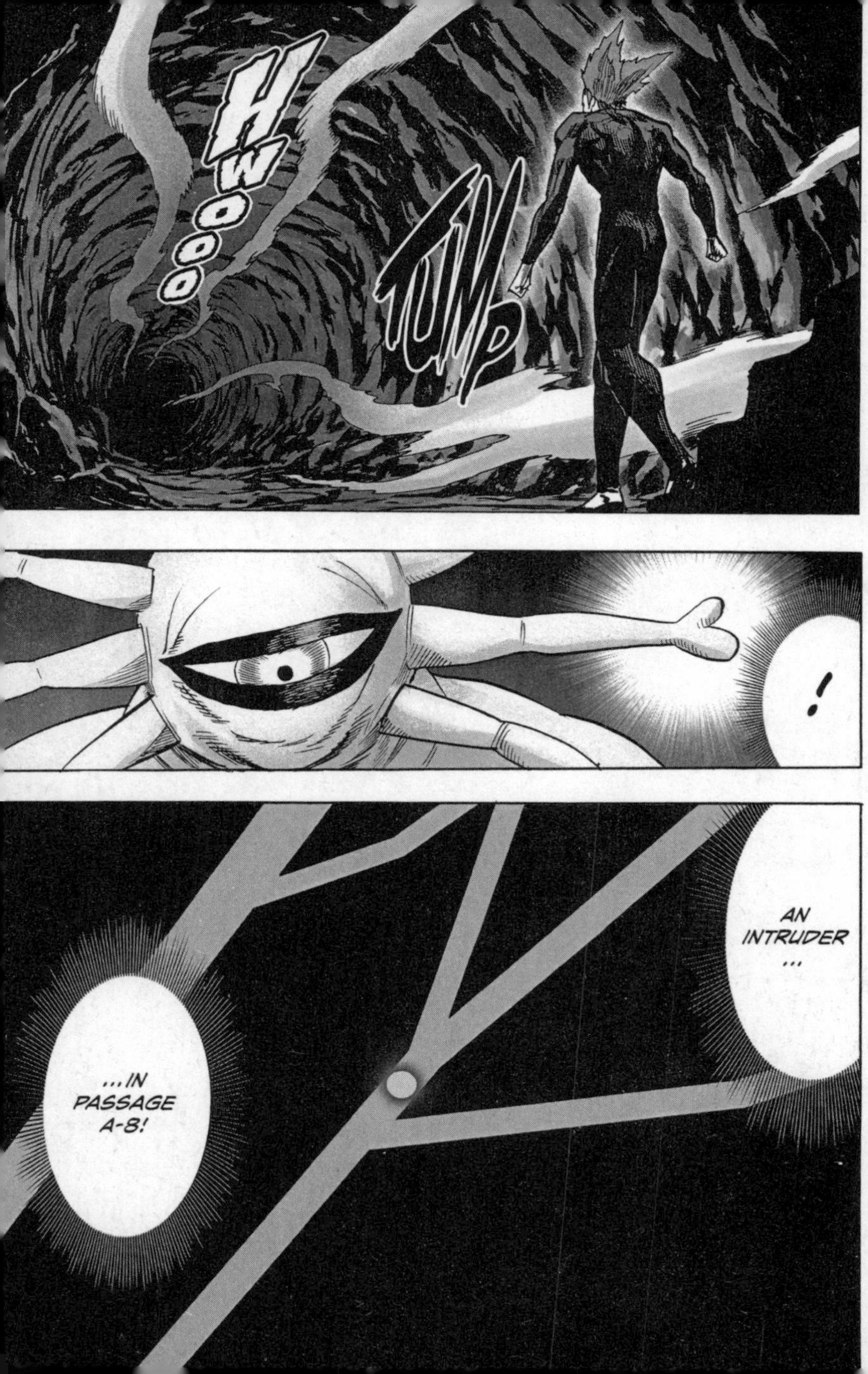
TUMP
HWOOO
!
AN INTRUDER ...
...IN PASSAGE A-8!

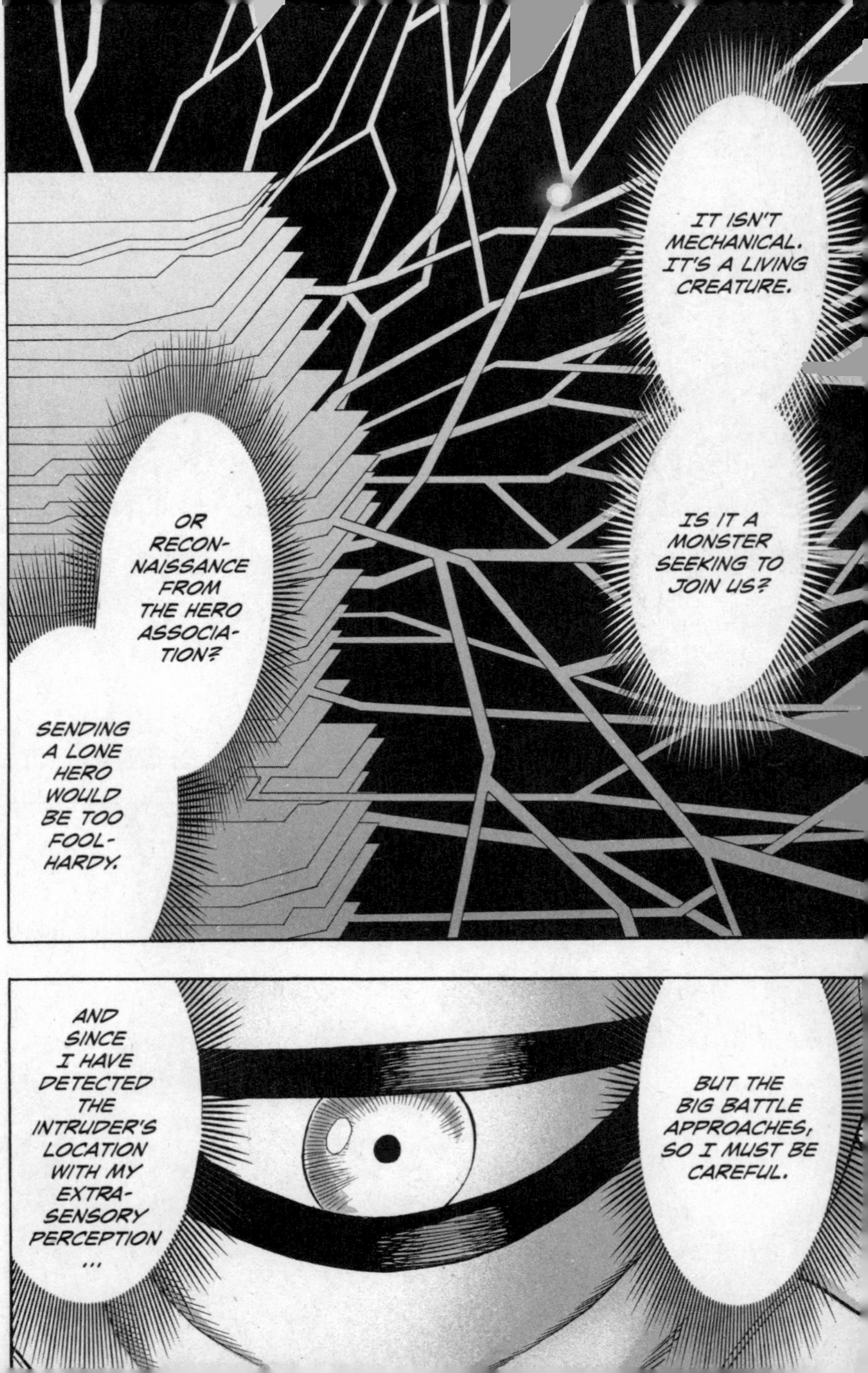
IT ISN'T MECHANICAL. IT'S A LIVING CREATURE.
IS IT A MONSTER SEEKING TO JOIN US?
OR RECONNAISSANCE FROM THE HERO ASSOCIATION?
SENDING A LONE HERO WOULD BE TOO FOOLHARDY.
BUT THE BIG BATTLE APPROACHES, SO I MUST BE CAREFUL.
AND SINCE I HAVE DETECTED THE INTRUDER'S LOCATION WITH MY EXTRASENSORY PERCEPTION...

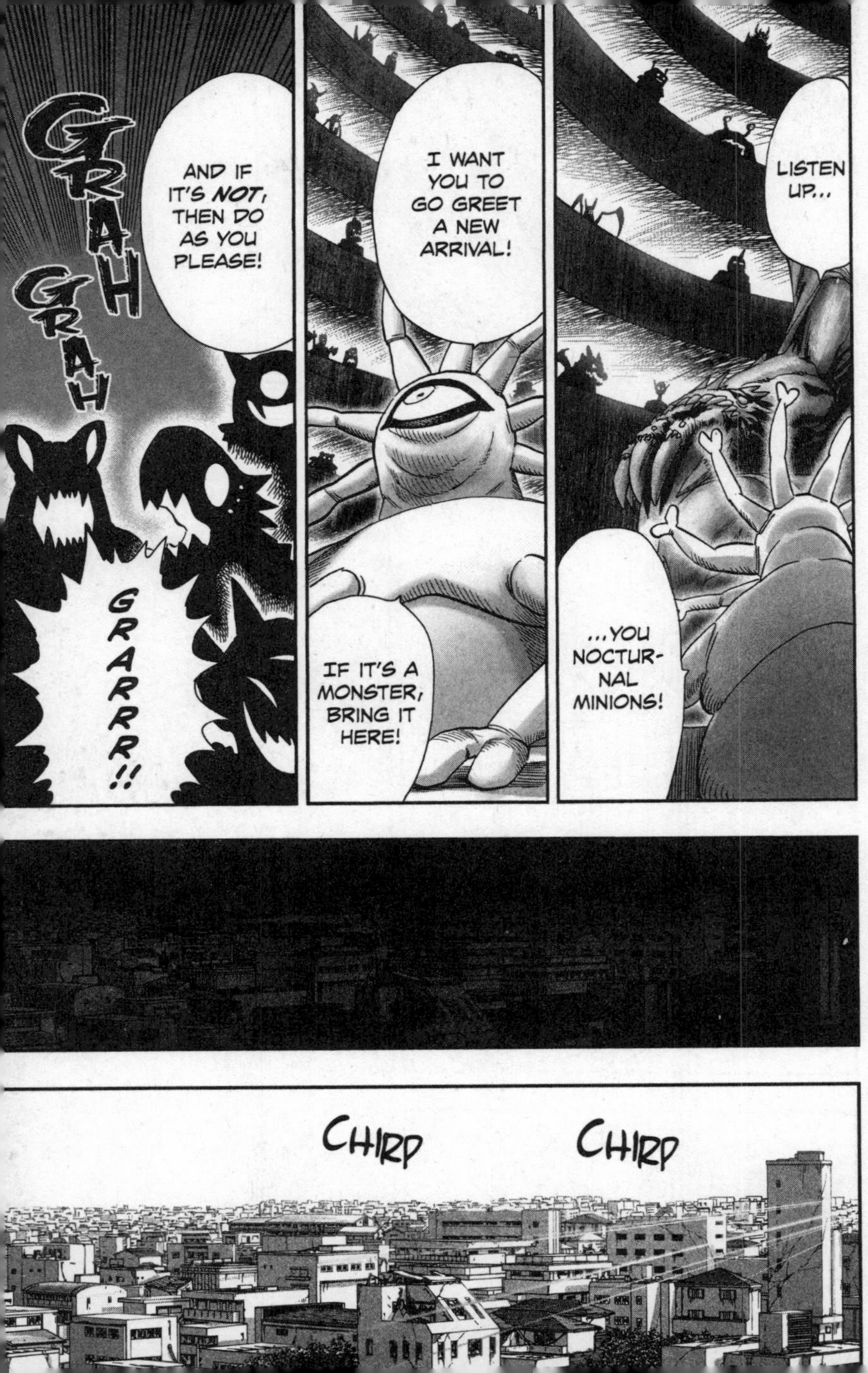
LISTEN UP...
...YOU NOCTURNAL MINIONS!
I WANT YOU TO GO GREET A NEW ARRIVAL!
IF IT'S A MONSTER, BRING IT HERE!
AND IF IT'S NOT, THEN DO AS YOU PLEASE!
GRAH
GRAH
GRARRR!!
CHIRP
CHIRP

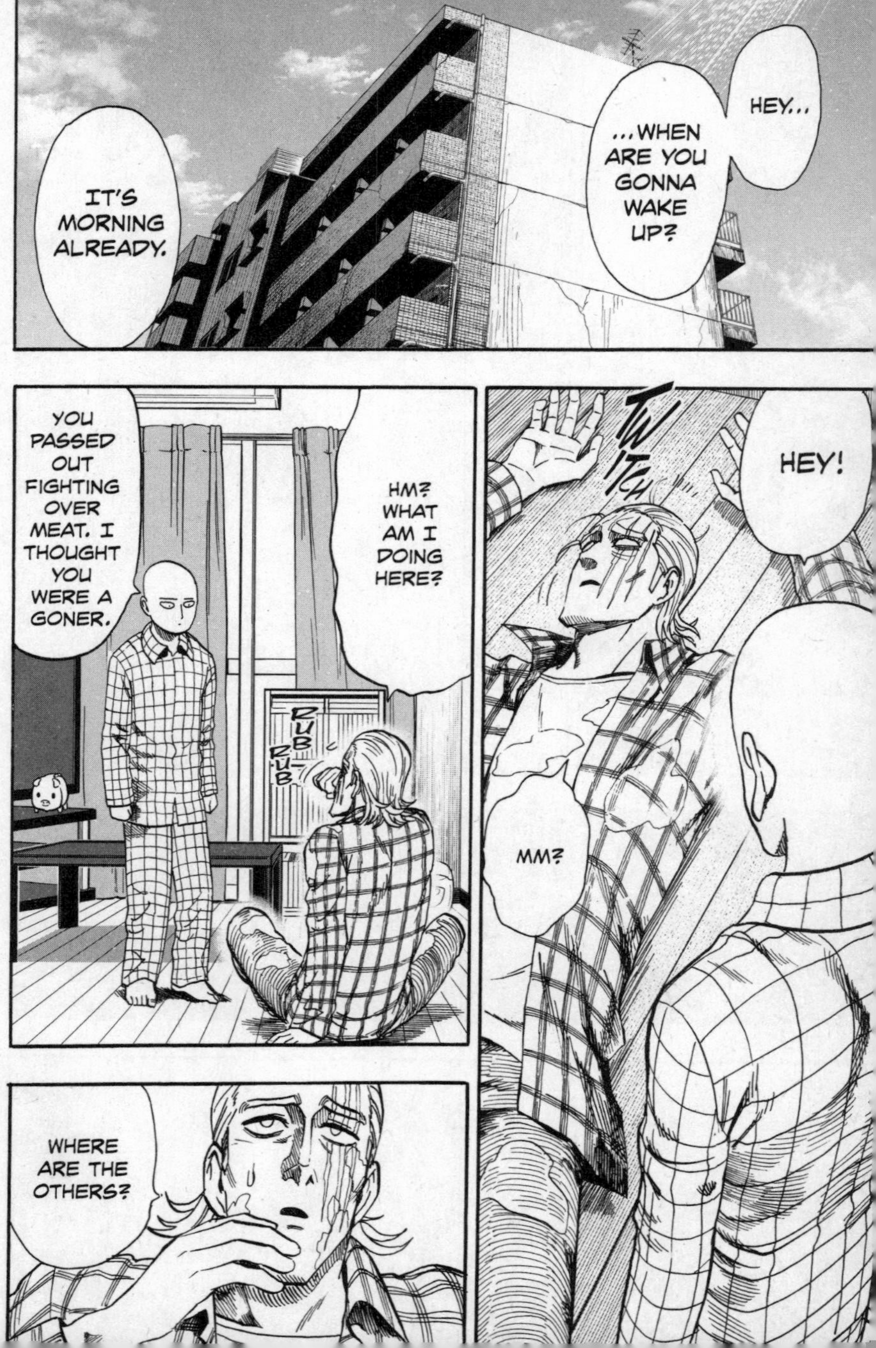
HEY...
...WHEN ARE YOU GONNA WAKE UP?
IT'S MORNING ALREADY.
TWITCH
HEY!
MM?
HM? WHAT AM I DOING HERE?
RUB RUB
YOU PASSED OUT FIGHTING OVER MEAT. I THOUGHT YOU WERE A GONER.
WHERE ARE THE OTHERS?

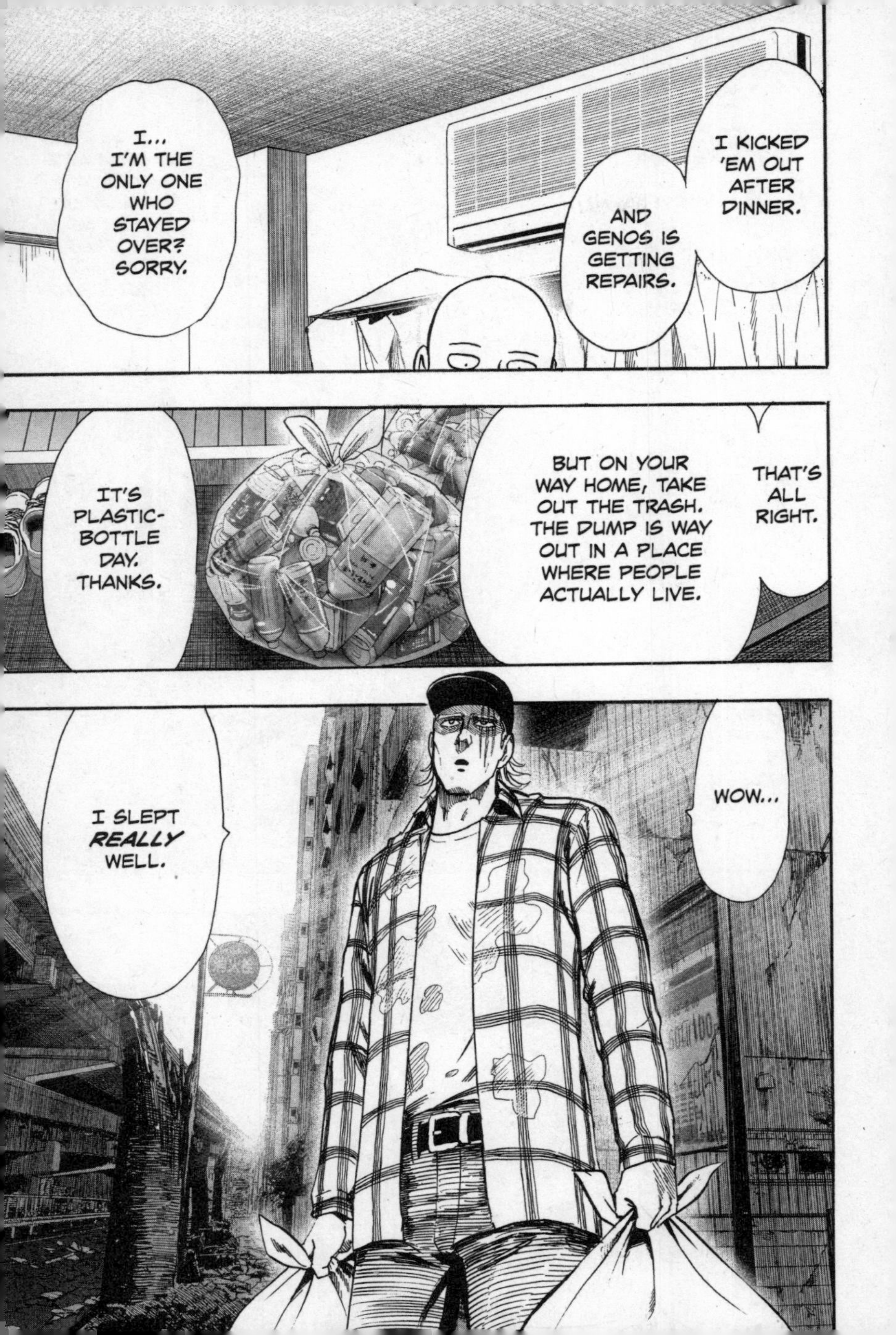
I KICKED 'EM OUT AFTER DINNER.
AND GENOS IS GETTING REPAIRS.
I... I'M THE ONLY ONE WHO STAYED OVER? SORRY.
THAT'S ALL RIGHT.
BUT ON YOUR WAY HOME, TAKE OUT THE TRASH. THE DUMP IS WAY OUT IN A PLACE WHERE PEOPLE ACTUALLY LIVE.
IT'S PLASTIC-BOTTLE DAY. THANKS.
WOW...
I SLEPT *REALLY* WELL.

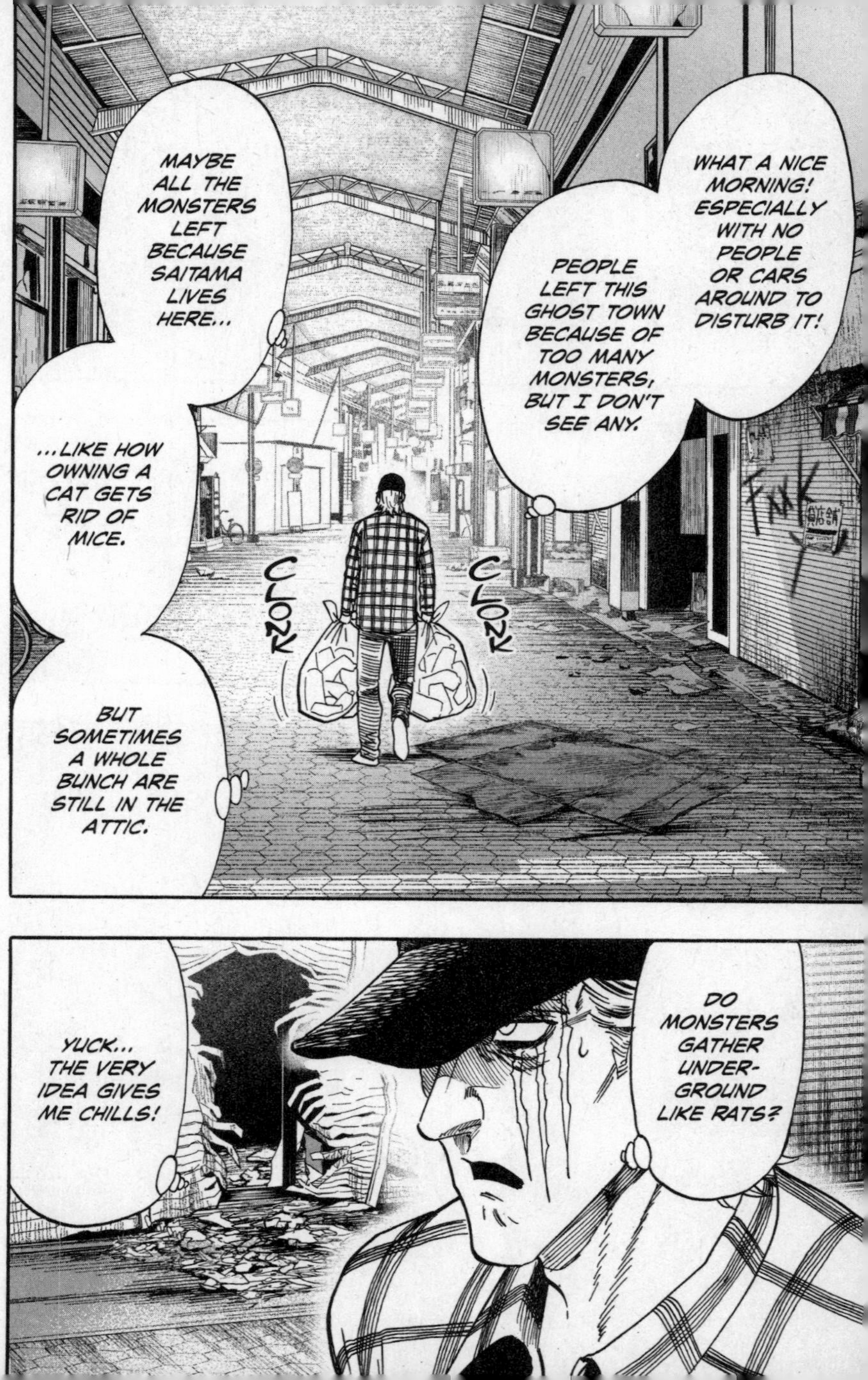
WHAT A NICE MORNING! ESPECIALLY WITH NO PEOPLE OR CARS AROUND TO DISTURB IT!
PEOPLE LEFT THIS GHOST TOWN BECAUSE OF TOO MANY MONSTERS, BUT I DON'T SEE ANY.
MAYBE ALL THE MONSTERS LEFT BECAUSE SAITAMA LIVES HERE...
...LIKE HOW OWNING A CAT GETS RID OF MICE.
CLONK
CLONK
BUT SOMETIMES A WHOLE BUNCH ARE STILL IN THE ATTIC.
DO MONSTERS GATHER UNDER-GROUND LIKE RATS?
YUCK... THE VERY IDEA GIVES ME CHILLS!

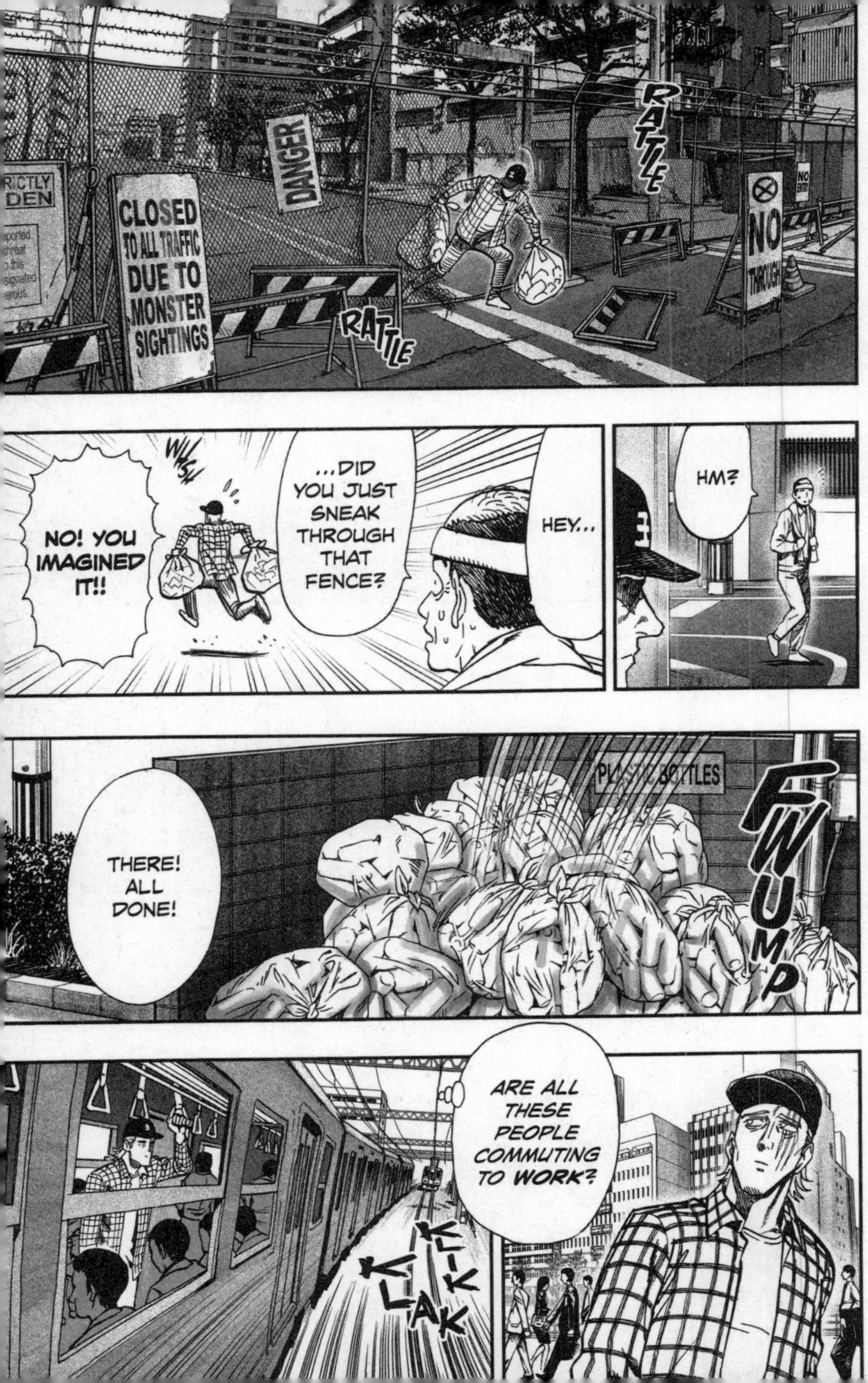
DANGER
CLOSED TO ALL TRAFFIC DUE TO MONSTER SIGHTINGS
NO THROUGH
NO EXIT
RATTLE
RATTLE
HM?
HEY...
...DID YOU JUST SNEAK THROUGH THAT FENCE?
WHSH
NO! YOU IMAGINED IT!!
FWUMP
THERE! ALL DONE!
ARE ALL THESE PEOPLE COMMUTING TO *WORK*?
KLIK
KLAK

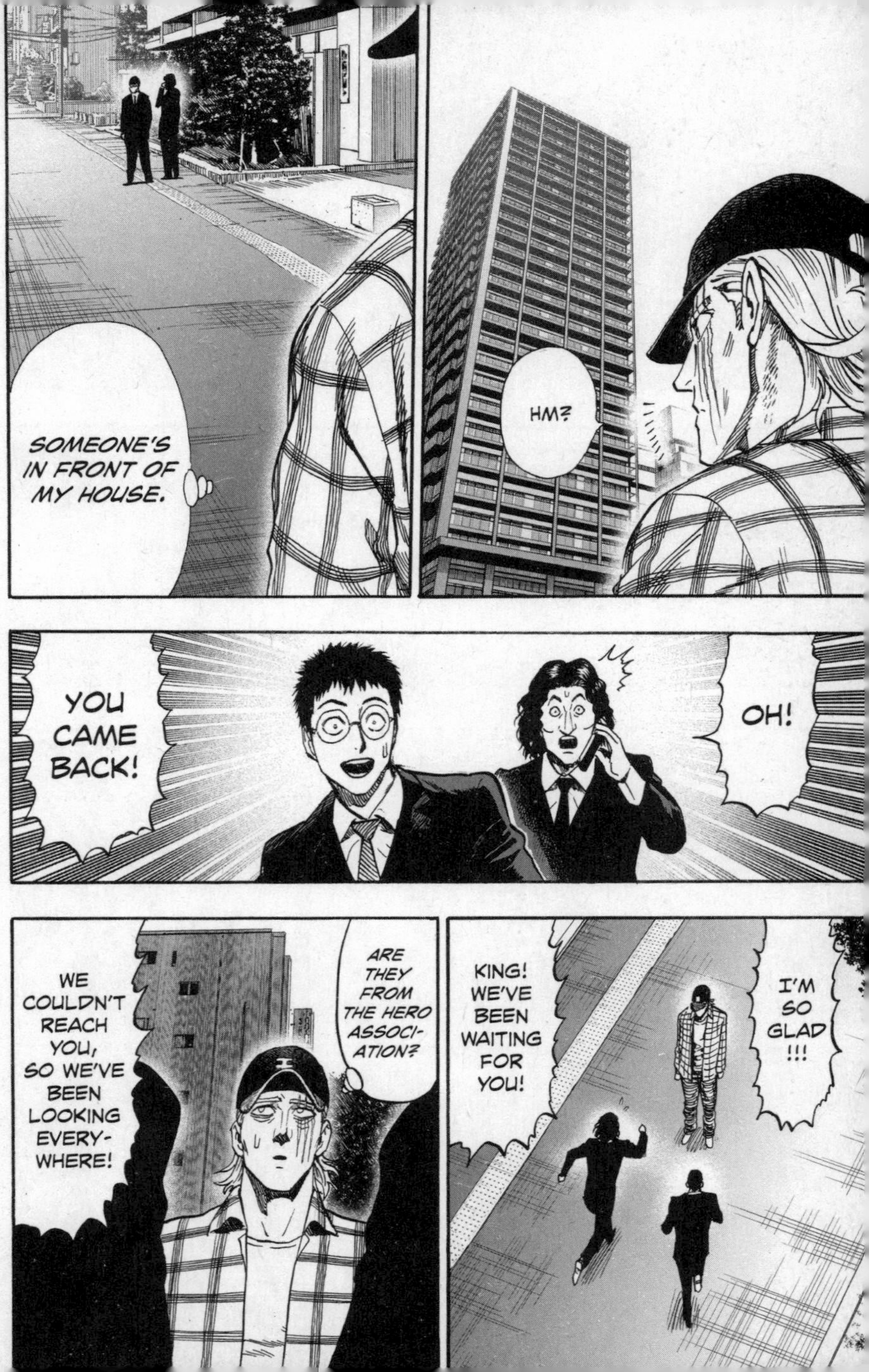
HM?
SOMEONE'S IN FRONT OF MY HOUSE.
OH!
YOU CAME BACK!
I'M SO GLAD!!!
KING! WE'VE BEEN WAITING FOR YOU!
ARE THEY FROM THE HERO ASSOCIATION?
WE COULDN'T REACH YOU, SO WE'VE BEEN LOOKING EVERYWHERE!

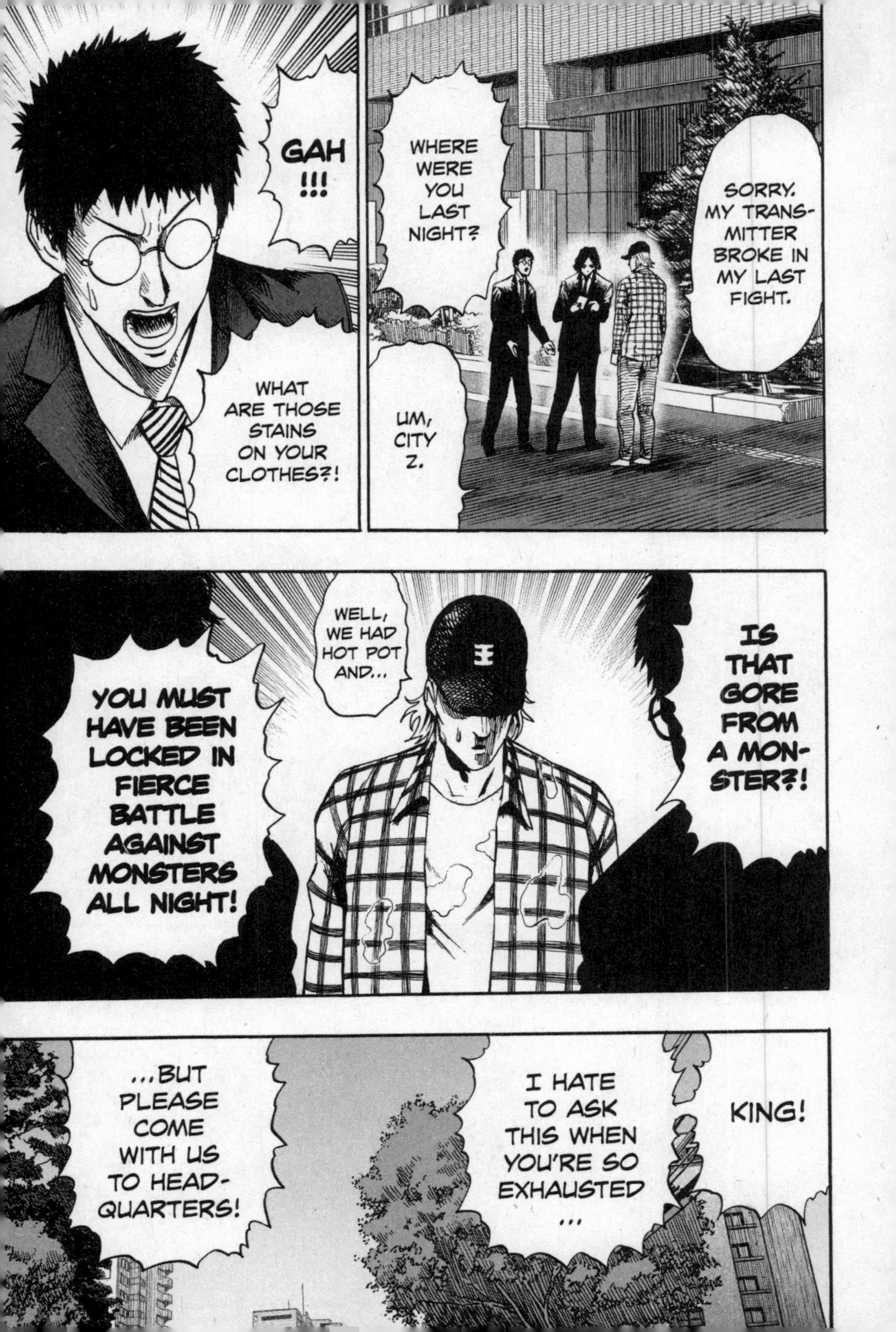

SORRY. MY TRANSMITTER BROKE IN MY LAST FIGHT.
WHERE WERE YOU LAST NIGHT?
UM, CITY Z.
GAH!!!
WHAT ARE THOSE STAINS ON YOUR CLOTHES?!
IS THAT GORE FROM A MONSTER?!
WELL, WE HAD HOT POT AND...
YOU MUST HAVE BEEN LOCKED IN FIERCE BATTLE AGAINST MONSTERS ALL NIGHT!
KING!
I HATE TO ASK THIS WHEN YOU'RE SO EXHAUSTED...
...BUT PLEASE COME WITH US TO HEADQUARTERS!

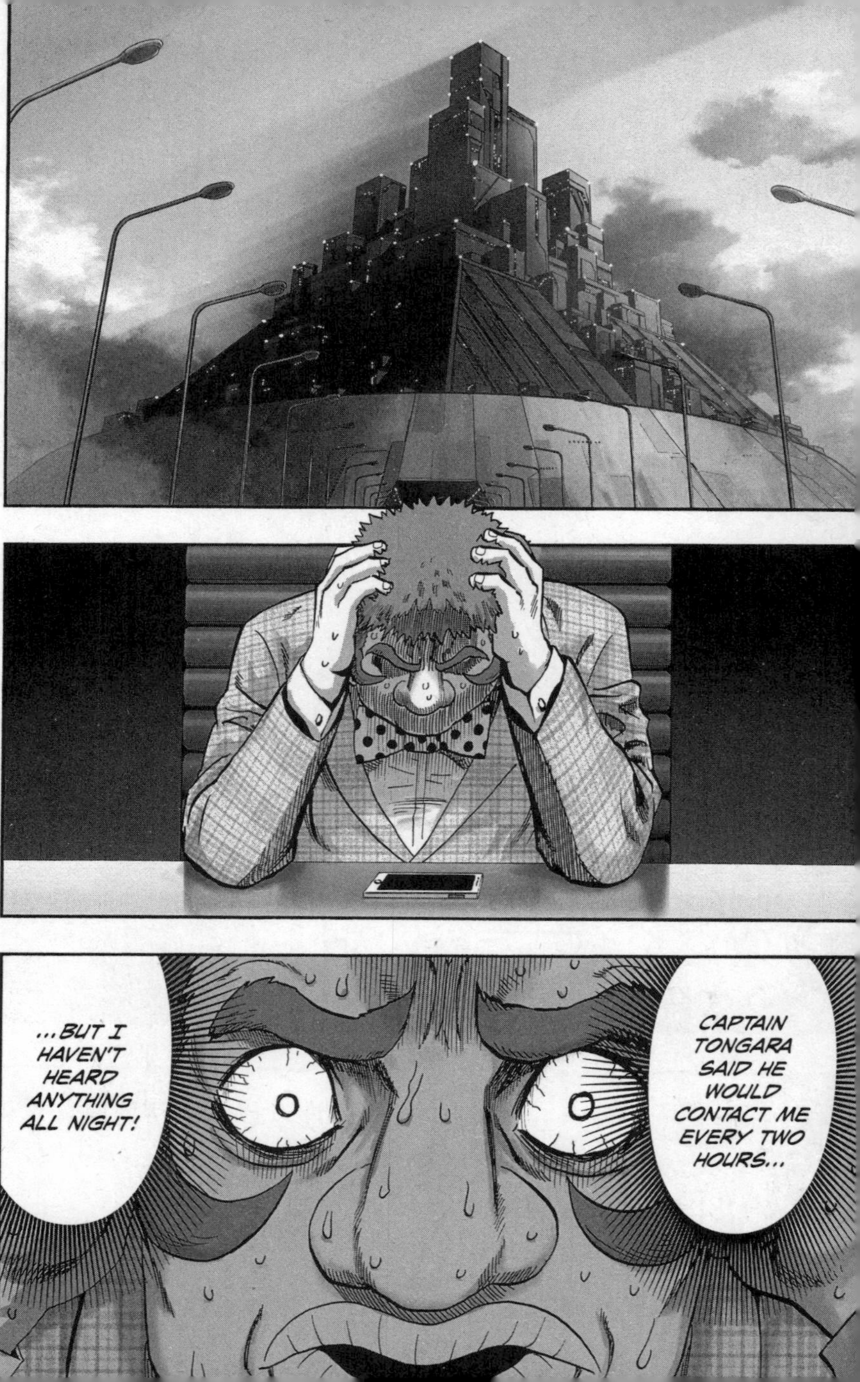

CAPTAIN TONGARA SAID HE WOULD CONTACT ME EVERY TWO HOURS...
...BUT I HAVEN'T HEARD ANYTHING ALL NIGHT!

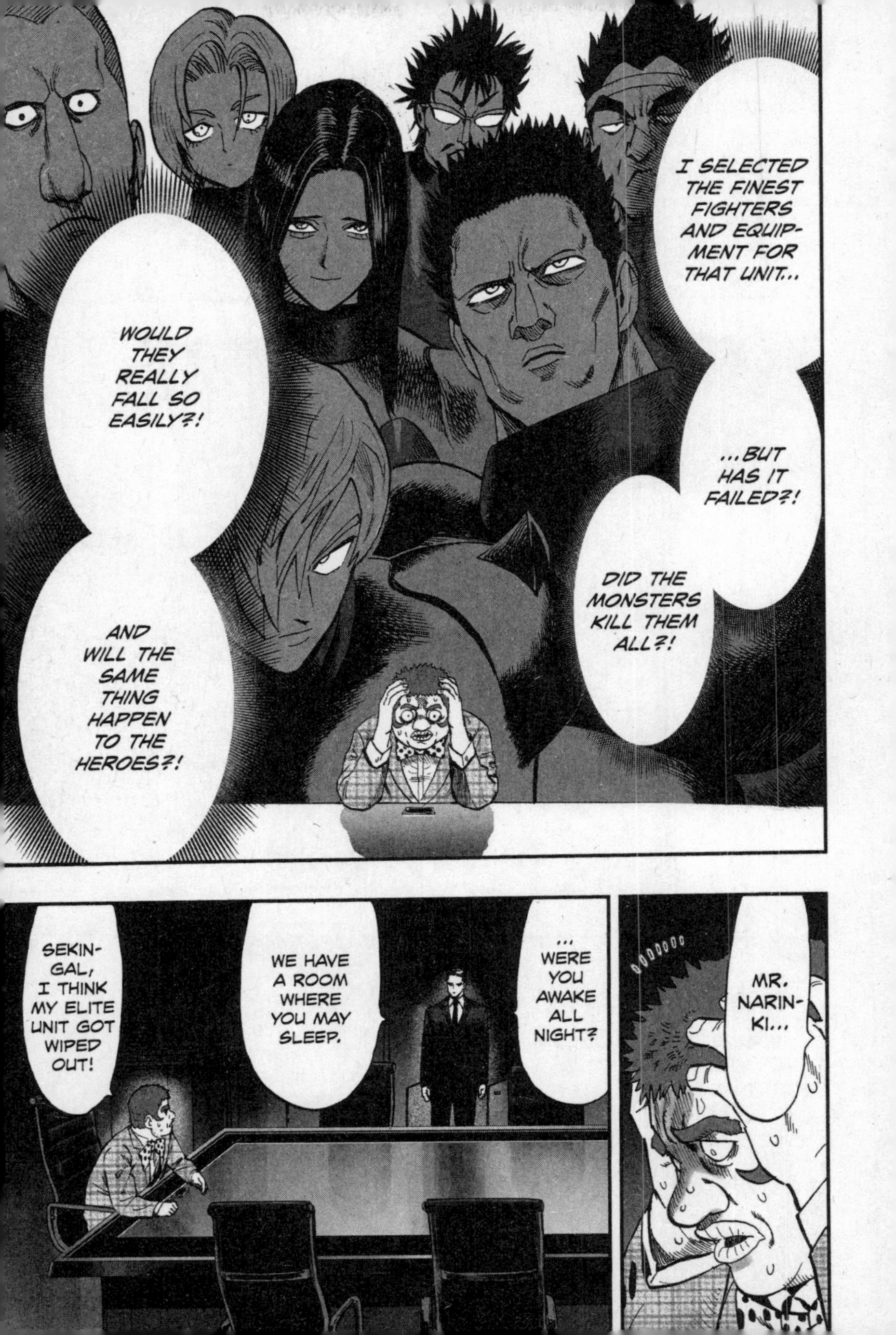
I SELECTED THE FINEST FIGHTERS AND EQUIPMENT FOR THAT UNIT...
...BUT HAS IT FAILED?!
DID THE MONSTERS KILL THEM ALL?!
WOULD THEY REALLY FALL SO EASILY?!
AND WILL THE SAME THING HAPPEN TO THE HEROES?!
MR. NARINKI...
...WERE YOU AWAKE ALL NIGHT?
WE HAVE A ROOM WHERE YOU MAY SLEEP.
SEKINGAL, I THINK MY ELITE UNIT GOT WIPED OUT!

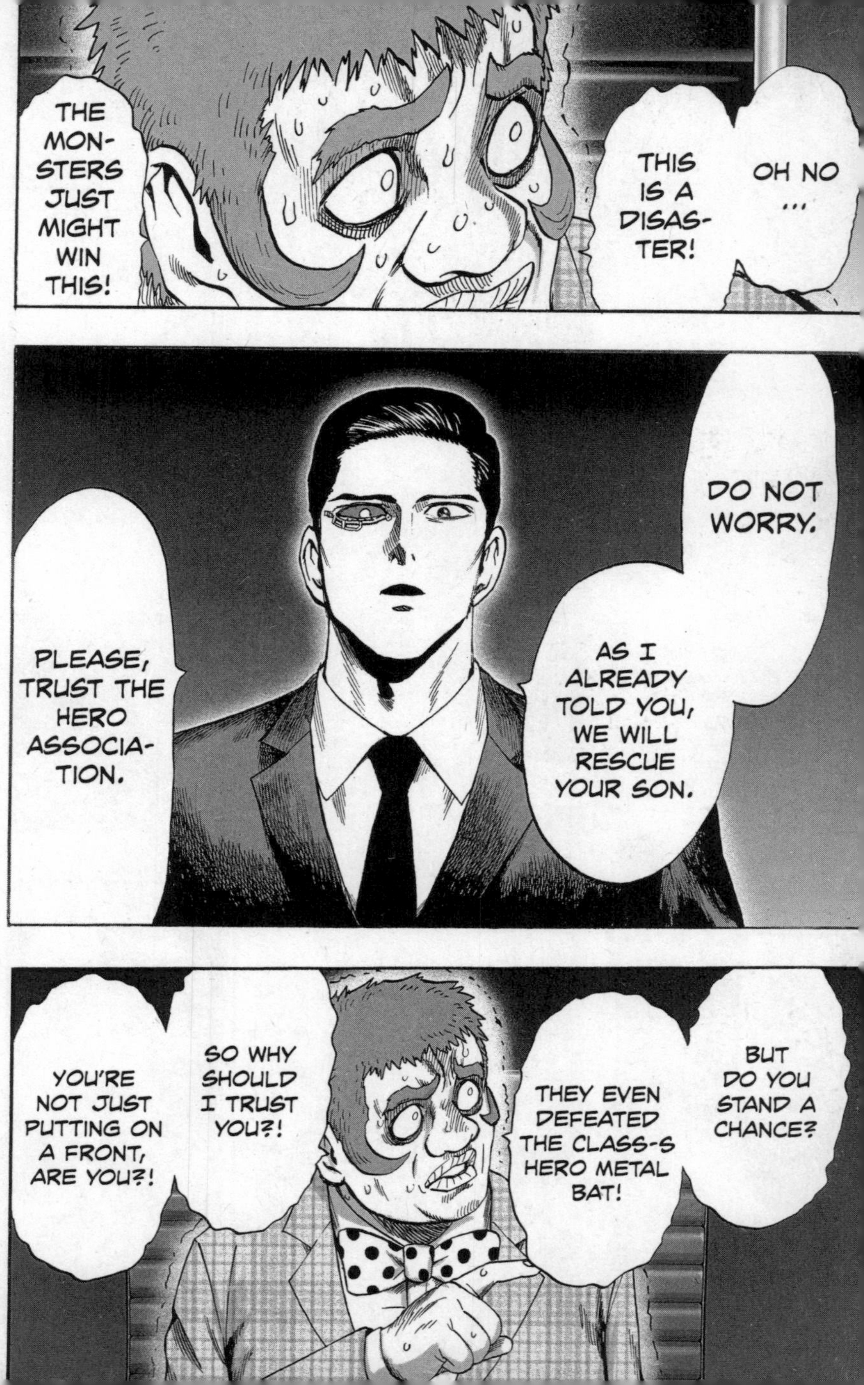
OH NO ...
THIS IS A DISASTER!
THE MONSTERS JUST MIGHT WIN THIS!
DO NOT WORRY.
AS I ALREADY TOLD YOU, WE WILL RESCUE YOUR SON.
PLEASE, TRUST THE HERO ASSOCIATION.
BUT DO YOU STAND A CHANCE?
THEY EVEN DEFEATED THE CLASS-S HERO METAL BAT!
SO WHY SHOULD I TRUST YOU?!
YOU'RE NOT JUST PUTTING ON A FRONT, ARE YOU?!

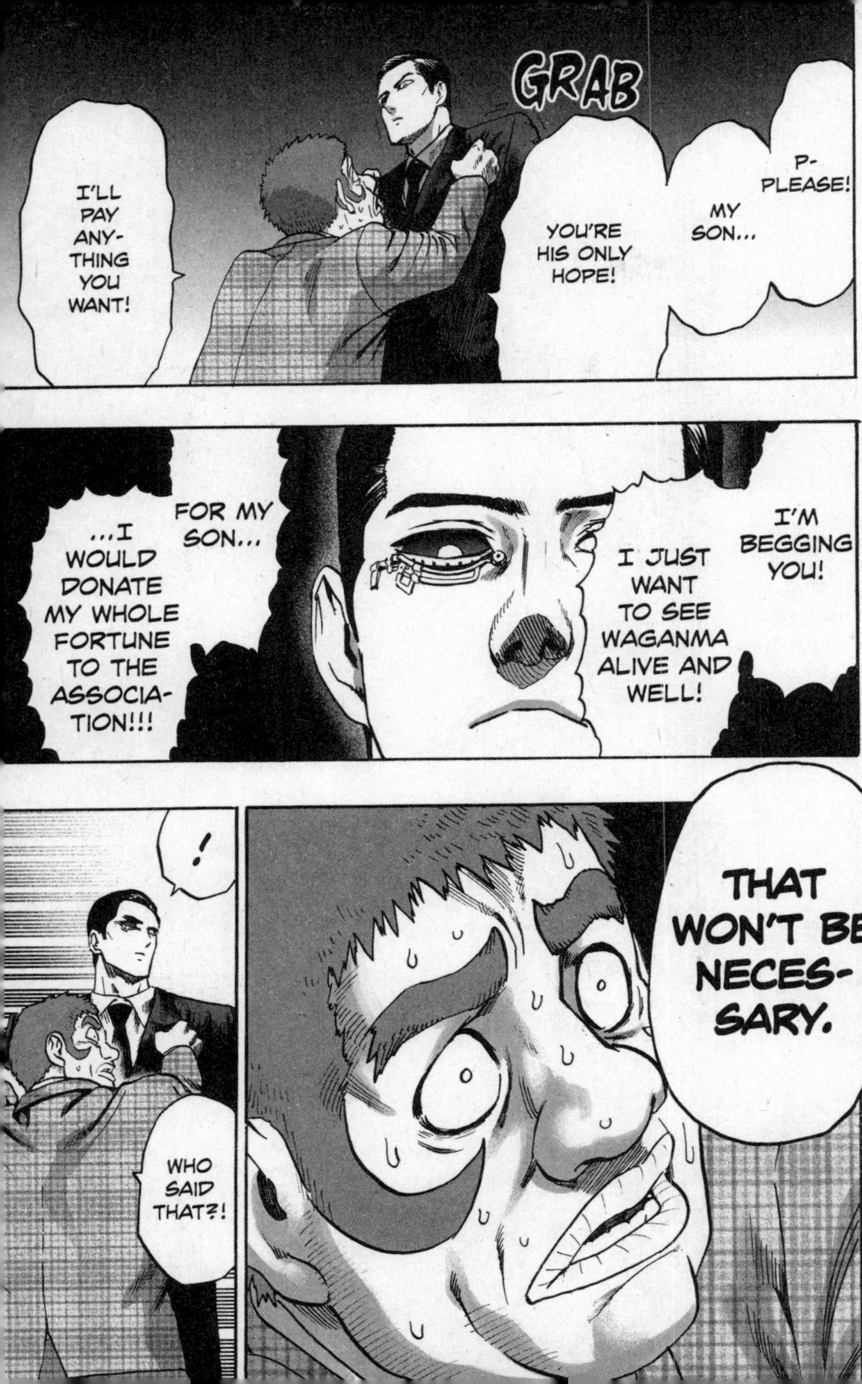
GRAB
P-PLEASE!
MY SON...
YOU'RE HIS ONLY HOPE!
I'LL PAY ANYTHING YOU WANT!
I'M BEGGING YOU!
I JUST WANT TO SEE WAGANMA ALIVE AND WELL!
FOR MY SON...
...I WOULD DONATE MY WHOLE FORTUNE TO THE ASSOCIATION!!!
THAT WON'T BE NECESSARY.
!
WHO SAID THAT?!

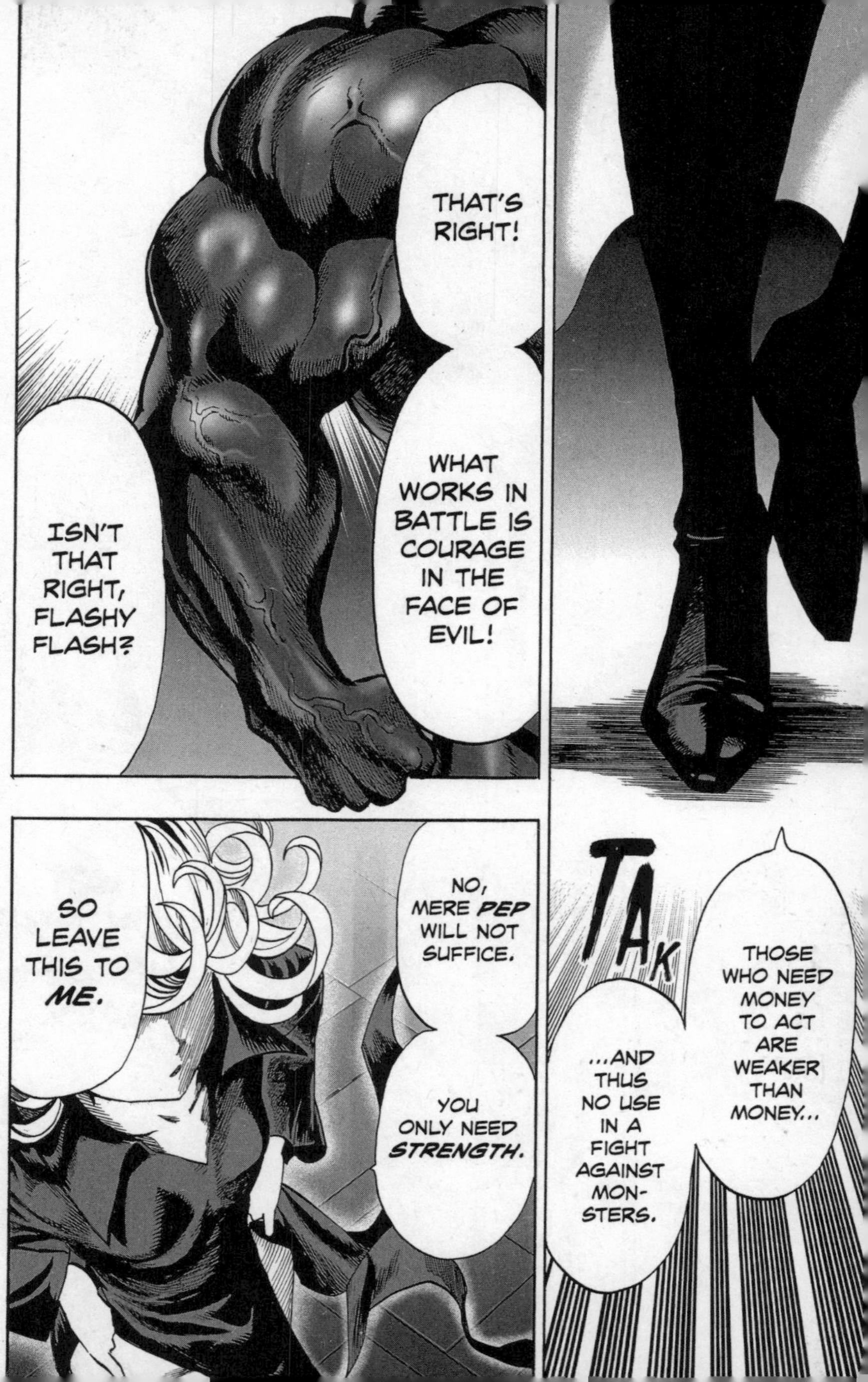
THAT'S RIGHT!
WHAT WORKS IN BATTLE IS COURAGE IN THE FACE OF EVIL!
ISN'T THAT RIGHT, FLASHY FLASH?
TAK
THOSE WHO NEED MONEY TO ACT ARE WEAKER THAN MONEY...
...AND THUS NO USE IN A FIGHT AGAINST MON-STERS.
NO, MERE *PEP* WILL NOT SUFFICE.
YOU ONLY NEED ***STRENGTH***.
SO LEAVE THIS TO ***ME***.

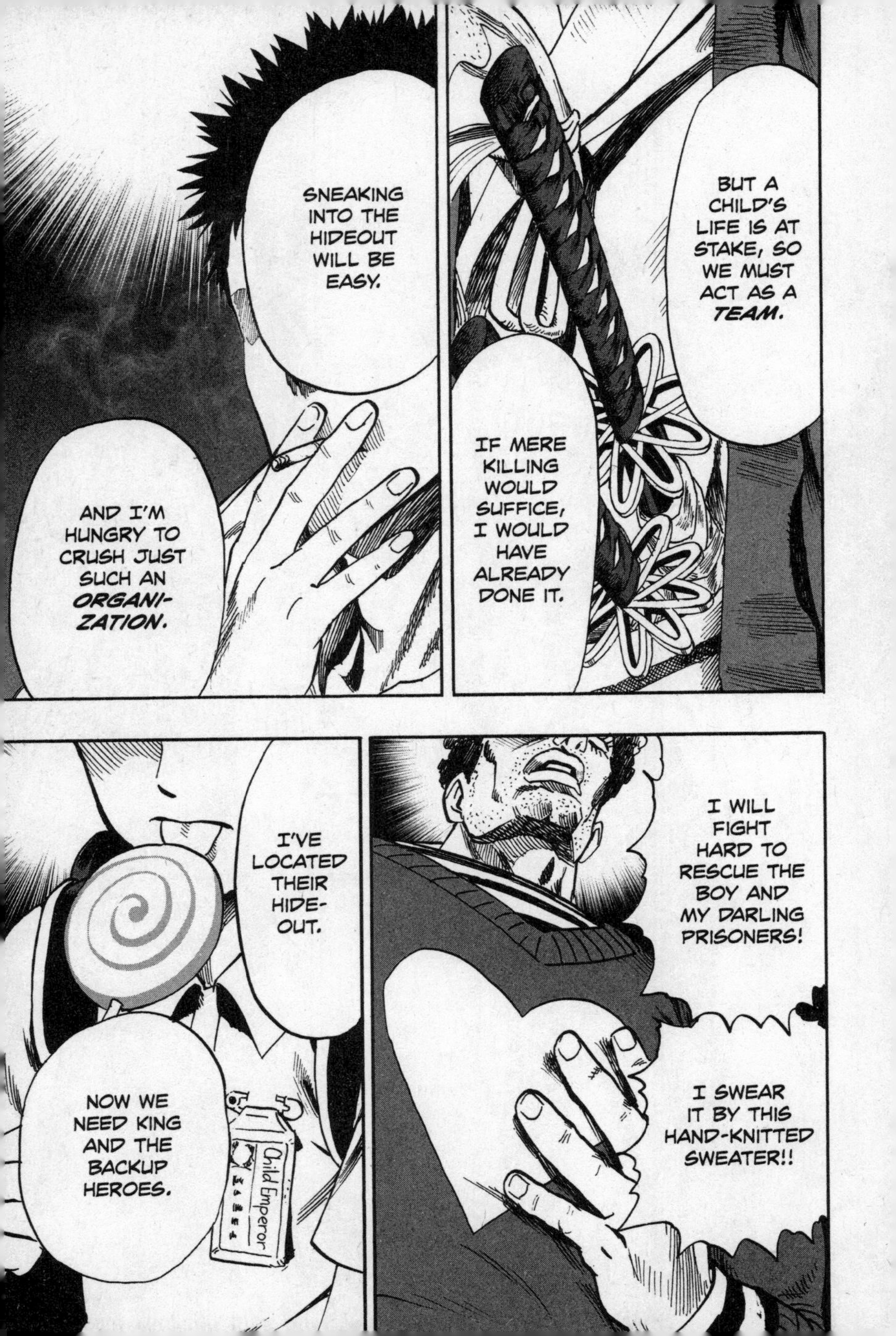
BUT A CHILD'S LIFE IS AT STAKE, SO WE MUST ACT AS A *TEAM*.
IF MERE KILLING WOULD SUFFICE, I WOULD HAVE ALREADY DONE IT.
SNEAKING INTO THE HIDEOUT WILL BE EASY.
AND I'M HUNGRY TO CRUSH JUST SUCH AN *ORGANI-ZATION*.
I WILL FIGHT HARD TO RESCUE THE BOY AND MY DARLING PRISONERS!
I SWEAR IT BY THIS HAND-KNITTED SWEATER!!
I'VE LOCATED THEIR HIDE-OUT.
NOW WE NEED KING AND THE BACKUP HEROES.
Child Emperor

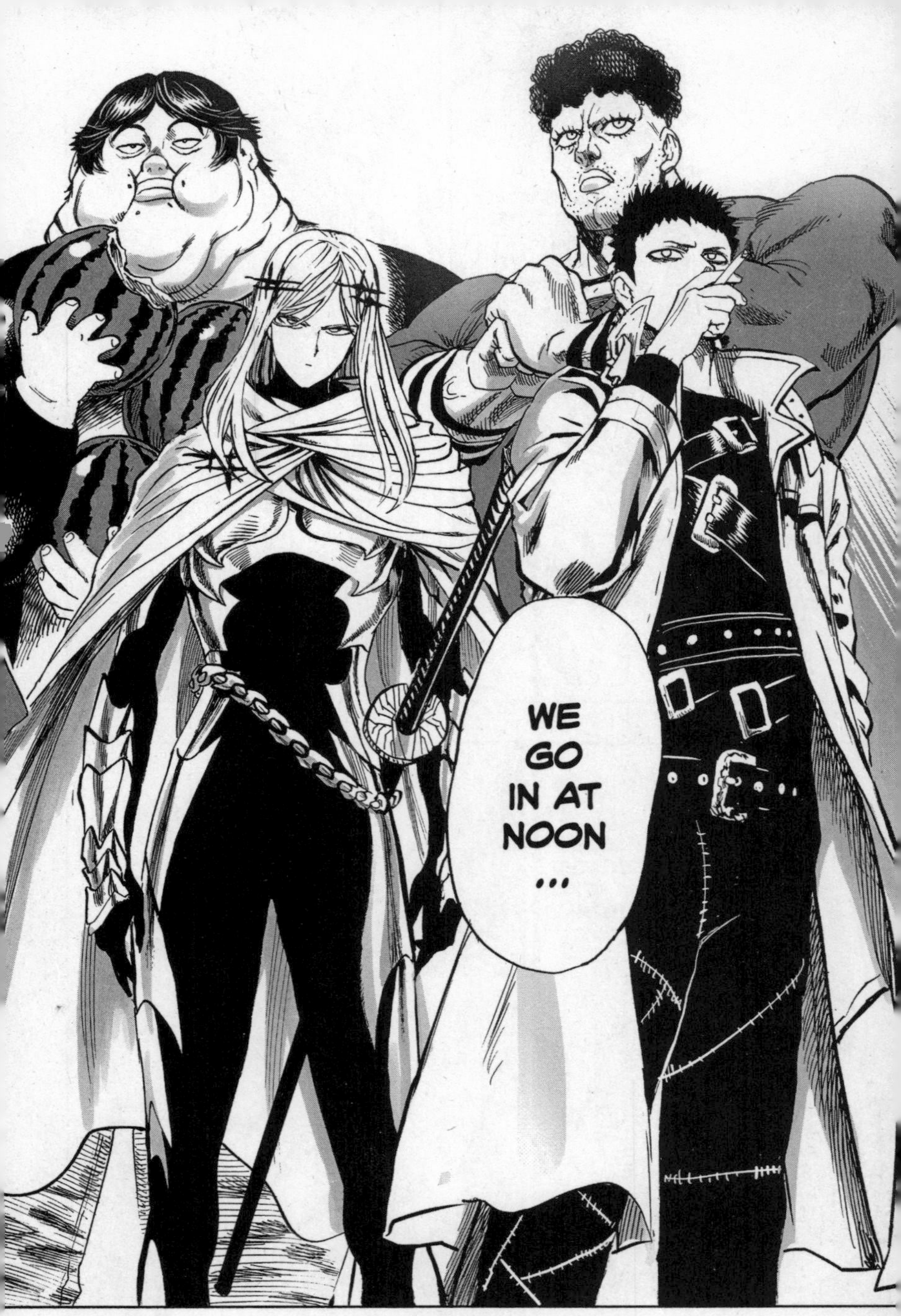
WE GO IN AT NOON ...

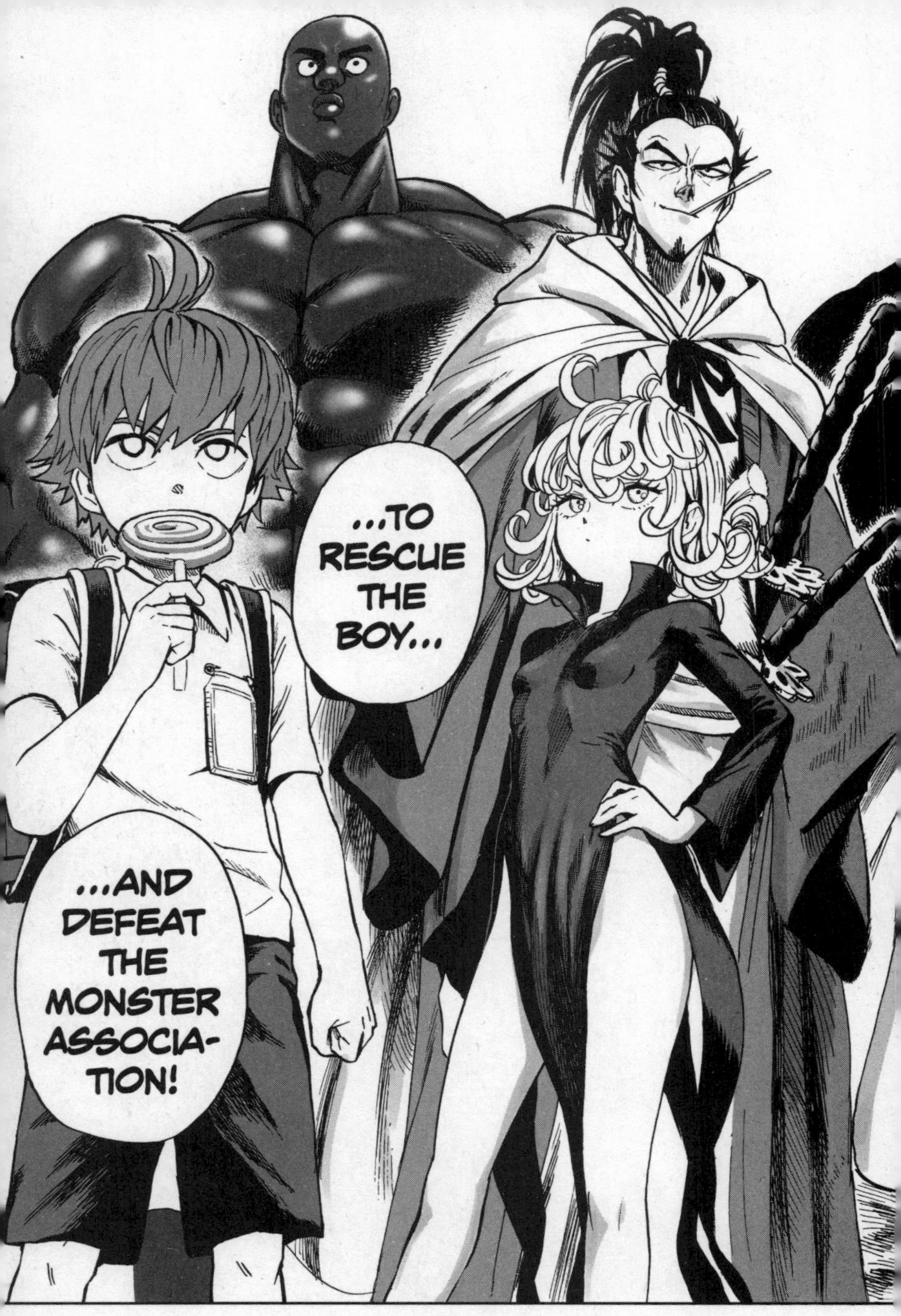
...TO RESCUE THE BOY...
...AND DEFEAT THE MONSTER ASSOCIA-TION!

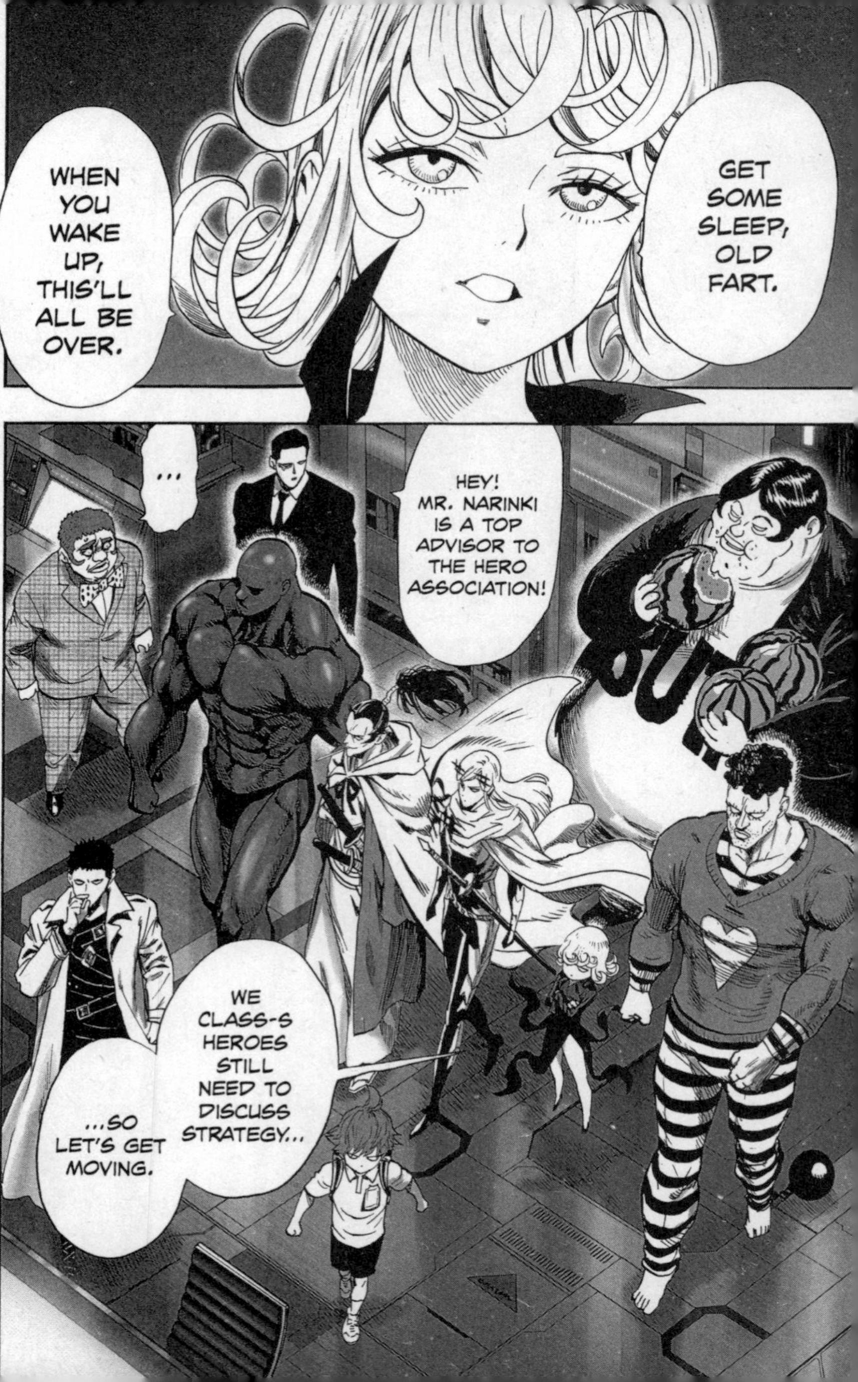
GET SOME SLEEP, OLD FART.
WHEN YOU WAKE UP, THIS'LL ALL BE OVER.
HEY! MR. NARINKI IS A TOP ADVISOR TO THE HERO ASSOCIATION!
...
WE CLASS-S HEROES STILL NEED TO DISCUSS STRATEGY...
...SO LET'S GET MOVING.

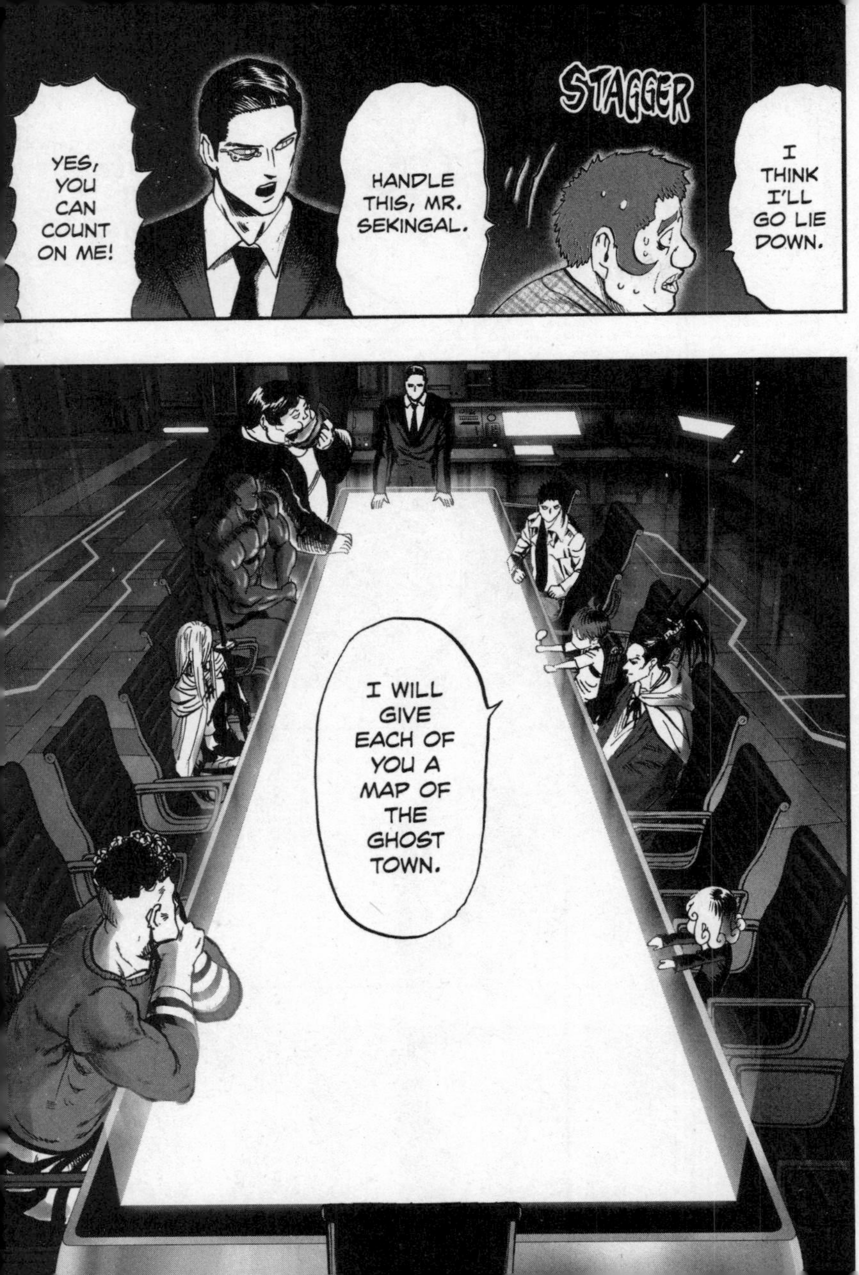
YES, YOU CAN COUNT ON ME!
HANDLE THIS, MR. SEKINGAL.
STAGGER
I THINK I'LL GO LIE DOWN.
I WILL GIVE EACH OF YOU A MAP OF THE GHOST TOWN.

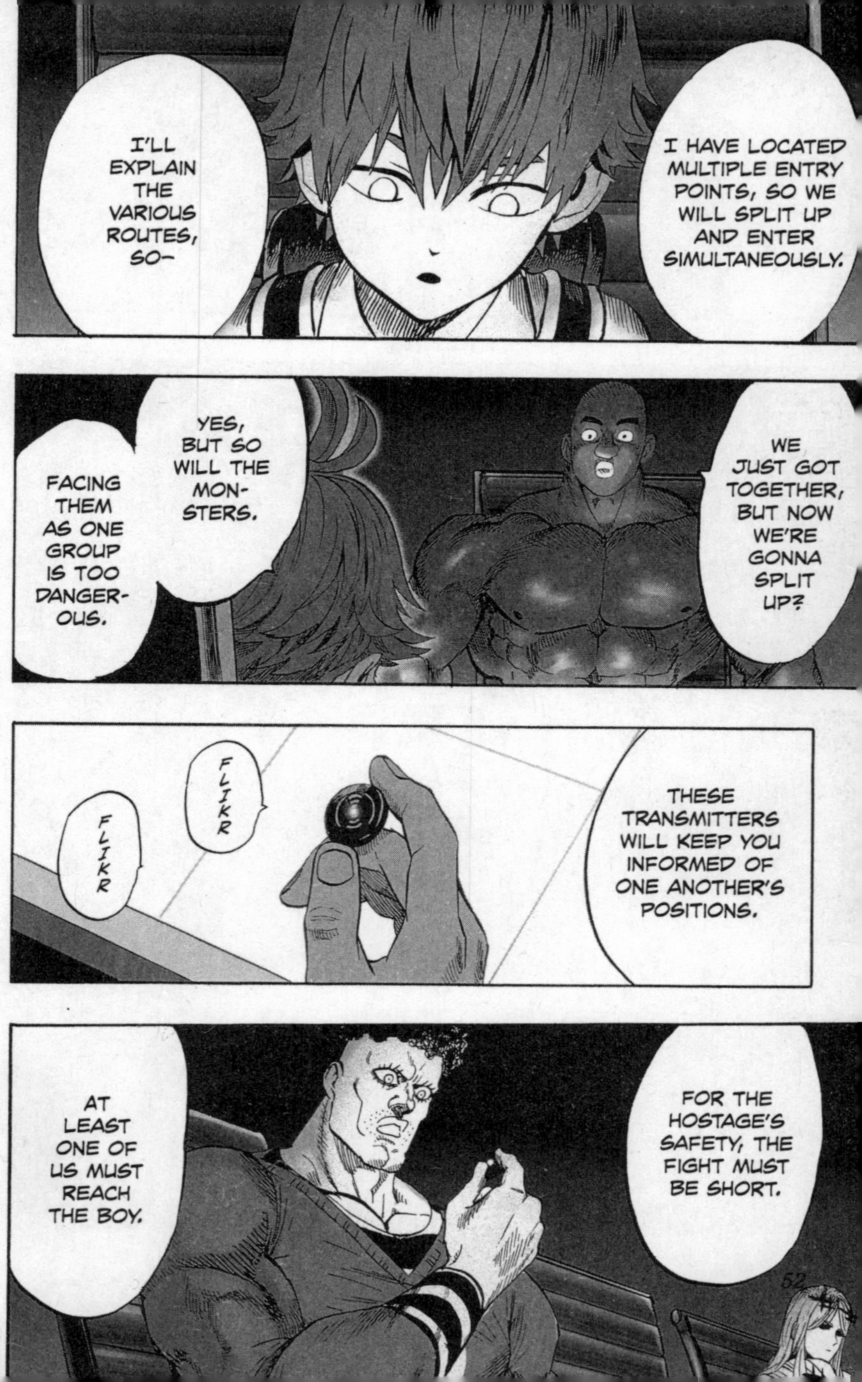
I HAVE LOCATED MULTIPLE ENTRY POINTS, SO WE WILL SPLIT UP AND ENTER SIMULTANEOUSLY.
I'LL EXPLAIN THE VARIOUS ROUTES, SO–
WE JUST GOT TOGETHER, BUT NOW WE'RE GONNA SPLIT UP?
YES, BUT SO WILL THE MON-STERS.
FACING THEM AS ONE GROUP IS TOO DANGER-OUS.
THESE TRANSMITTERS WILL KEEP YOU INFORMED OF ONE ANOTHER'S POSITIONS.
FLIKR
FLIKR
FOR THE HOSTAGE'S SAFETY, THE FIGHT MUST BE SHORT.
AT LEAST ONE OF US MUST REACH THE BOY.

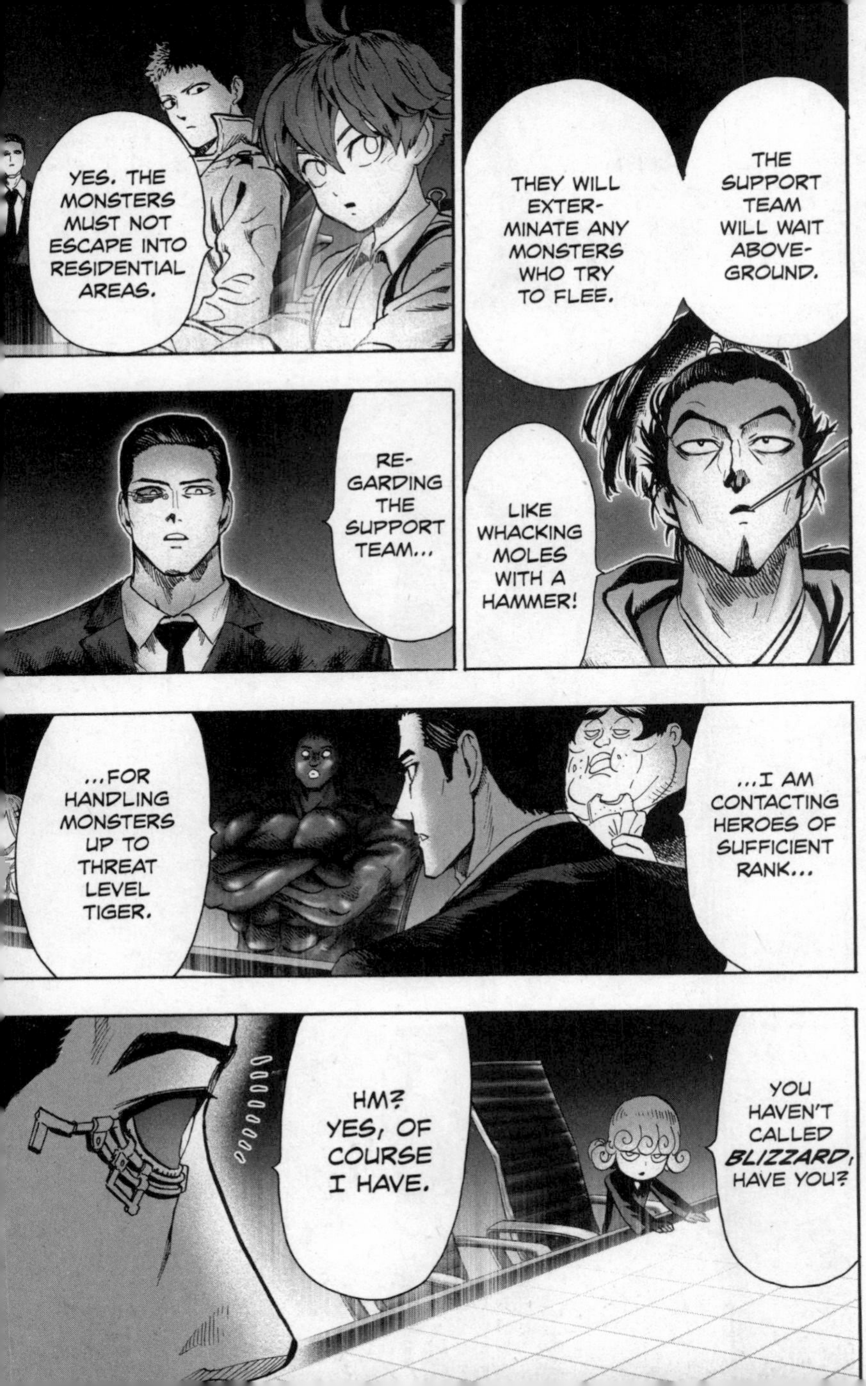
THE SUPPORT TEAM WILL WAIT ABOVE-GROUND.
THEY WILL EXTER-MINATE ANY MONSTERS WHO TRY TO FLEE.
LIKE WHACKING MOLES WITH A HAMMER!
YES. THE MONSTERS MUST NOT ESCAPE INTO RESIDENTIAL AREAS.
RE-GARDING THE SUPPORT TEAM...
...I AM CONTACTING HEROES OF SUFFICIENT RANK...
...FOR HANDLING MONSTERS UP TO THREAT LEVEL TIGER.
YOU HAVEN'T CALLED *BLIZZARD*, HAVE YOU?
HM? YES, OF COURSE I HAVE.

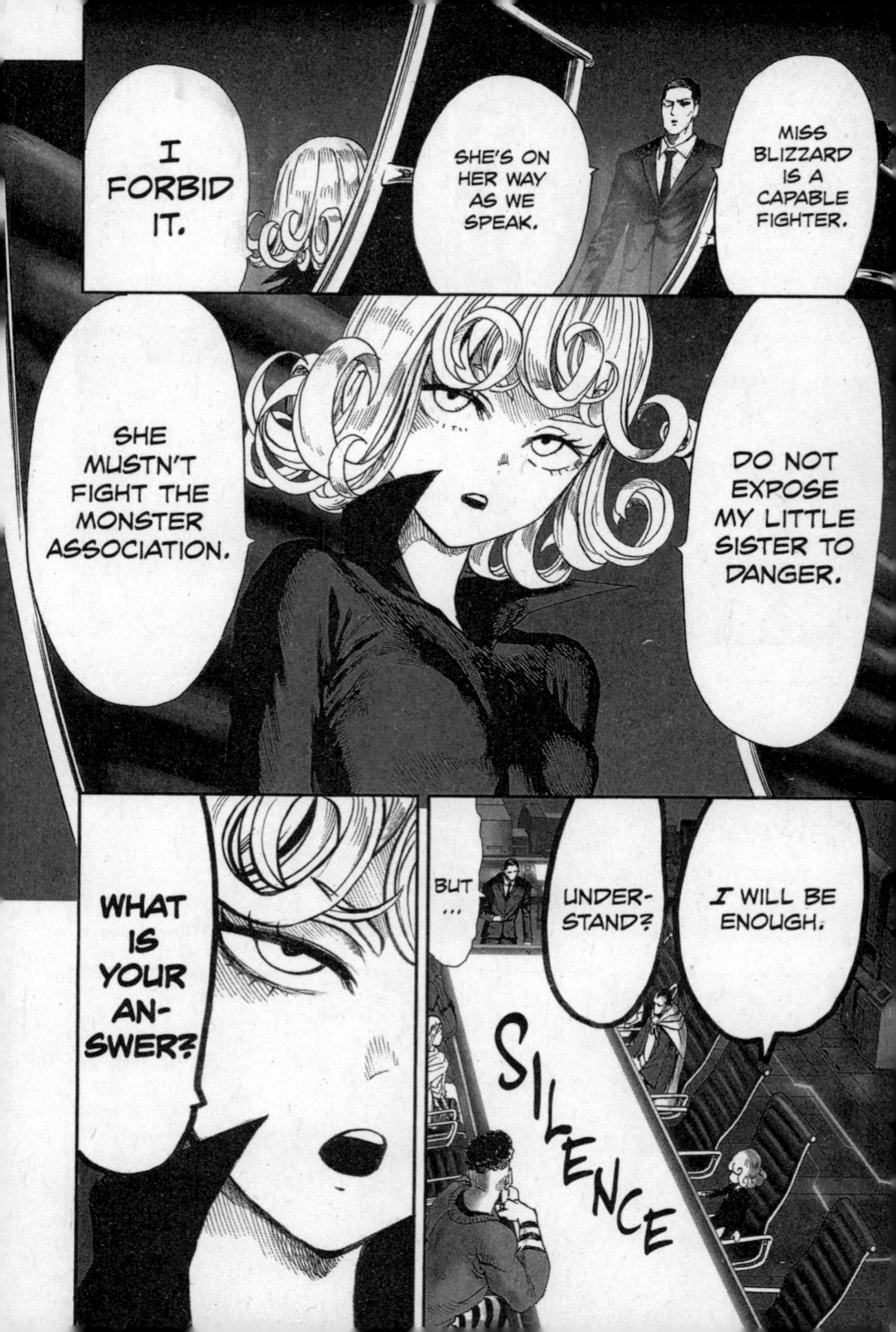
MISS BLIZZARD IS A CAPABLE FIGHTER.
SHE'S ON HER WAY AS WE SPEAK.
I FORBID IT.
DO NOT EXPOSE MY LITTLE SISTER TO DANGER.
SHE MUSTN'T FIGHT THE MONSTER ASSOCIATION.
I WILL BE ENOUGH.
UNDER-STAND?
BUT ...
SILENCE
WHAT IS YOUR AN-SWER?

I'LL TELL HER TO STAND DOWN.

UM... VERY WELL.

GOOD MORNING. HAVE YOU BEEN A GOOD BOY?

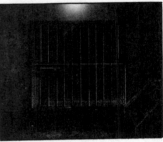

YIKES!

CRINGE

DOZE

DOZE

ZZZ

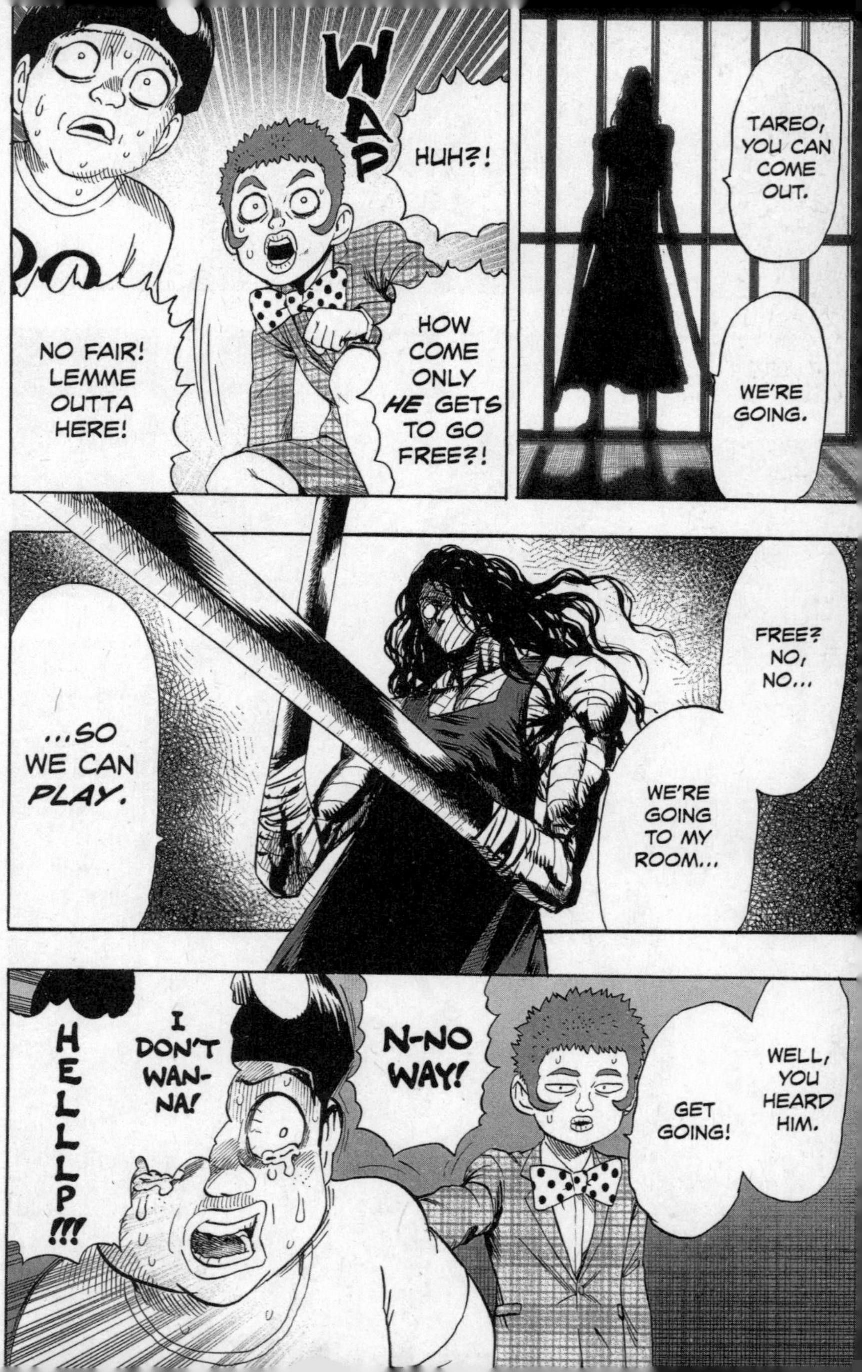
TAREO, YOU CAN COME OUT.
WE'RE GOING.
WAP
HUH?!
HOW COME ONLY *HE* GETS TO GO FREE?!
NO FAIR! LEMME OUTTA HERE!
FREE? NO, NO...
WE'RE GOING TO MY ROOM...
...SO WE CAN *PLAY*.
WELL, YOU HEARD HIM.
GET GOING!
N-NO WAY!
I DON'T WAN-NA!
HELLLP!!!

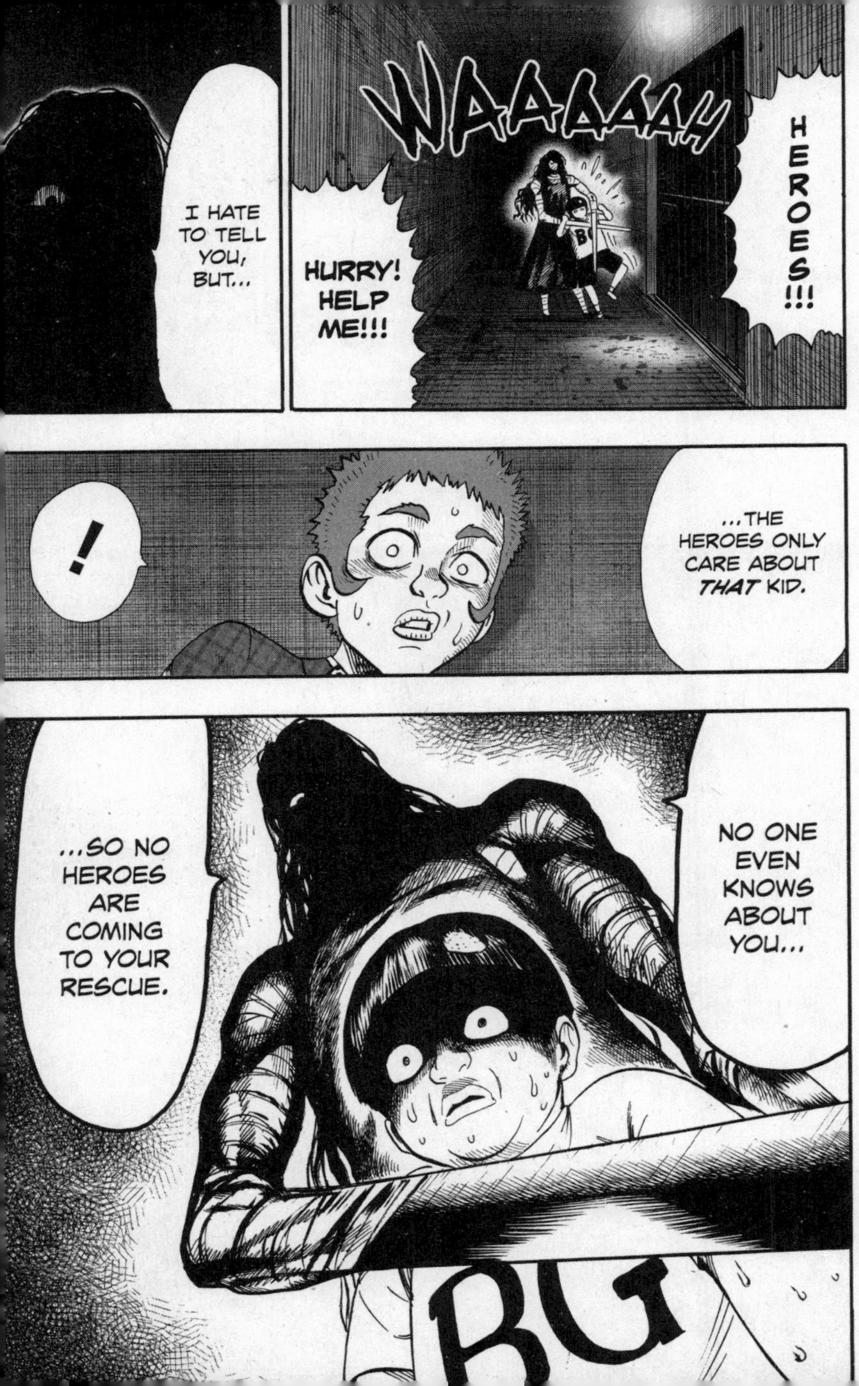
WAAAAAH
HEROES!!!
HURRY! HELP ME!!!
I HATE TO TELL YOU, BUT...
...THE HEROES ONLY CARE ABOUT *THAT* KID.
!
NO ONE EVEN KNOWS ABOUT YOU...
...SO NO HEROES ARE COMING TO YOUR RESCUE.
BG

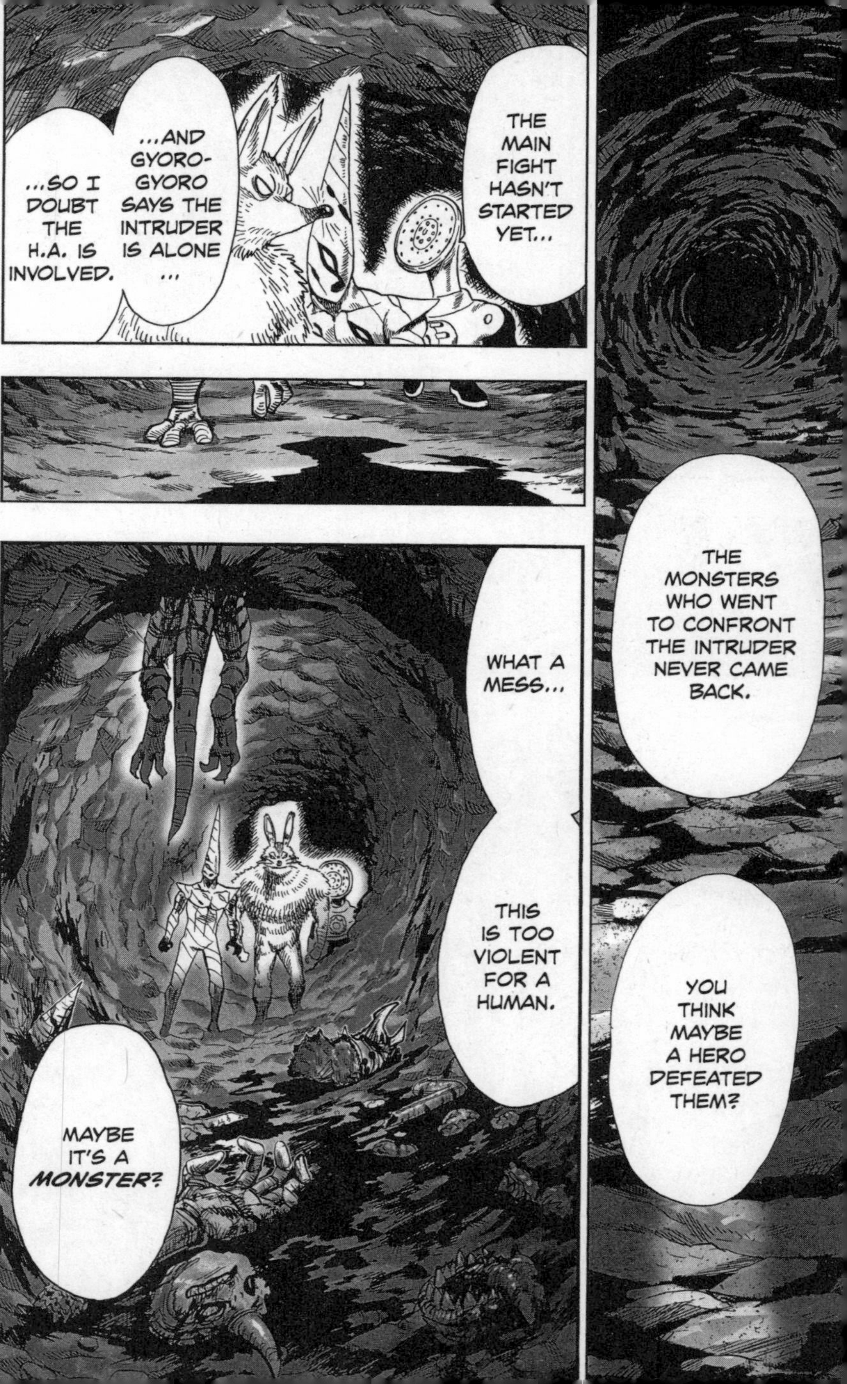
THE MONSTERS WHO WENT TO CONFRONT THE INTRUDER NEVER CAME BACK.
YOU THINK MAYBE A HERO DEFEATED THEM?
THE MAIN FIGHT HASN'T STARTED YET...
...AND GYORO-GYORO SAYS THE INTRUDER IS ALONE...
...SO I DOUBT THE H.A. IS INVOLVED.
WHAT A MESS...
THIS IS TOO VIOLENT FOR A HUMAN.
MAYBE IT'S A *MONSTER*?

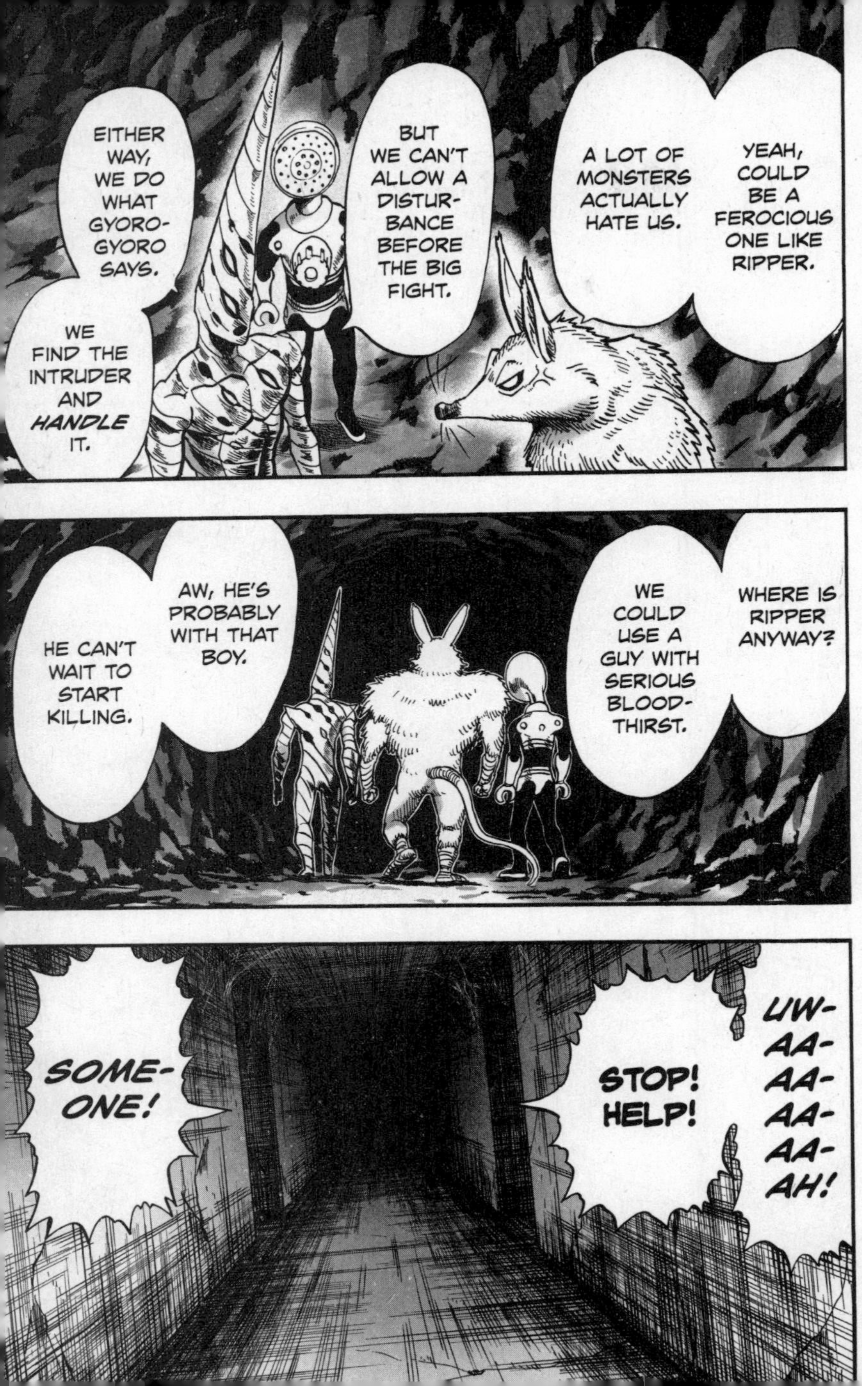
YEAH, COULD BE A FEROCIOUS ONE LIKE RIPPER.
A LOT OF MONSTERS ACTUALLY HATE US.
BUT WE CAN'T ALLOW A DISTUR-BANCE BEFORE THE BIG FIGHT.
EITHER WAY, WE DO WHAT GYORO-GYORO SAYS.
WE FIND THE INTRUDER AND *HANDLE* IT.
WHERE IS RIPPER ANYWAY?
WE COULD USE A GUY WITH SERIOUS BLOOD-THIRST.
AW, HE'S PROBABLY WITH THAT BOY.
HE CAN'T WAIT TO START KILLING.
UW-AA-AA-AA-AA-AH!
STOP! HELP!
SOME-ONE!

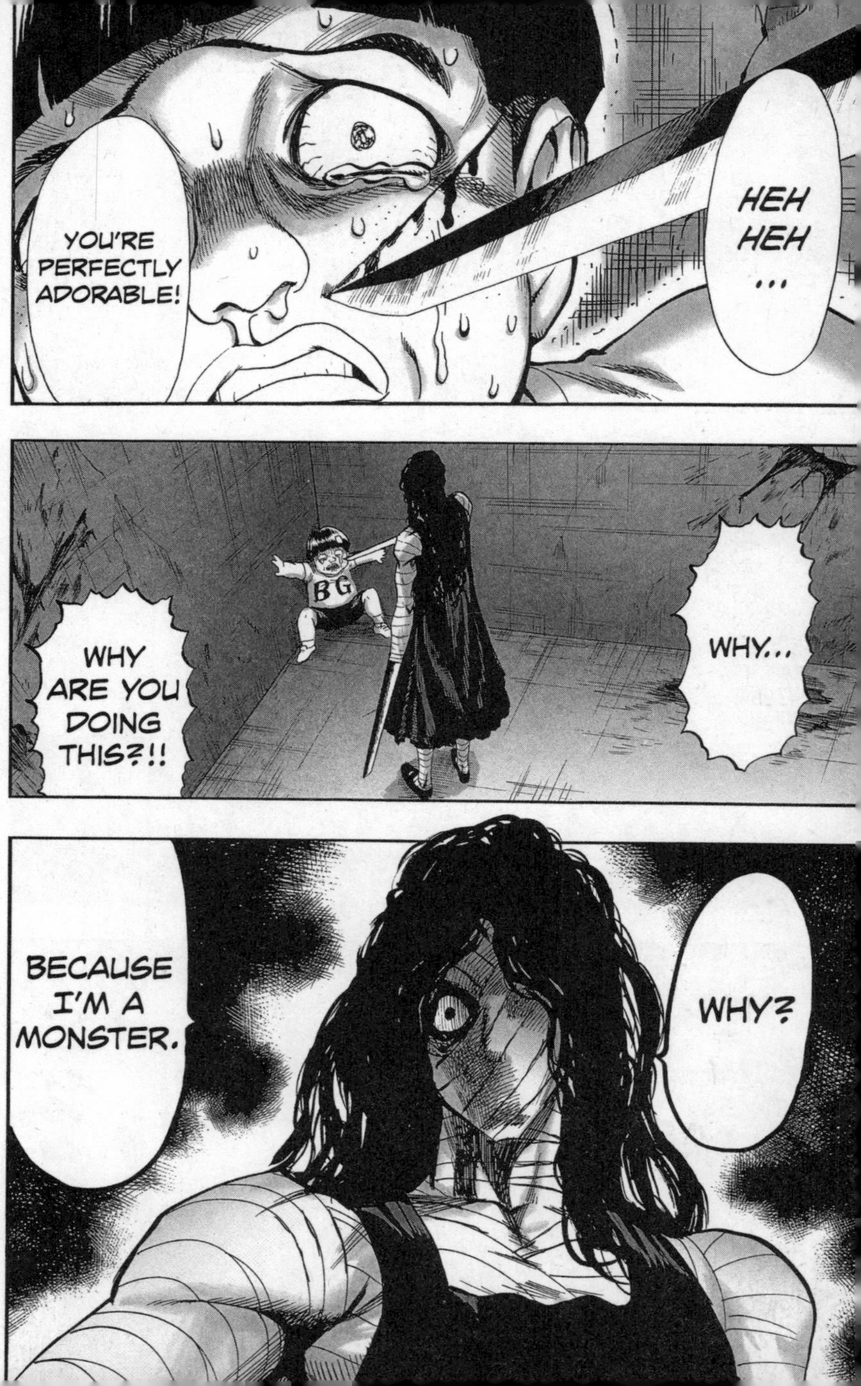
HEH HEH ...
YOU'RE PERFECTLY ADORABLE!
WHY...
WHY ARE YOU DOING THIS?!!
WHY?
BECAUSE I'M A MONSTER.

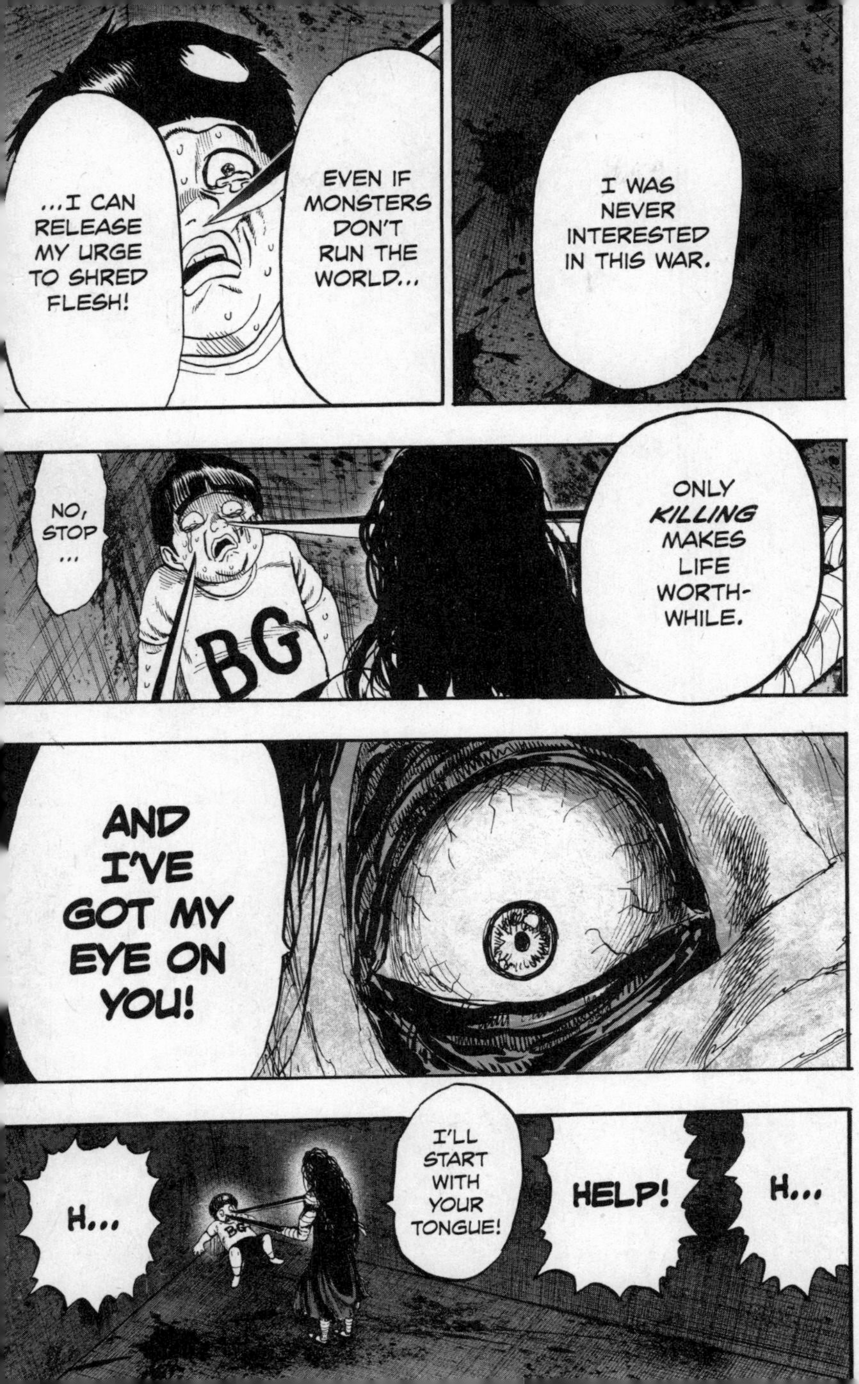
I WAS NEVER INTERESTED IN THIS WAR.
EVEN IF MONSTERS DON'T RUN THE WORLD...
...I CAN RELEASE MY URGE TO SHRED FLESH!
ONLY *KILLING* MAKES LIFE WORTH-WHILE.
NO, STOP ...
AND I'VE GOT MY EYE ON YOU!
H...
HELP!
I'LL START WITH YOUR TONGUE!
H...

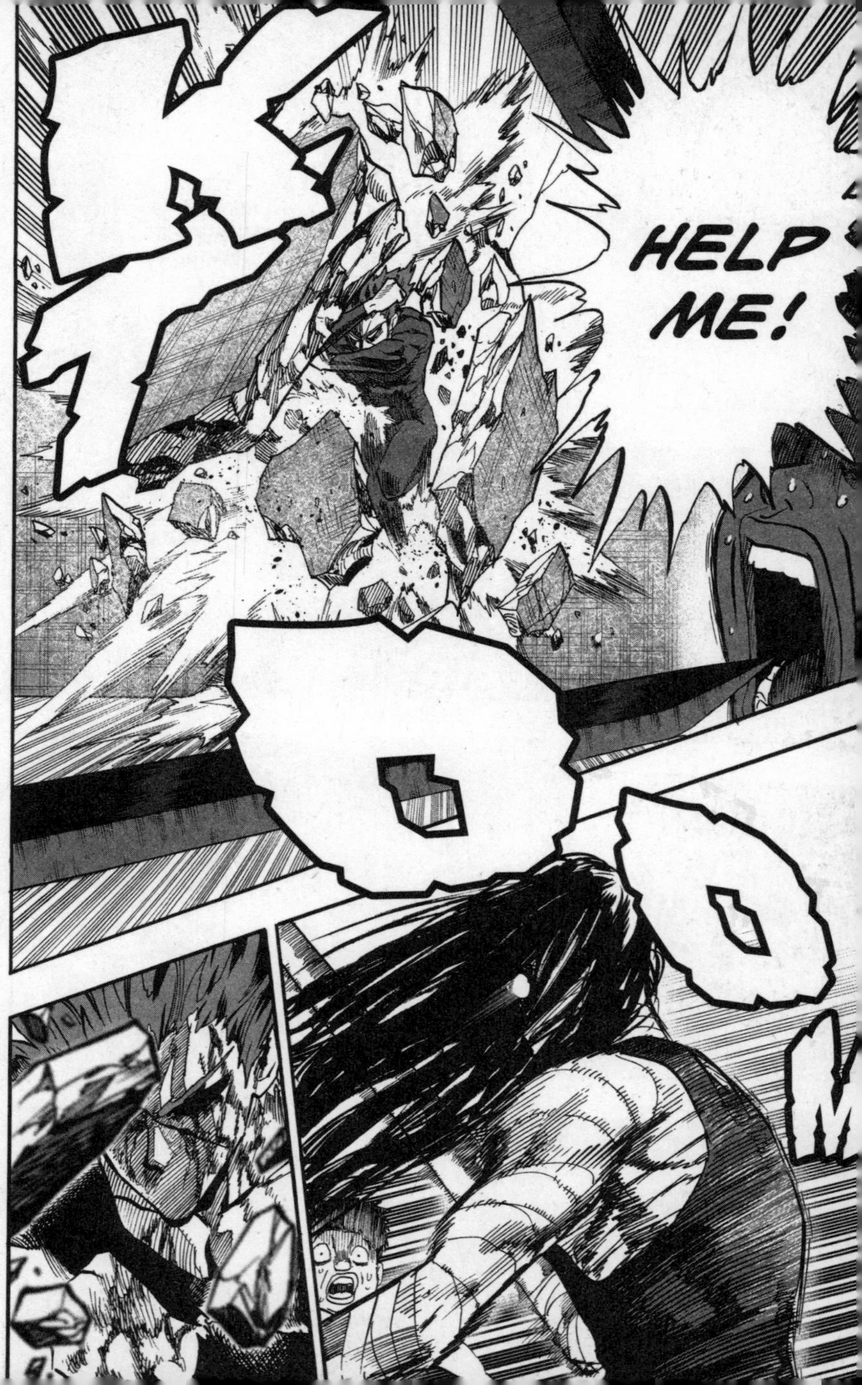
HELP ME!

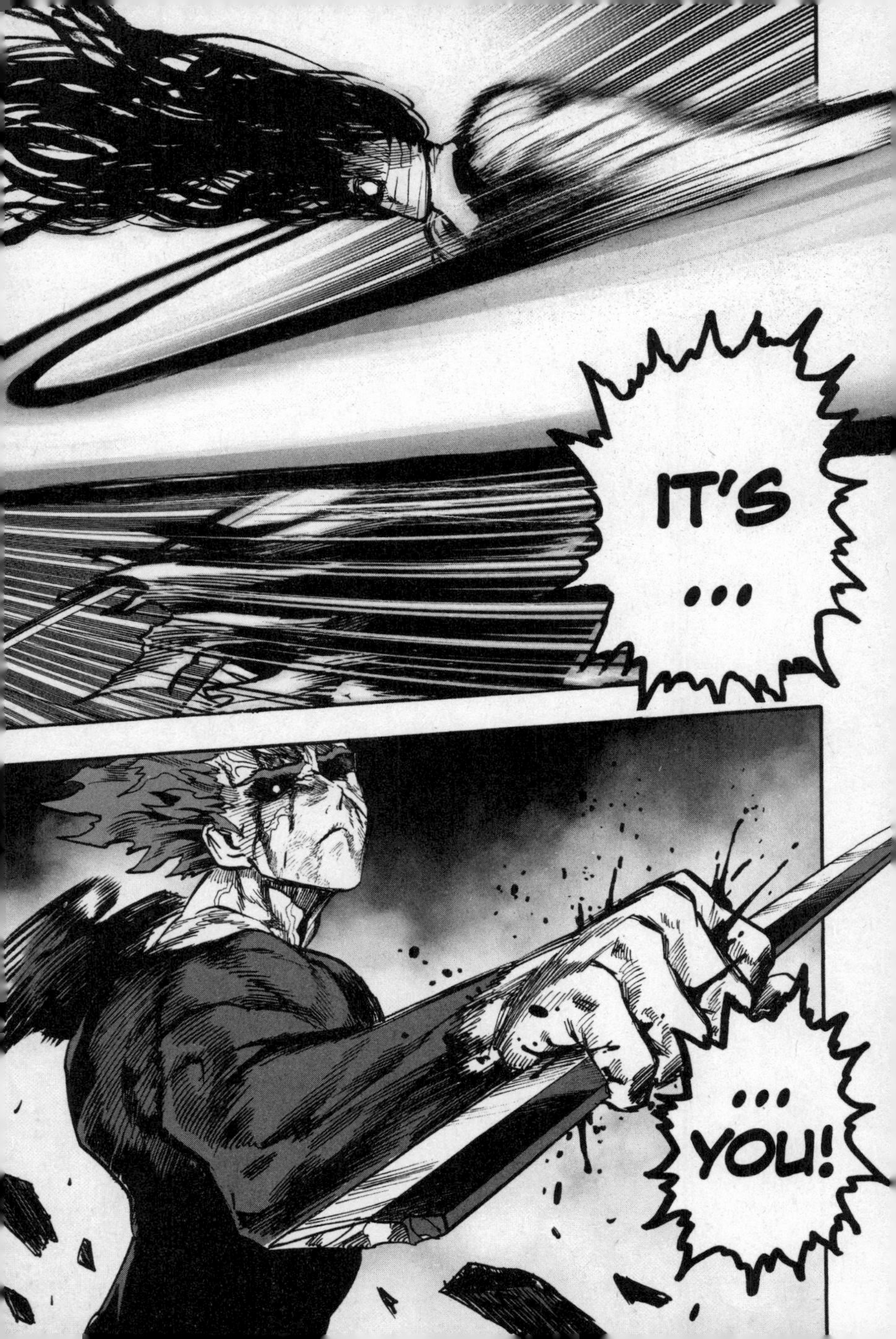
IT'S ...
... YOU!

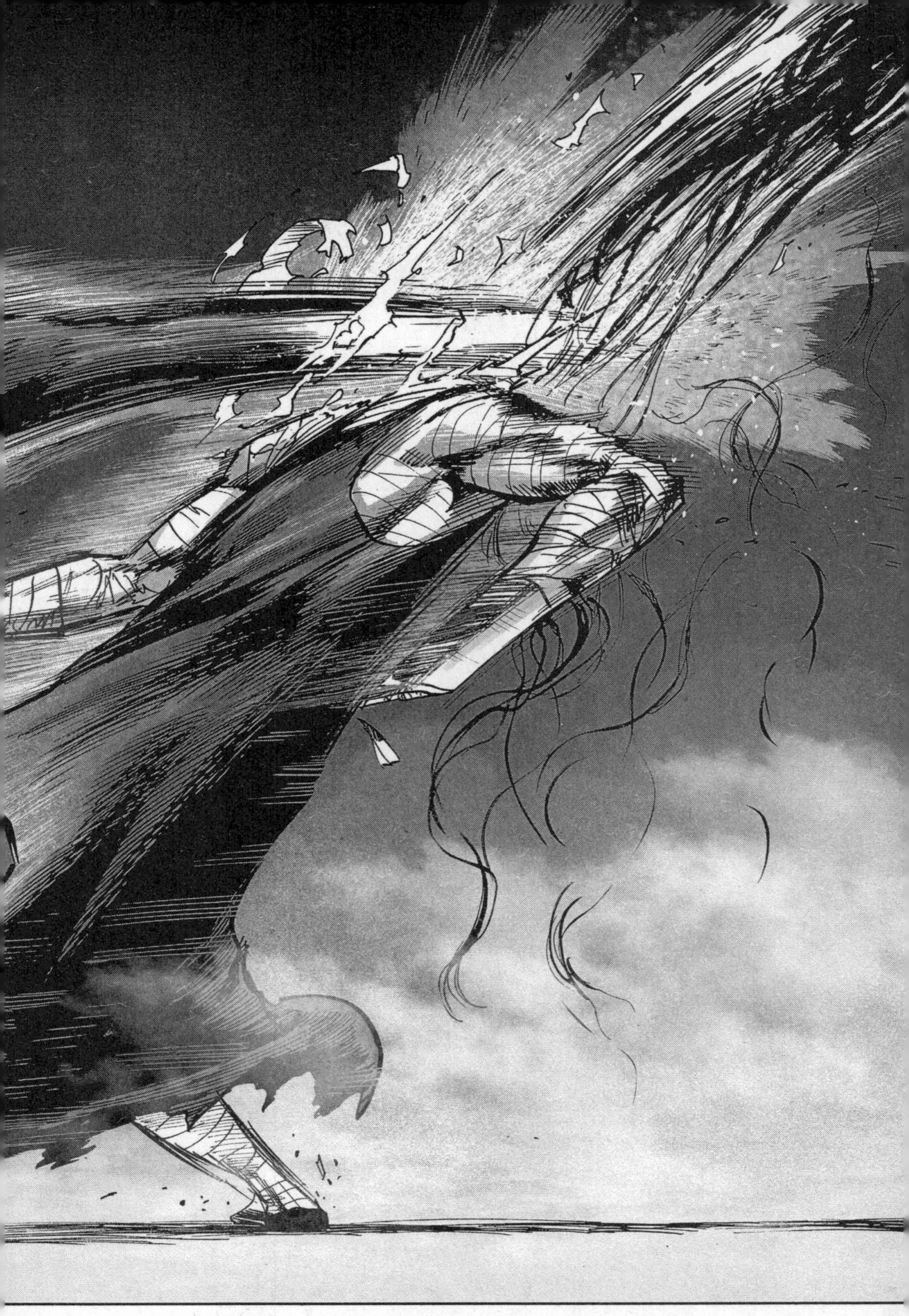

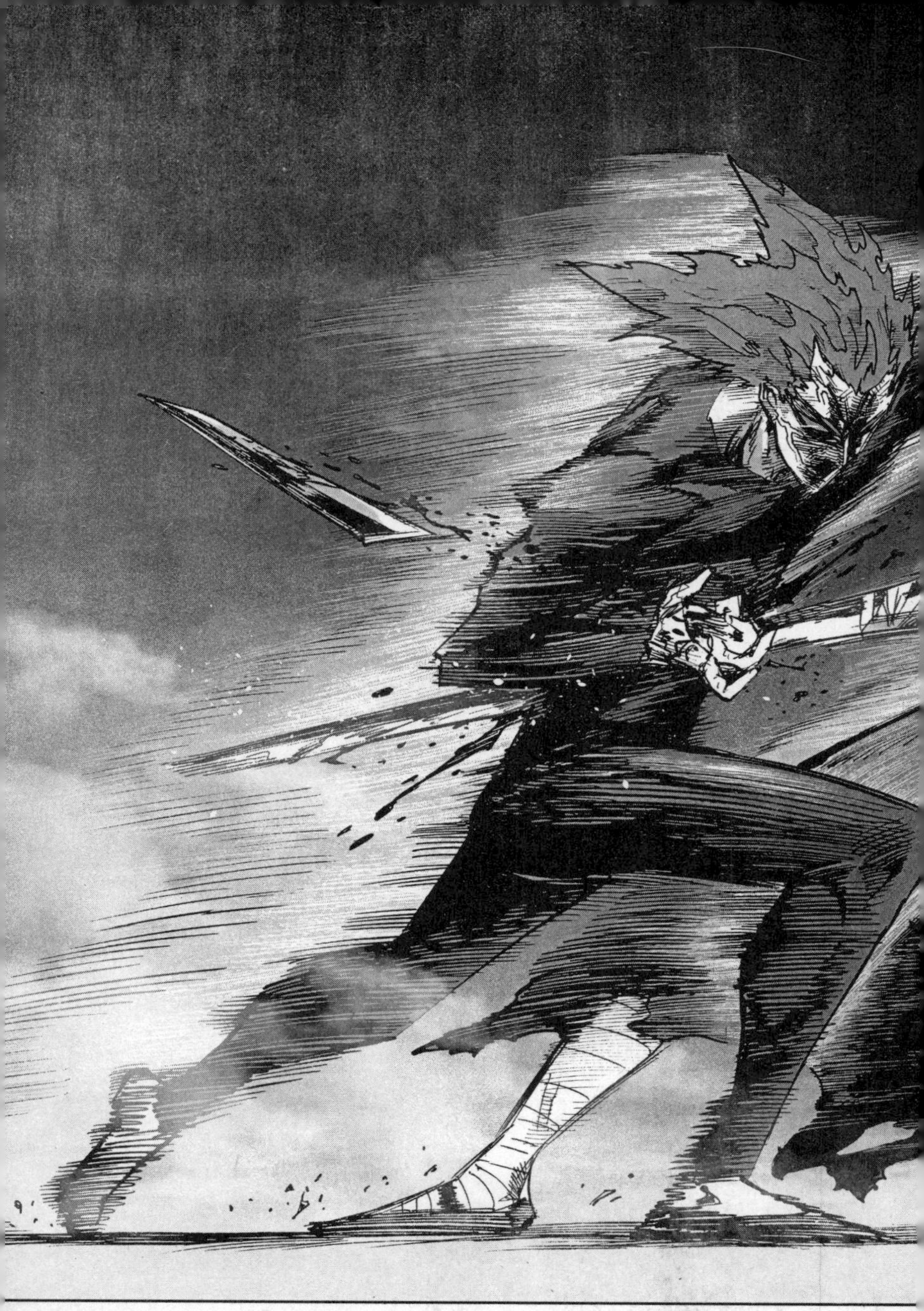

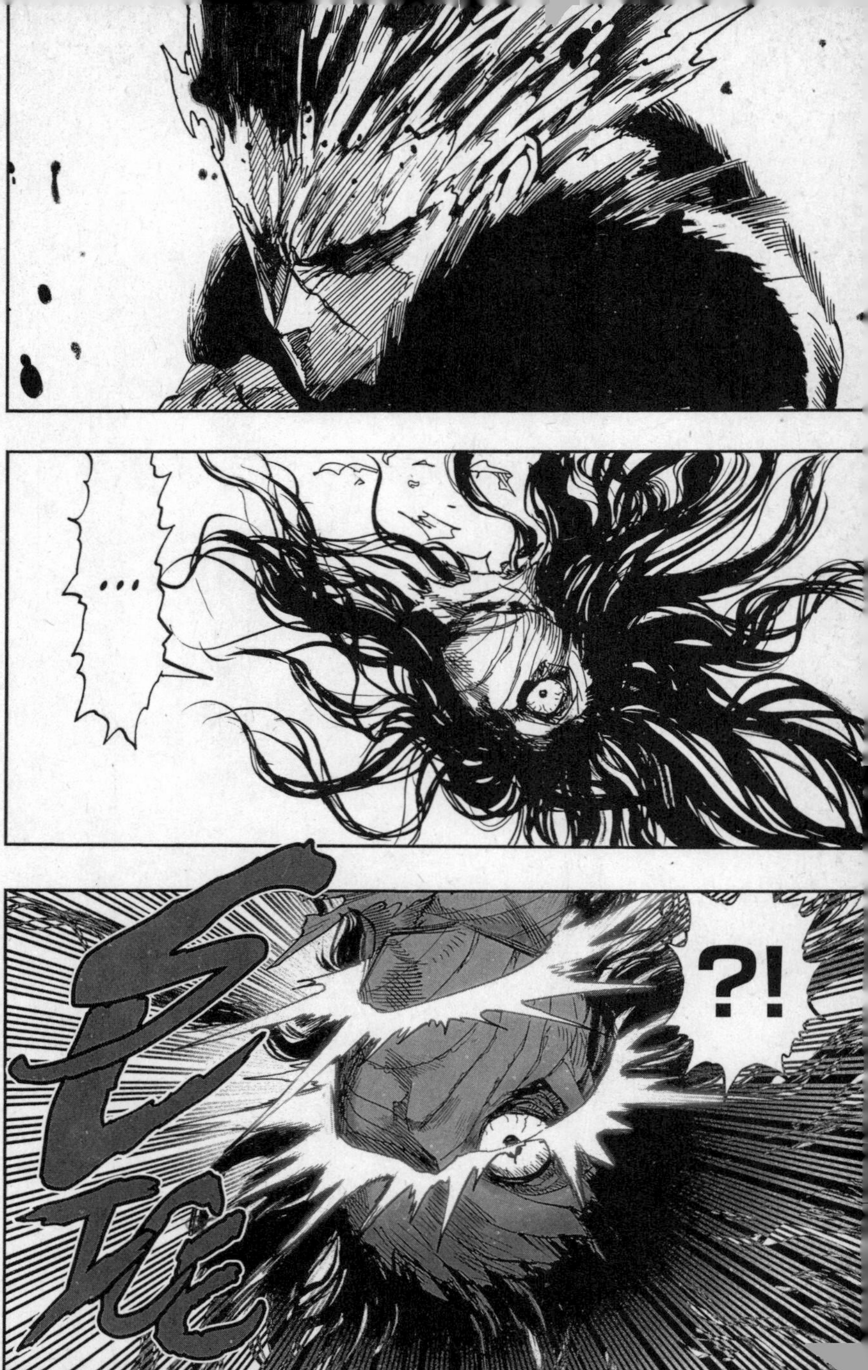
...
?!

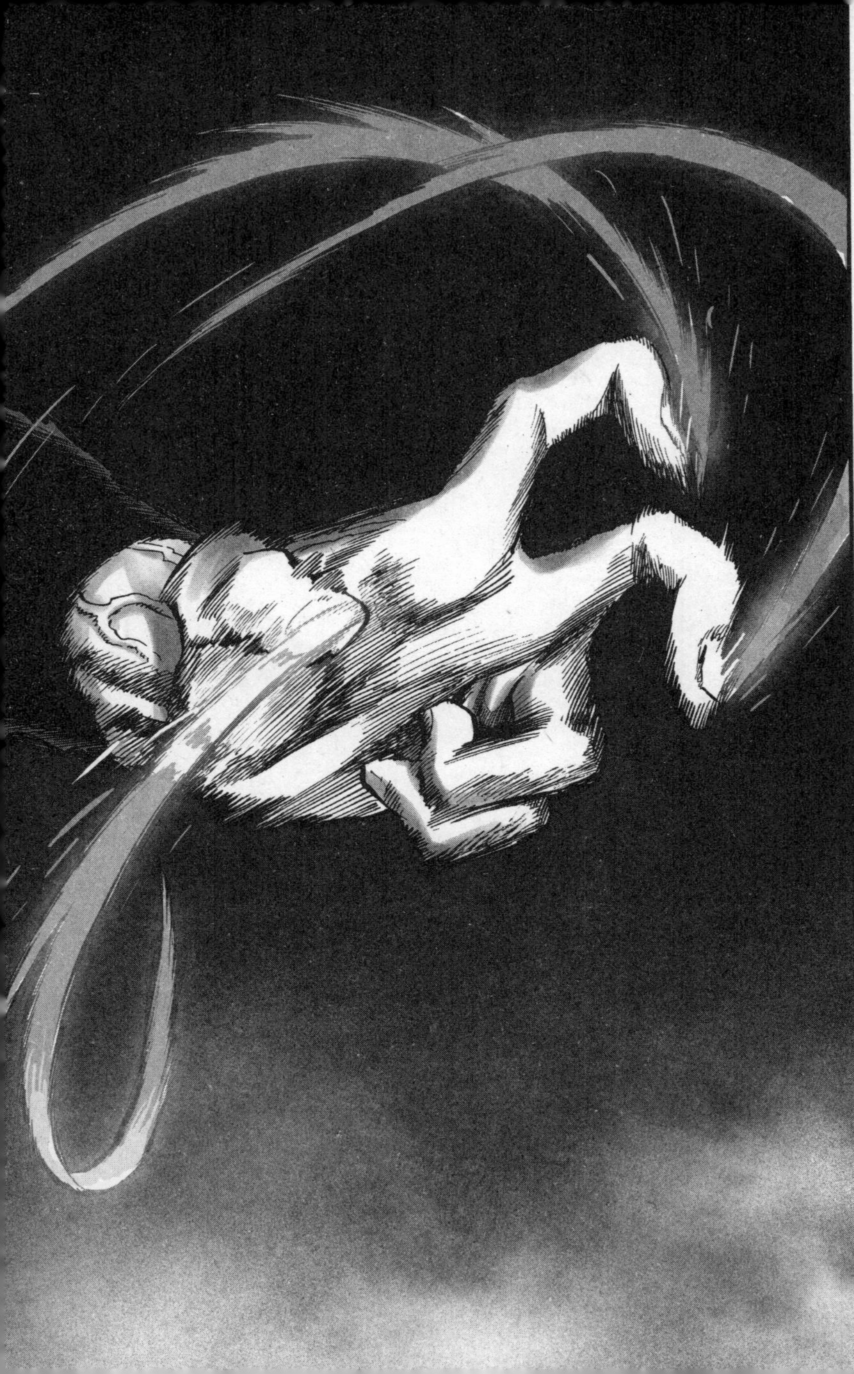

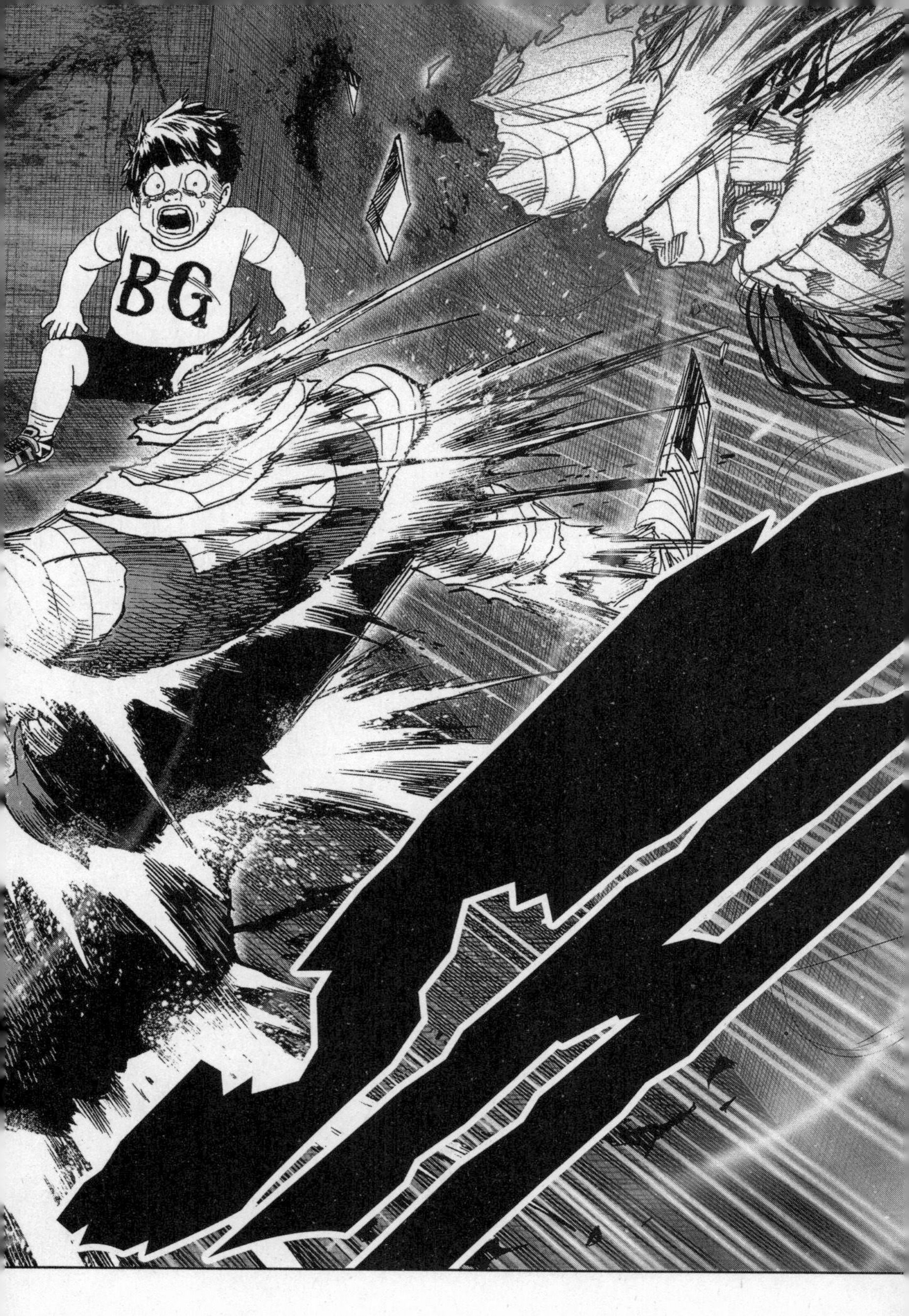
BG

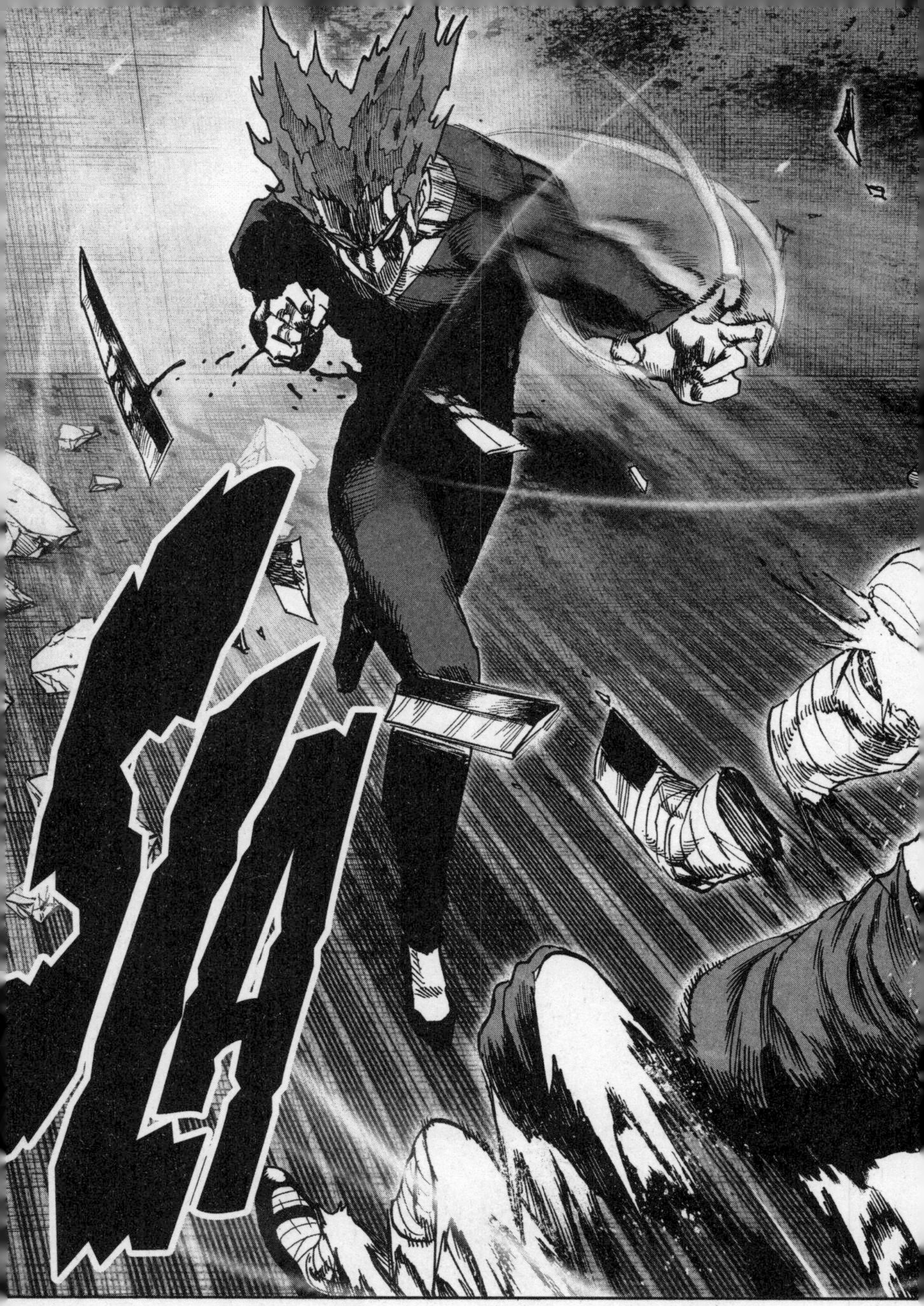

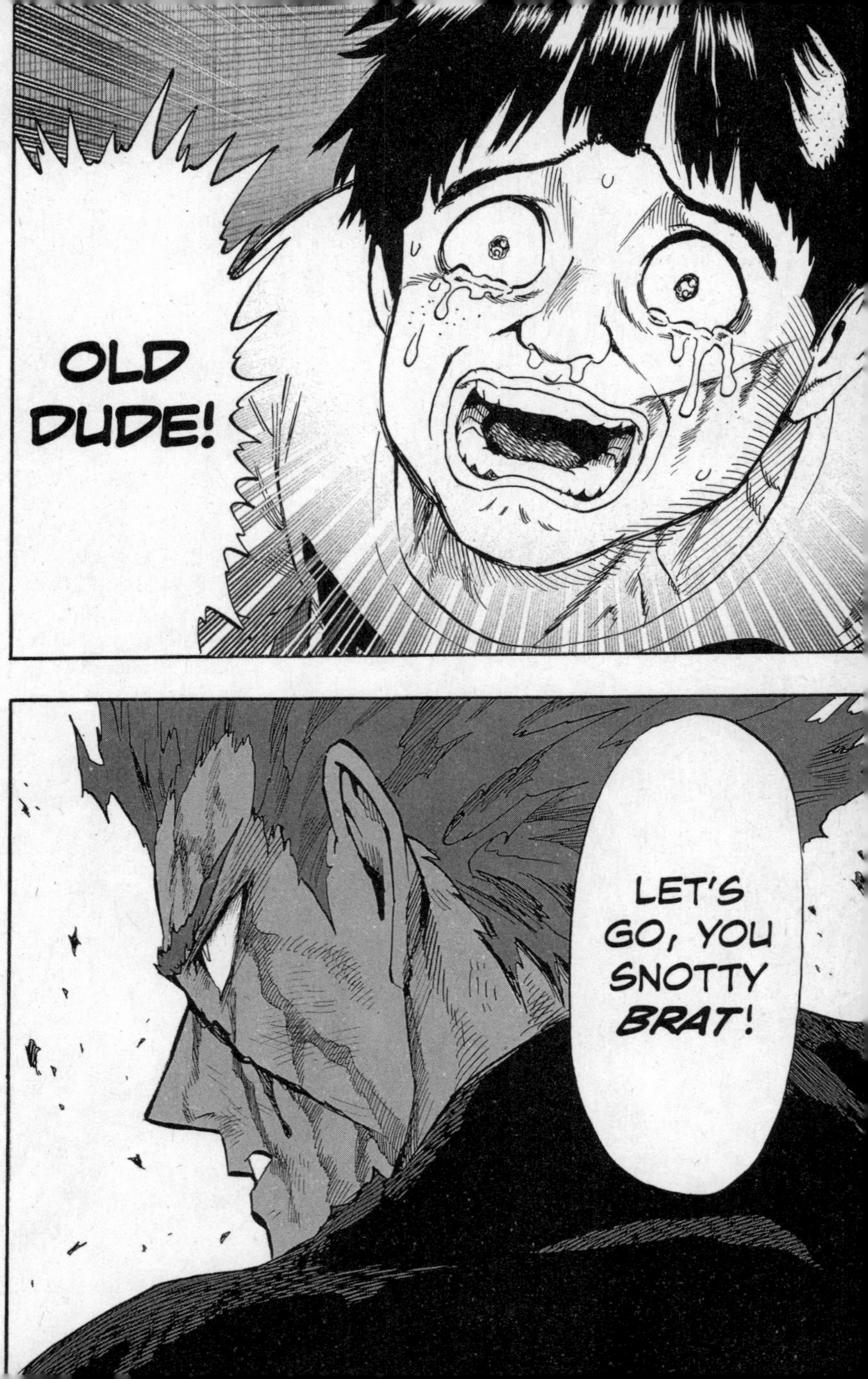
OLD DUDE!
LET'S GO, YOU SNOTTY BRAT!

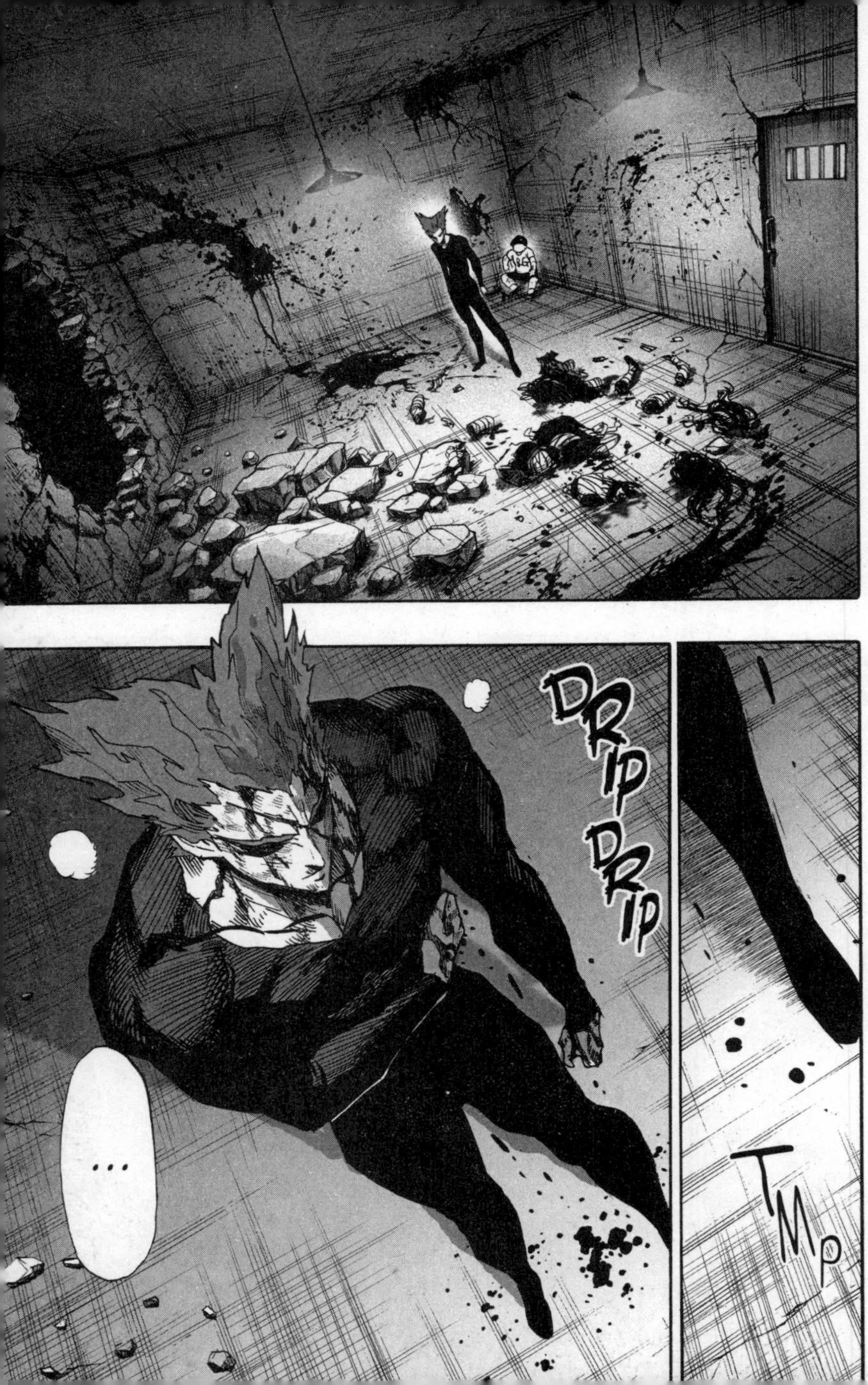
DRIP DRIP
...
TMP

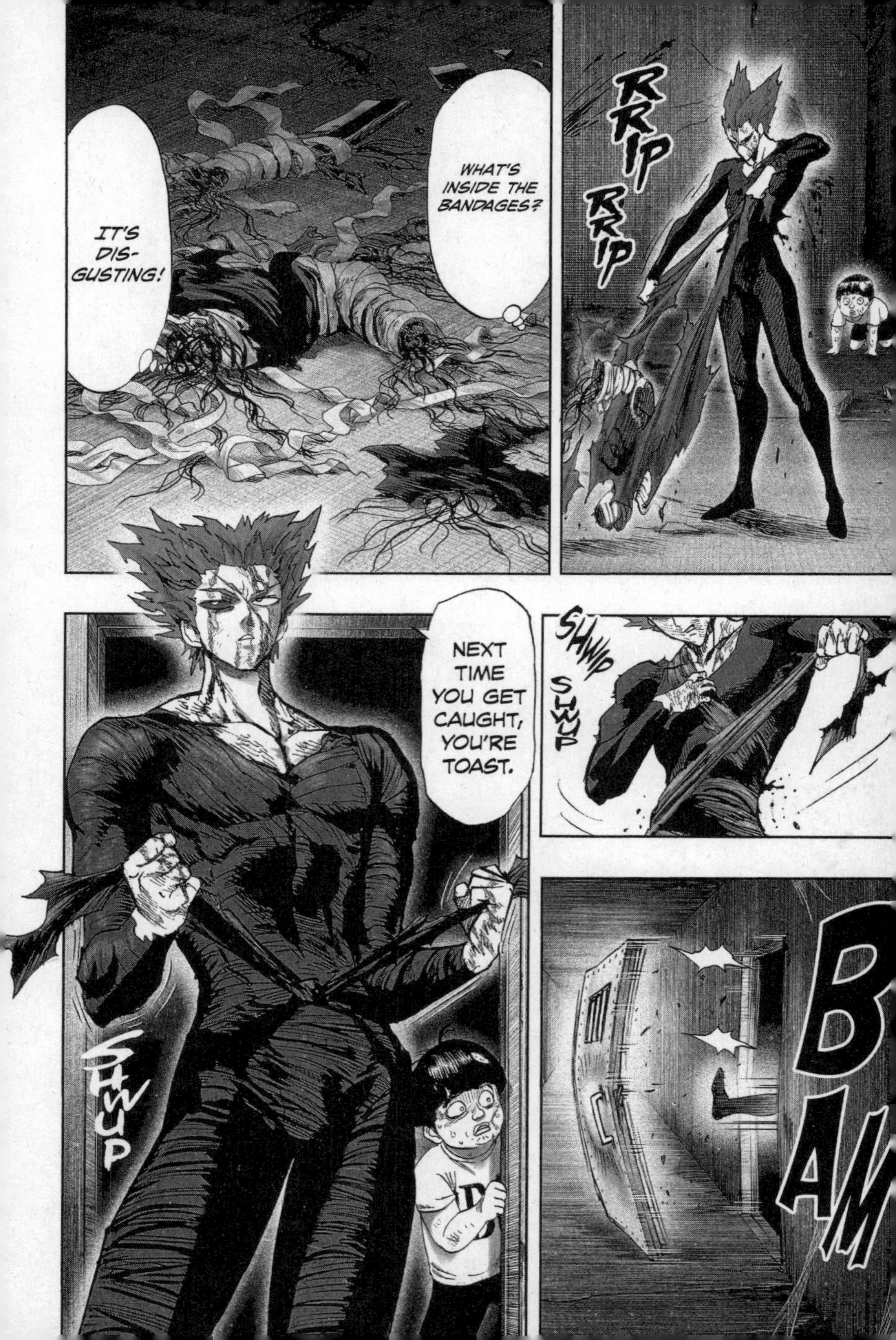
RRIP
RRIP
WHAT'S INSIDE THE BANDAGES?
IT'S DIS-GUSTING!
SHWUP
SHWUP
BAM
NEXT TIME YOU GET CAUGHT, YOU'RE TOAST.
SHWUP

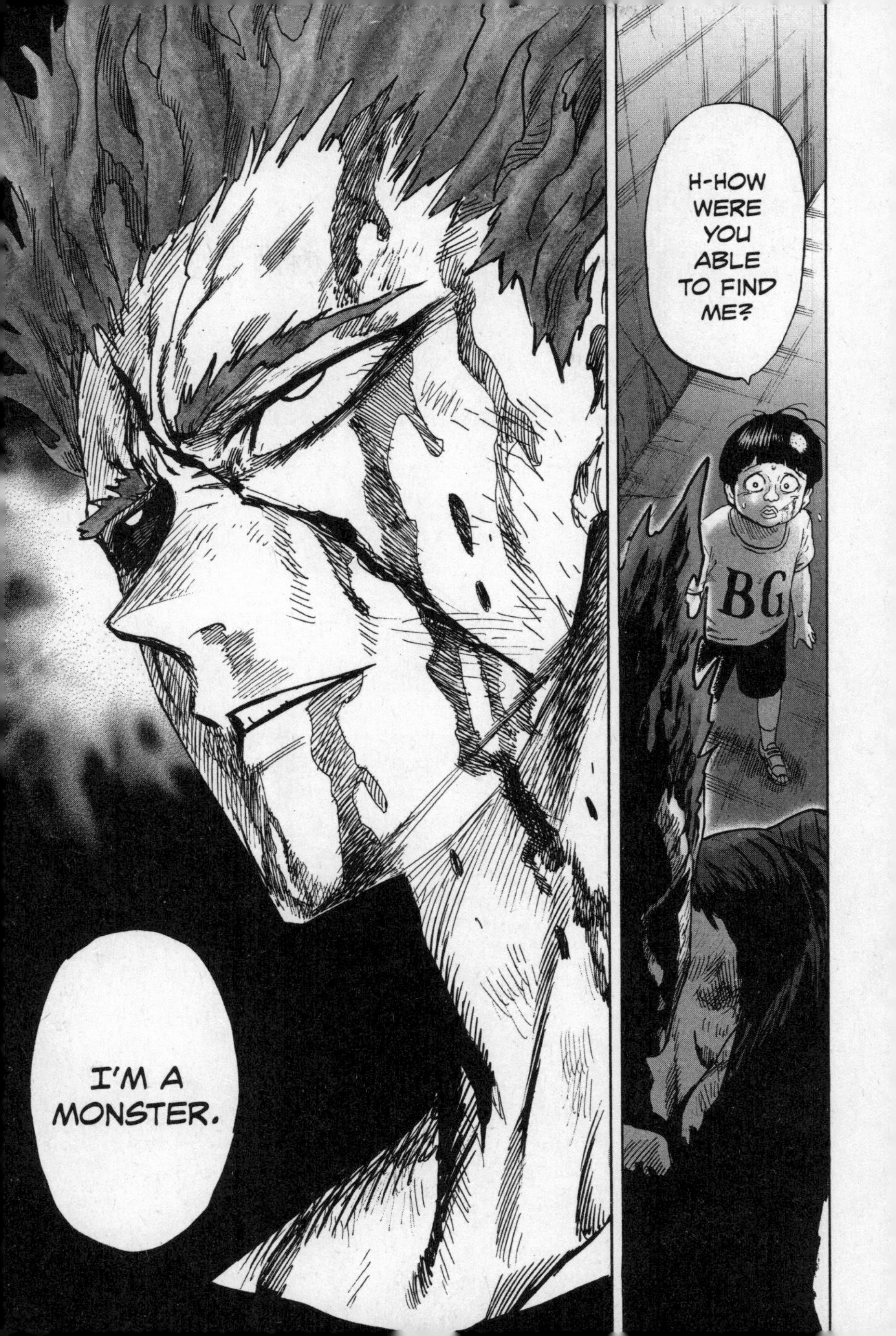
H-HOW WERE YOU ABLE TO FIND ME?
BG
I'M A MONSTER.

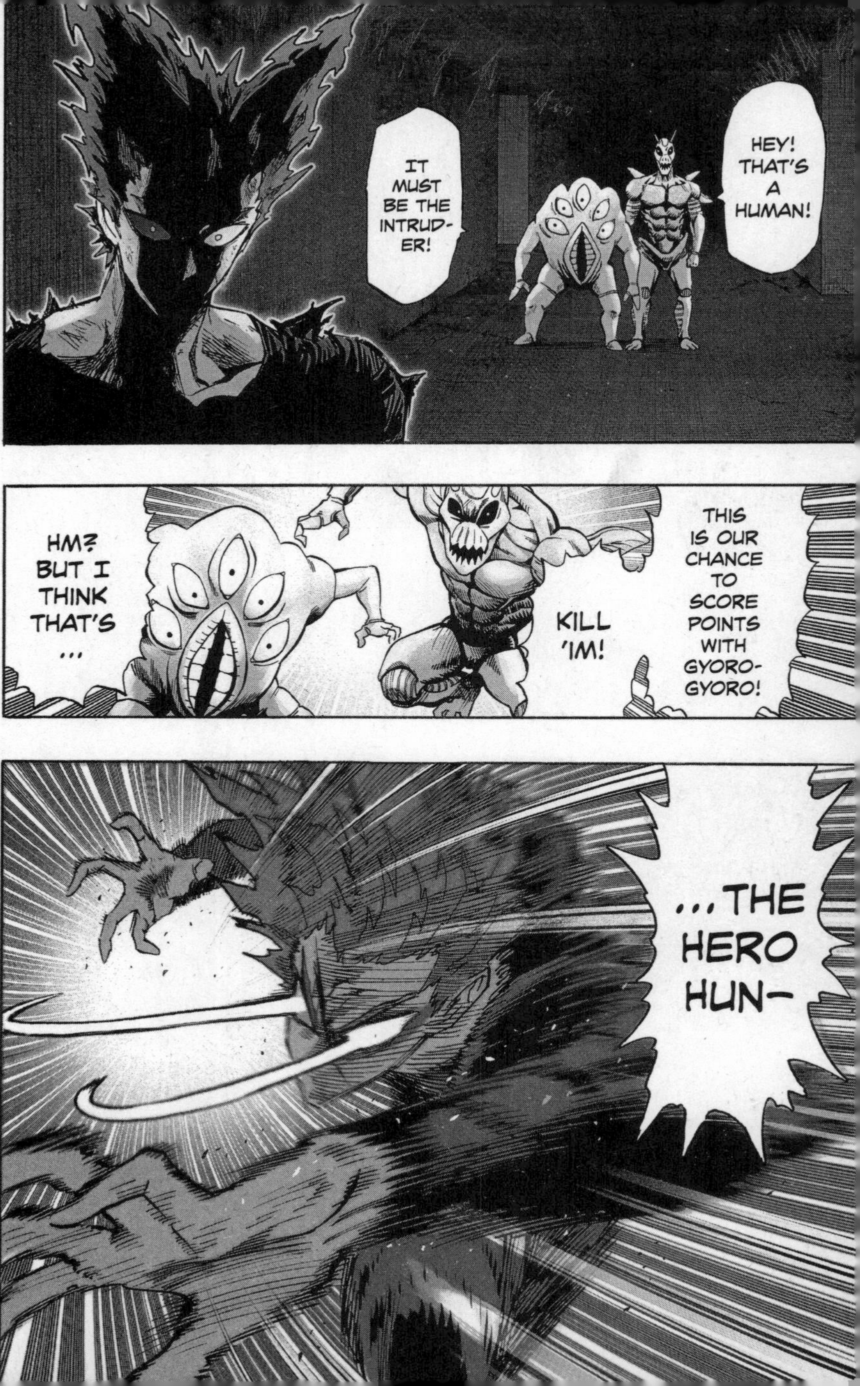
HEY! THAT'S A HUMAN!
IT MUST BE THE INTRUDER!
THIS IS OUR CHANCE TO SCORE POINTS WITH GYORO-GYORO!
KILL 'IM!
HM? BUT I THINK THAT'S ...
...THE HERO HUN-

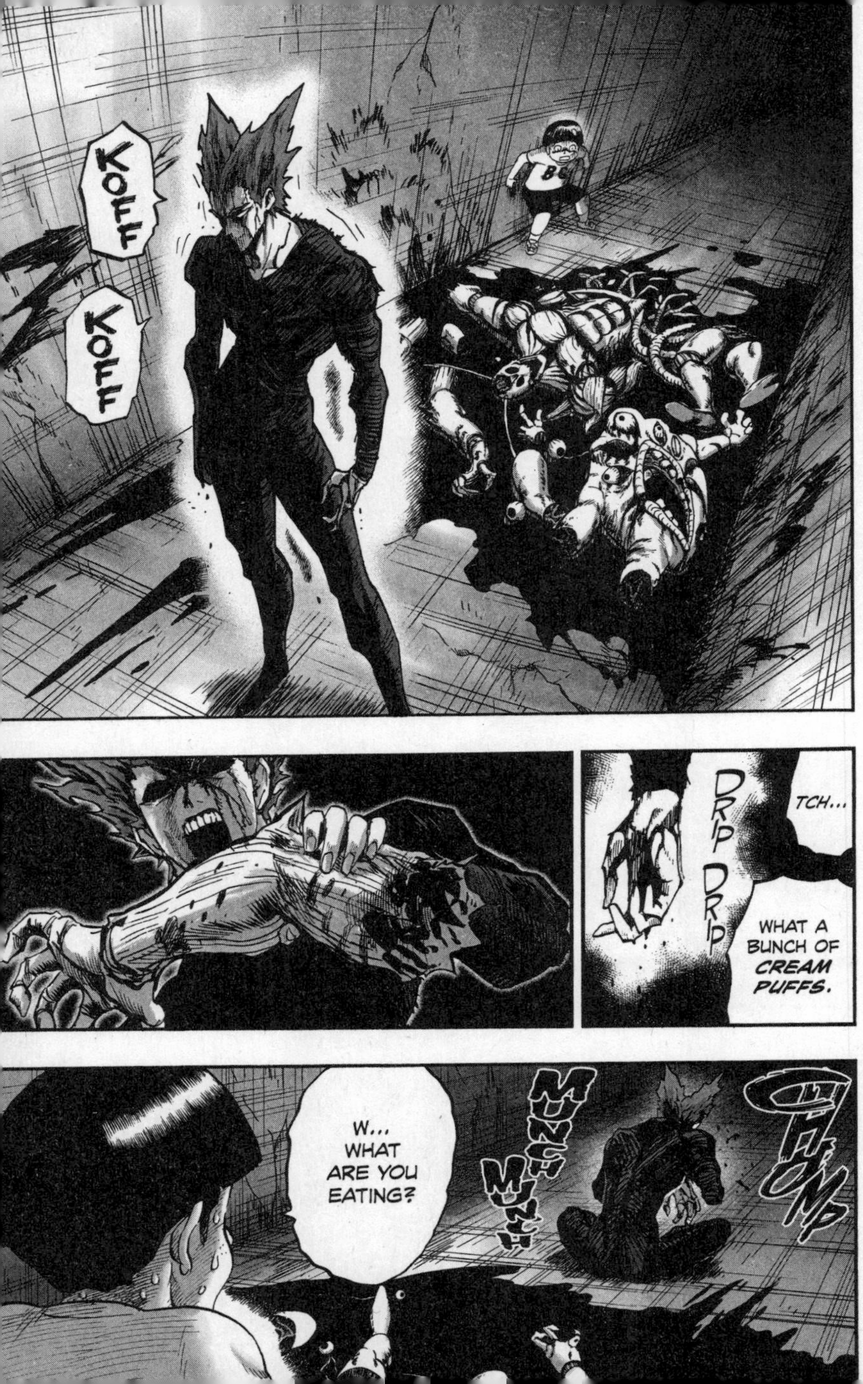
KOFF
KOFF
TCH...
DRIP DRIP DRIP
WHAT A BUNCH OF *CREAM PUFFS.*
CHOMP
MUNCH MUNCH
W... WHAT ARE YOU EATING?

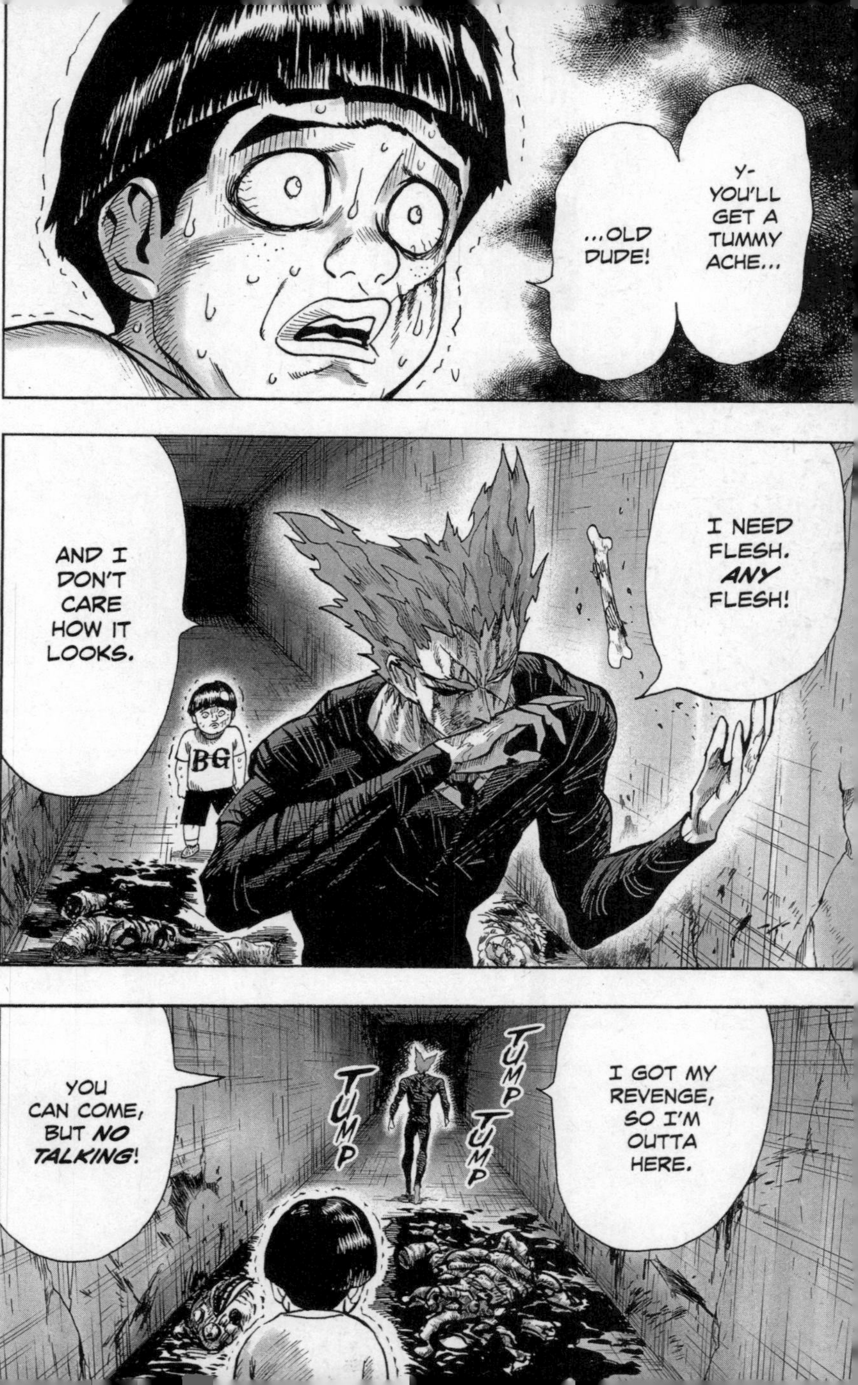
Y- YOU'LL GET A TUMMY ACHE...
...OLD DUDE!
I NEED FLESH. *ANY* FLESH!
AND I DON'T CARE HOW IT LOOKS.
I GOT MY REVENGE, SO I'M OUTTA HERE.
TUMP TUMP
TUMP
YOU CAN COME, BUT *NO TALKING*!

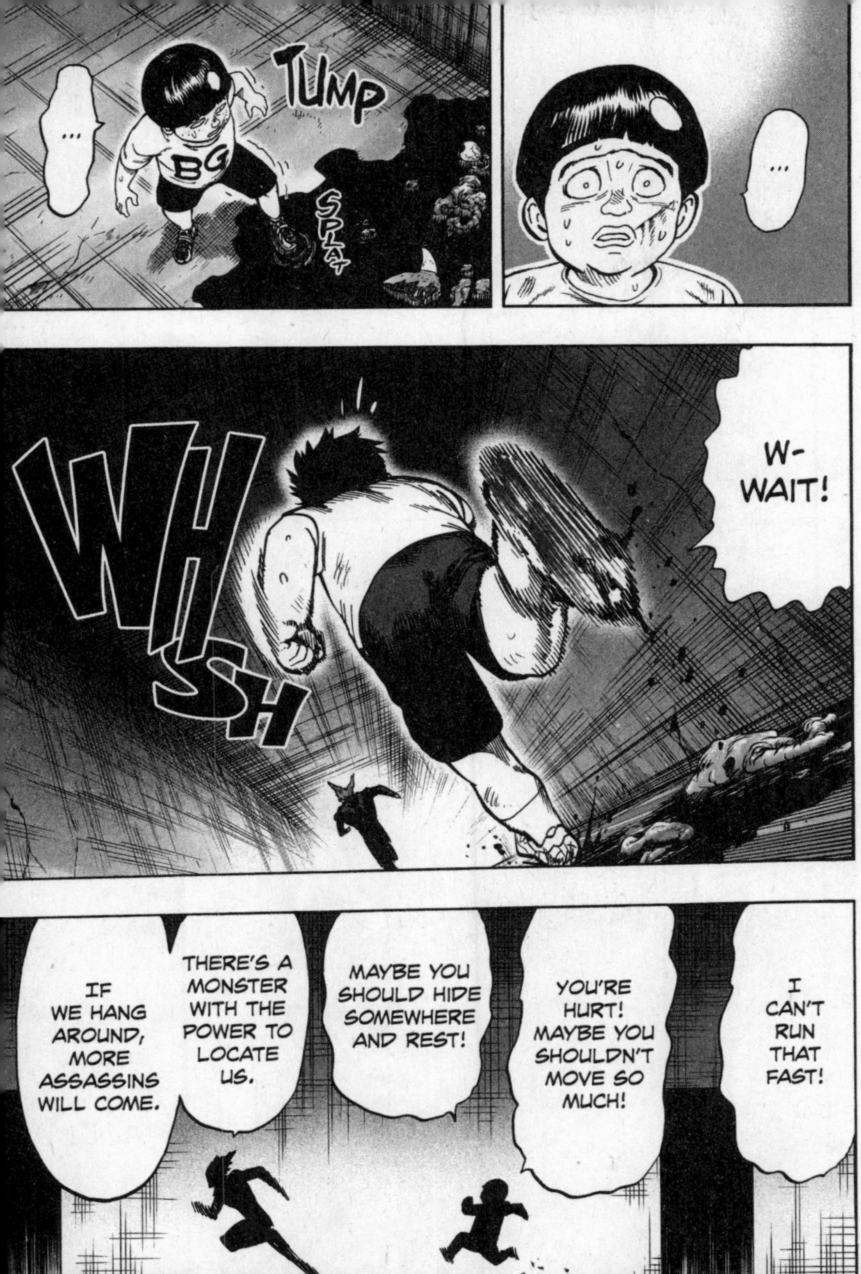
...
...
TUMP
SPLAT
W- WAIT!
WHISH
I CAN'T RUN THAT FAST!
YOU'RE HURT! MAYBE YOU SHOULDN'T MOVE SO MUCH!
MAYBE YOU SHOULD HIDE SOMEWHERE AND REST!
THERE'S A MONSTER WITH THE POWER TO LOCATE US.
IF WE HANG AROUND, MORE ASSASSINS WILL COME.

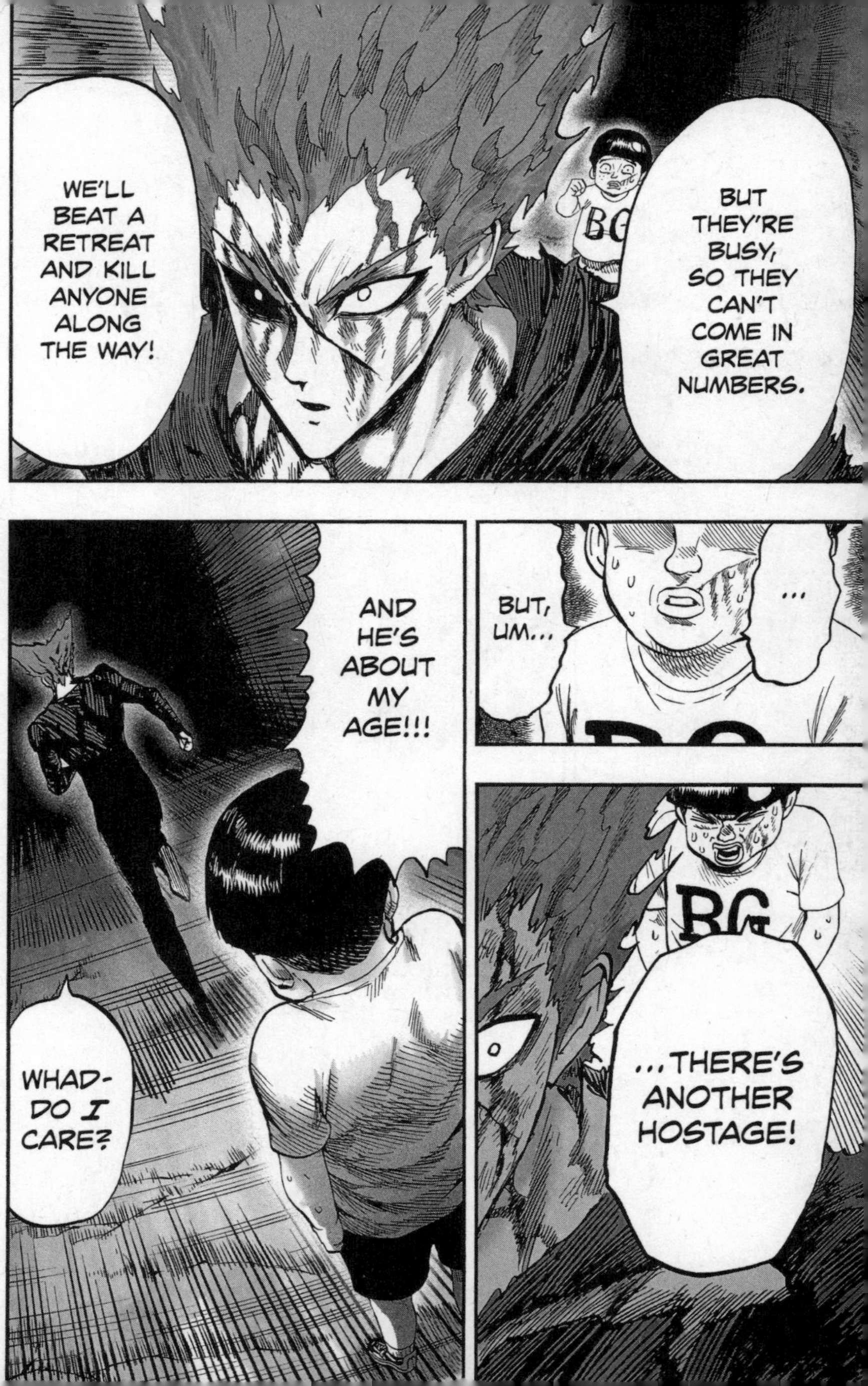
BUT THEY'RE BUSY, SO THEY CAN'T COME IN GREAT NUMBERS.
WE'LL BEAT A RETREAT AND KILL ANYONE ALONG THE WAY!
...
BUT, UM...
...THERE'S ANOTHER HOSTAGE!
AND HE'S ABOUT MY AGE!!!
WHAD-DO I CARE?

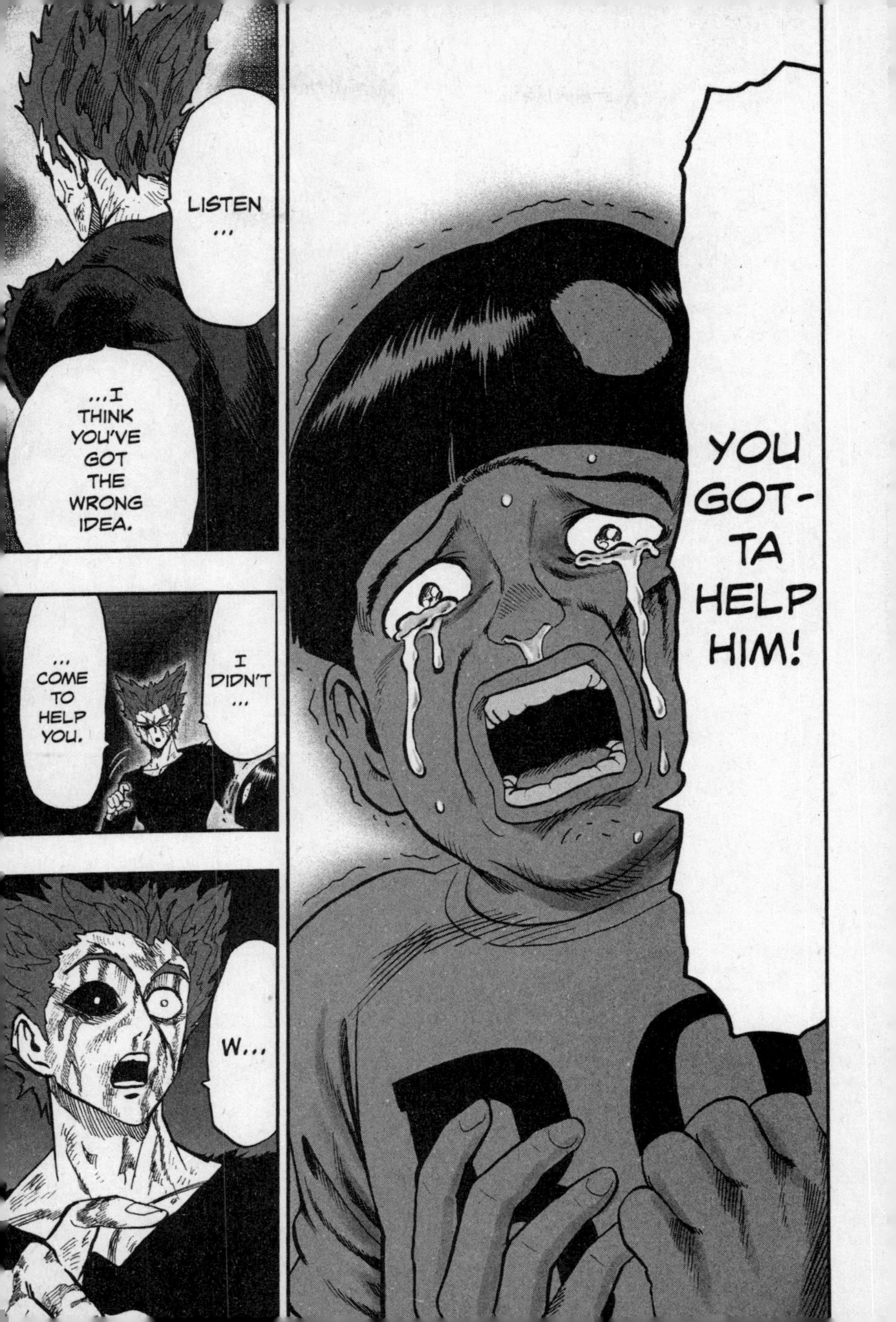

YOU GOT-TA HELP HIM!
LISTEN ...
...I THINK YOU'VE GOT THE WRONG IDEA.
I DIDN'T ...
... COME TO HELP YOU.
W...

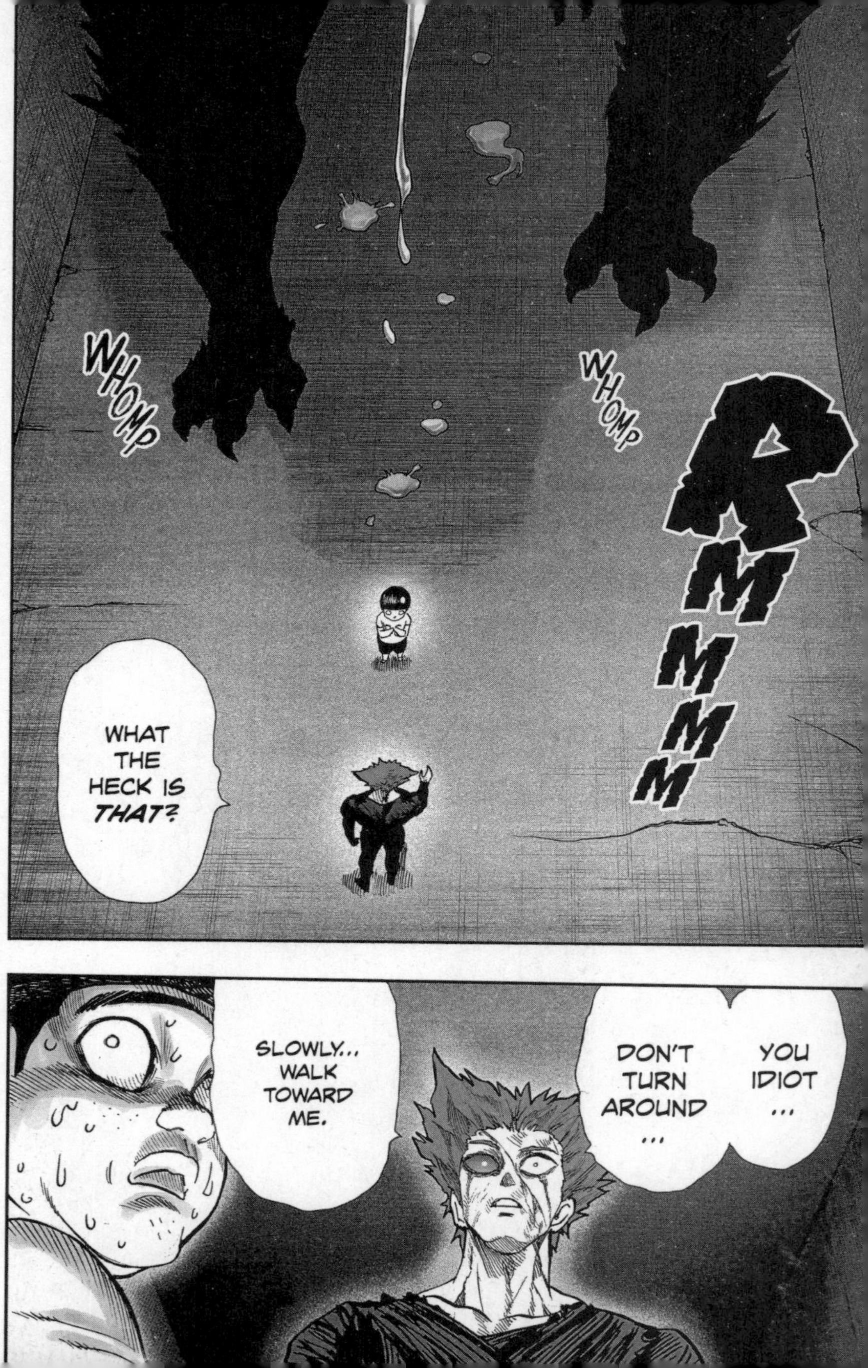
WHOMP
WHOMP
RMMMMM
WHAT THE HECK IS *THAT?*
YOU IDIOT ...
DON'T TURN AROUND ...
SLOWLY... WALK TOWARD ME.

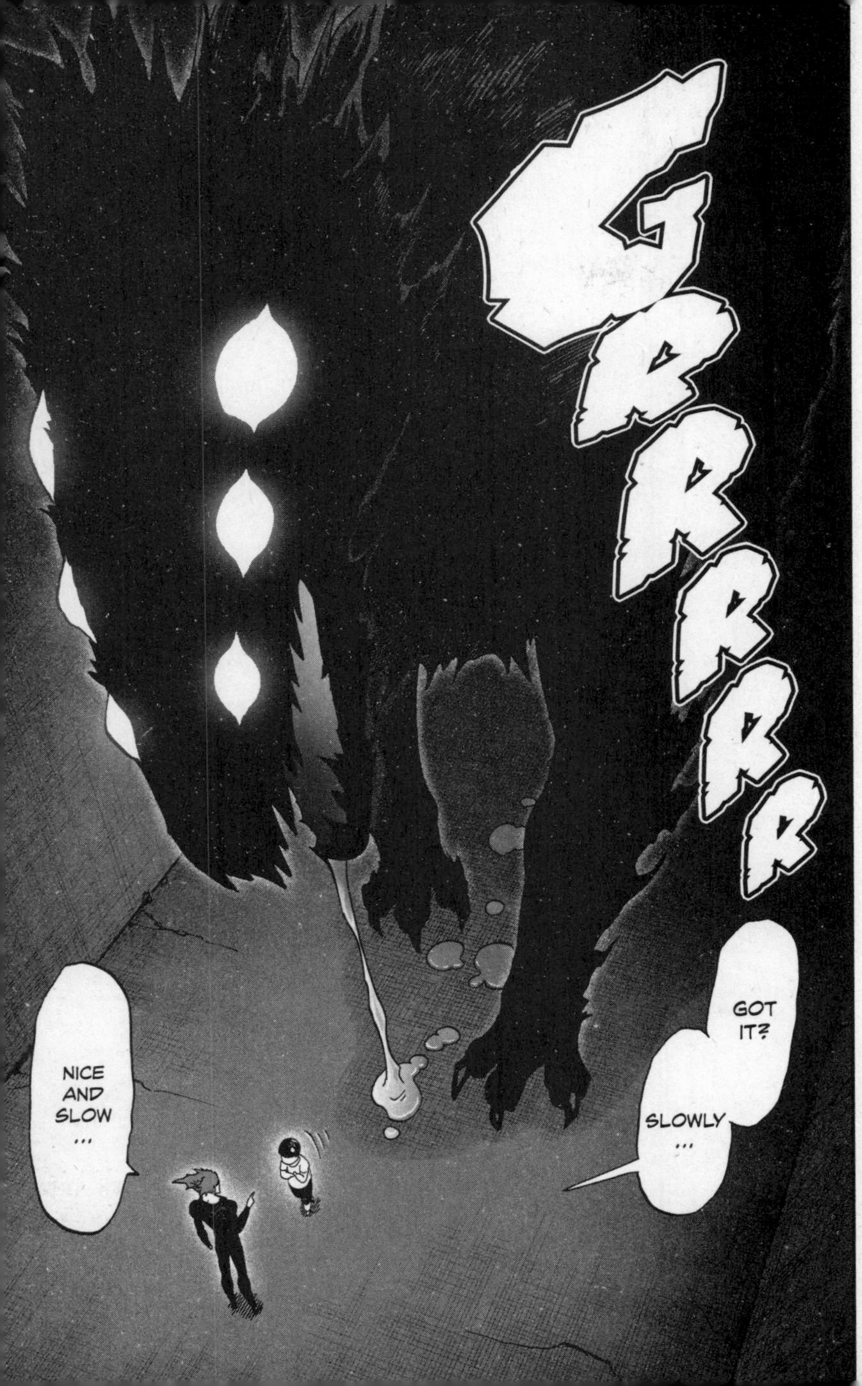
GRRRRR
GOT IT?
SLOWLY...
NICE AND SLOW...

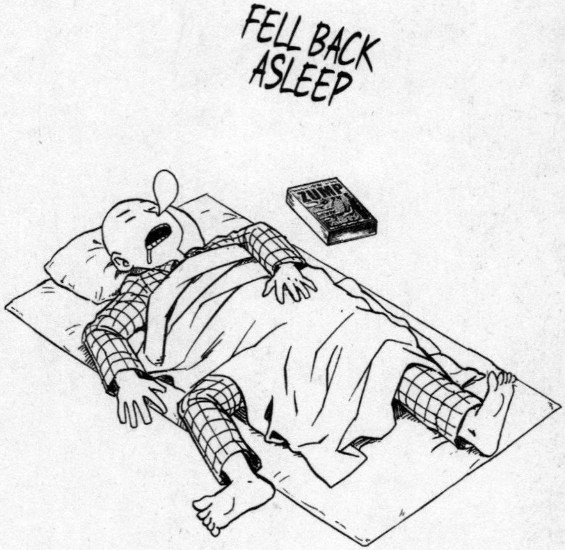
FELL BACK ASLEEP
ZUMP

PUNCH 93:
POCHI

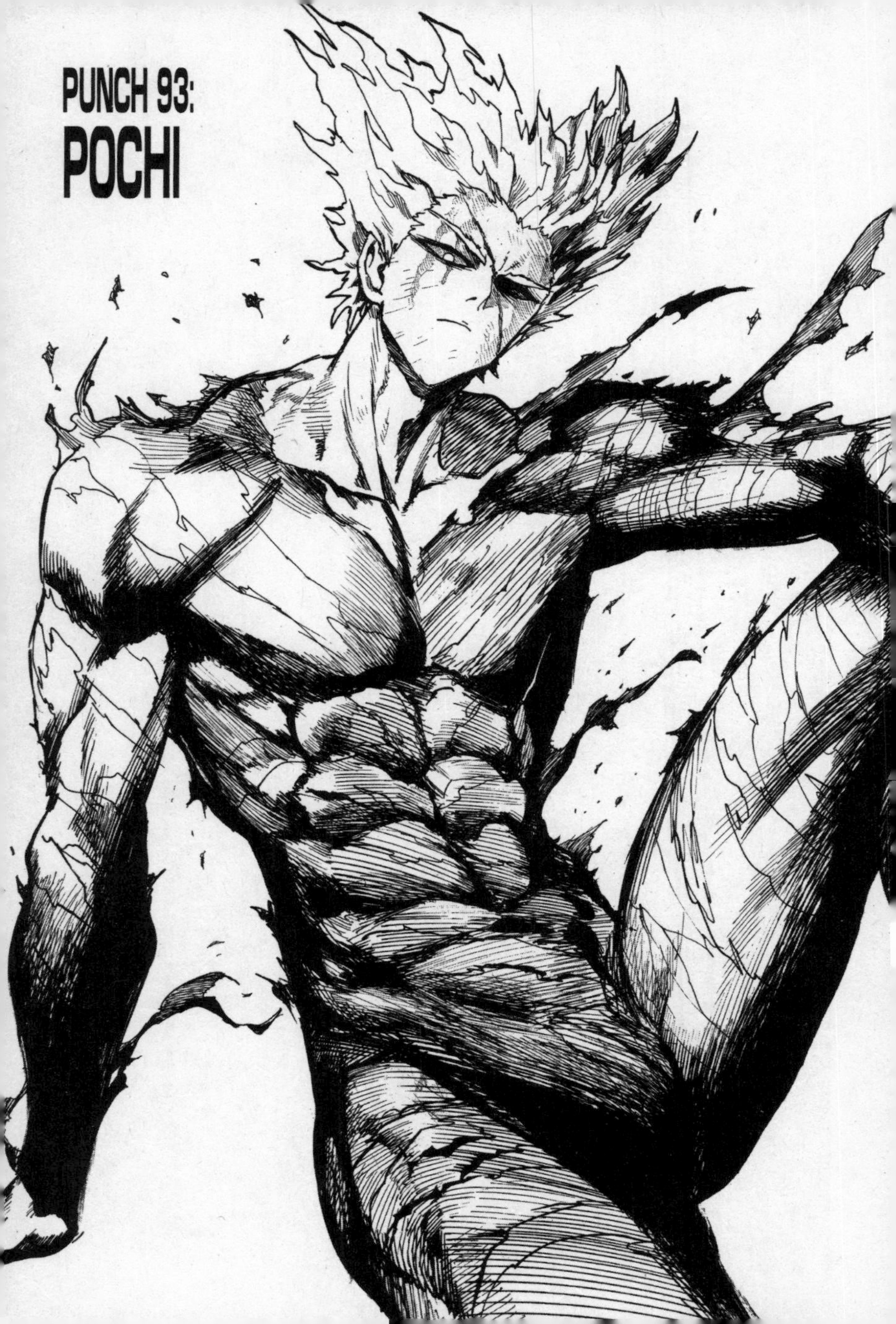

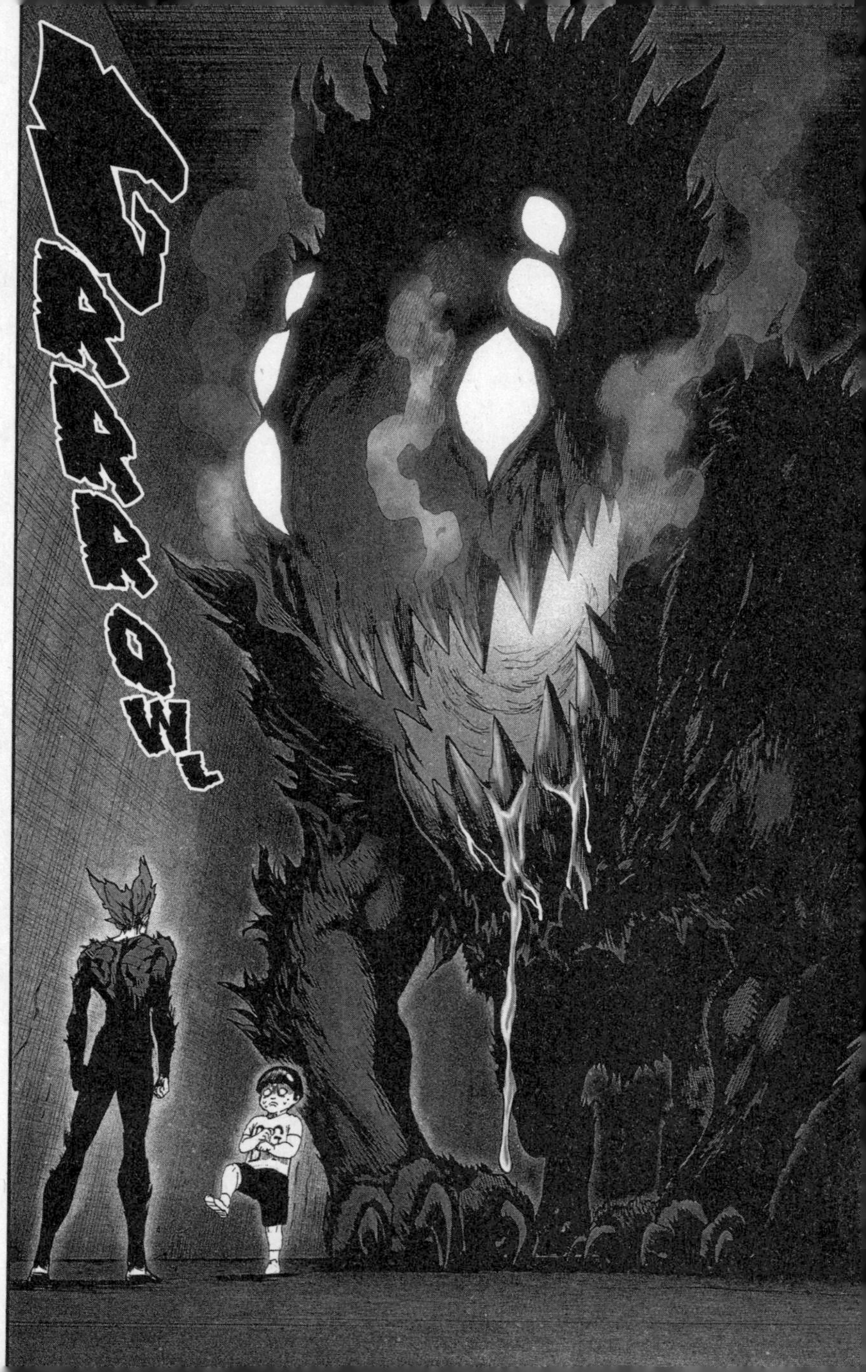
GRRROWL

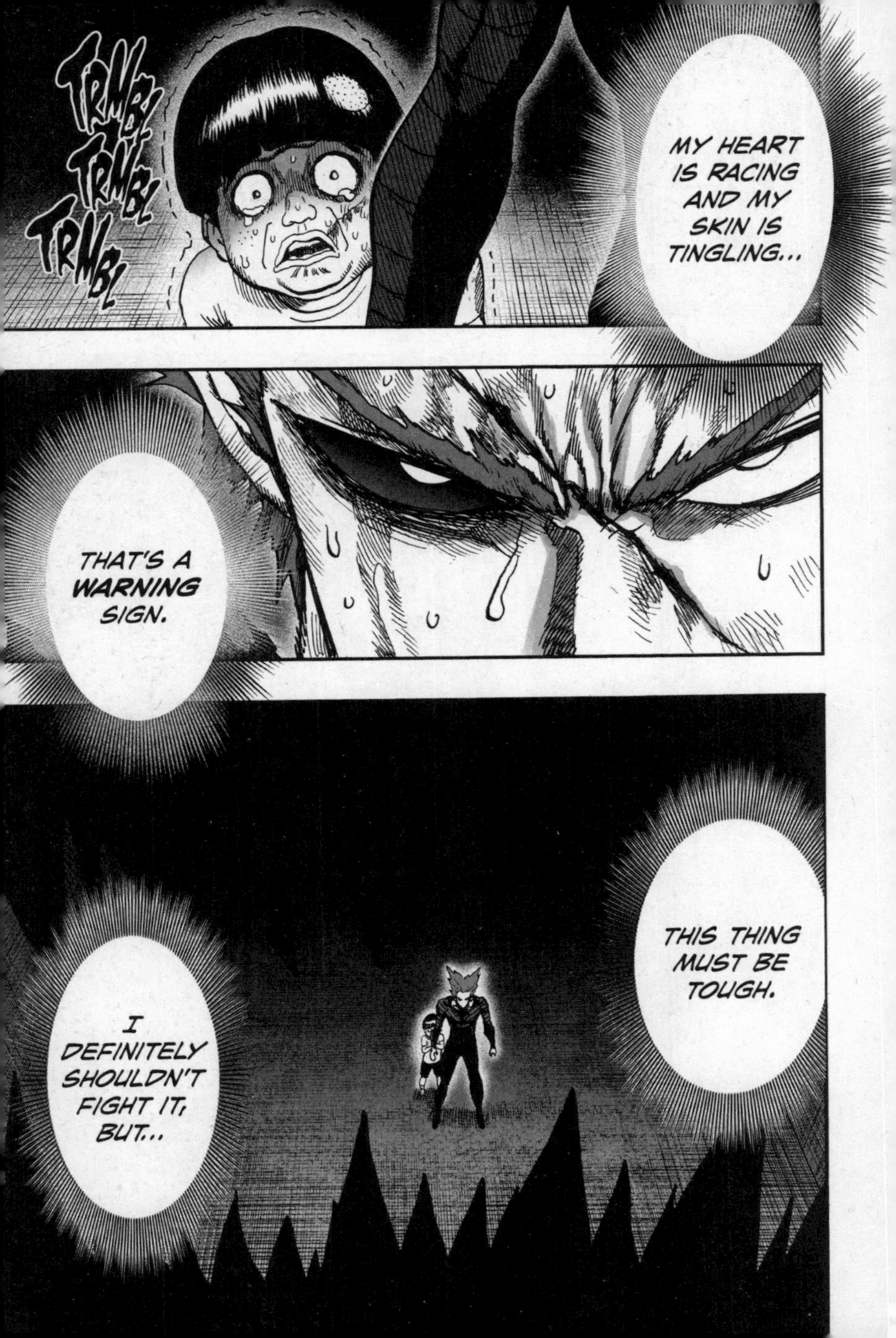
MY HEART IS RACING AND MY SKIN IS TINGLING...
TRMBL TRMBL TRMBL
THAT'S A WARNING SIGN.
THIS THING MUST BE TOUGH.
I DEFINITELY SHOULDN'T FIGHT IT, BUT...

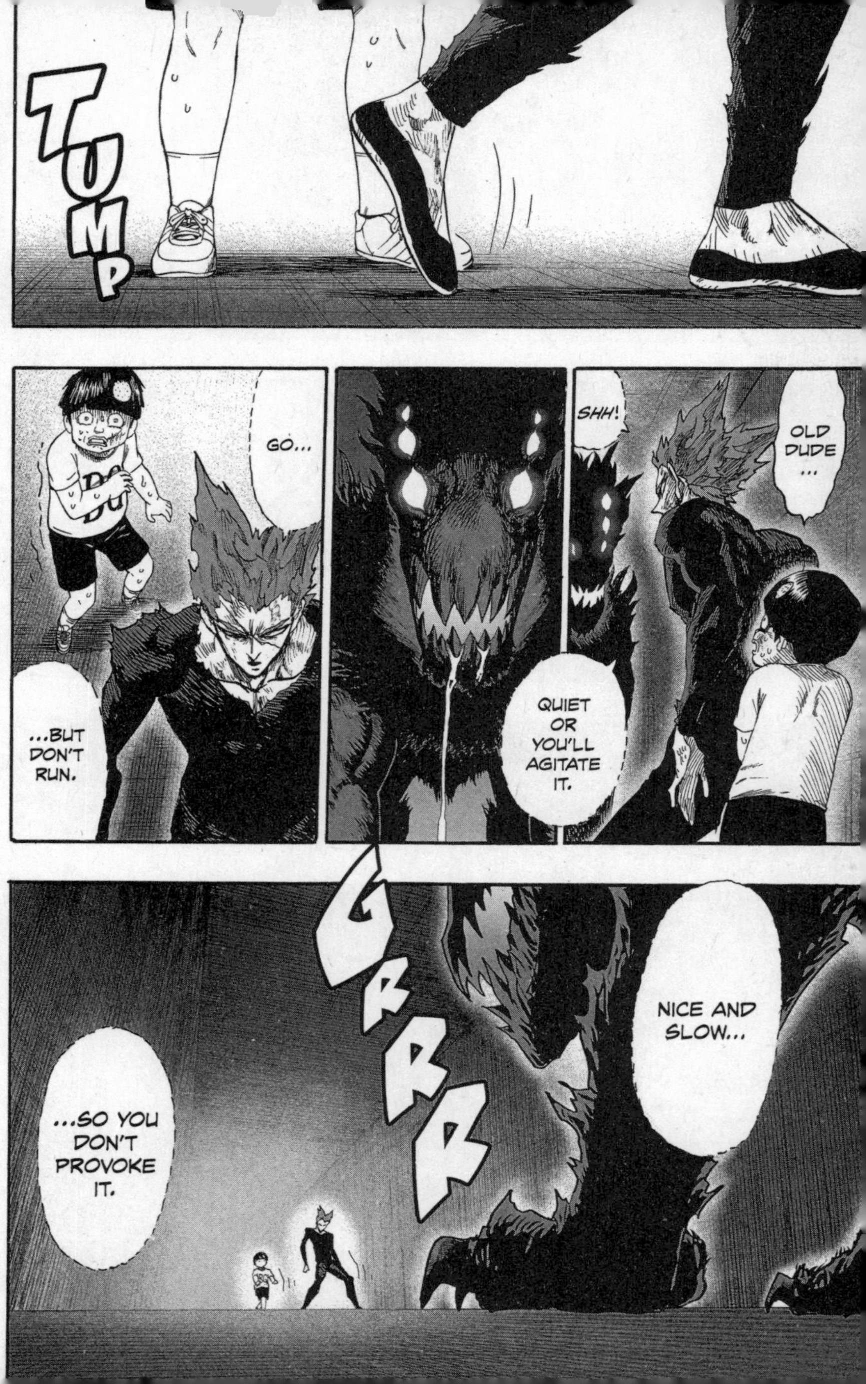

TUMP
GO...
...BUT DON'T RUN.
QUIET OR YOU'LL AGITATE IT.
SHH!
OLD DUDE...
GRRR
NICE AND SLOW...
...SO YOU DON'T PROVOKE IT.

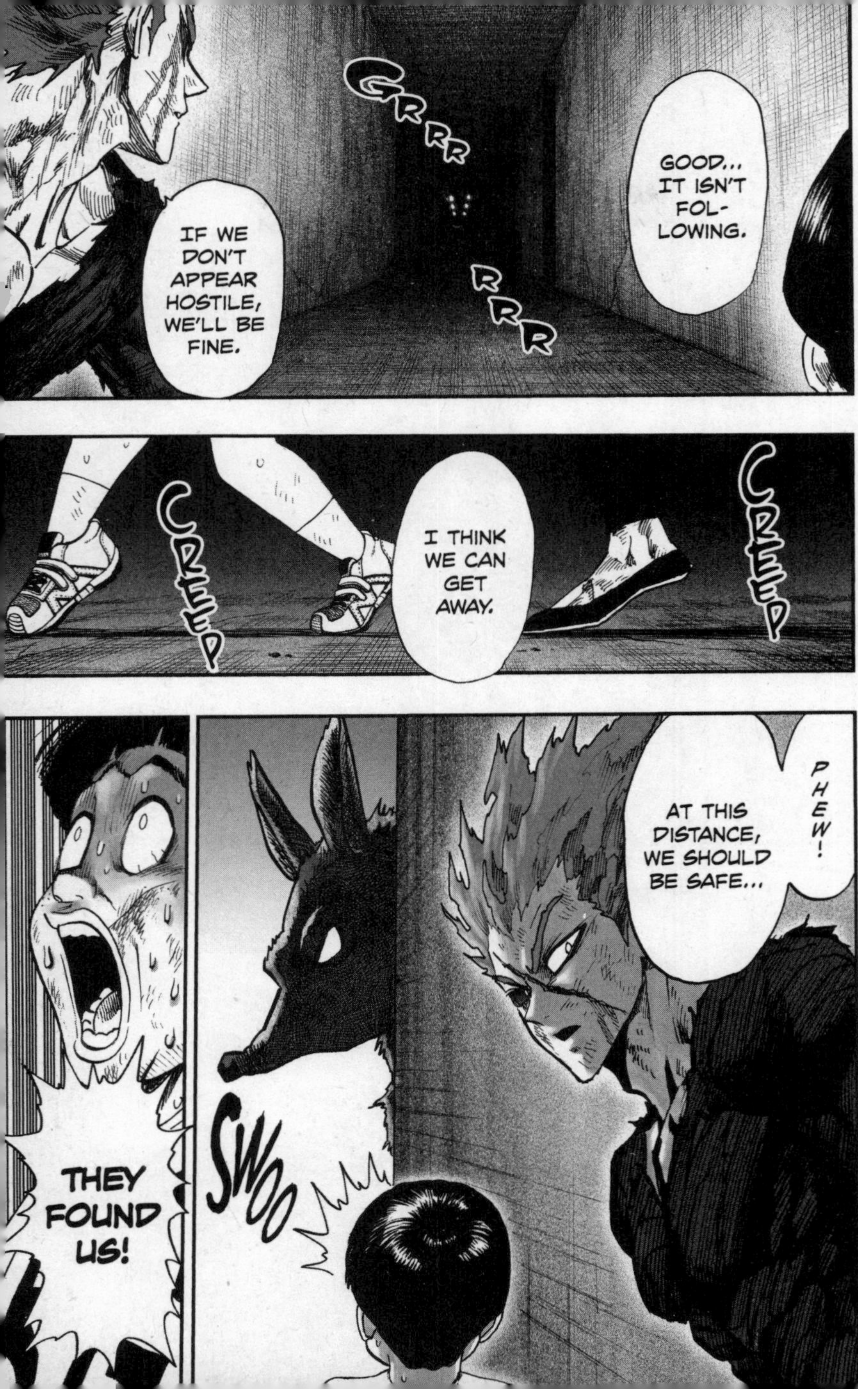
GOOD... IT ISN'T FOL-LOWING.
GRRR
RRRR
IF WE DON'T APPEAR HOSTILE, WE'LL BE FINE.
CREEP
I THINK WE CAN GET AWAY.
CREEP
PHEW!
AT THIS DISTANCE, WE SHOULD BE SAFE...
SWOO
THEY FOUND US!

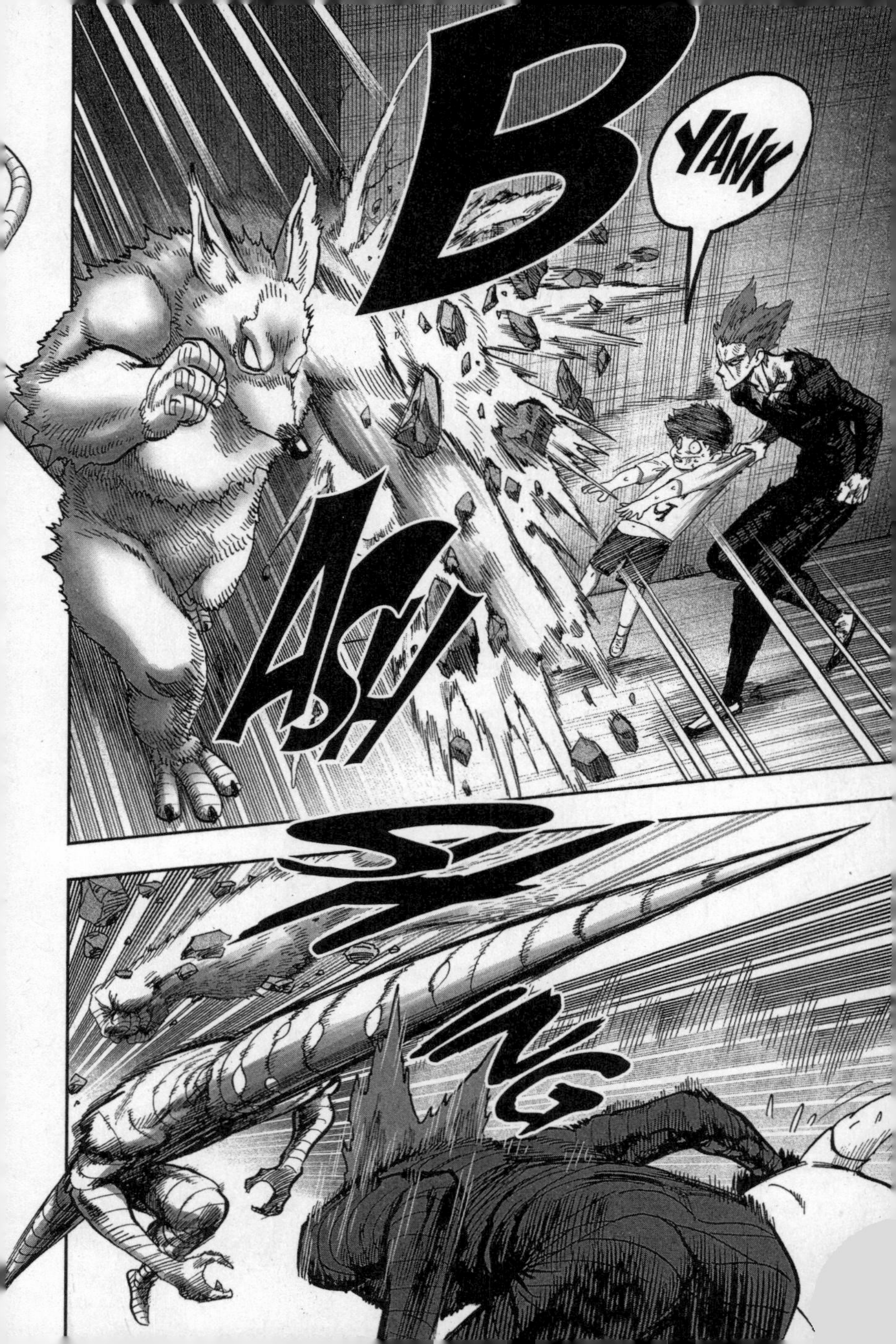

YANK
BASH!
SHING

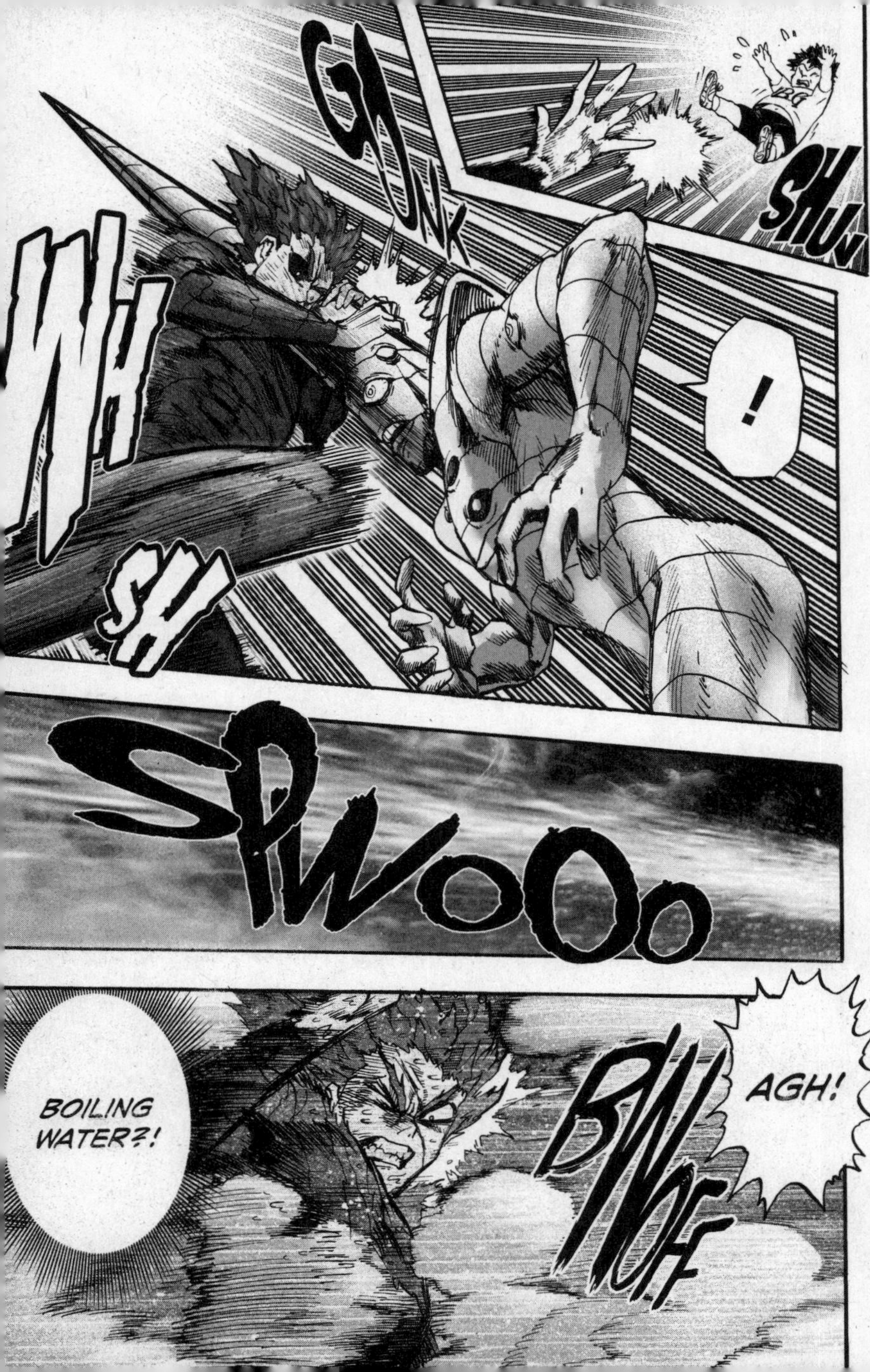
SHUN
!
SPWOOO
AGH!
BOILING WATER?!

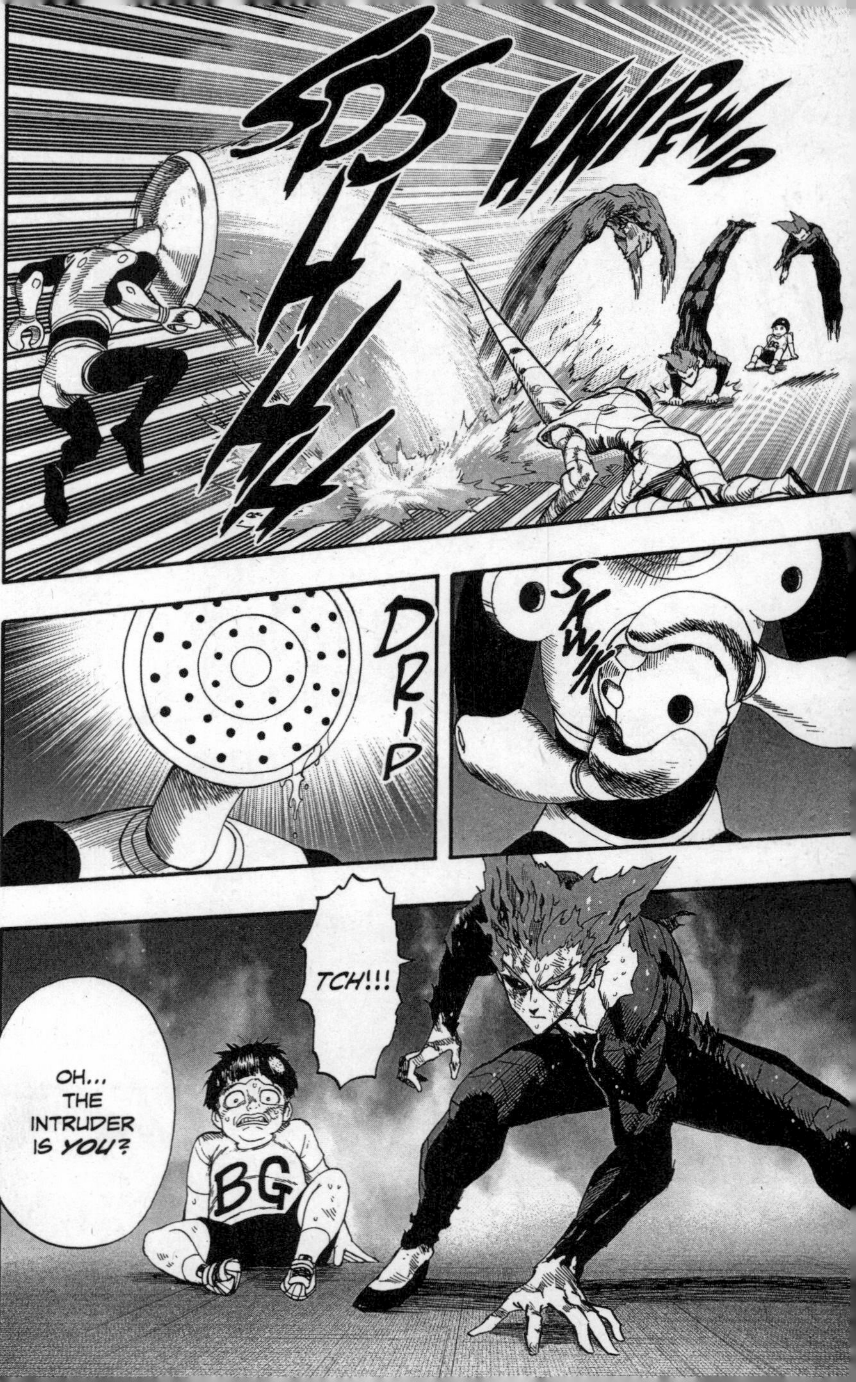

DRIP
SKWIK
TCH!!!
OH... THE INTRUDER IS *YOU*?

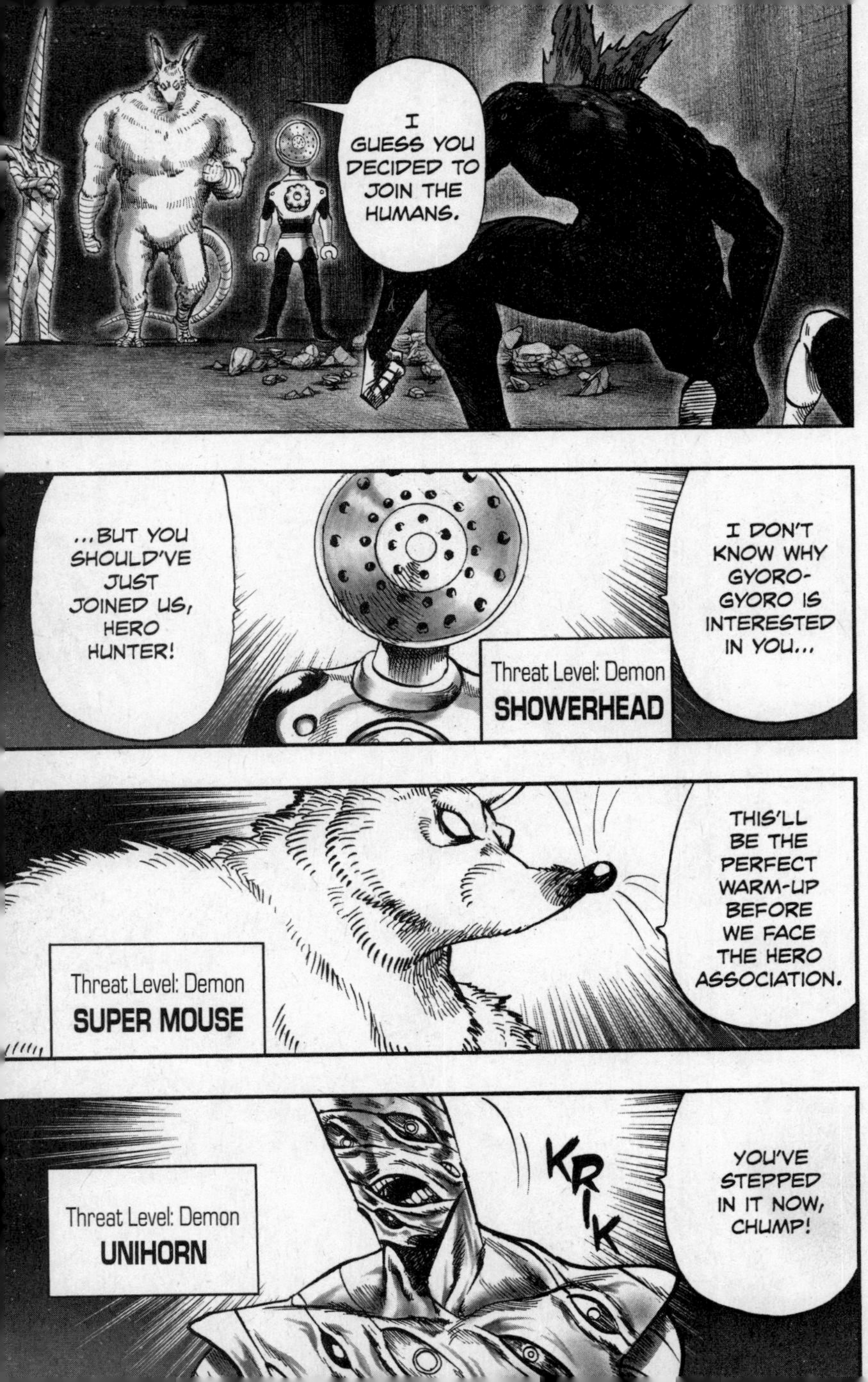
I GUESS YOU DECIDED TO JOIN THE HUMANS.
I DON'T KNOW WHY GYORO-GYORO IS INTERESTED IN YOU...
...BUT YOU SHOULD'VE JUST JOINED US, HERO HUNTER!
Threat Level: Demon
SHOWERHEAD
THIS'LL BE THE PERFECT WARM-UP BEFORE WE FACE THE HERO ASSOCIATION.
Threat Level: Demon
SUPER MOUSE
KRIK
YOU'VE STEPPED IN IT NOW, CHUMP!
Threat Level: Demon
UNIHORN

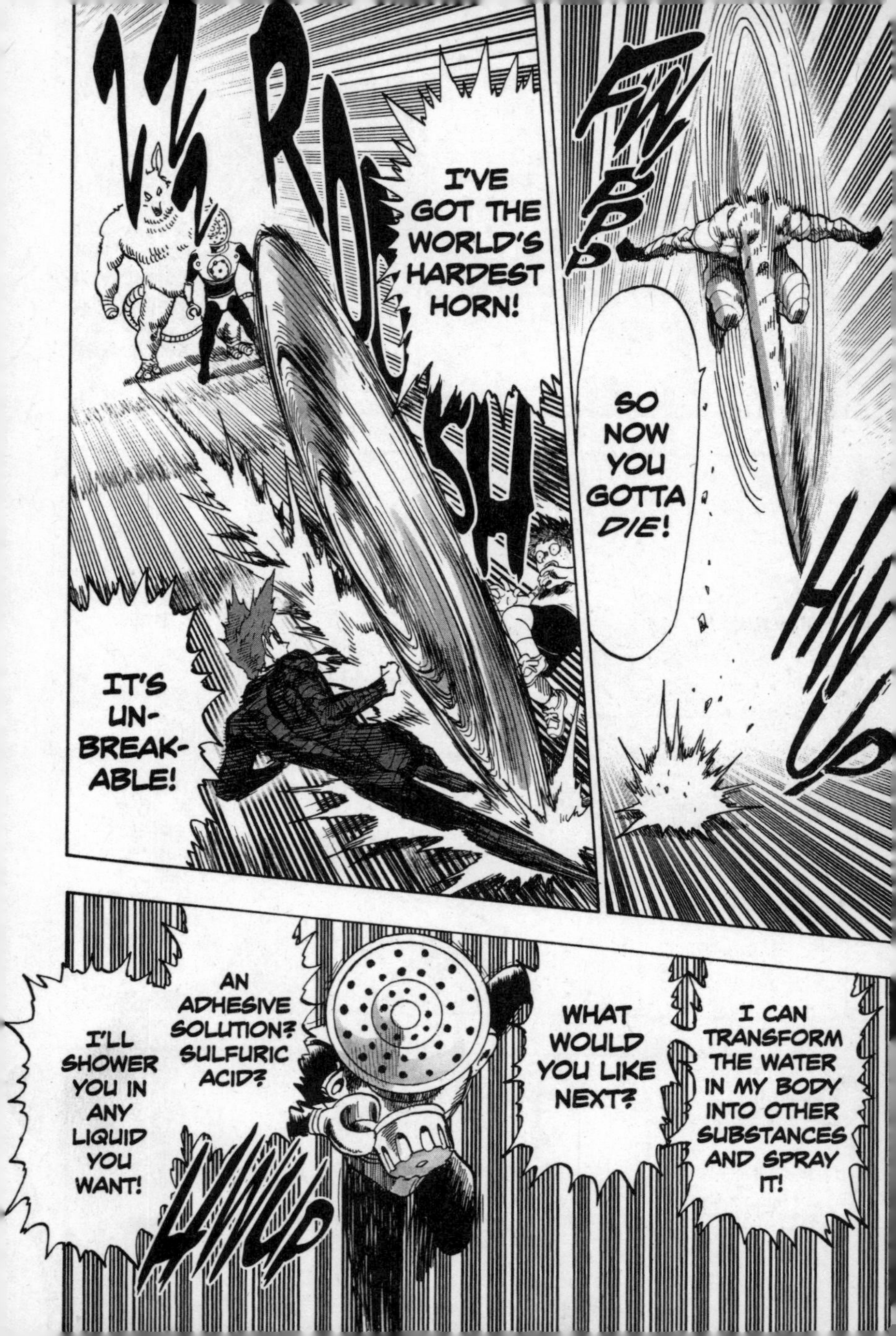
I'VE GOT THE WORLD'S HARDEST HORN!
IT'S UN-BREAK-ABLE!
SO NOW YOU GOTTA *DIE*!
I CAN TRANSFORM THE WATER IN MY BODY INTO OTHER SUBSTANCES AND SPRAY IT!
WHAT WOULD YOU LIKE NEXT?
AN ADHESIVE SOLUTION? SULFURIC ACID?
I'LL SHOWER YOU IN ANY LIQUID YOU WANT!

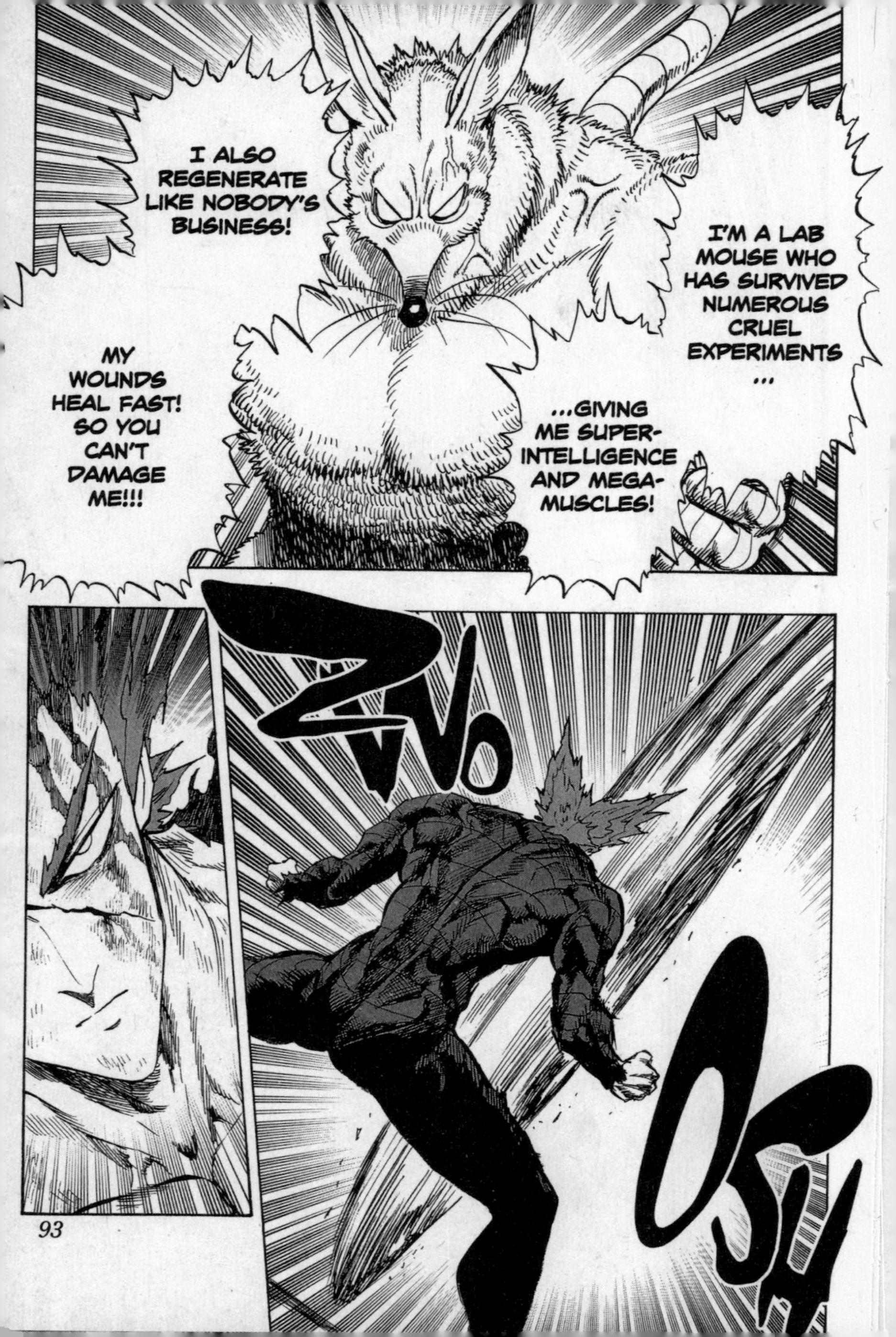

I'M A LAB MOUSE WHO HAS SURVIVED NUMEROUS CRUEL EXPERIMENTS...
...GIVING ME SUPER-INTELLIGENCE AND MEGA-MUSCLES!
I ALSO REGENERATE LIKE NOBODY'S BUSINESS!
MY WOUNDS HEAL FAST! SO YOU CAN'T DAMAGE ME!!!
ZWO
OSH

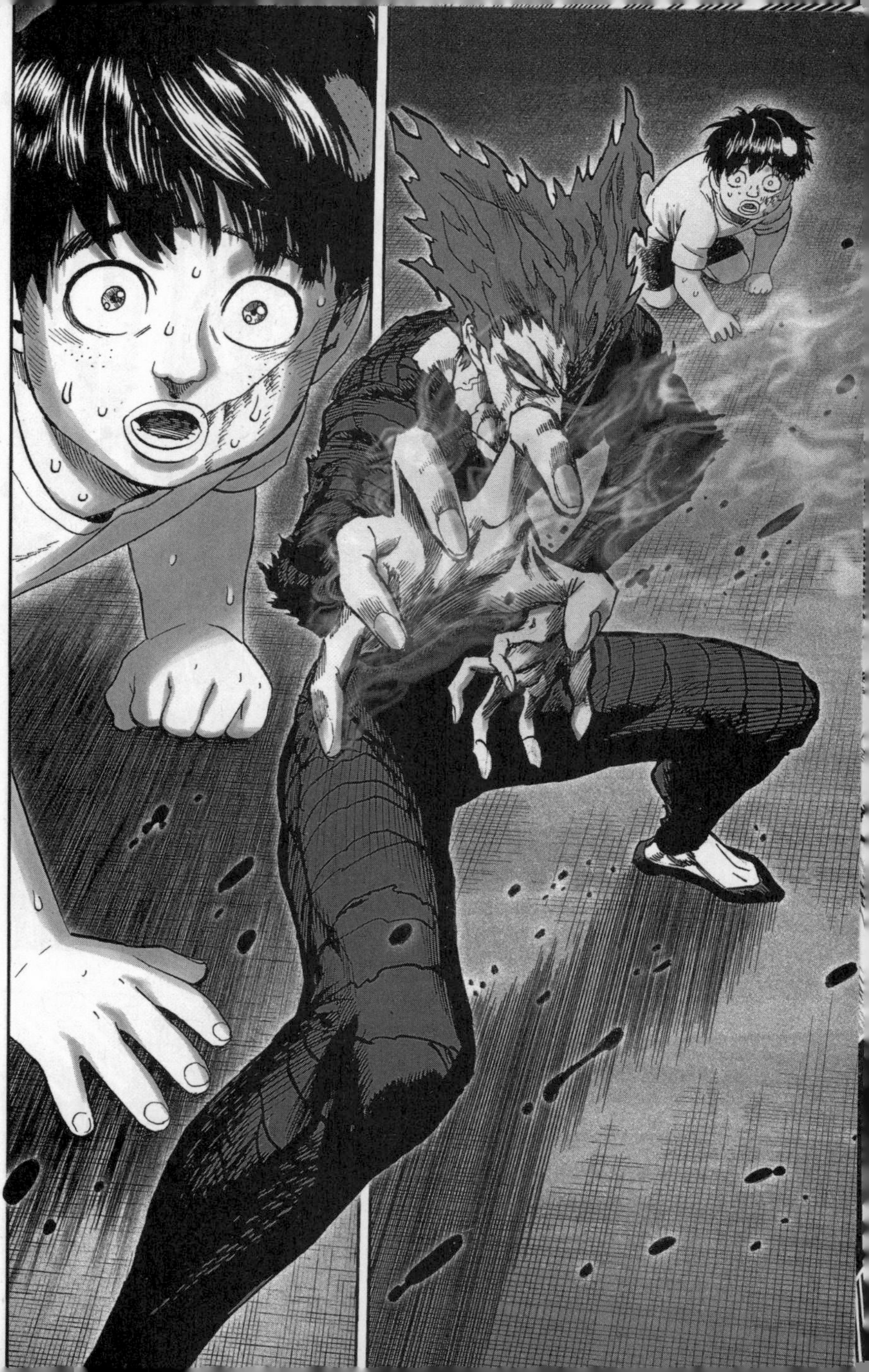

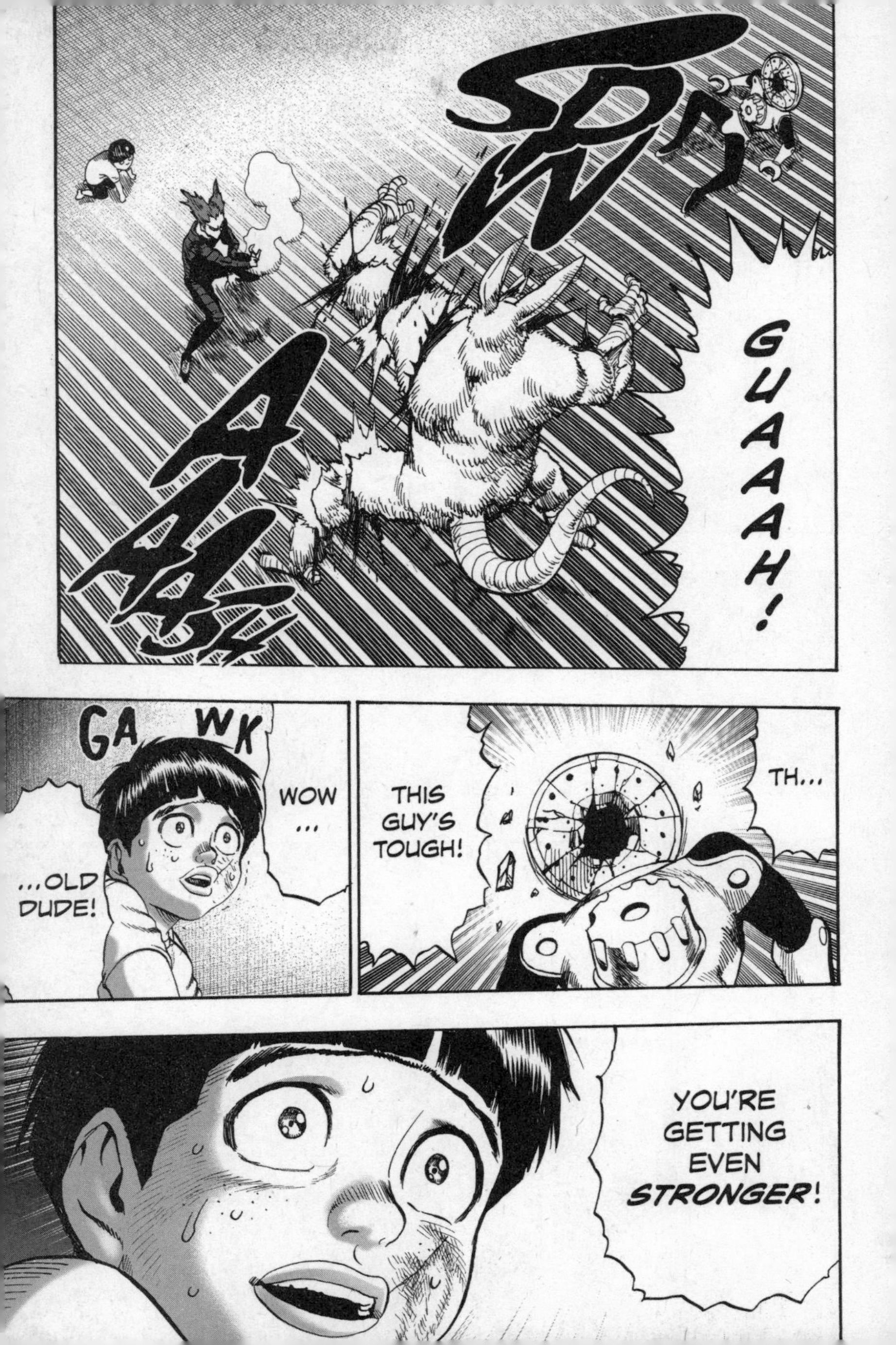
GUAAAAH!
TH...
THIS GUY'S TOUGH!
GAWK
WOW ...
...OLD DUDE!
YOU'RE GETTING EVEN **STRONGER**!

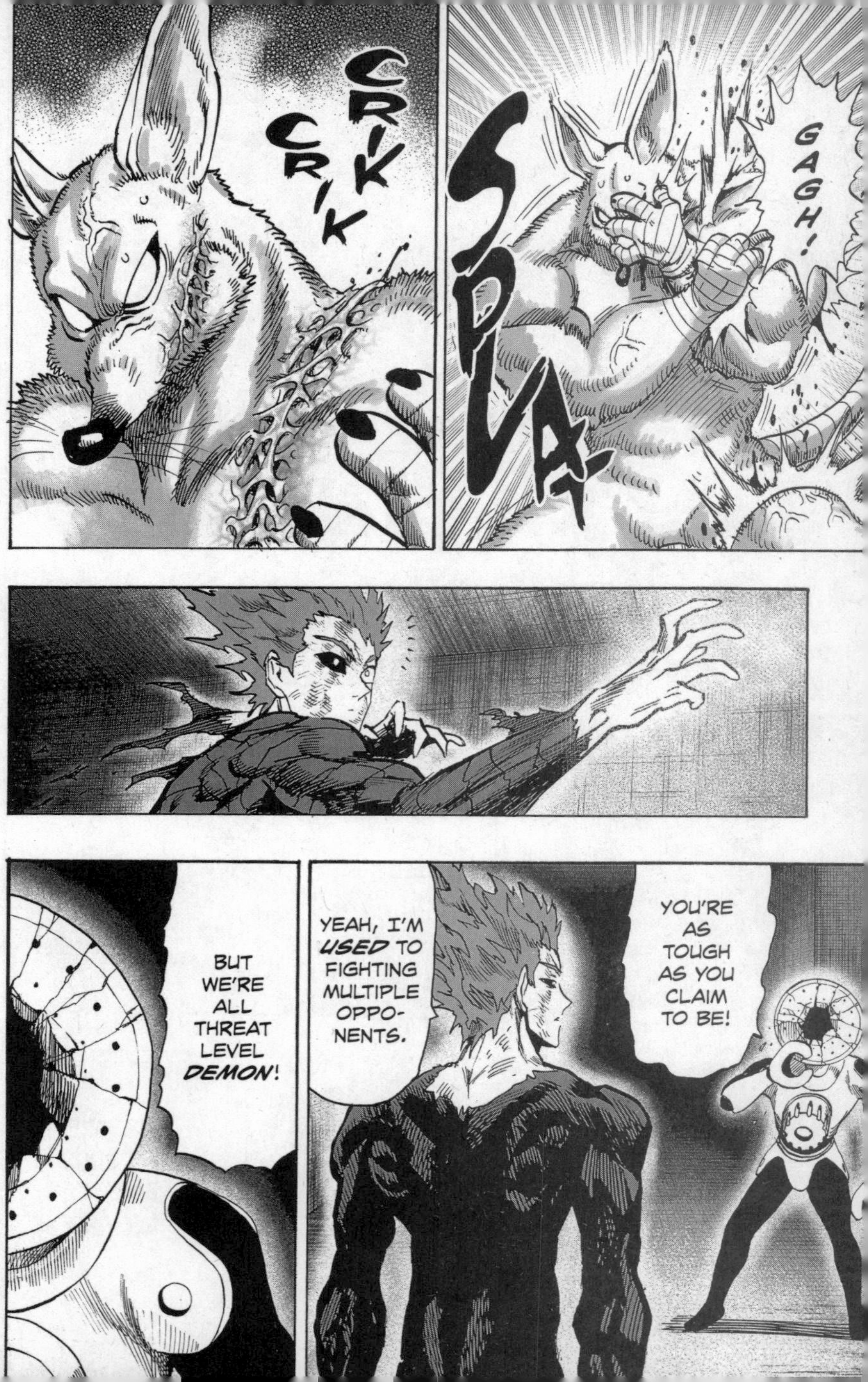
GAGH!
SPLAT
CRIK CRIK CRIK
YOU'RE AS TOUGH AS YOU CLAIM TO BE!
YEAH, I'M *USED* TO FIGHTING MULTIPLE OPPO-NENTS.
BUT WE'RE ALL THREAT LEVEL *DEMON*!

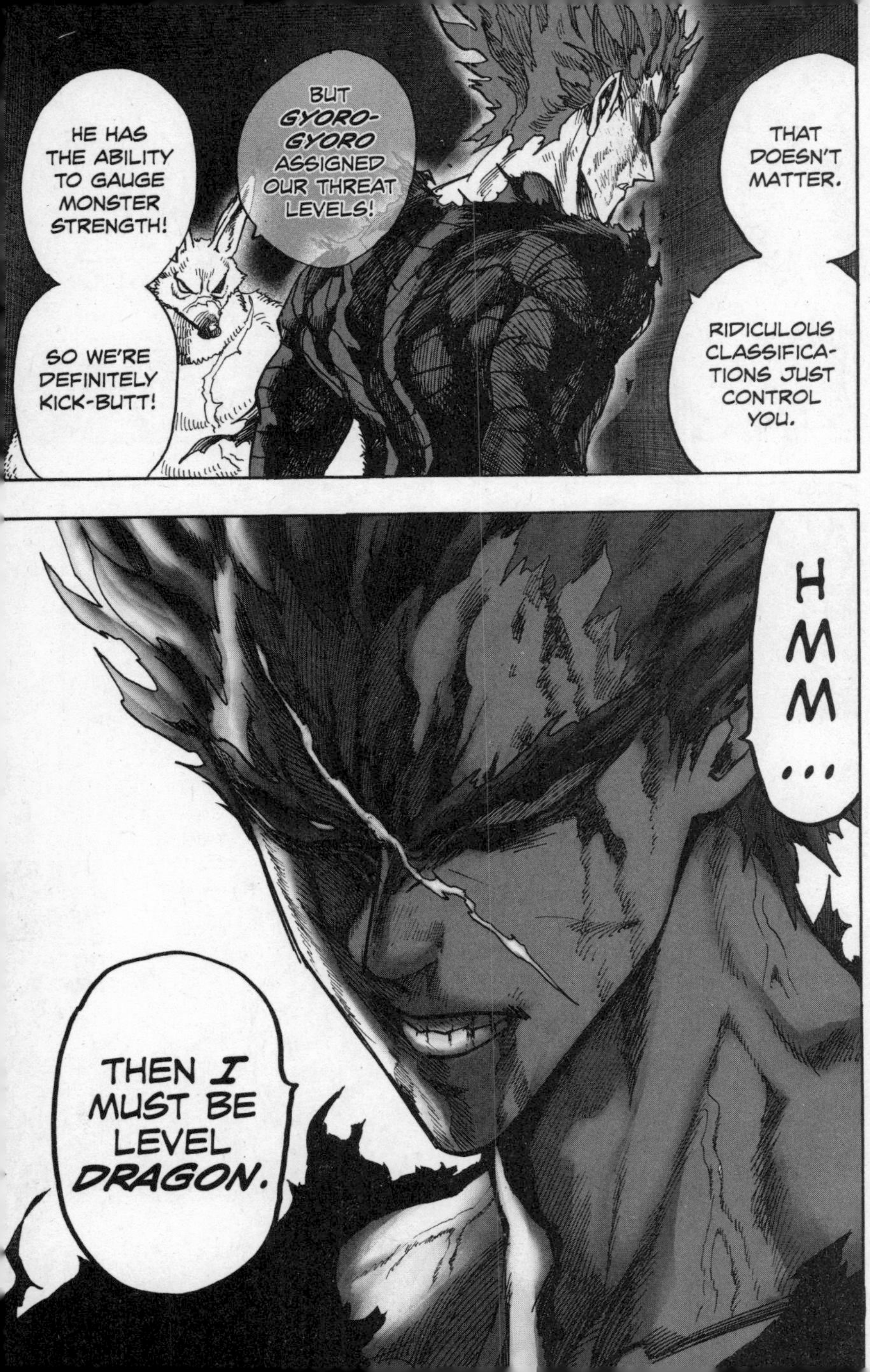

BUT GYORO-GYORO ASSIGNED OUR THREAT LEVELS!
HE HAS THE ABILITY TO GAUGE MONSTER STRENGTH!
SO WE'RE DEFINITELY KICK-BUTT!
THAT DOESN'T MATTER.
RIDICULOUS CLASSIFICA-TIONS JUST CONTROL YOU.
HMM...
THEN *I* MUST BE LEVEL ***DRAGON***.

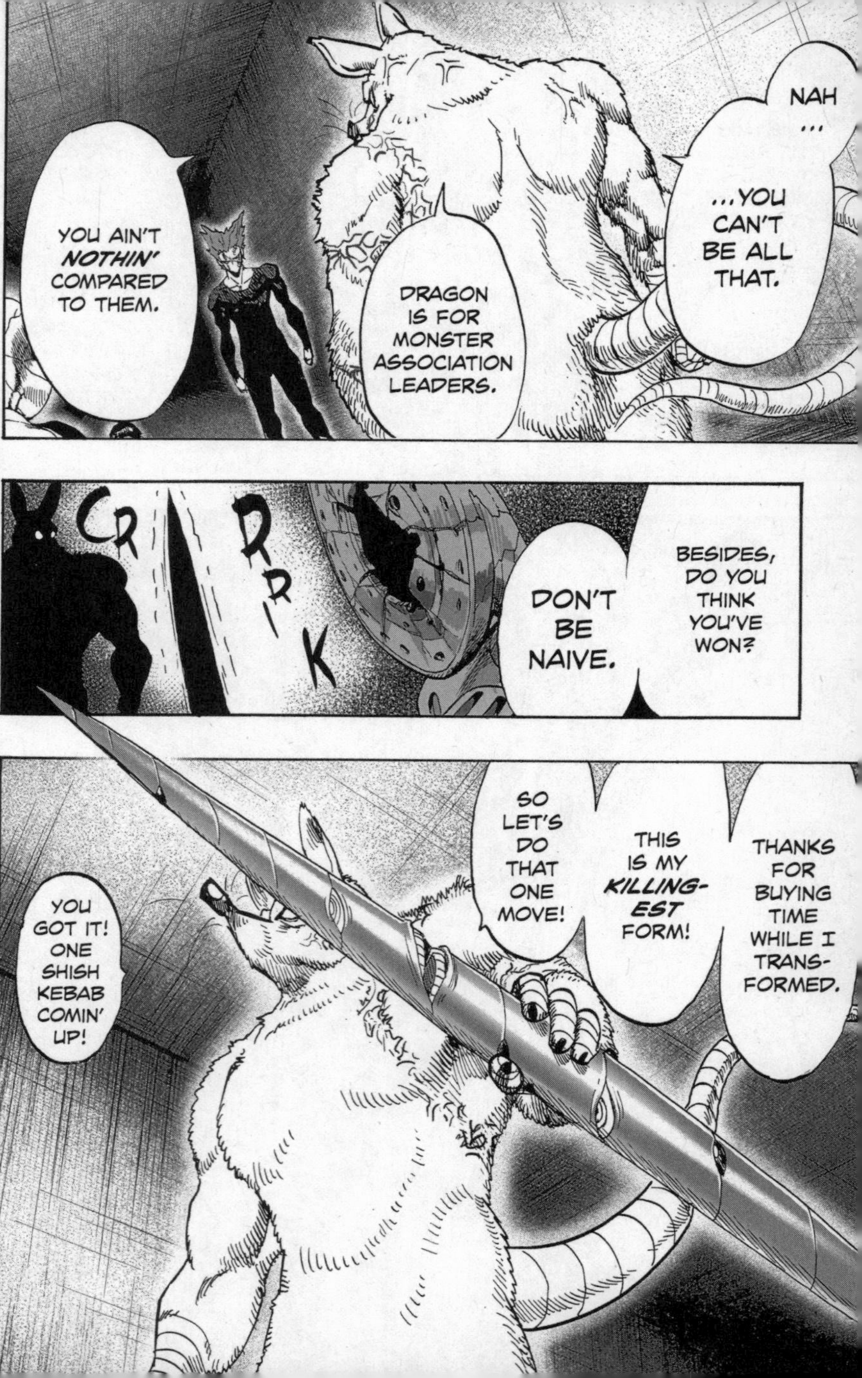

NAH ...
...YOU CAN'T BE ALL THAT.
DRAGON IS FOR MONSTER ASSOCIATION LEADERS.
YOU AIN'T *NOTHIN'* COMPARED TO THEM.
BESIDES, DO YOU THINK YOU'VE WON?
DON'T BE NAIVE.
CRRIK
THANKS FOR BUYING TIME WHILE I TRANS-FORMED.
THIS IS MY *KILLING-EST* FORM!
SO LET'S DO THAT ONE MOVE!
YOU GOT IT! ONE SHISH KEBAB COMIN' UP!

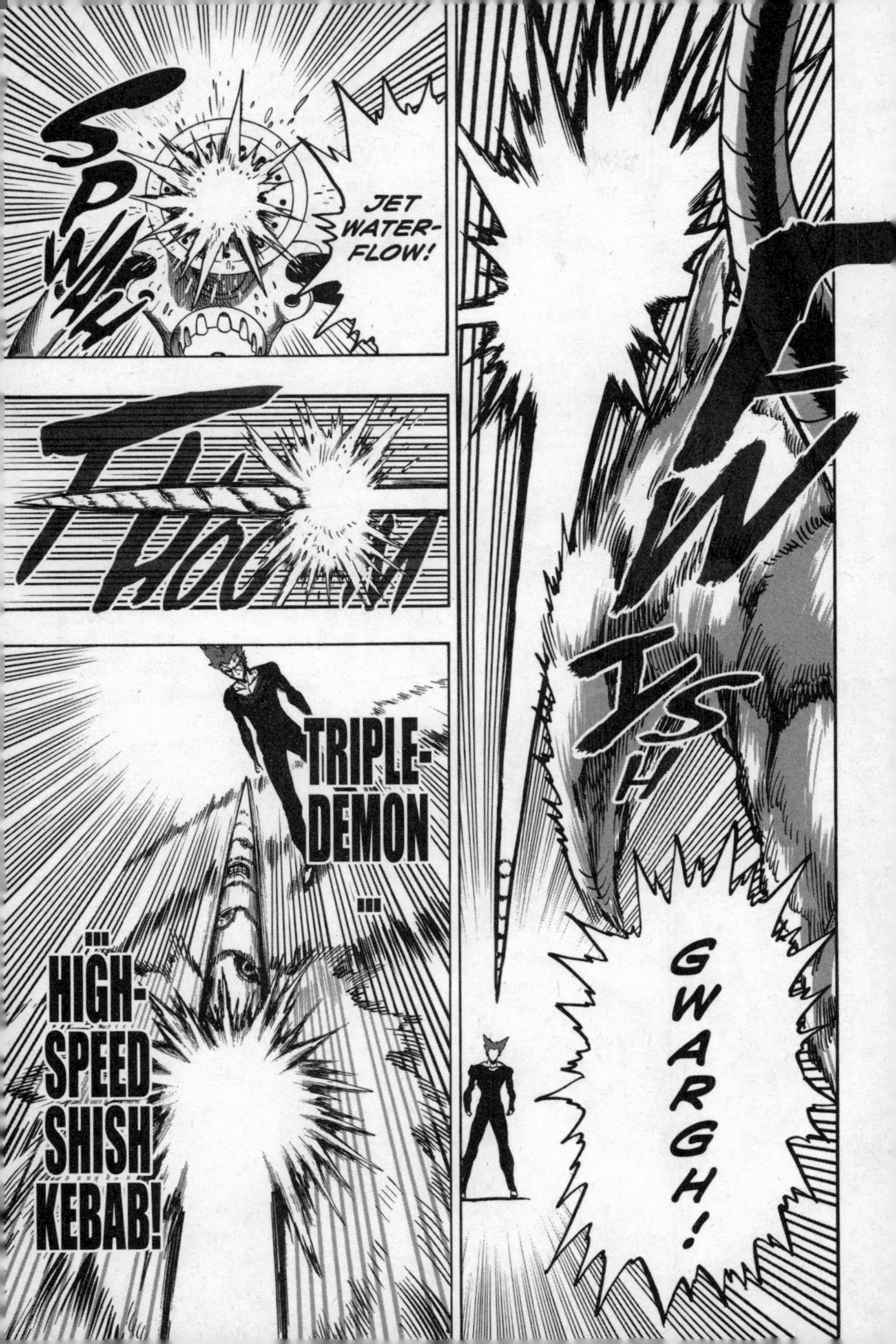

GWARGH!
JET WATER-FLOW!
TRIPLE-DEMON...
...HIGH-SPEED SHISH KEBAB!

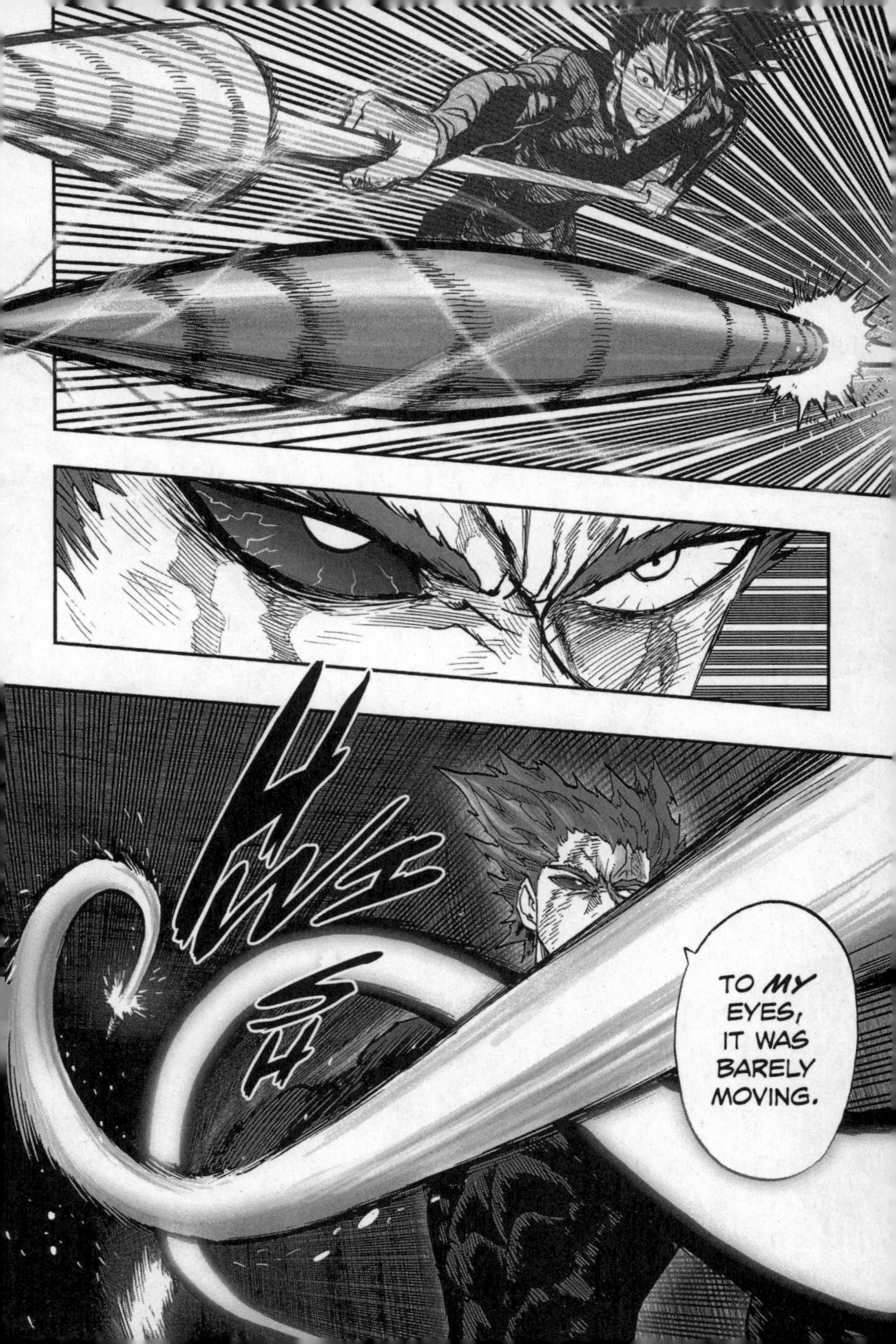
TO MY EYES, IT WAS BARELY MOVING.

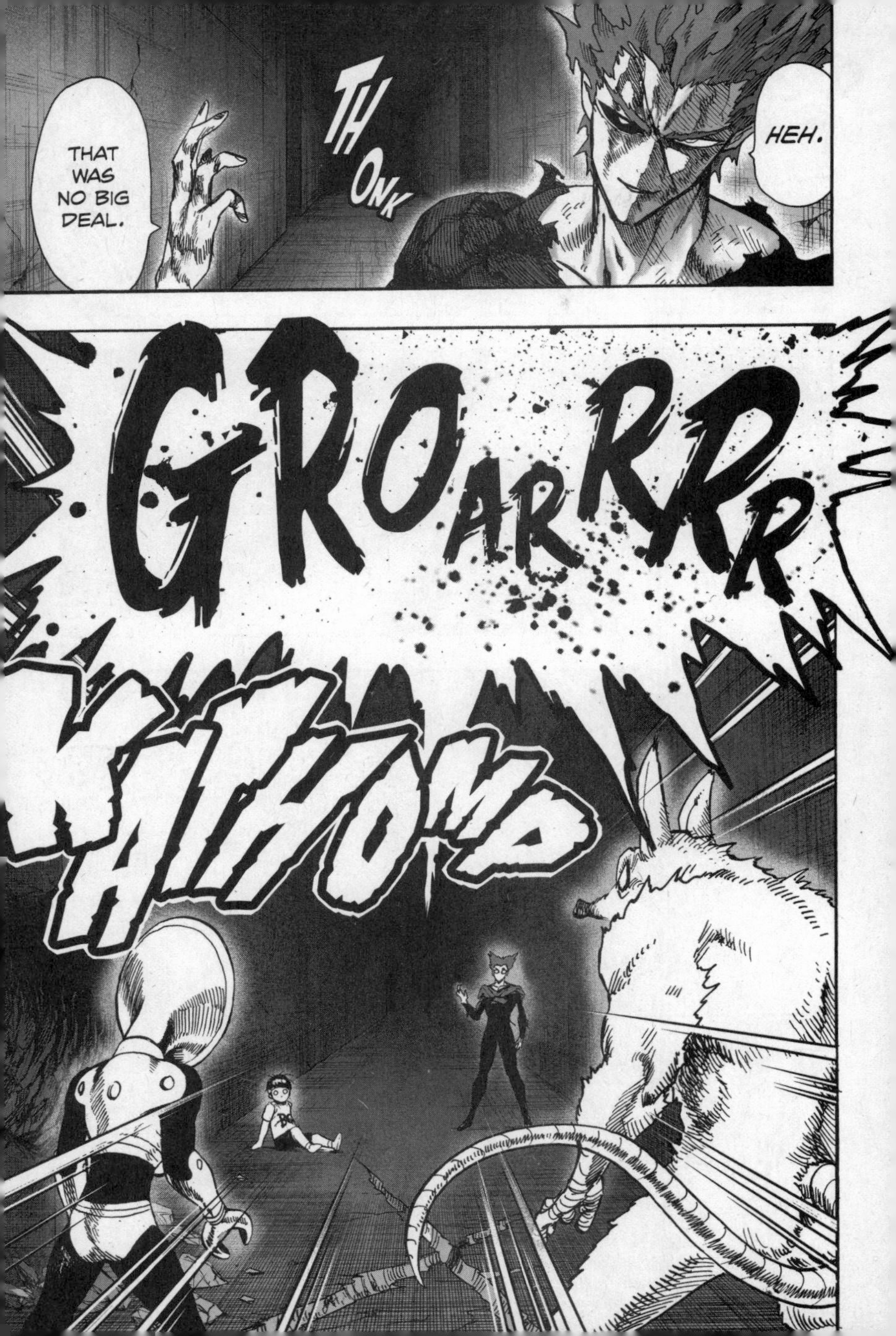
HEH.
THONK
THAT WAS NO BIG DEAL.
GROARRRR
WHOMP

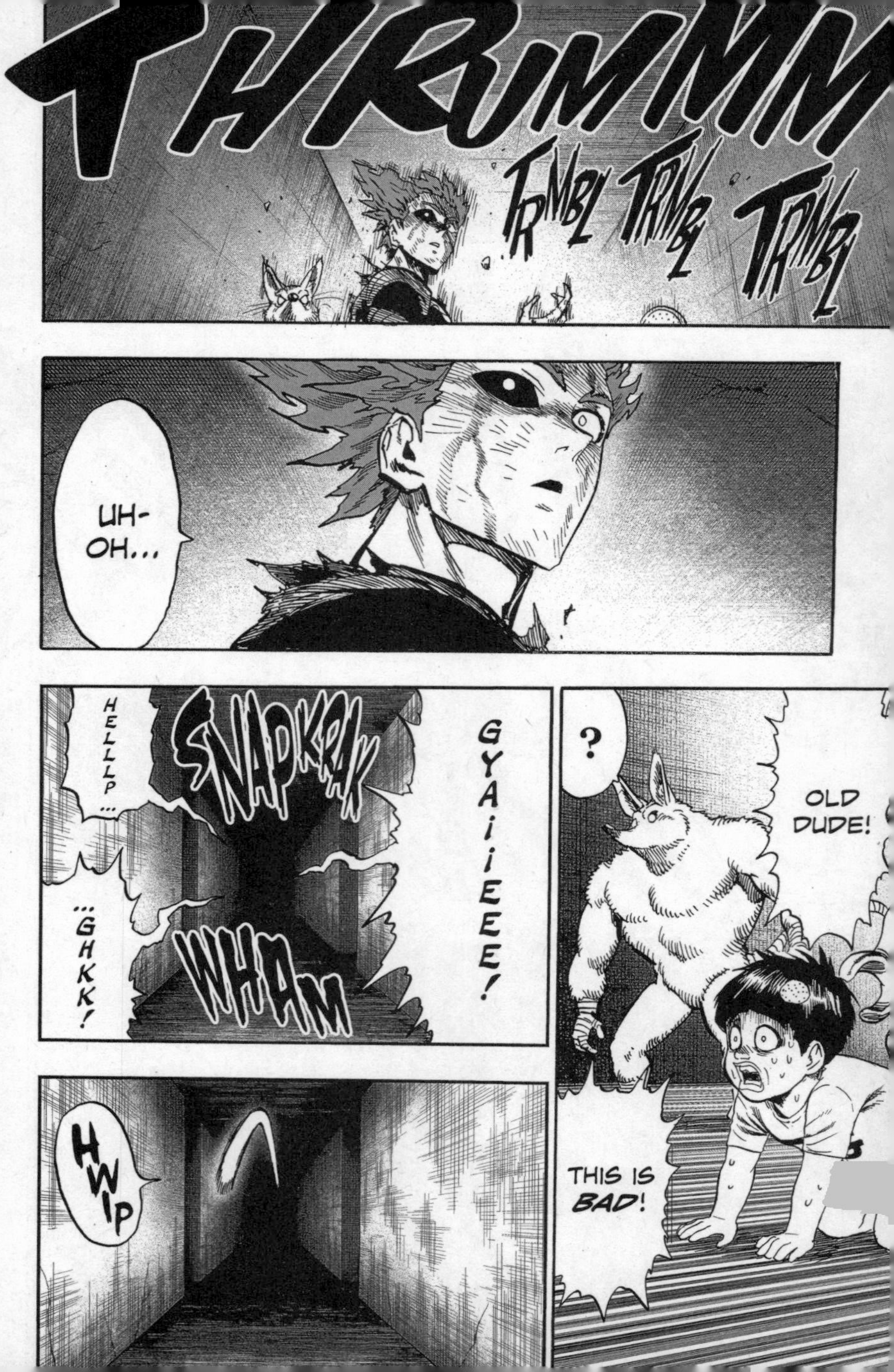
THRUMMM
TRMBL TRMBL TRMBL
UH-OH...
OLD DUDE!
?
GYAiiiEEEE!
SNAPKRAK
HELLLP...
WHAM
...GHKK!
THIS IS BAD!
HWIP

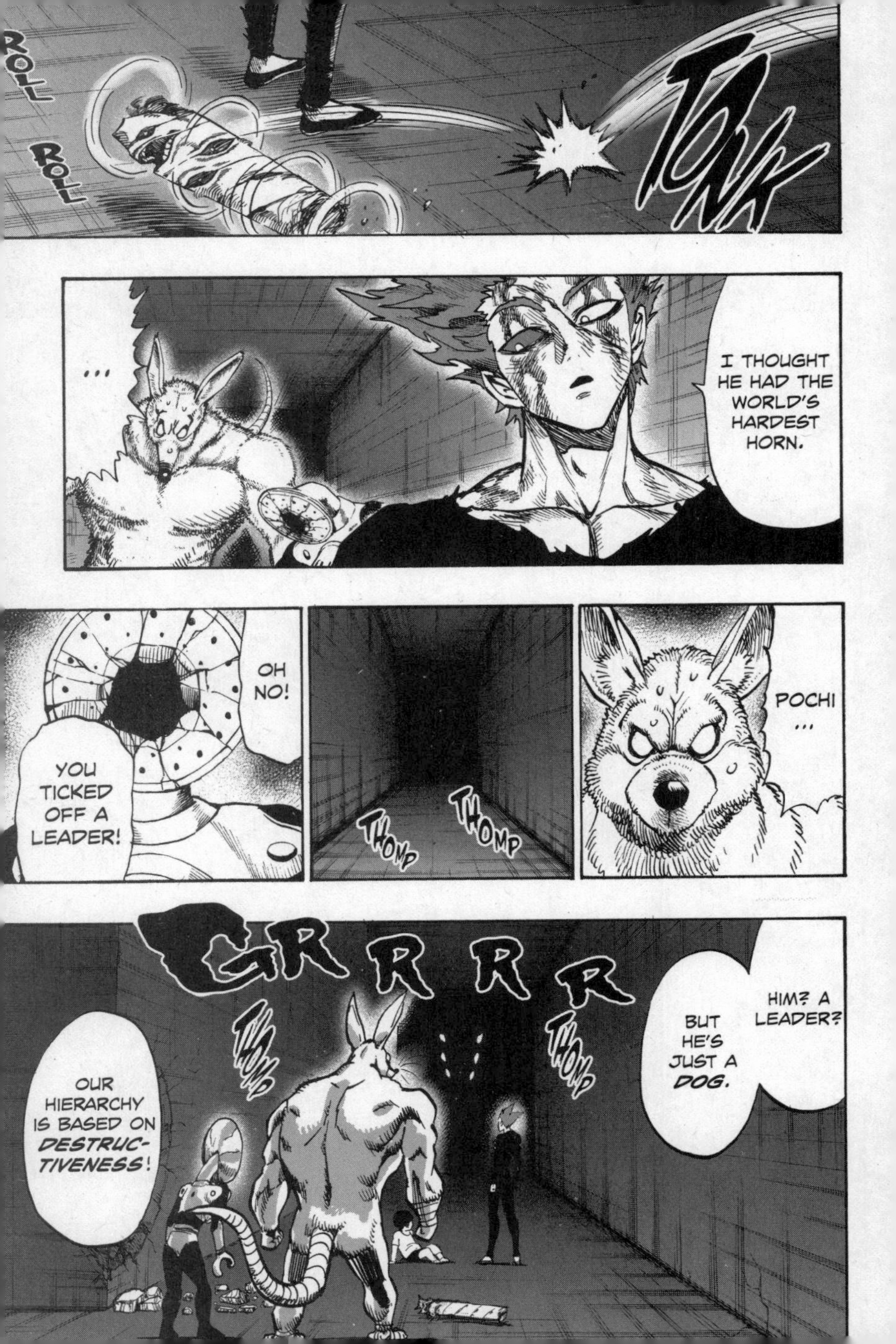
TONK
ROLL ROLL
I THOUGHT HE HAD THE WORLD'S HARDEST HORN.
...
POCHI ...
THOMP THOMP
OH NO!
YOU TICKED OFF A LEADER!
GRRRR
HIM? A LEADER?
BUT HE'S JUST A DOG.
THOMP THOMP
OUR HIERARCHY IS BASED ON DESTRUCTIVENESS!

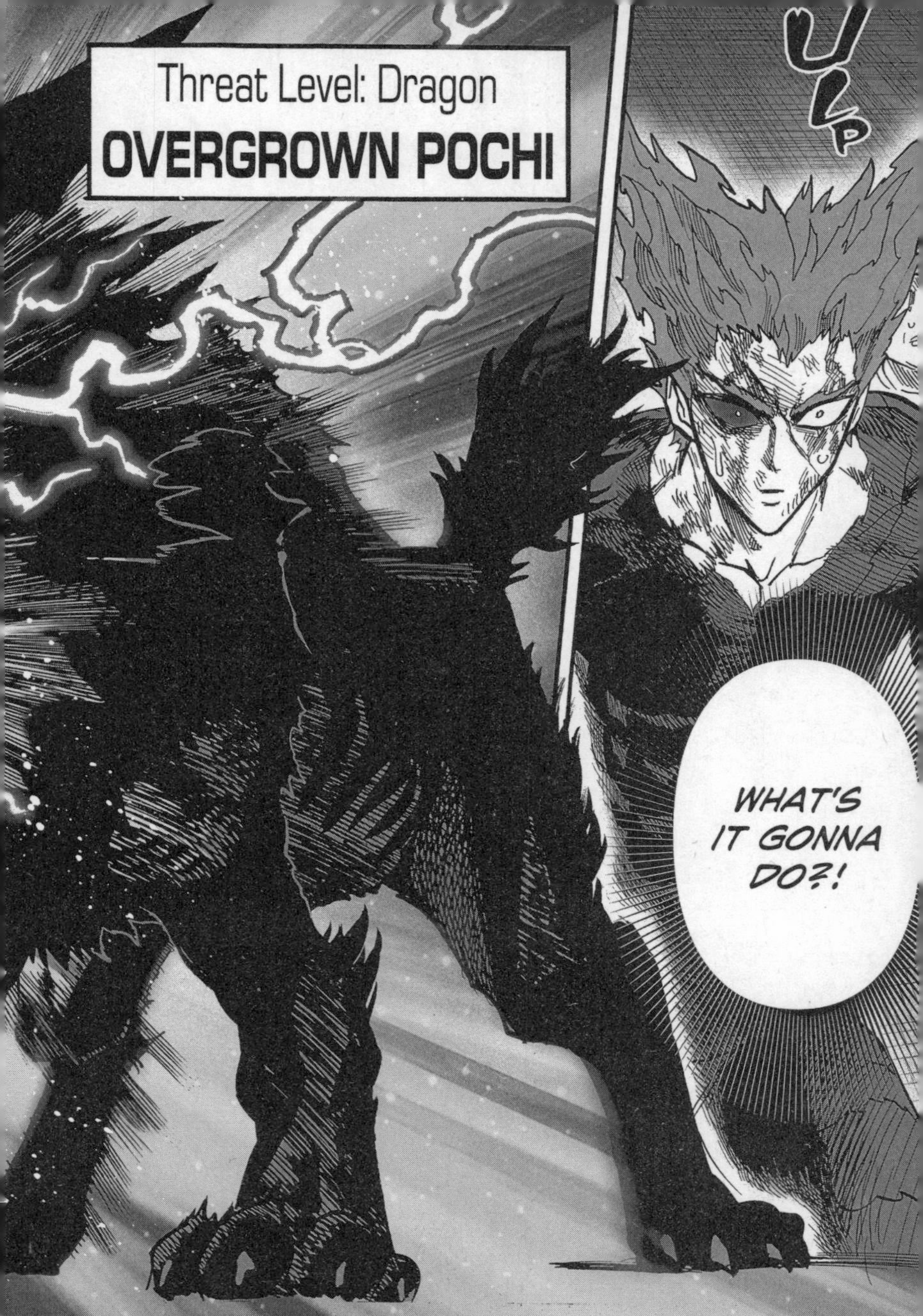
Threat Level: Dragon
OVERGROWN POCHI
ULP
WHAT'S IT GONNA DO?!

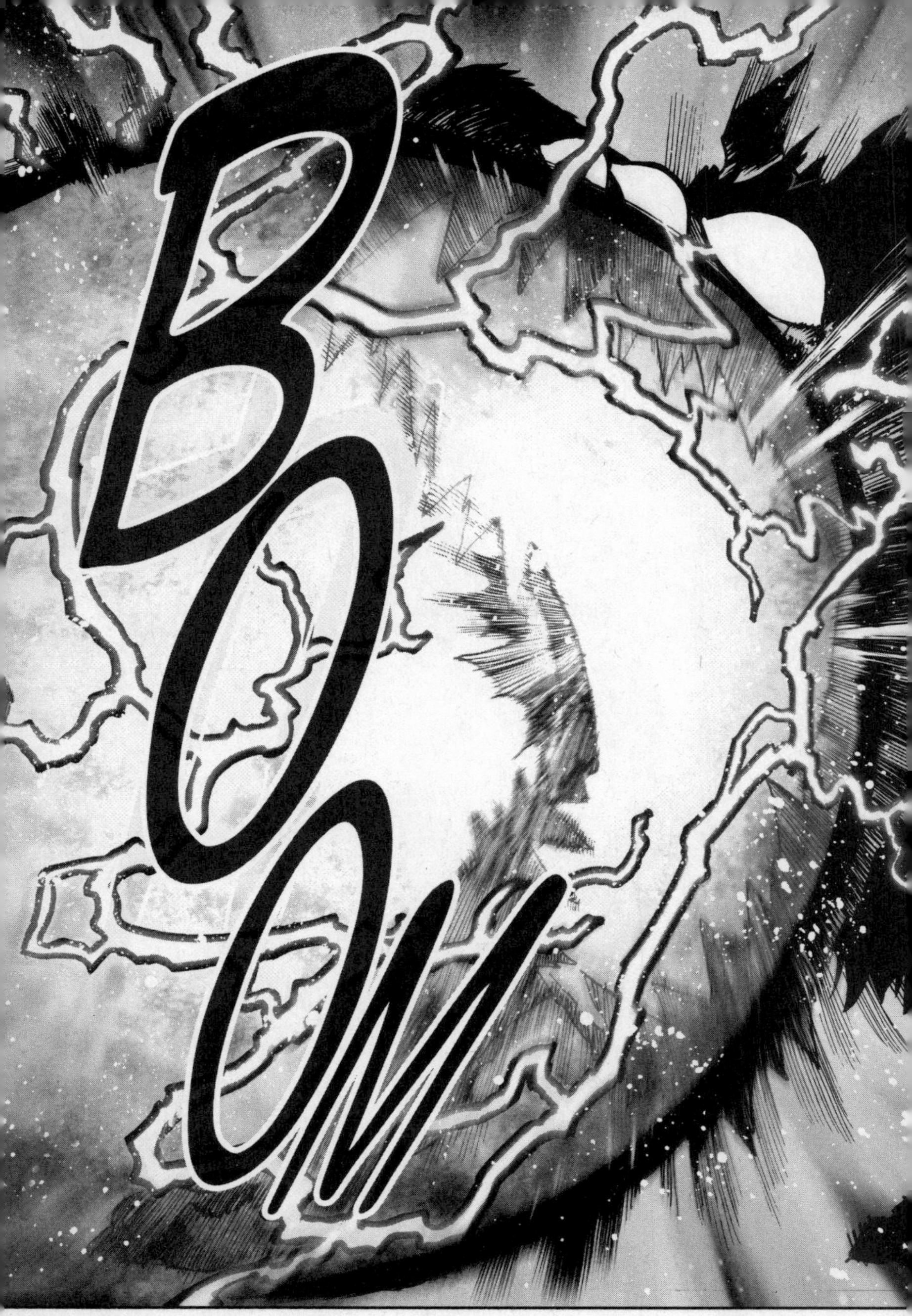
BOOM

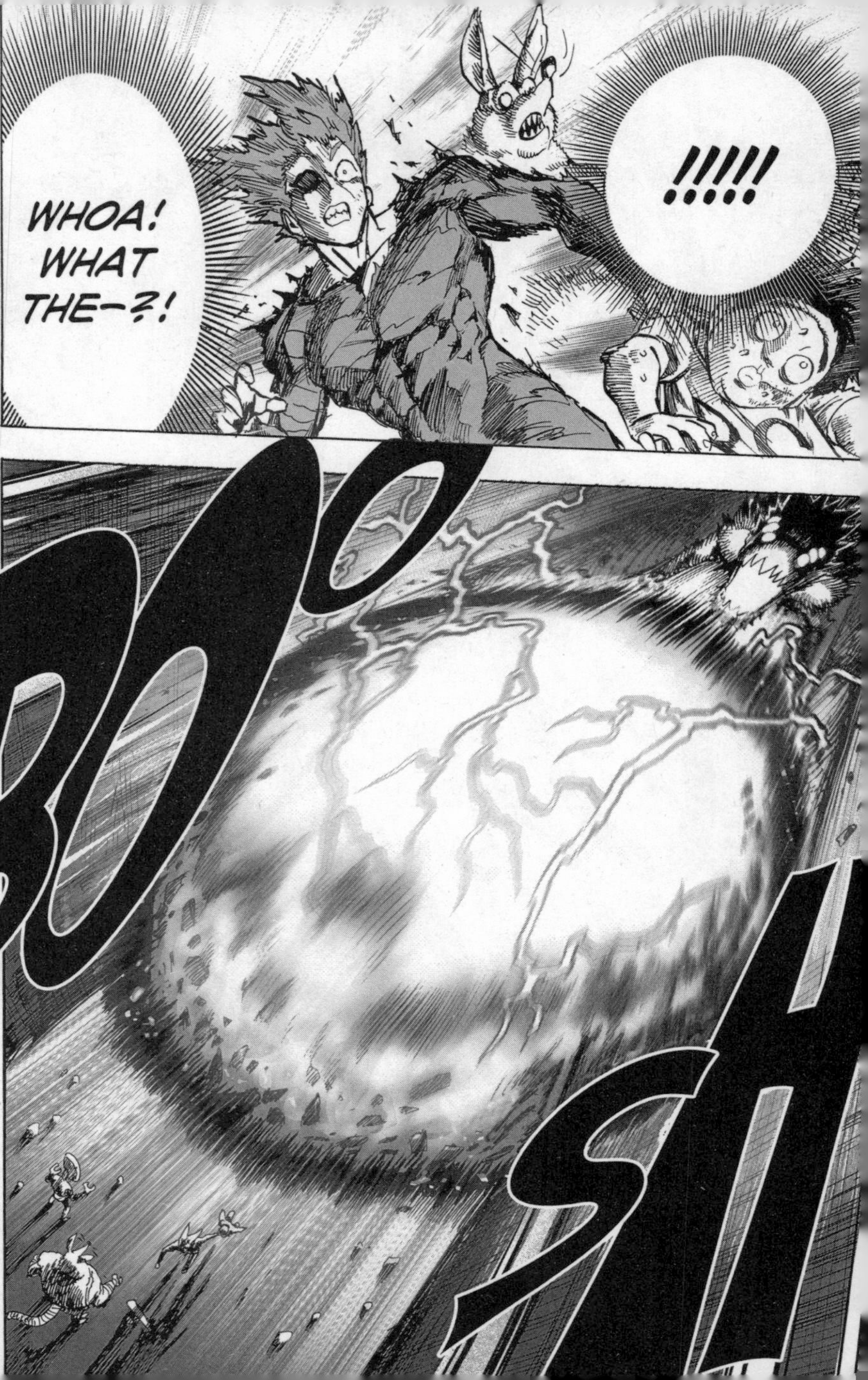
!!!!!
WHOA! WHAT THE—?!
BOOOSH

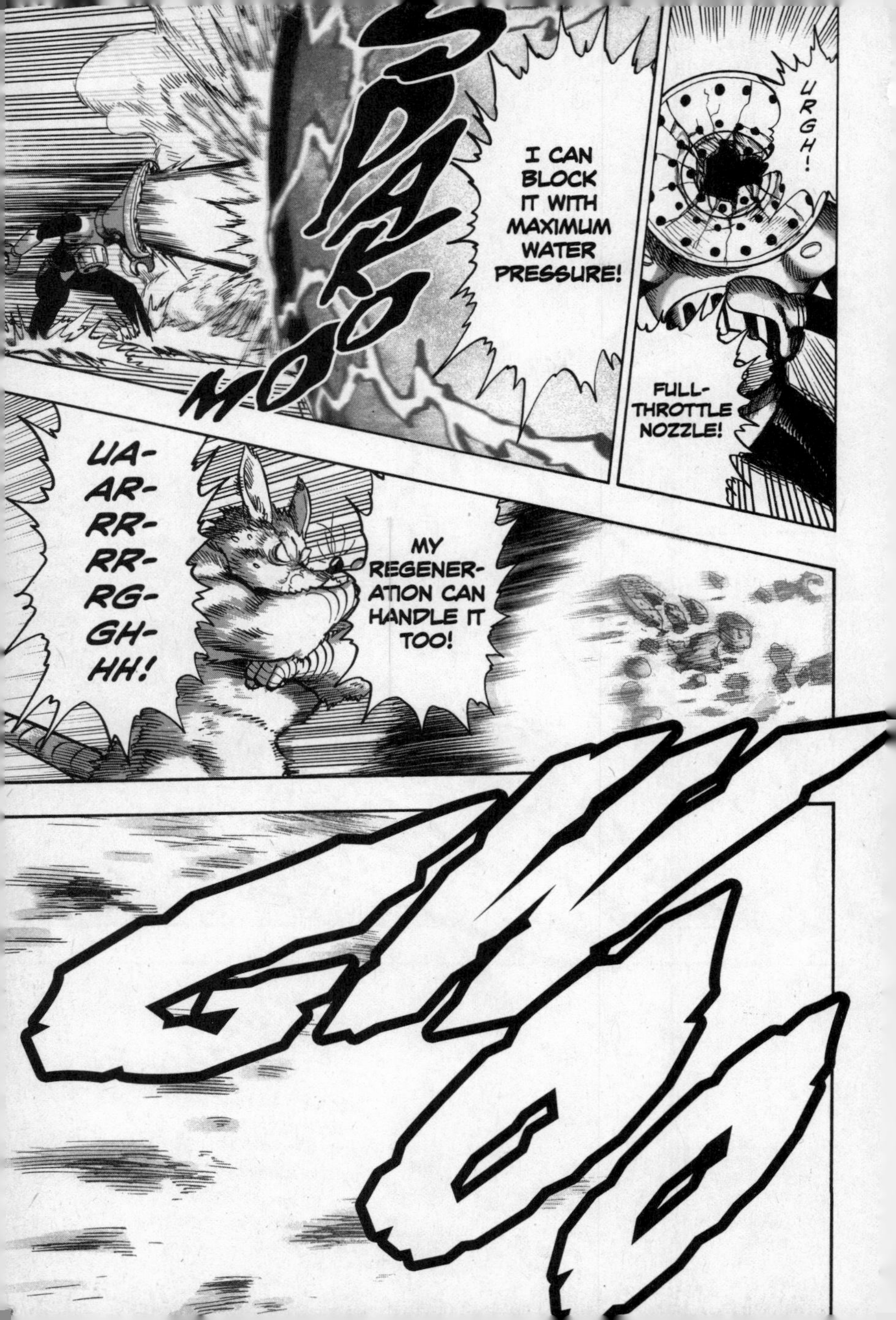
URGH!
FULL-THROTTLE NOZZLE!
SPAKOOM
I CAN BLOCK IT WITH MAXIMUM WATER PRESSURE!
MY REGENERATION CAN HANDLE IT TOO!
UAARRRRRRGHHH!
GWOO

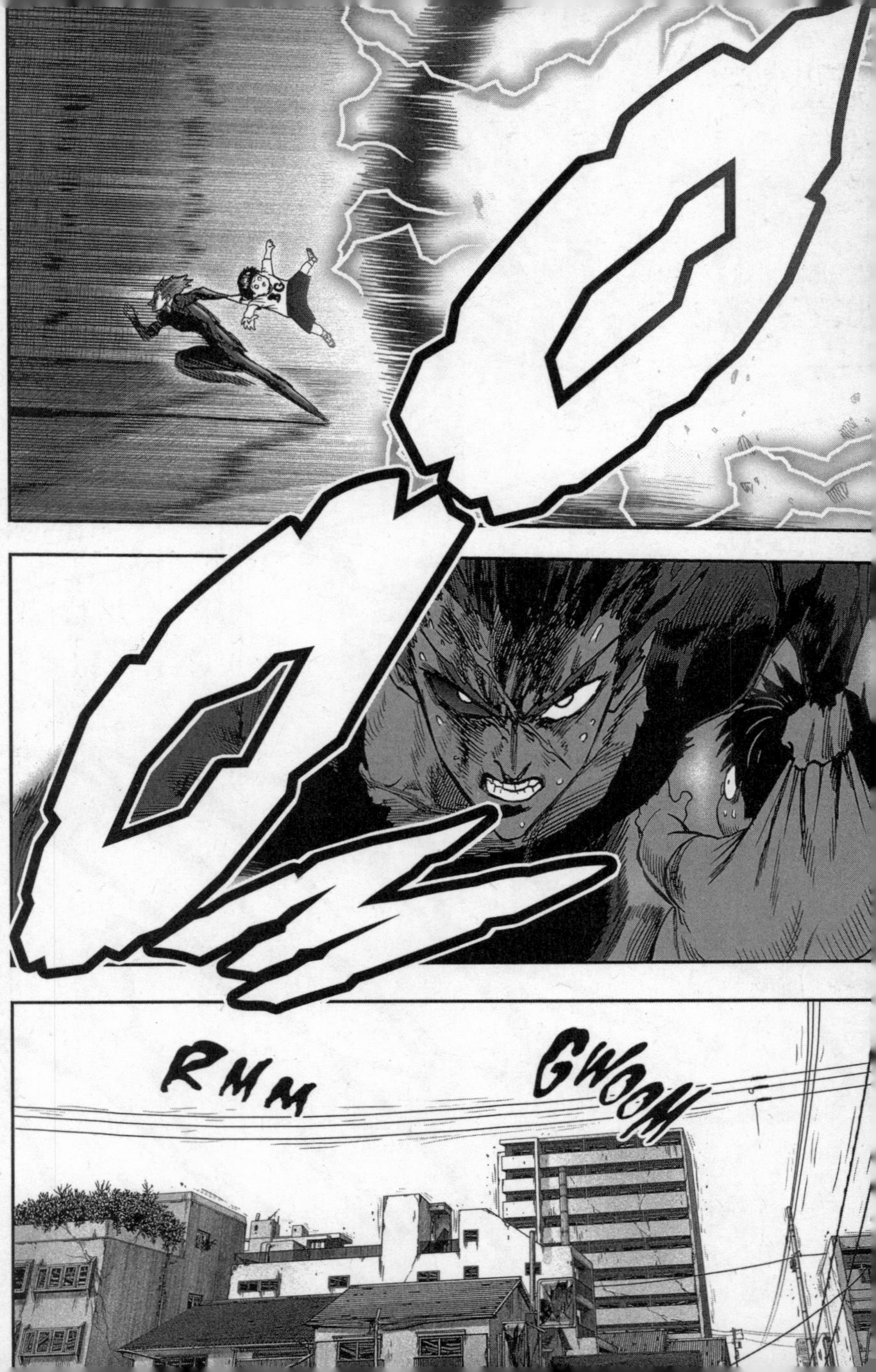
RMM
GWOOM

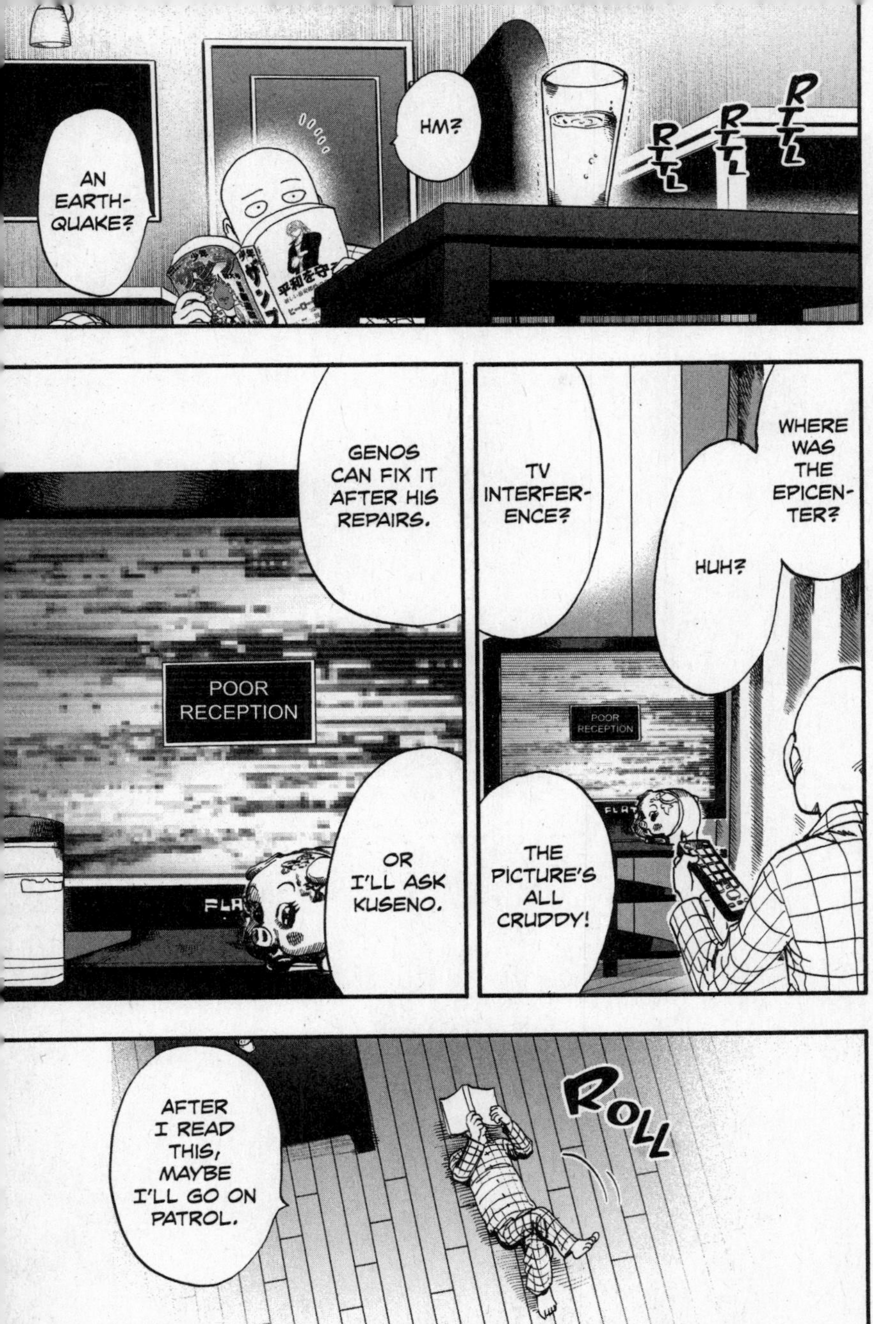
RTTL RTTL RTTL
HM?
AN EARTHQUAKE?
WHERE WAS THE EPICENTER?
HUH?
TV INTERFERENCE?
THE PICTURE'S ALL CRUDDY!
POOR RECEPTION
GENOS CAN FIX IT AFTER HIS REPAIRS.
OR I'LL ASK KUSENO.
POOR RECEPTION
ROLL
AFTER I READ THIS, MAYBE I'LL GO ON PATROL.

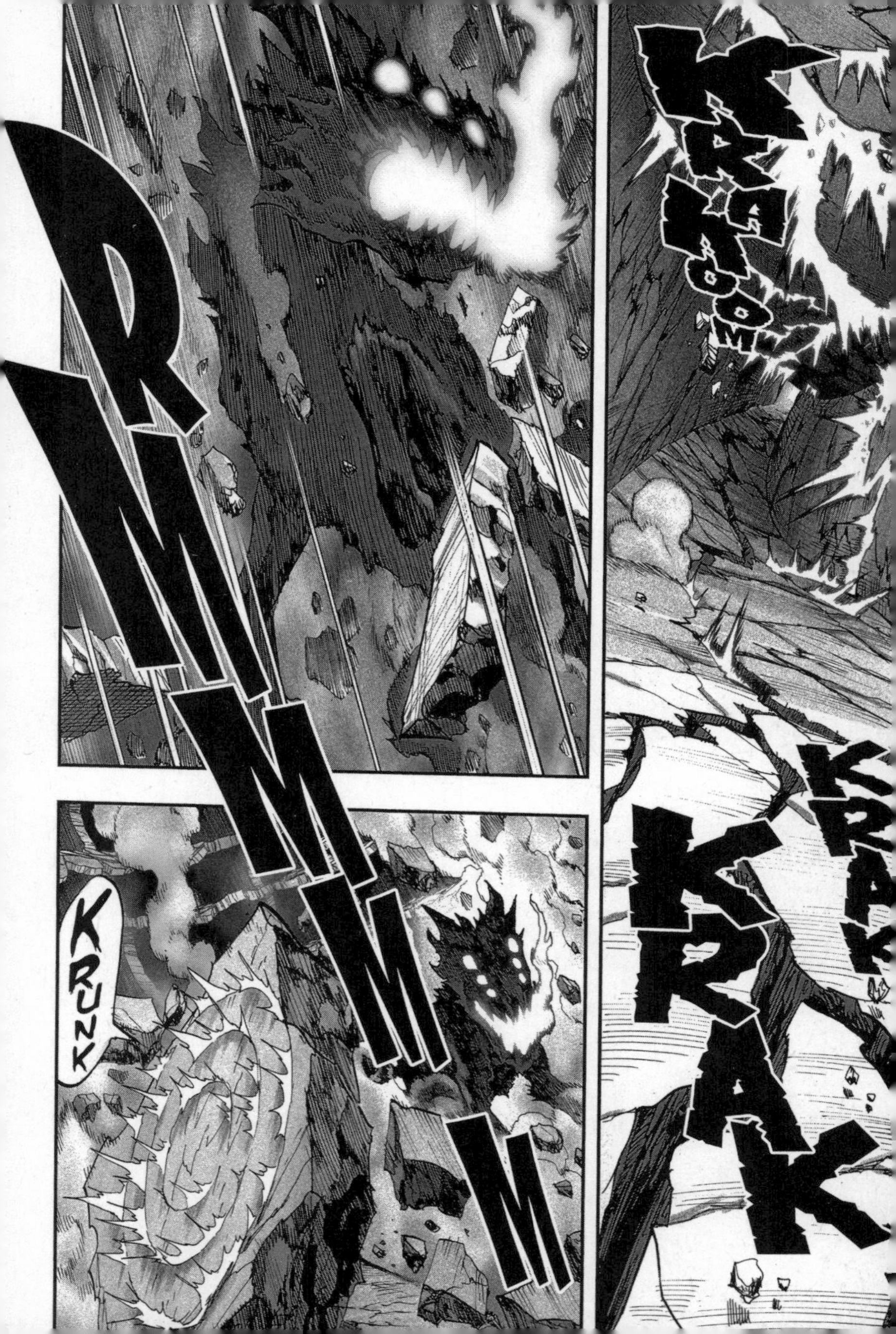
KABOOM
KRAK
KRAK
RMMMMMMM
KRUNK

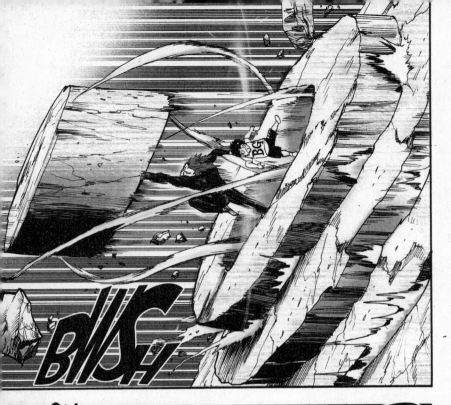

BWSH

SHUN

THIS IS HOW STRONG THEIR LEADERS ARE?

RMMMM

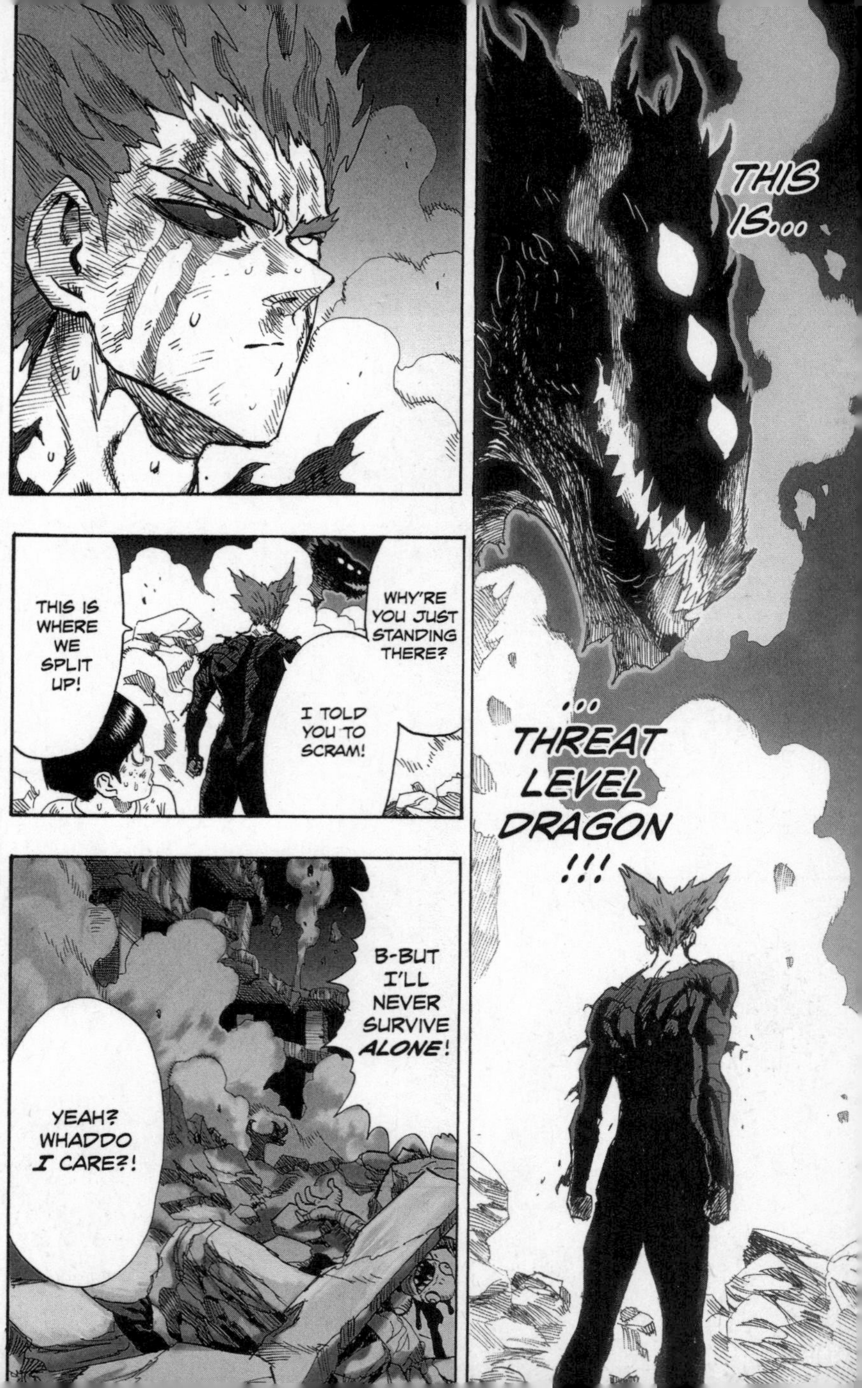
THIS IS...
...THREAT LEVEL DRAGON!!!
WHY'RE YOU JUST STANDING THERE?
I TOLD YOU TO SCRAM!
THIS IS WHERE WE SPLIT UP!
B-BUT I'LL NEVER SURVIVE ALONE!
YEAH? WHADDO I CARE?!

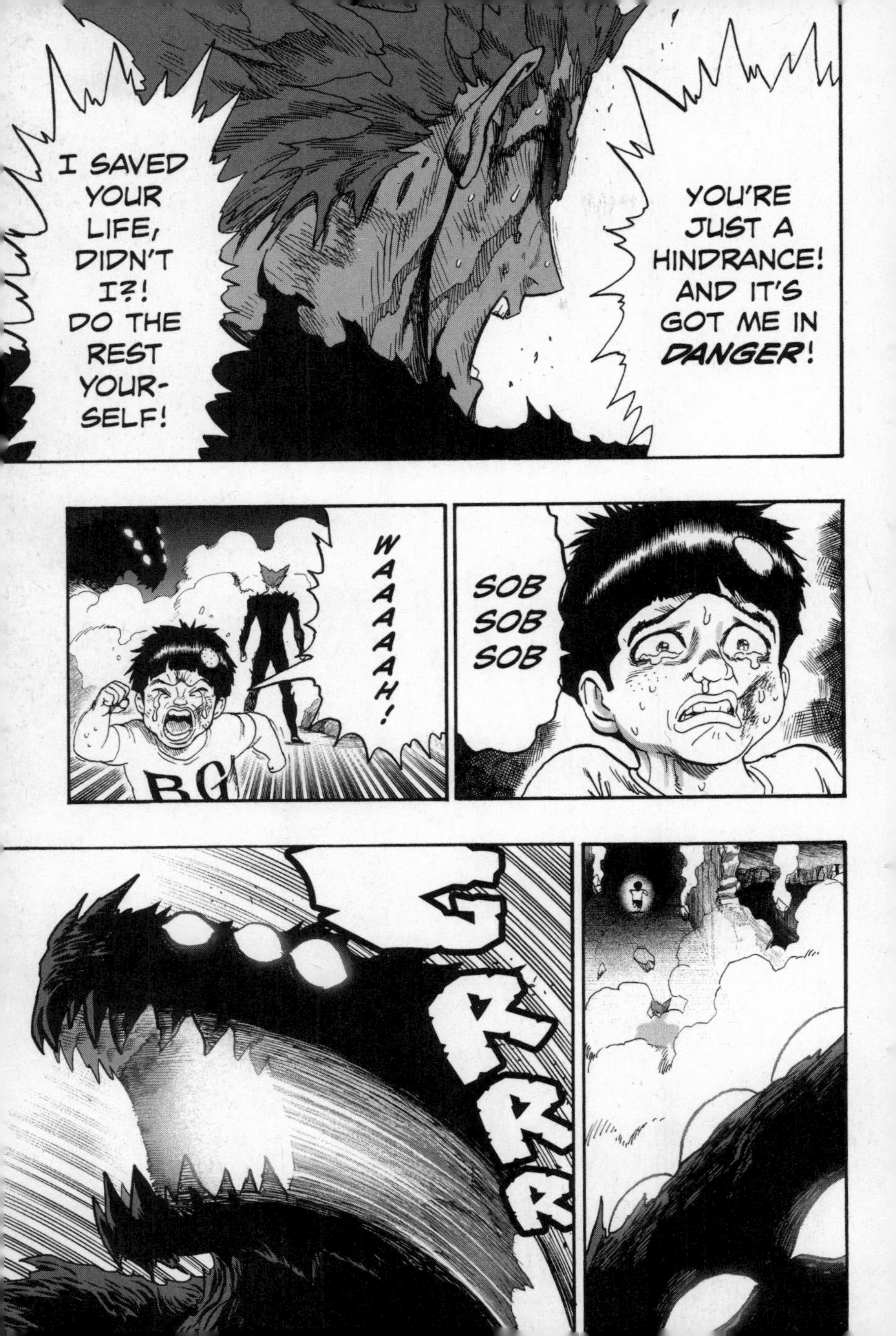
YOU'RE JUST A HINDRANCE! AND IT'S GOT ME IN DANGER!
I SAVED YOUR LIFE, DIDN'T I?! DO THE REST YOURSELF!
SOB SOB SOB
WAAAAAAH!
BG
GRRR

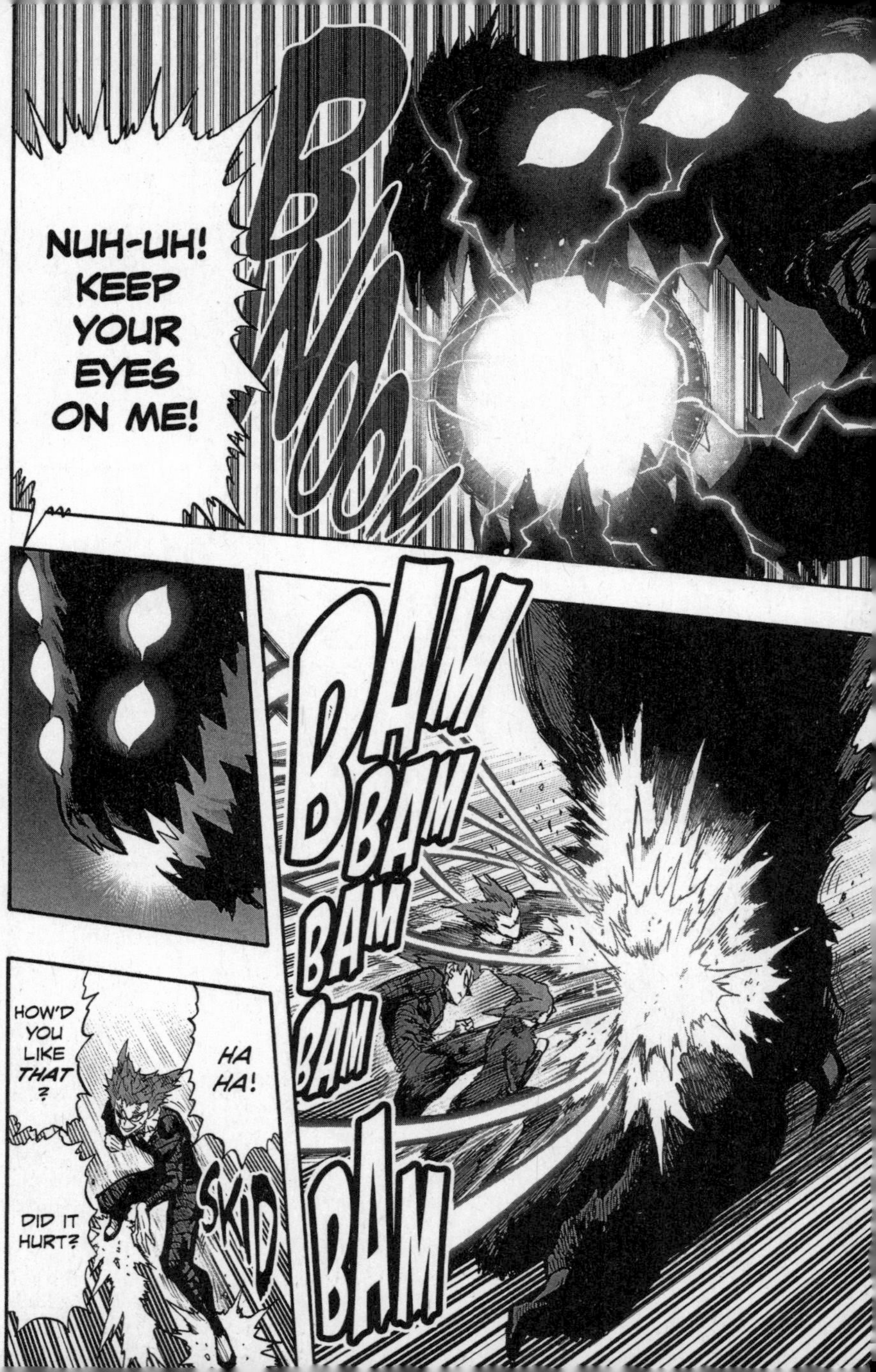
NUH-UH! KEEP YOUR EYES ON ME!
BAM
BAM
BAM
BAM
BAM
BAM
HA HA!
HOW'D YOU LIKE THAT?
SKID
DID IT HURT?

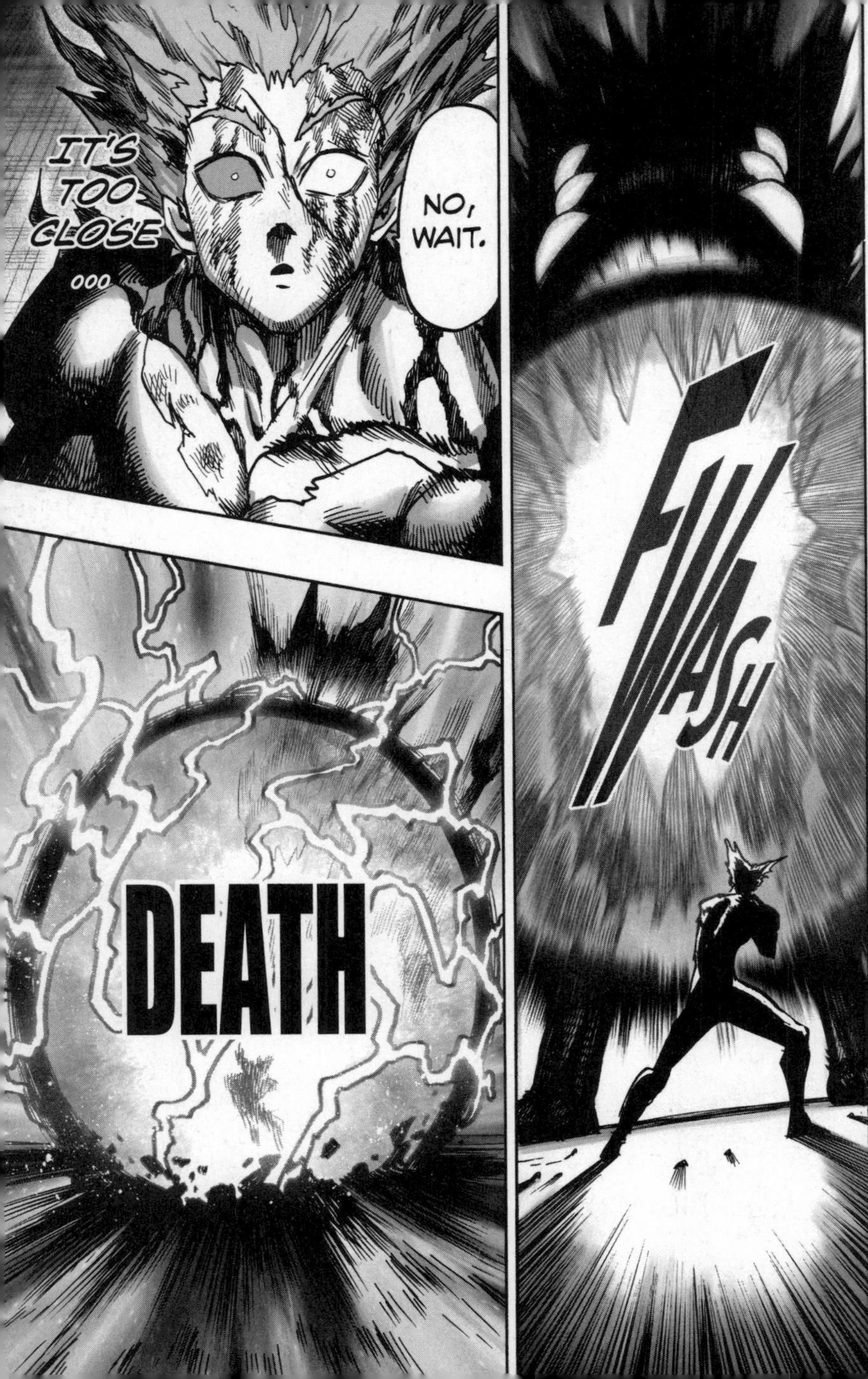
FLASH
NO, WAIT.
IT'S TOO CLOSE
...
DEATH

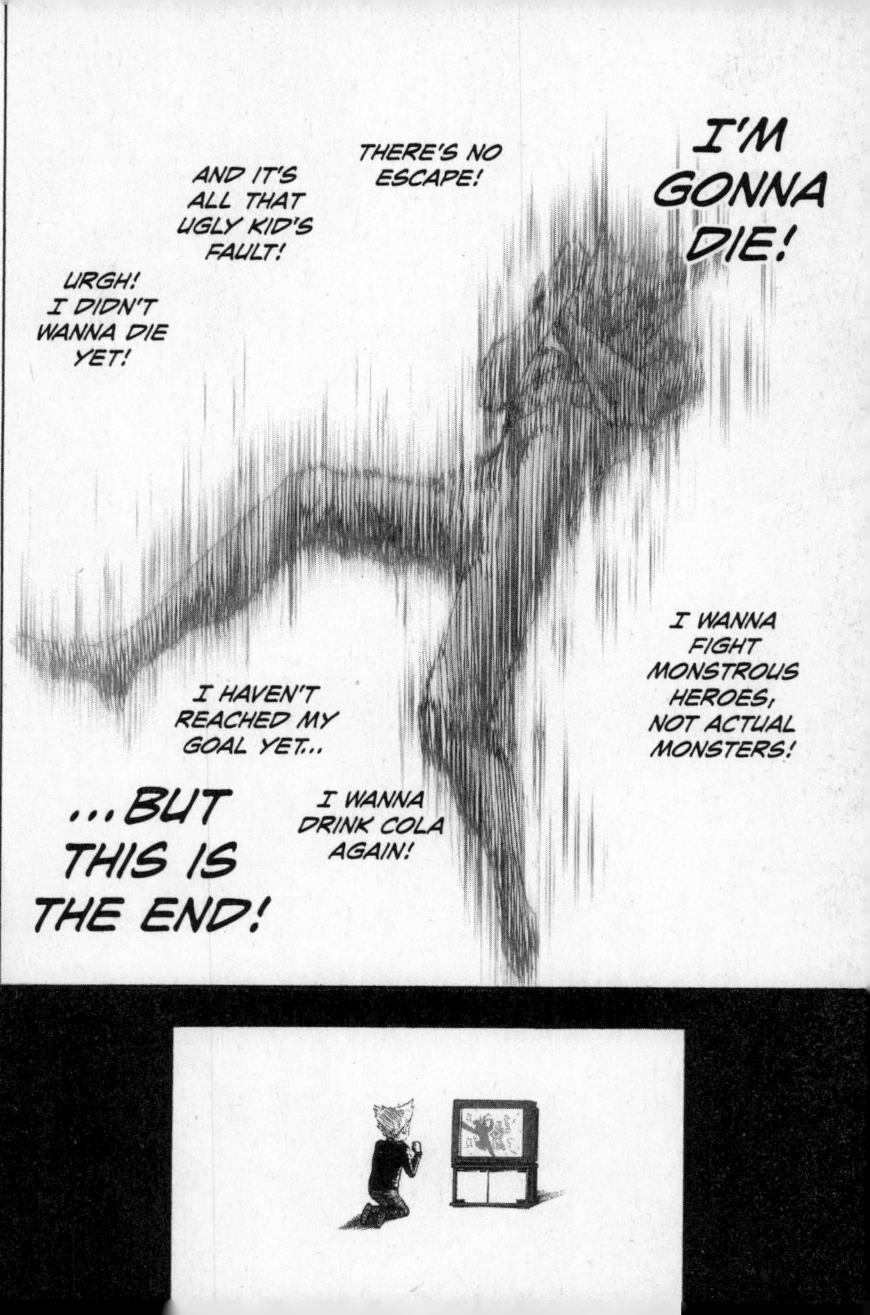
I'M GONNA DIE!
THERE'S NO ESCAPE!
AND IT'S ALL THAT UGLY KID'S FAULT!
URGH! I DIDN'T WANNA DIE YET!
I WANNA FIGHT MONSTROUS HEROES, NOT ACTUAL MONSTERS!
I WANNA DRINK COLA AGAIN!
I HAVEN'T REACHED MY GOAL YET...
...BUT THIS IS THE END!

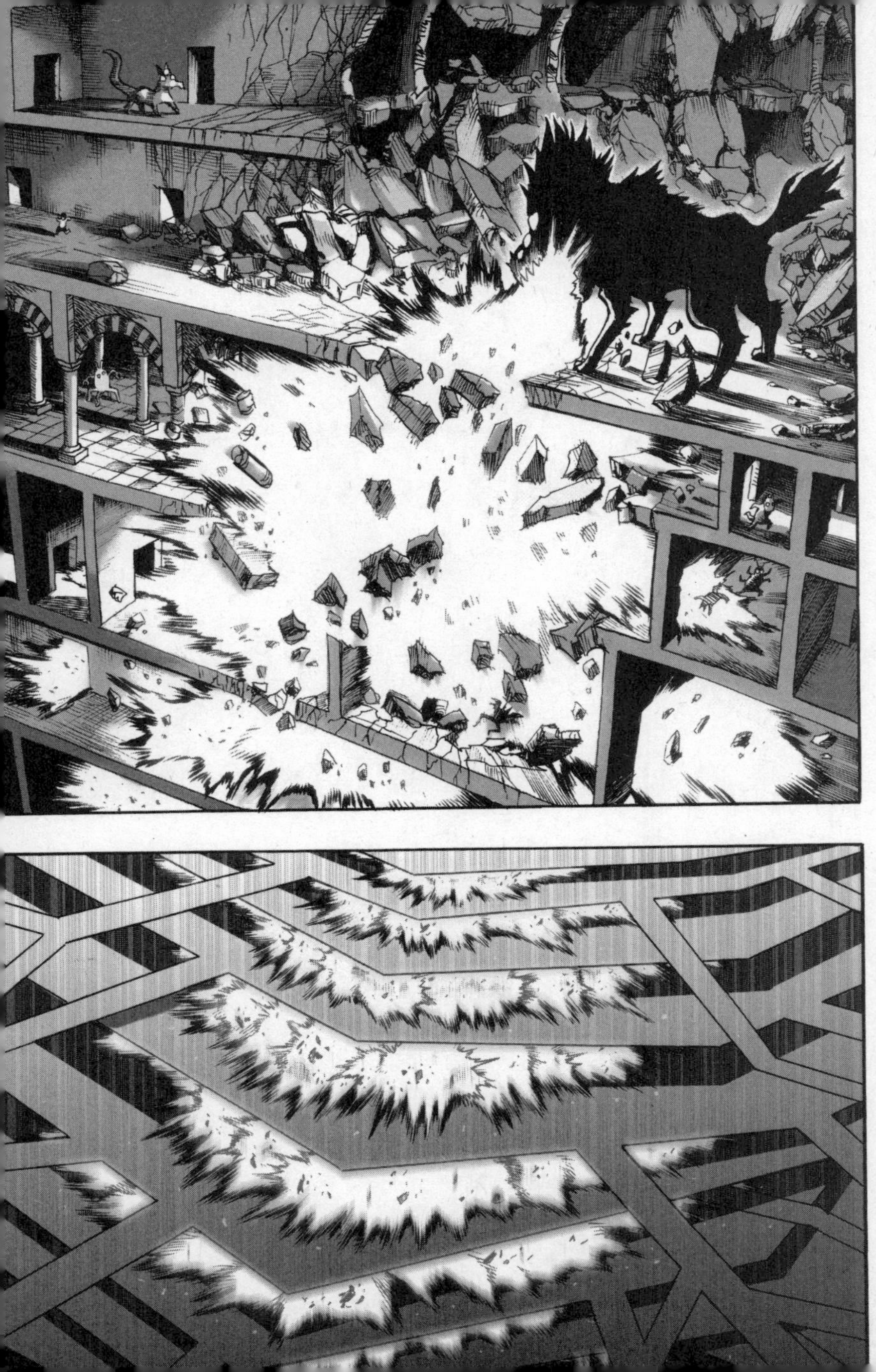

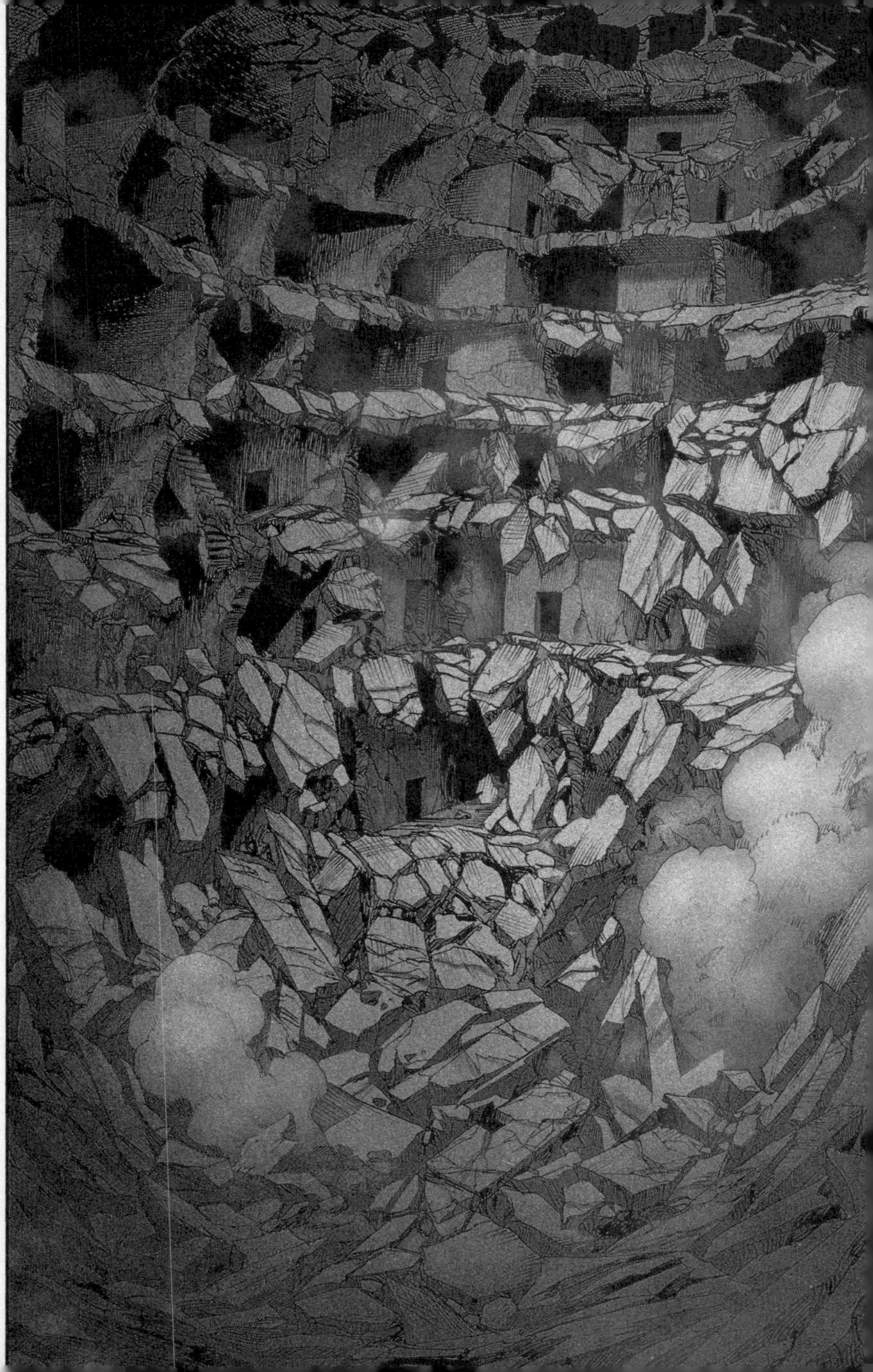

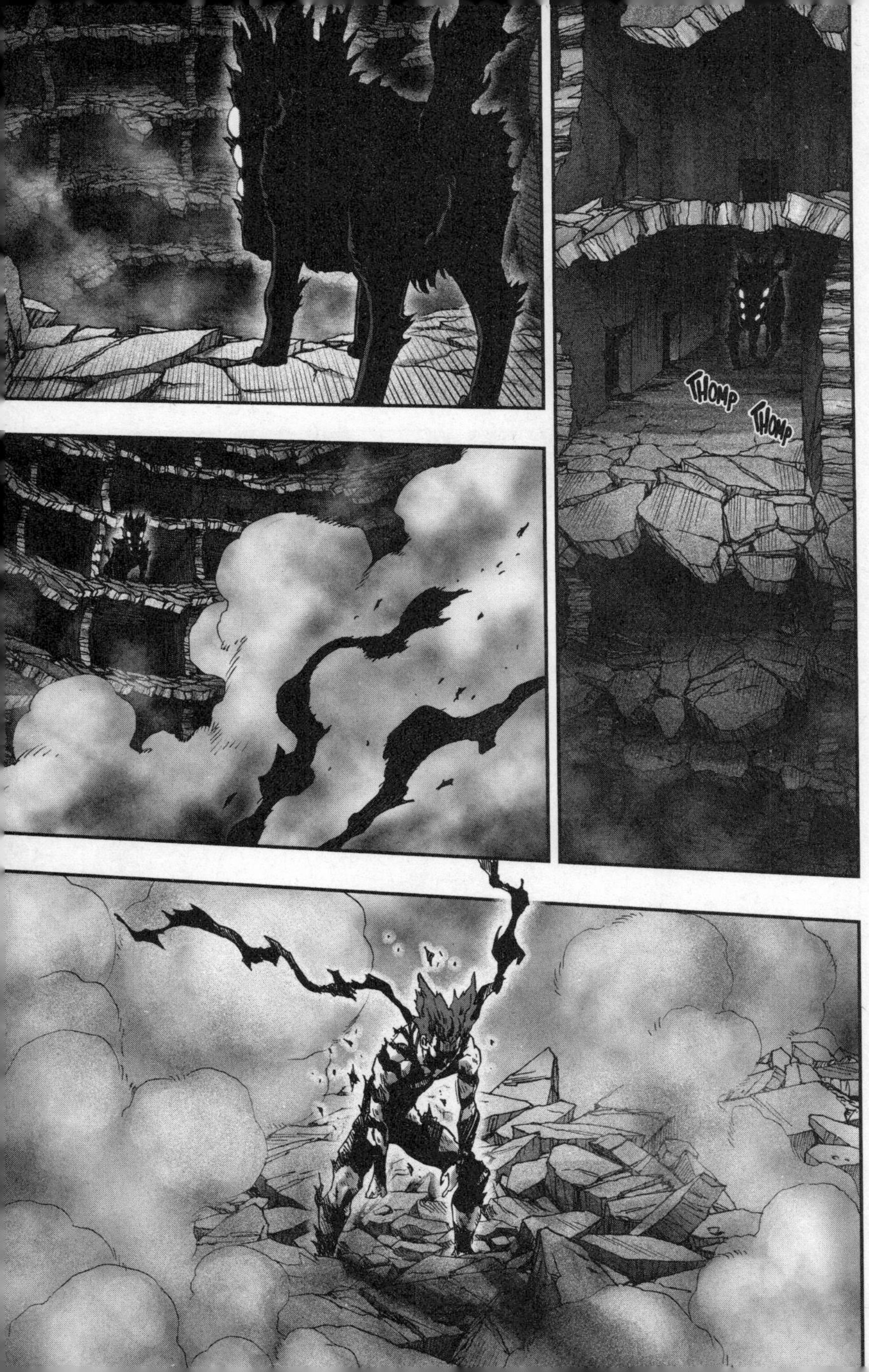
THOMP
THOMP

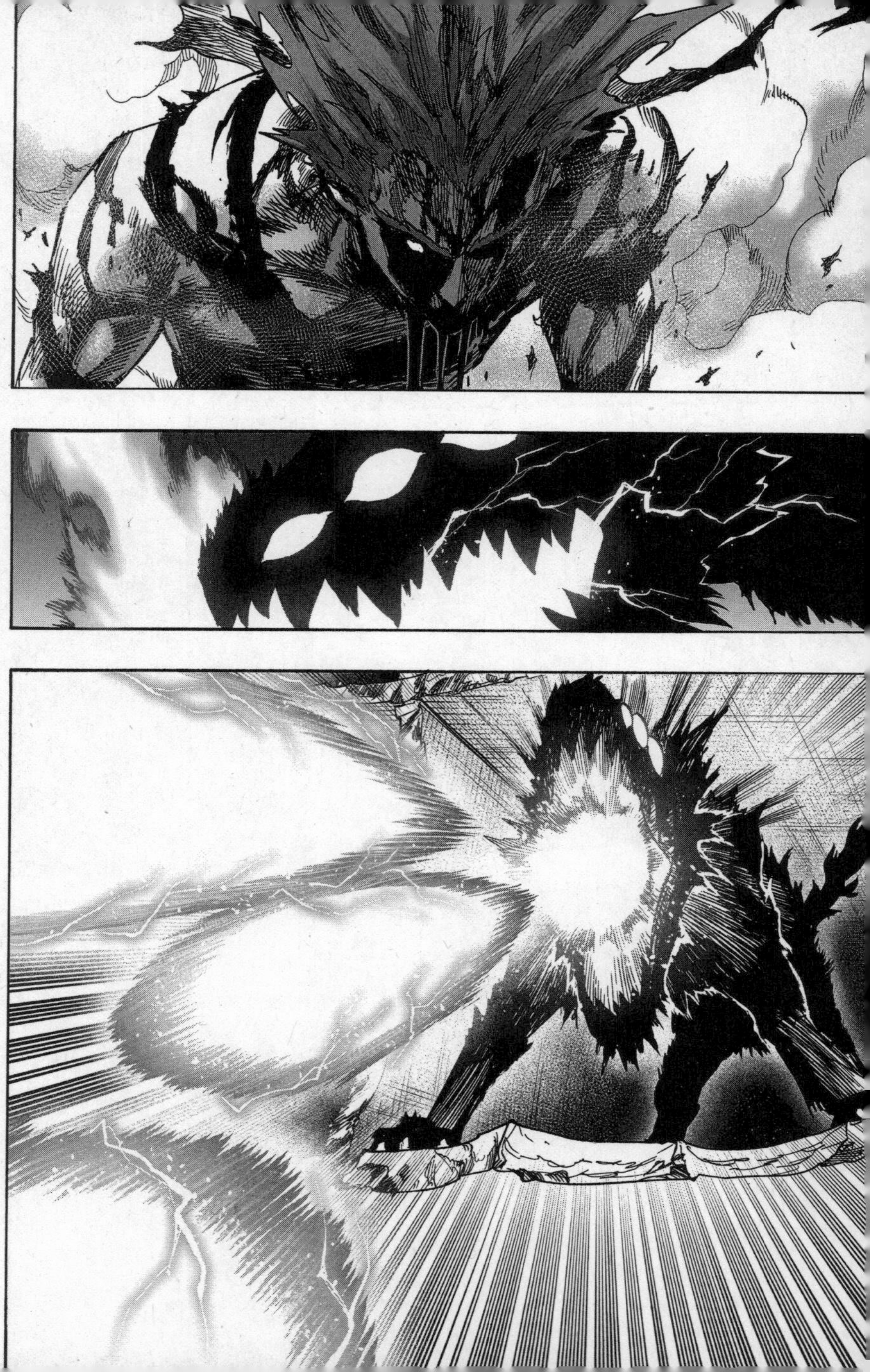

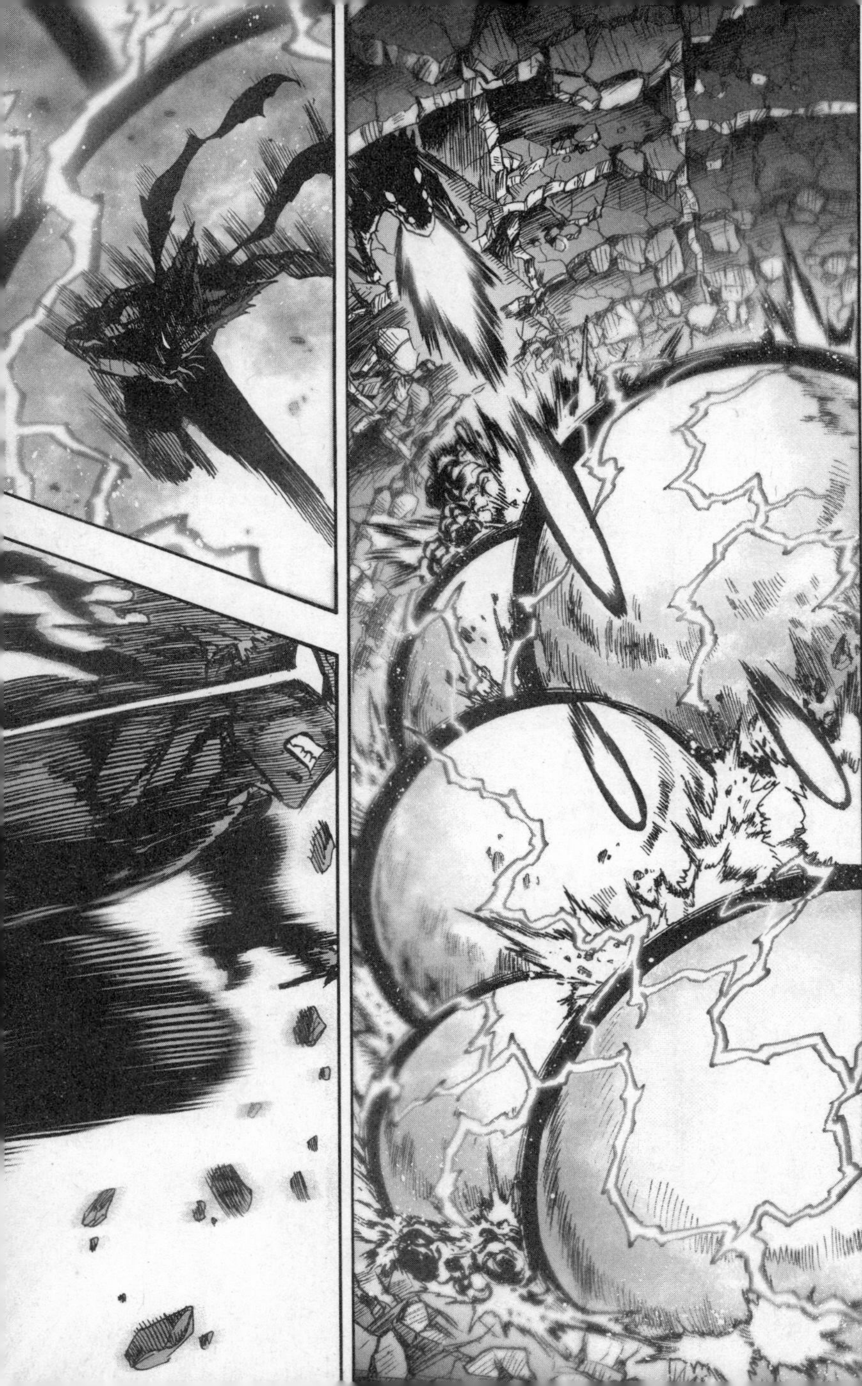

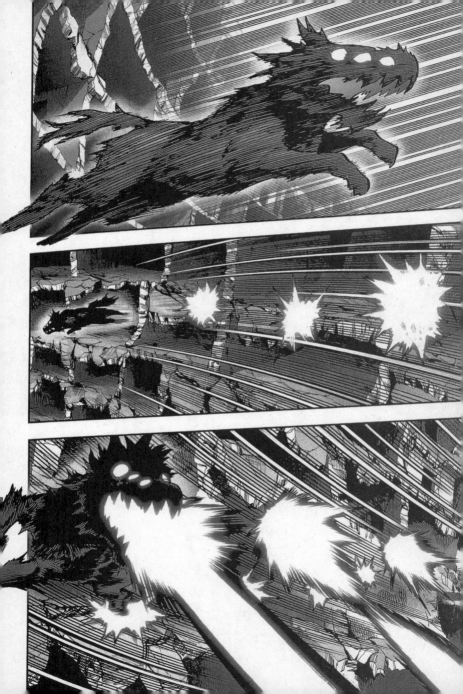

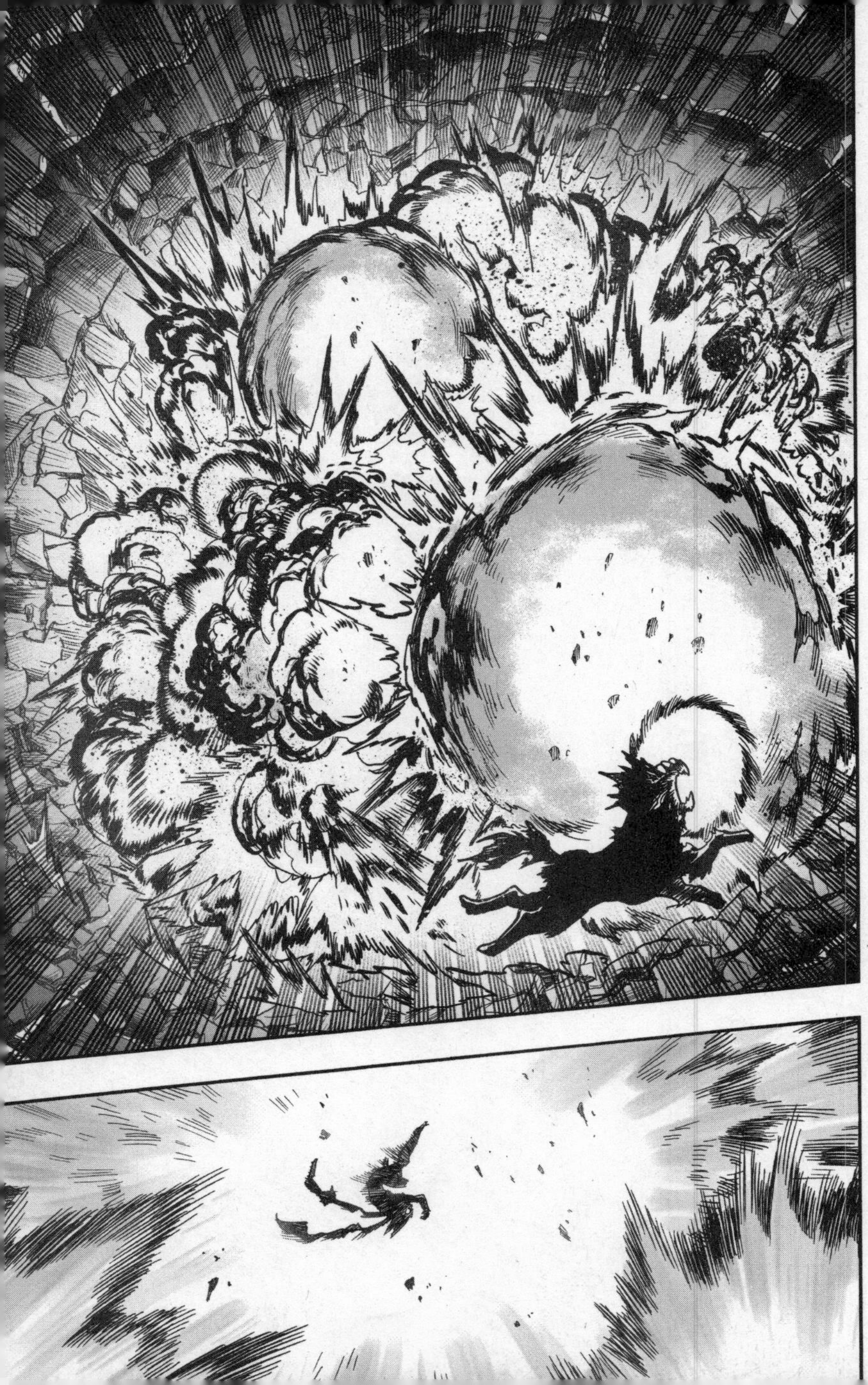

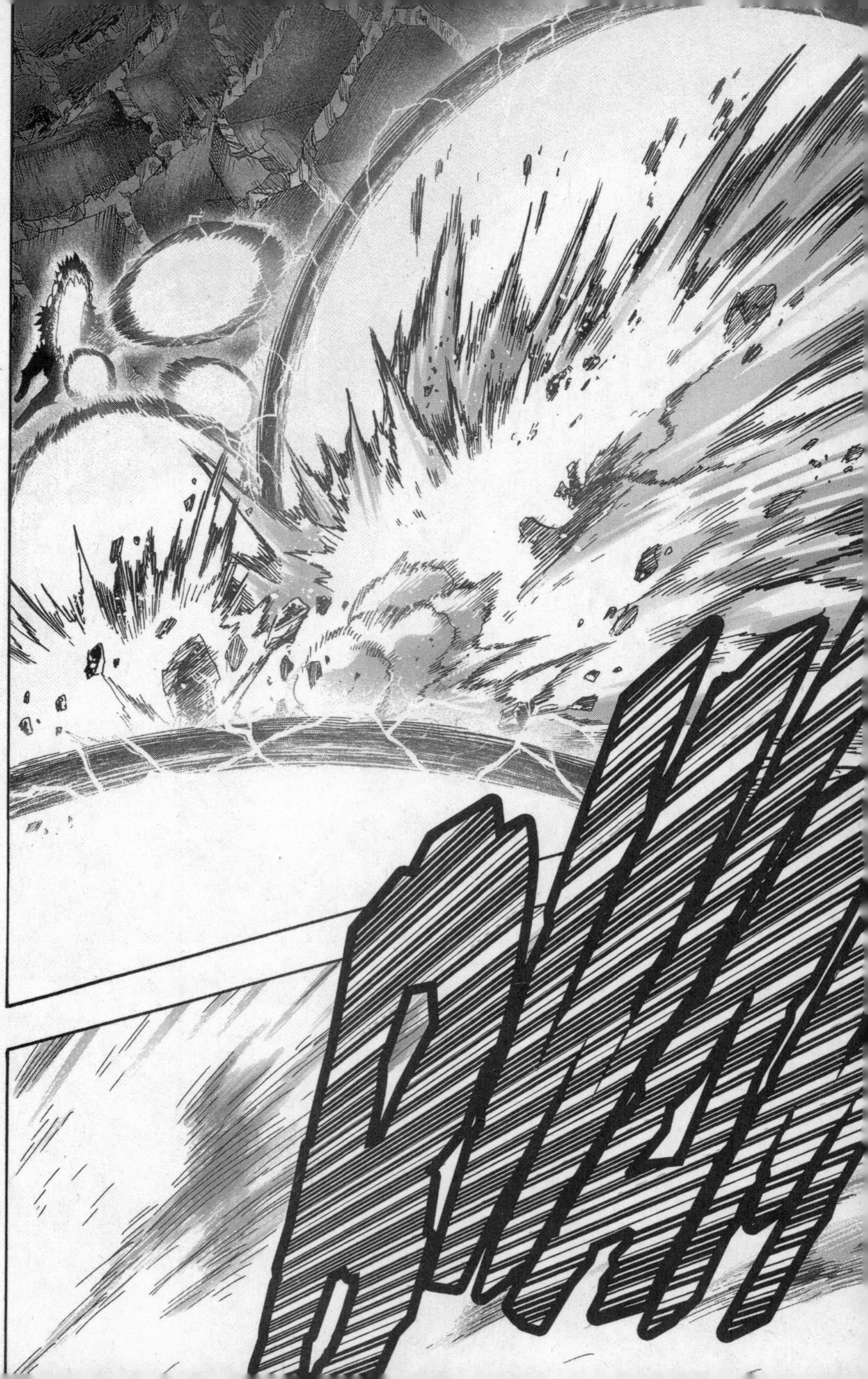

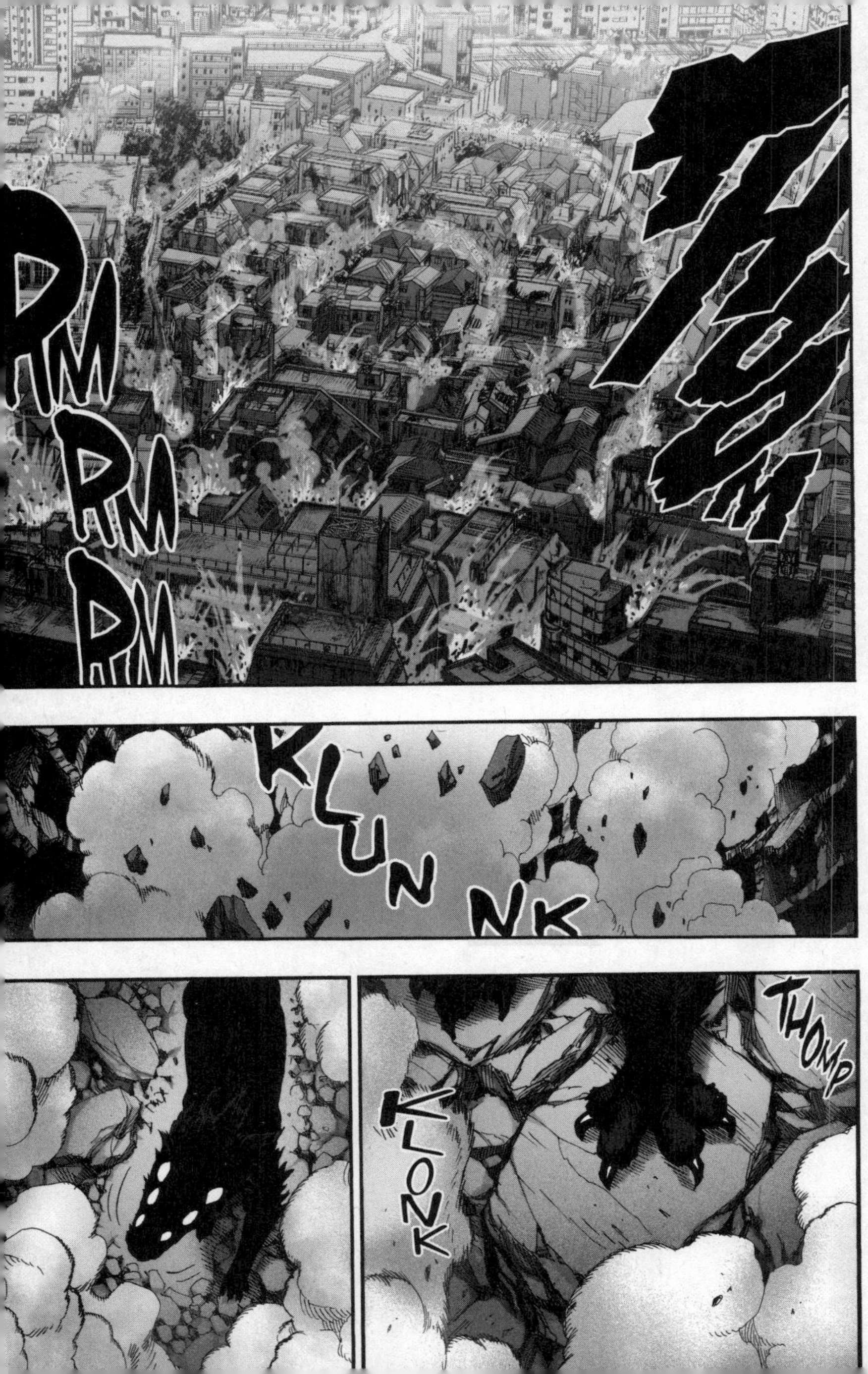
DRM DRM DRM DRM
KLUNNK
THOMP
KLONK

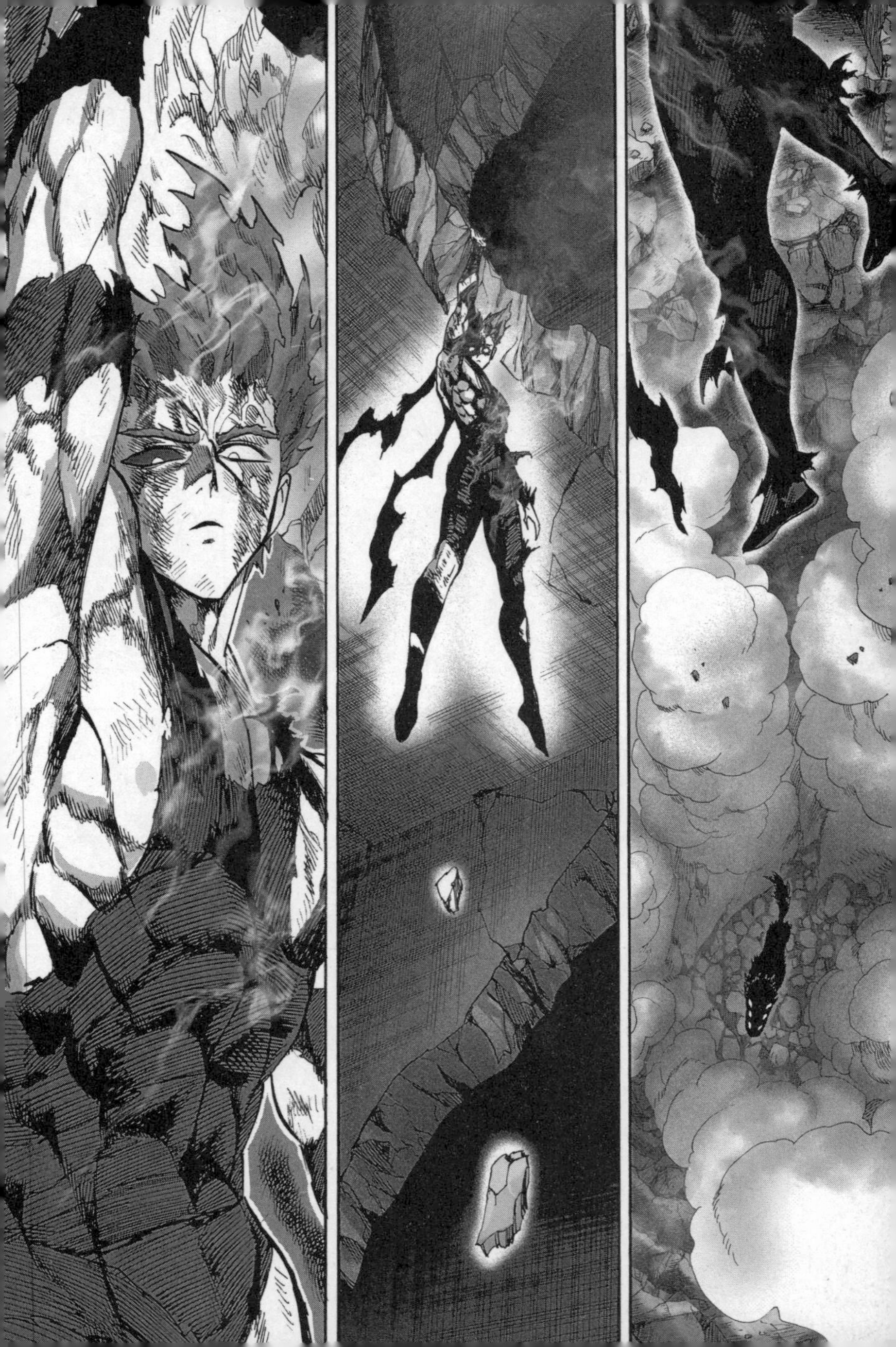

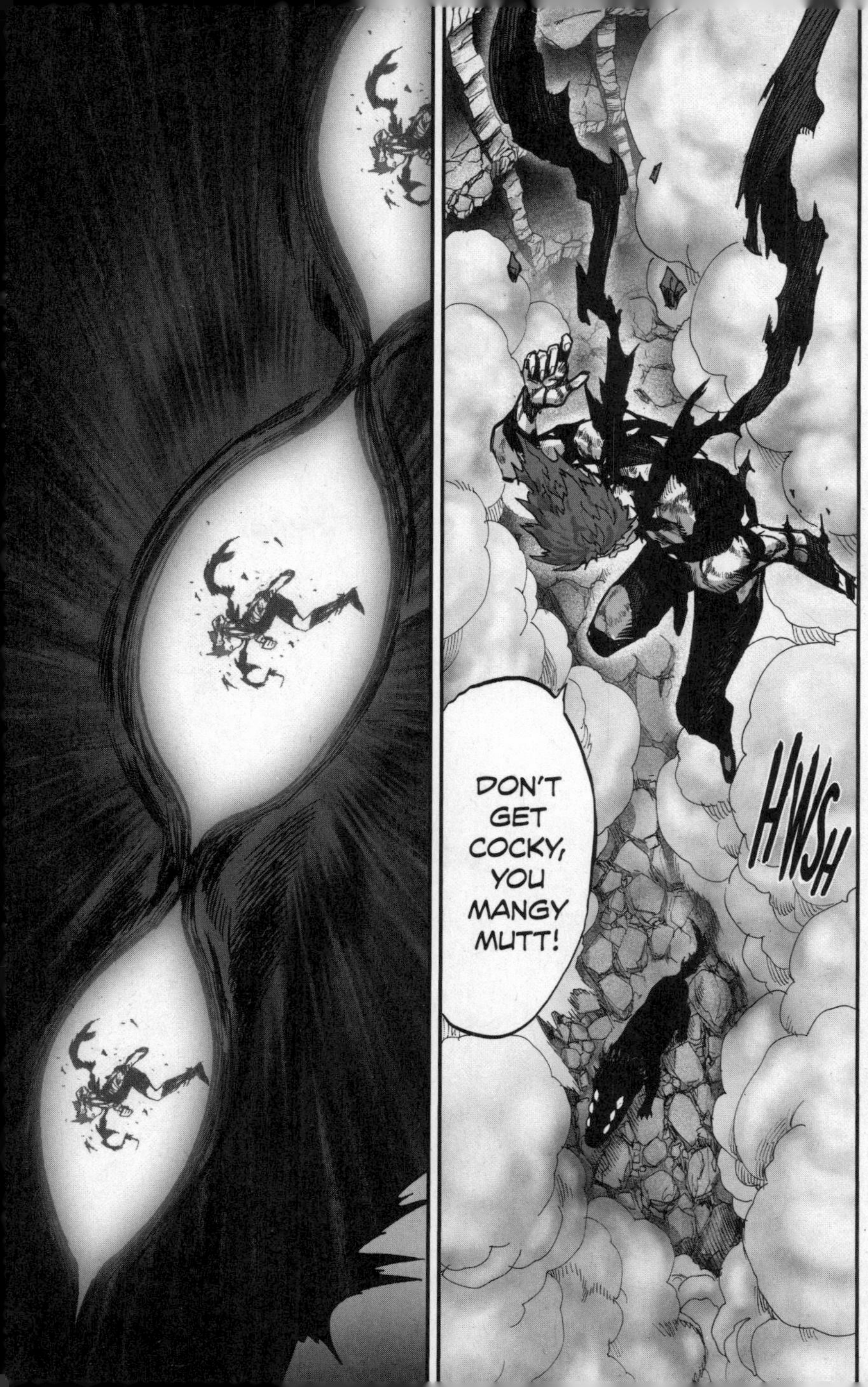
DON'T GET COCKY, YOU MANGY MUTT!
HWSH

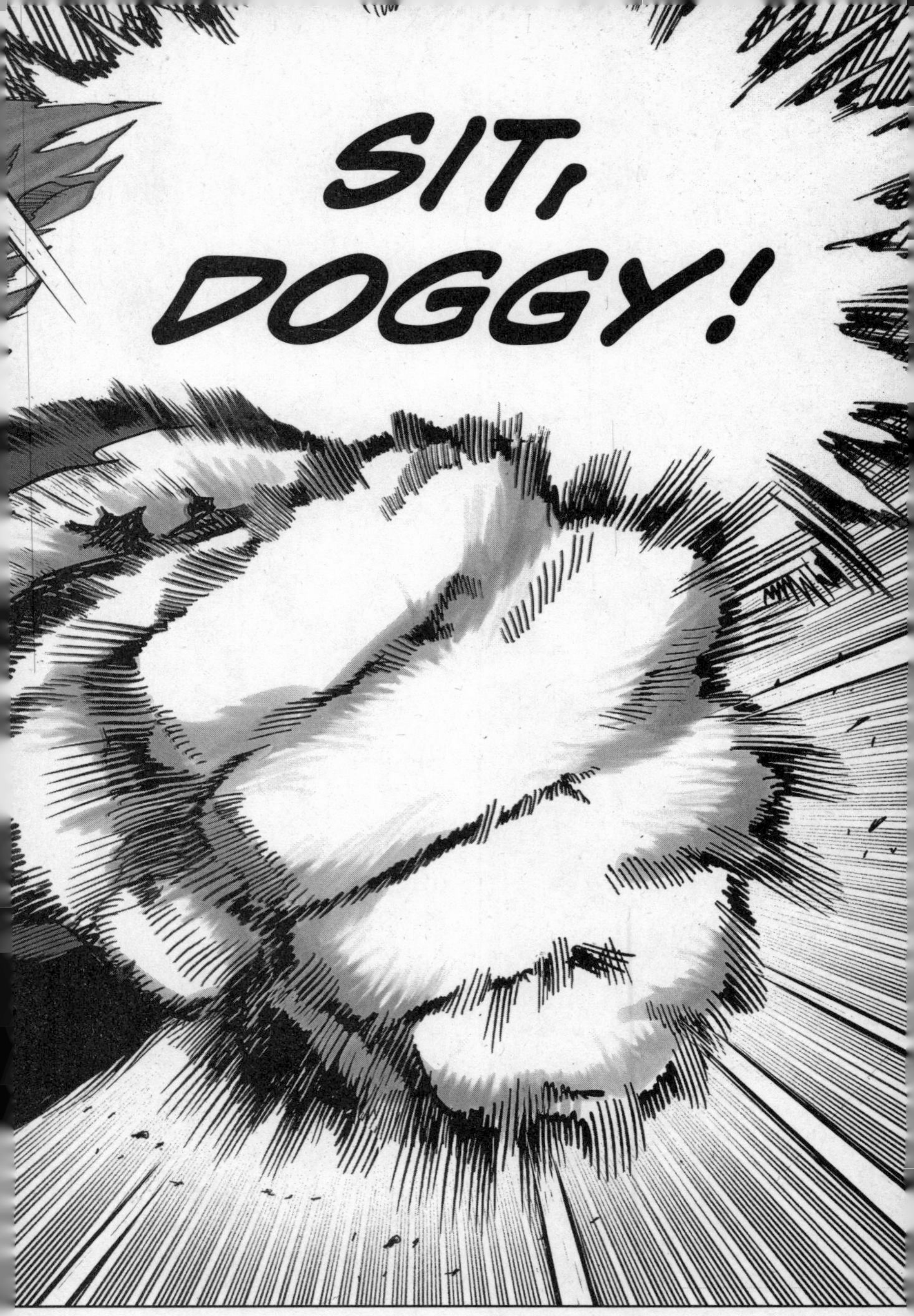
SIT, DOGGY!

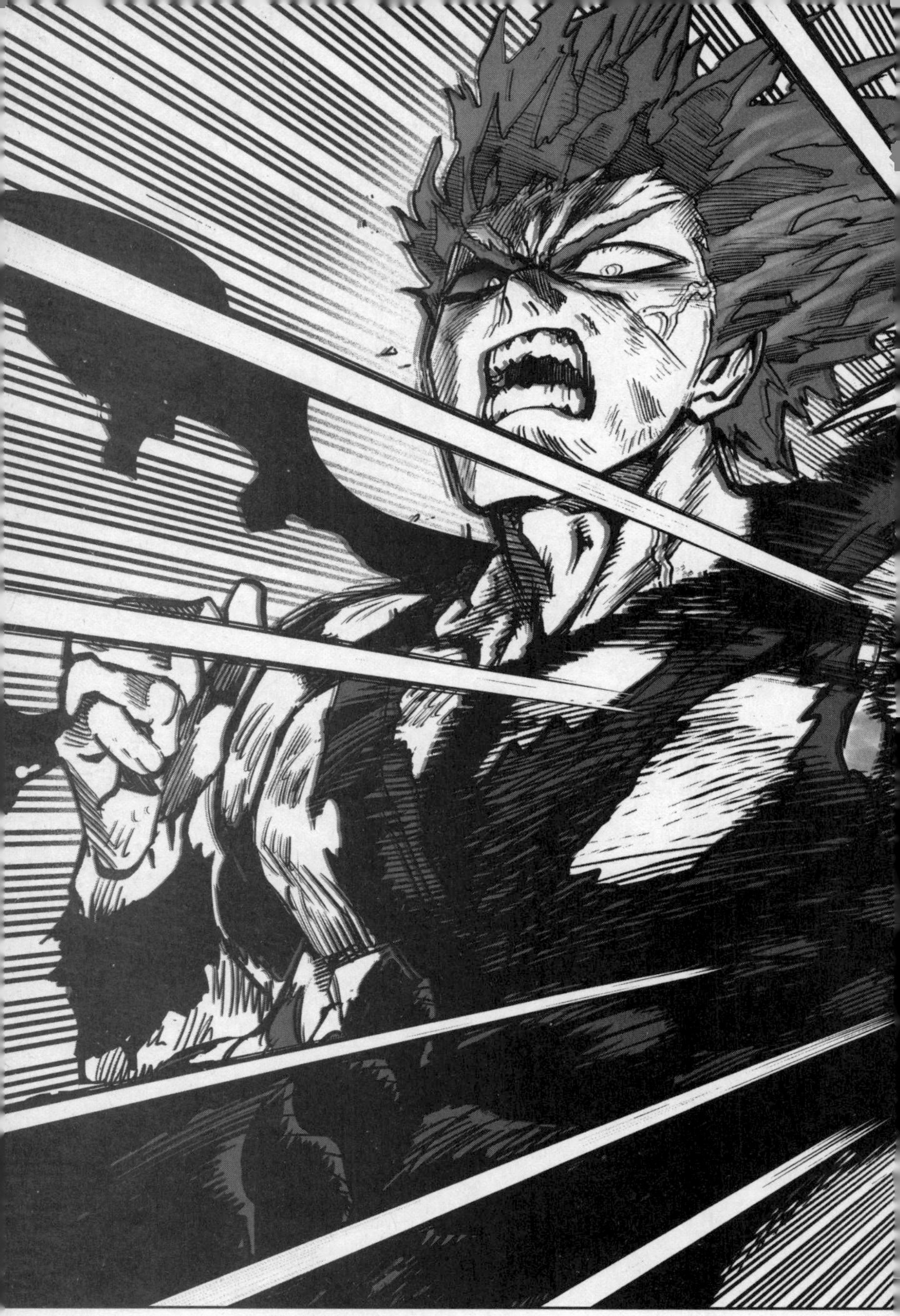

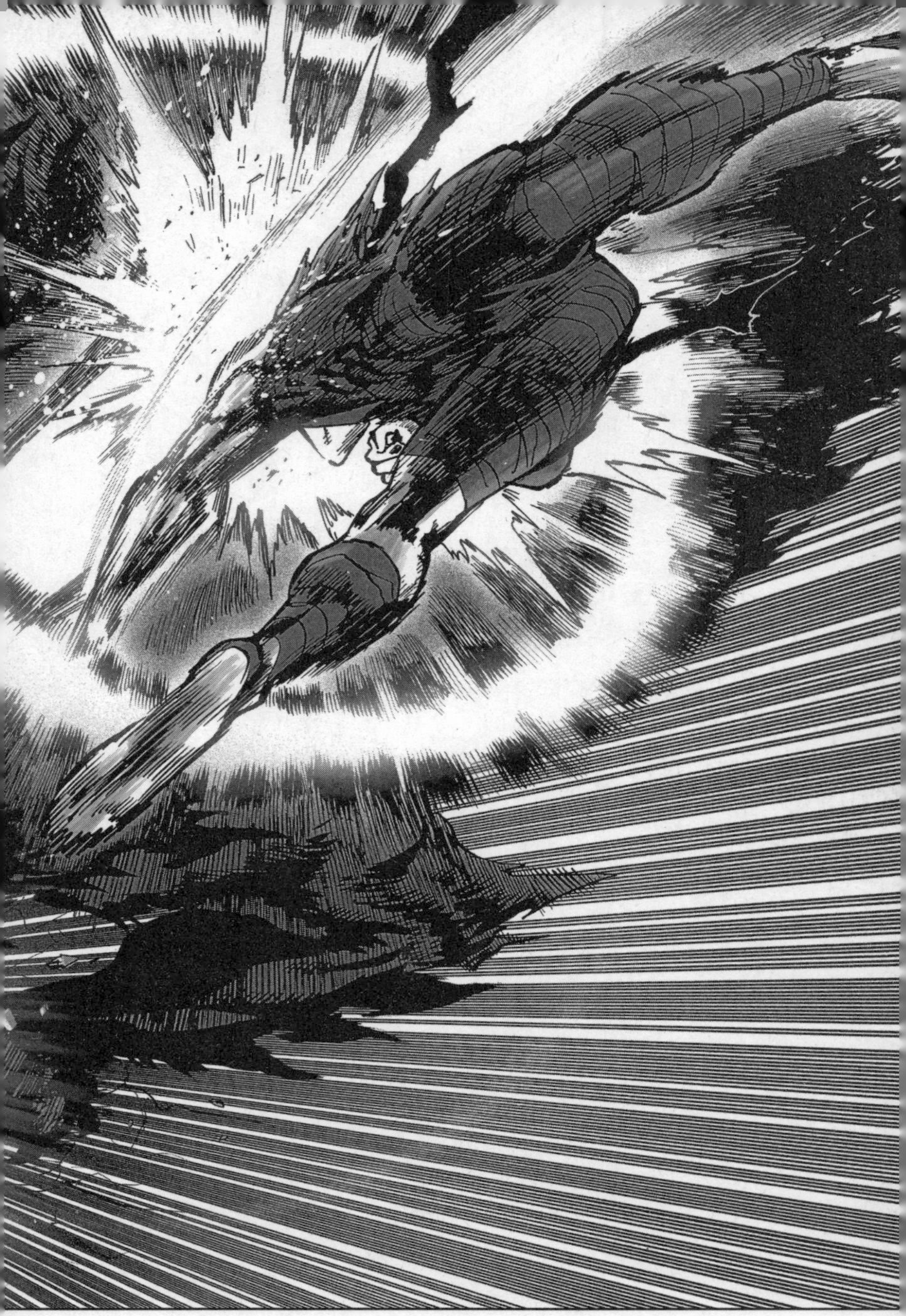

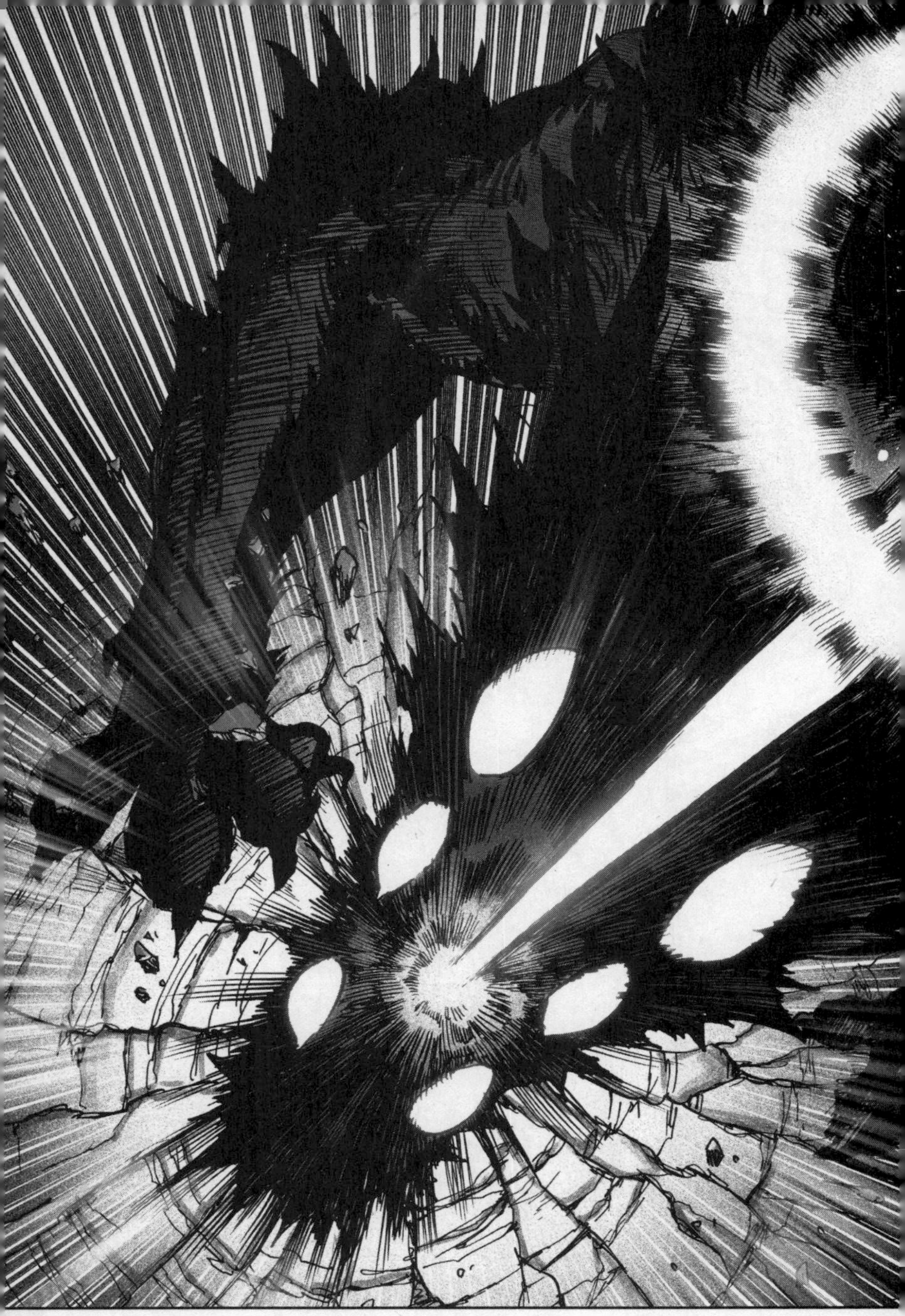

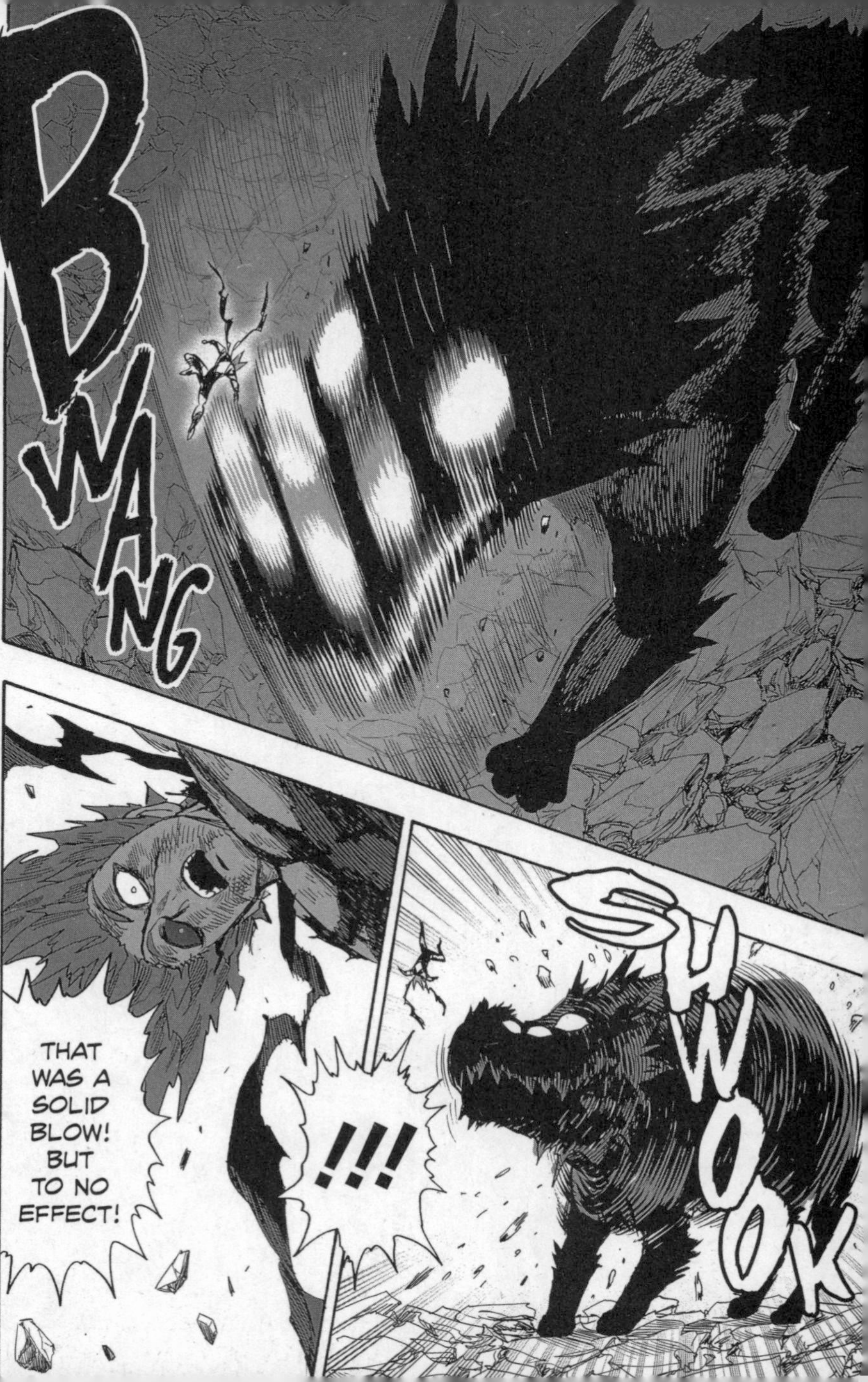
BWANG
SHWOOK
THAT WAS A SOLID BLOW! BUT TO NO EFFECT!
!!!

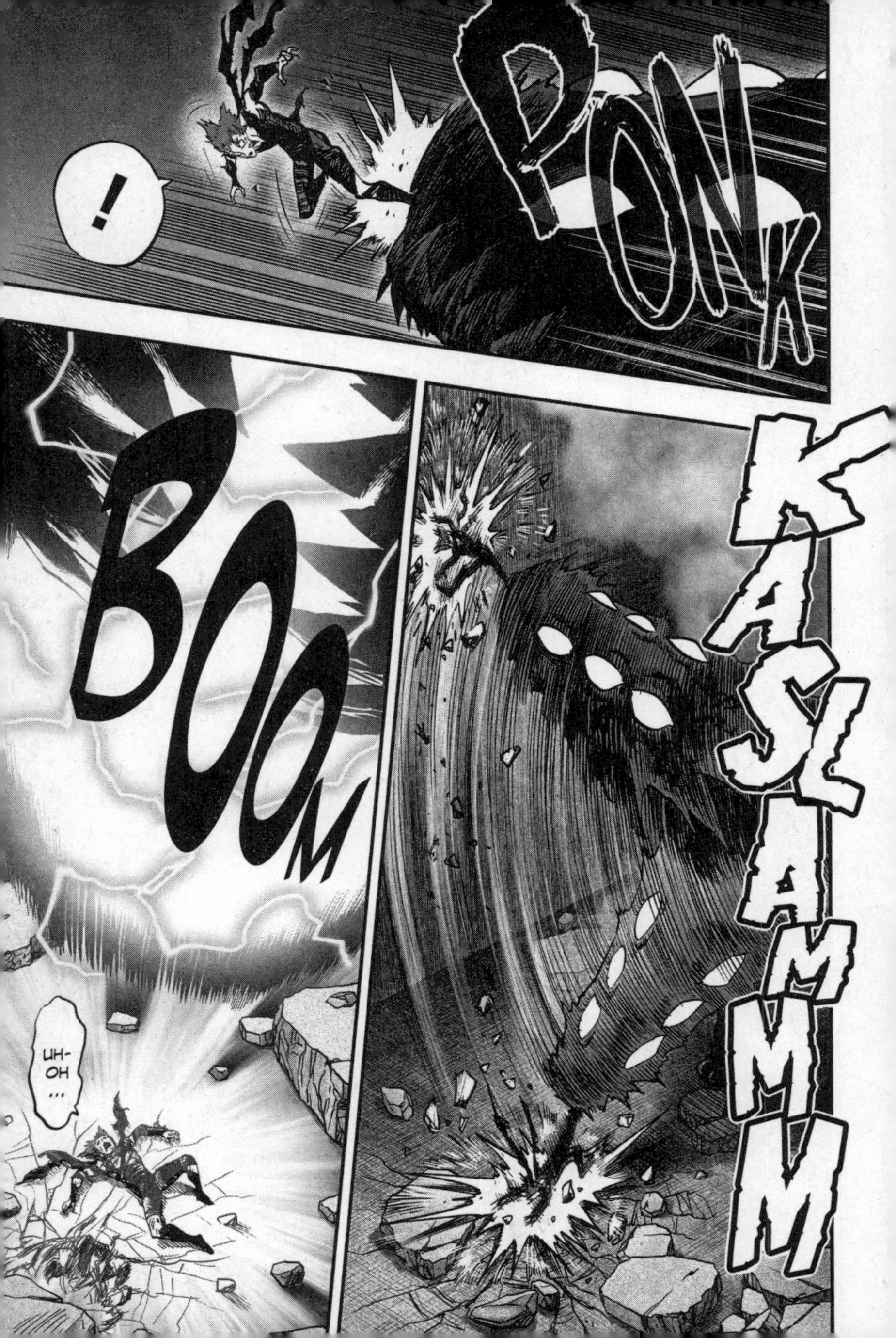
PONK
!
KASLAMMMM
BOOM
UH-OH ...

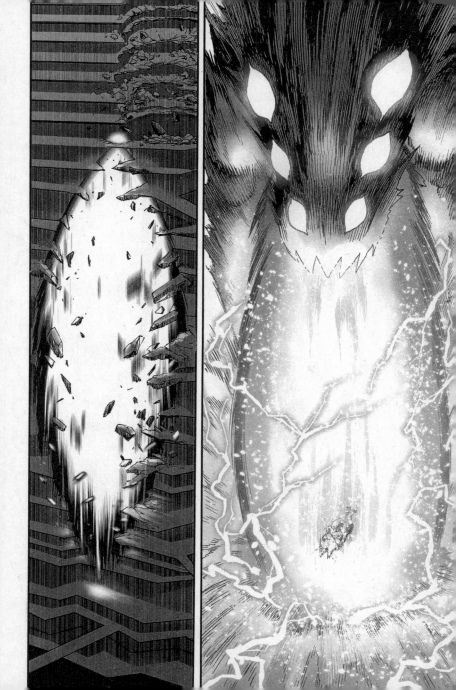

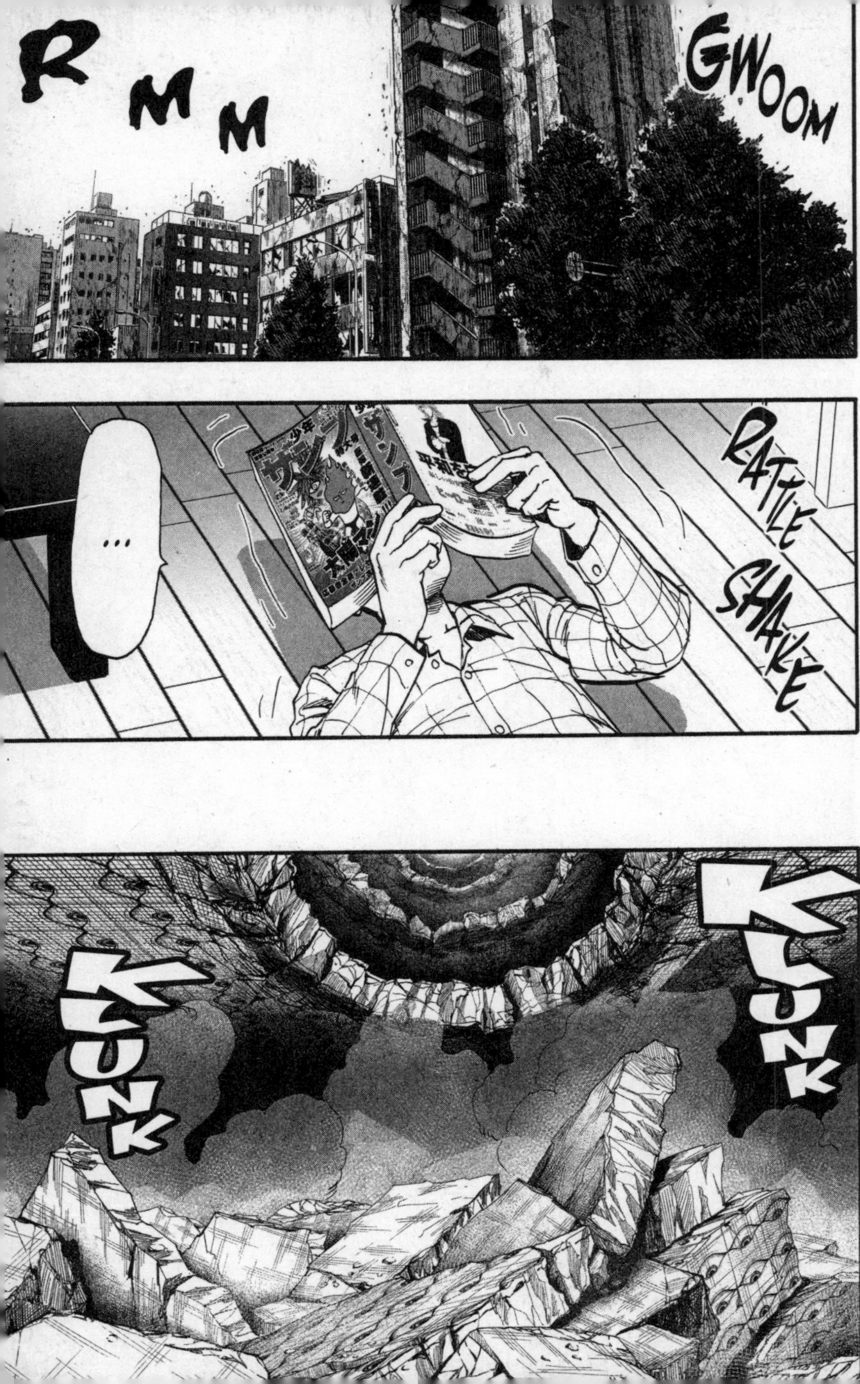
GWOOM
RMMM
RATTLE SHAKE
...
KLUNK
KLUNK

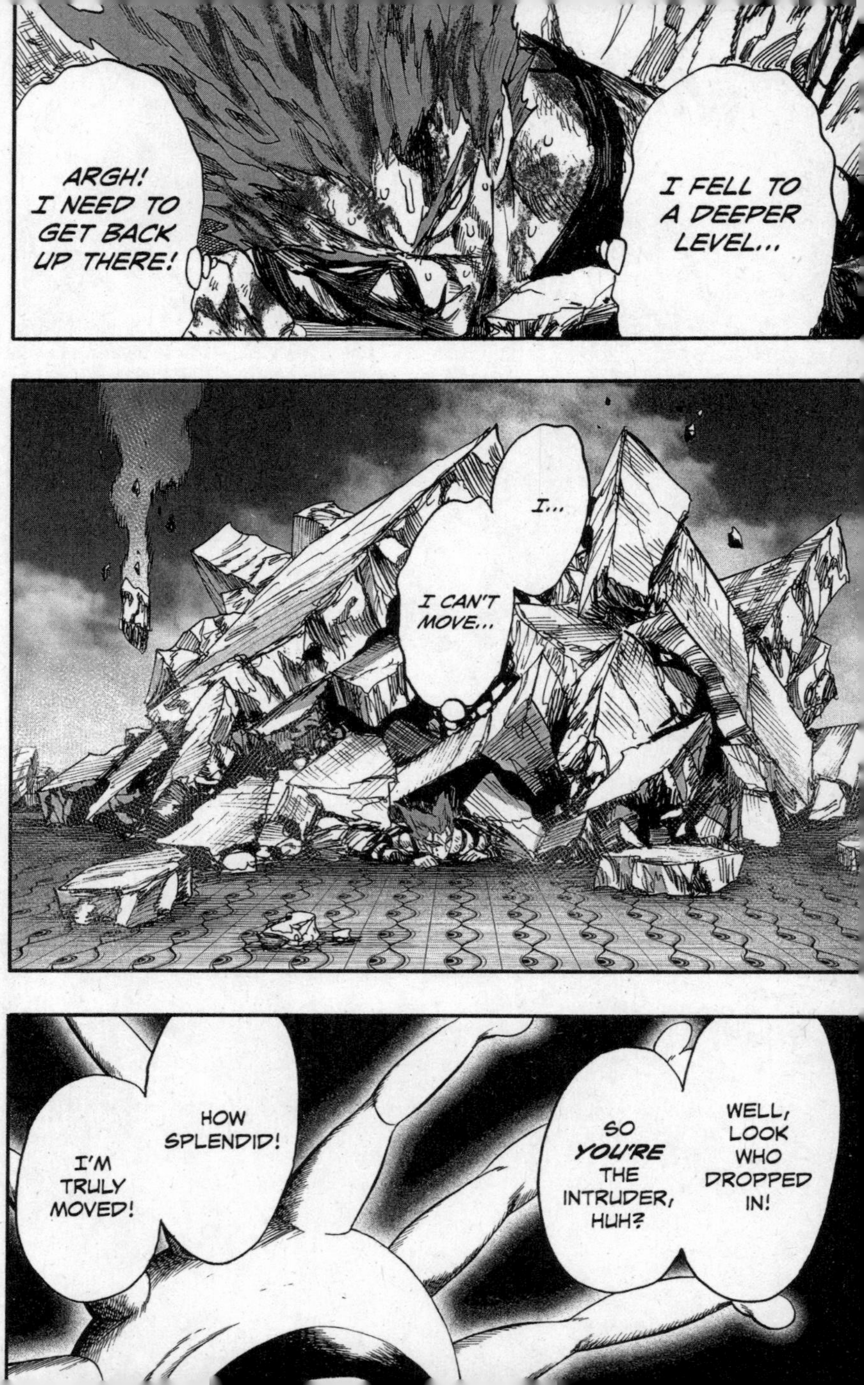
I FELL TO A DEEPER LEVEL...
ARGH! I NEED TO GET BACK UP THERE!
I...
I CAN'T MOVE...
WELL, LOOK WHO DROPPED IN!
SO *YOU'RE* THE INTRUDER, HUH?
HOW SPLENDID!
I'M TRULY MOVED!

JUST AS I SUSPECTED...

...YOU HAVE SATISFIED MY EXPECTATIONS.

YOU DIDN'T DIE AFTER ALL.

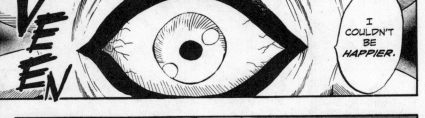

VEEN

I COULDN'T BE *HAPPIER.*

FWUP

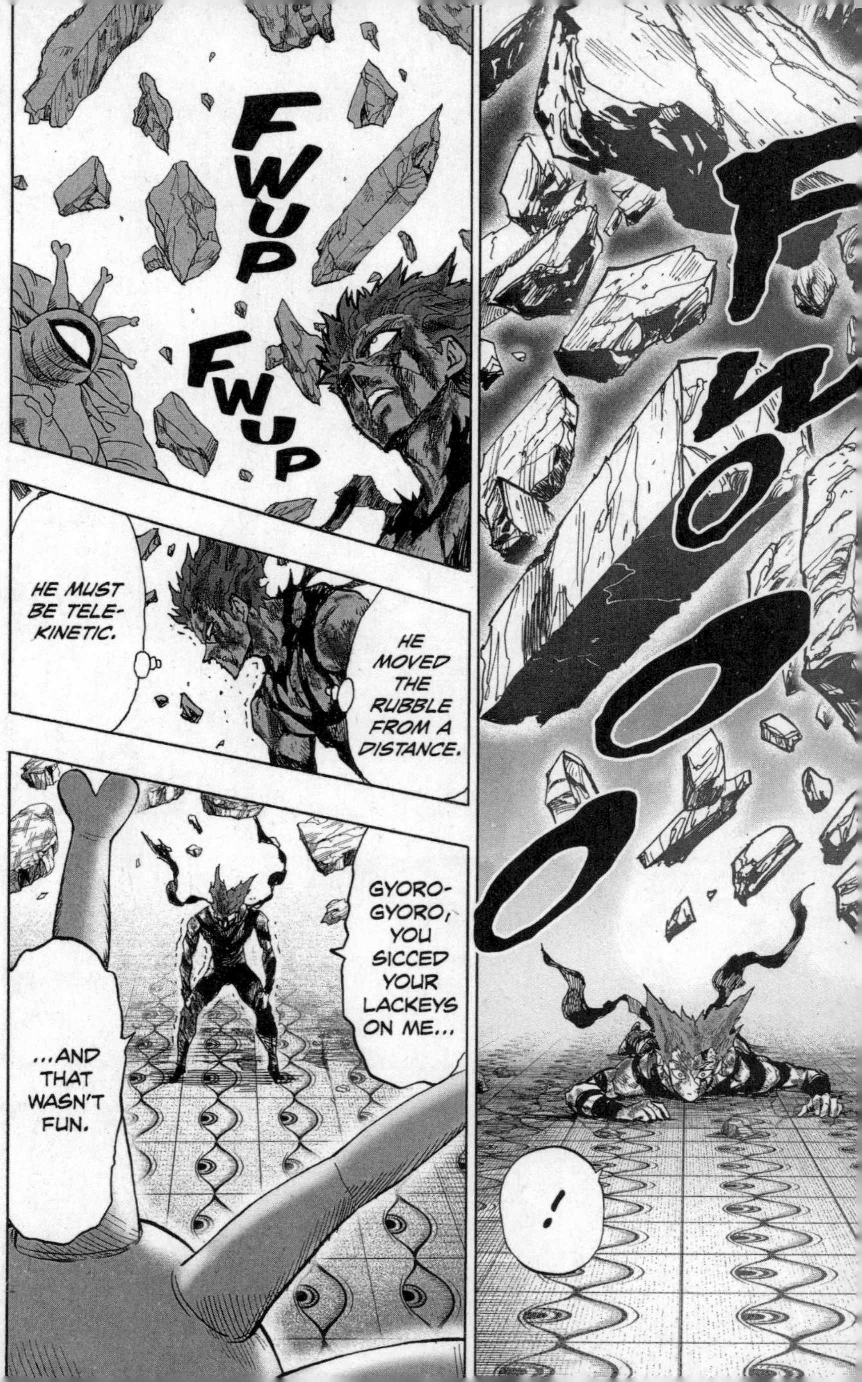

FWOOOOO
!
FWUP
FWUP
HE MOVED THE RUBBLE FROM A DISTANCE.
HE MUST BE TELE-KINETIC.
GYORO-GYORO, YOU SICCED YOUR LACKEYS ON ME...
...AND THAT WASN'T FUN.

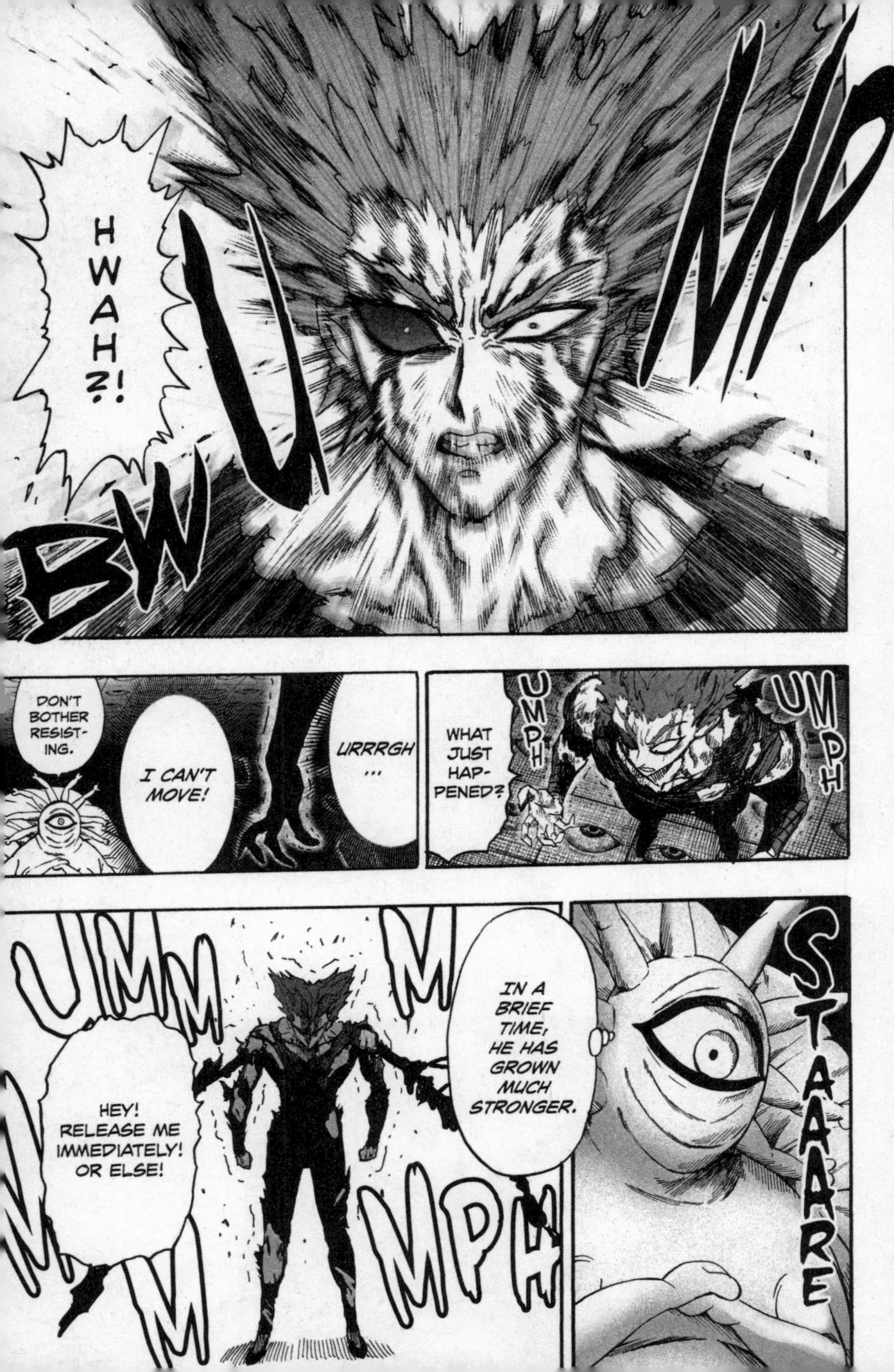
BWUMP
HWAH?!
UMPH
UMPH
WHAT JUST HAPPENED?
URRRGH ...
I CAN'T MOVE!
DON'T BOTHER RESISTING.
STAARE
IN A BRIEF TIME, HE HAS GROWN MUCH STRONGER.
UMMMMMPH
HEY! RELEASE ME IMMEDIATELY! OR ELSE!

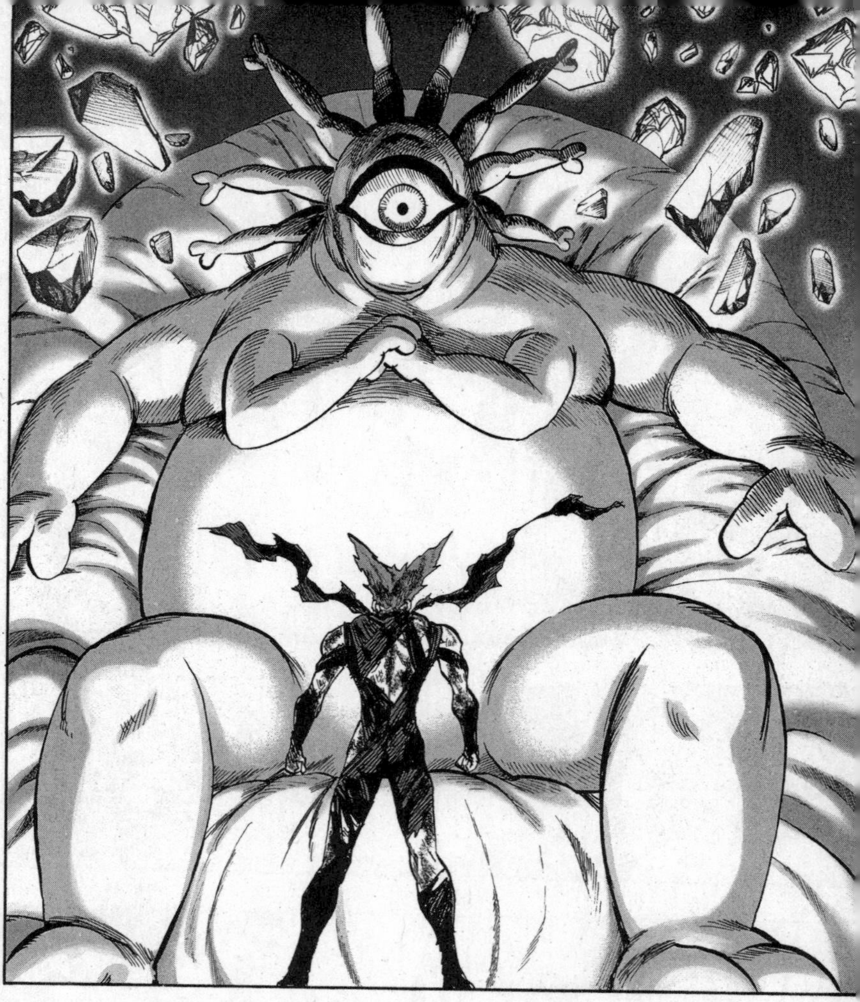

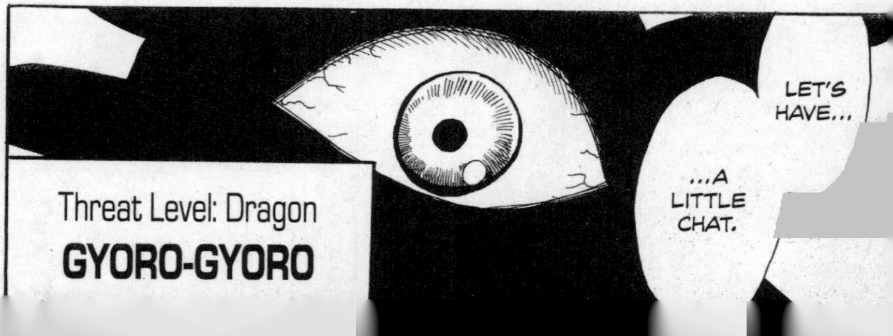
LET'S HAVE...
...A LITTLE CHAT.
Threat Level: Dragon
GYORO-GYORO

PUNCH 94: MANHOLE

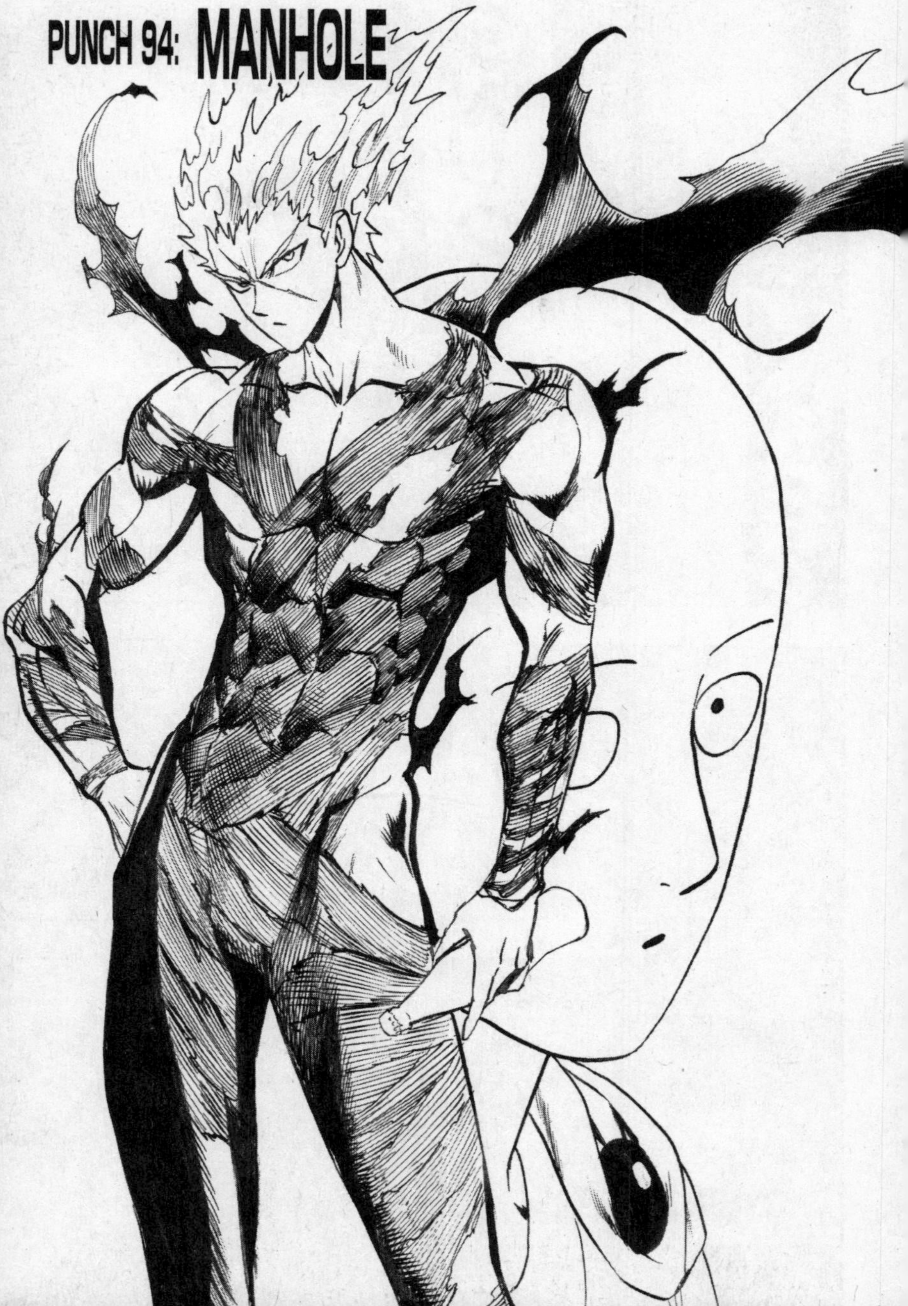

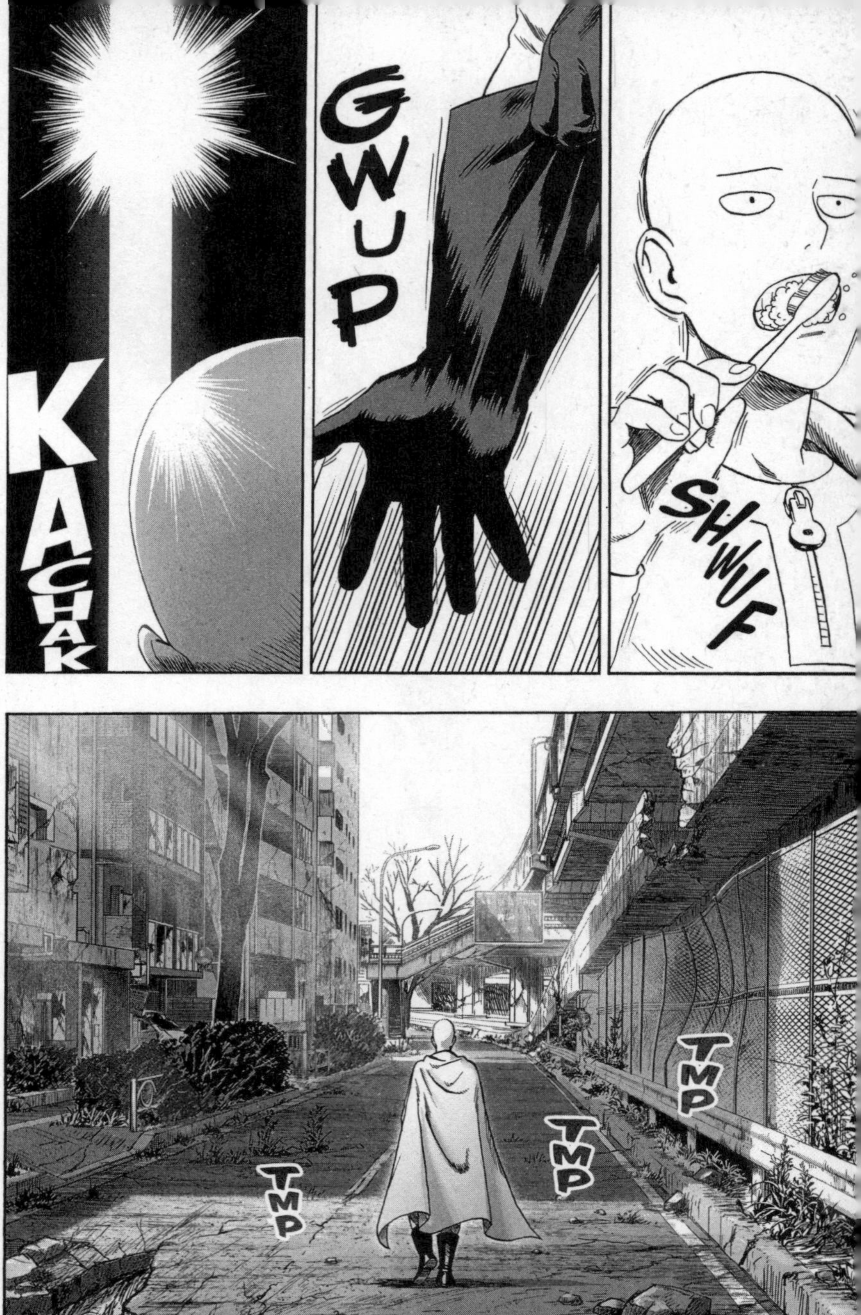
SHWUF
GWUP
KACHAK
TMP
TMP
TMP

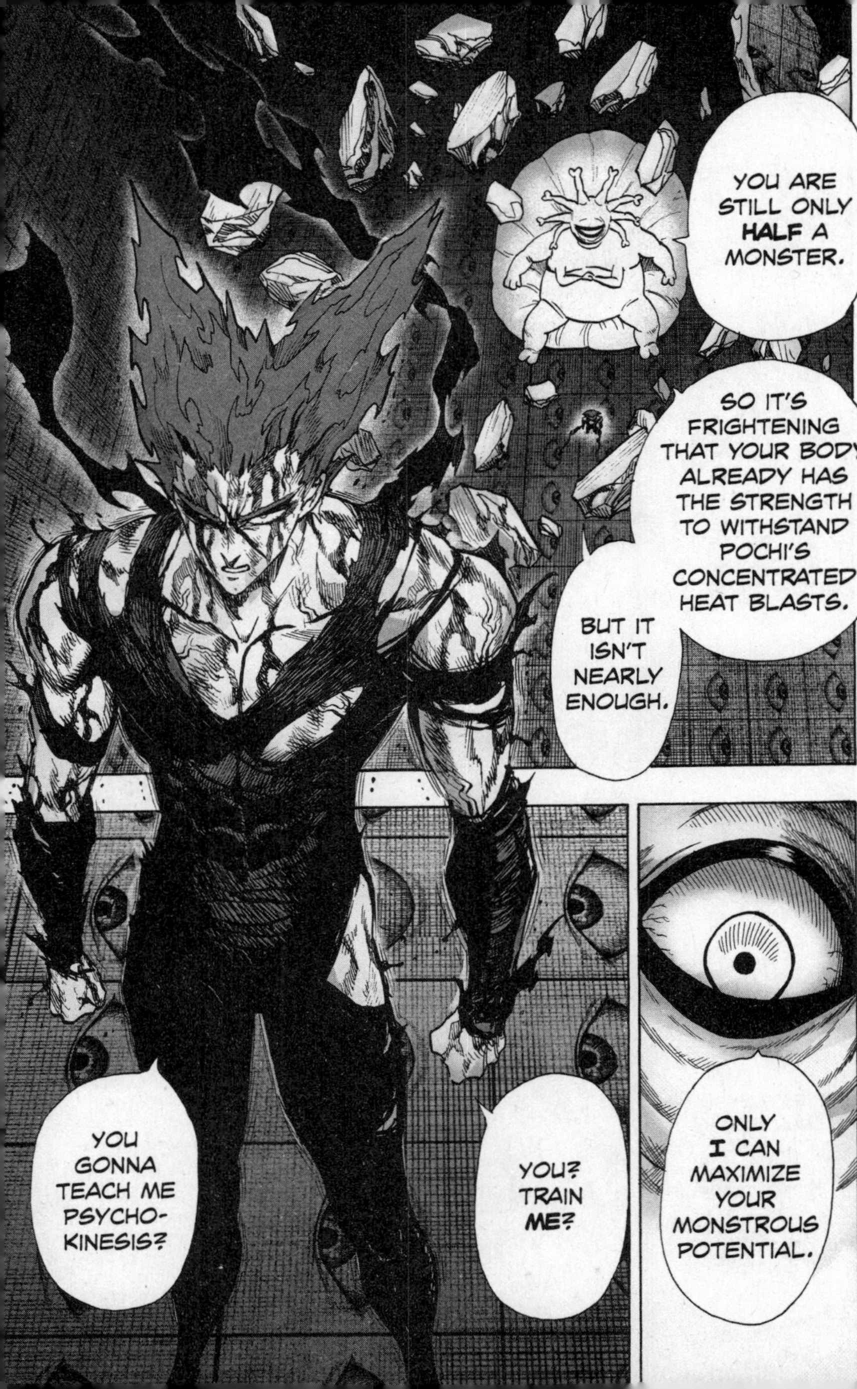
YOU ARE STILL ONLY **HALF** A MONSTER.
SO IT'S FRIGHTENING THAT YOUR BODY ALREADY HAS THE STRENGTH TO WITHSTAND POCHI'S CONCENTRATED HEAT BLASTS.
BUT IT ISN'T NEARLY ENOUGH.
ONLY **I** CAN MAXIMIZE YOUR MONSTROUS POTENTIAL.
YOU? TRAIN **ME**?
YOU GONNA TEACH ME PSYCHO-KINESIS?

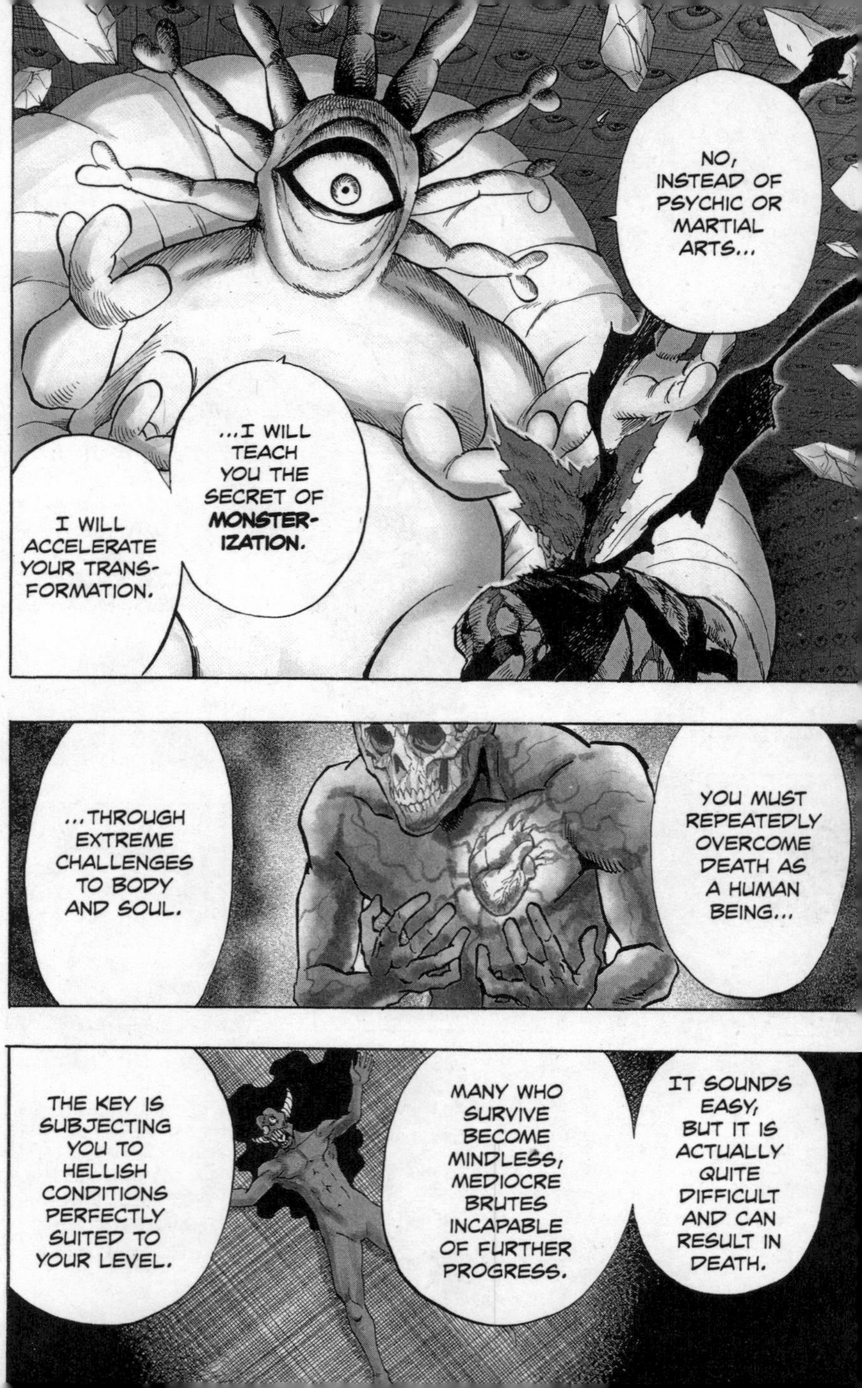
NO, INSTEAD OF PSYCHIC OR MARTIAL ARTS...
...I WILL TEACH YOU THE SECRET OF **MONSTERIZATION.**
I WILL ACCELERATE YOUR TRANSFORMATION.
YOU MUST REPEATEDLY OVERCOME DEATH AS A HUMAN BEING...
...THROUGH EXTREME CHALLENGES TO BODY AND SOUL.
IT SOUNDS EASY, BUT IT IS ACTUALLY QUITE DIFFICULT AND CAN RESULT IN DEATH.
MANY WHO SURVIVE BECOME MINDLESS, MEDIOCRE BRUTES INCAPABLE OF FURTHER PROGRESS.
THE KEY IS SUBJECTING YOU TO HELLISH CONDITIONS PERFECTLY SUITED TO YOUR LEVEL.

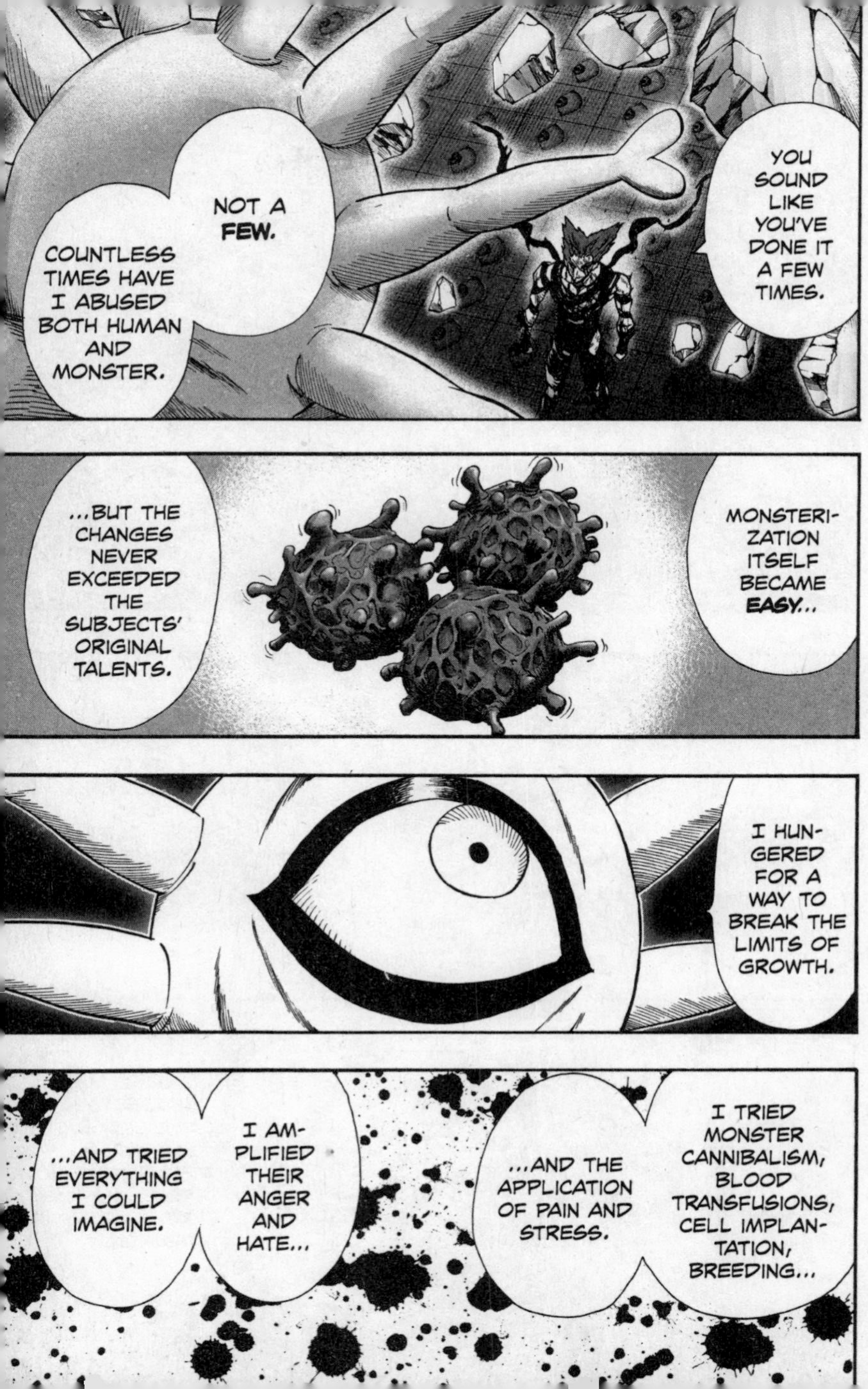
YOU SOUND LIKE YOU'VE DONE IT A FEW TIMES.
NOT A **FEW.**
COUNTLESS TIMES HAVE I ABUSED BOTH HUMAN AND MONSTER.
MONSTERIZATION ITSELF BECAME **EASY...**
...BUT THE CHANGES NEVER EXCEEDED THE SUBJECTS' ORIGINAL TALENTS.
I HUNGERED FOR A WAY TO BREAK THE LIMITS OF GROWTH.
I TRIED MONSTER CANNIBALISM, BLOOD TRANSFUSIONS, CELL IMPLANTATION, BREEDING...
...AND THE APPLICATION OF PAIN AND STRESS.
I AMPLIFIED THEIR ANGER AND HATE...
...AND TRIED EVERYTHING I COULD IMAGINE.

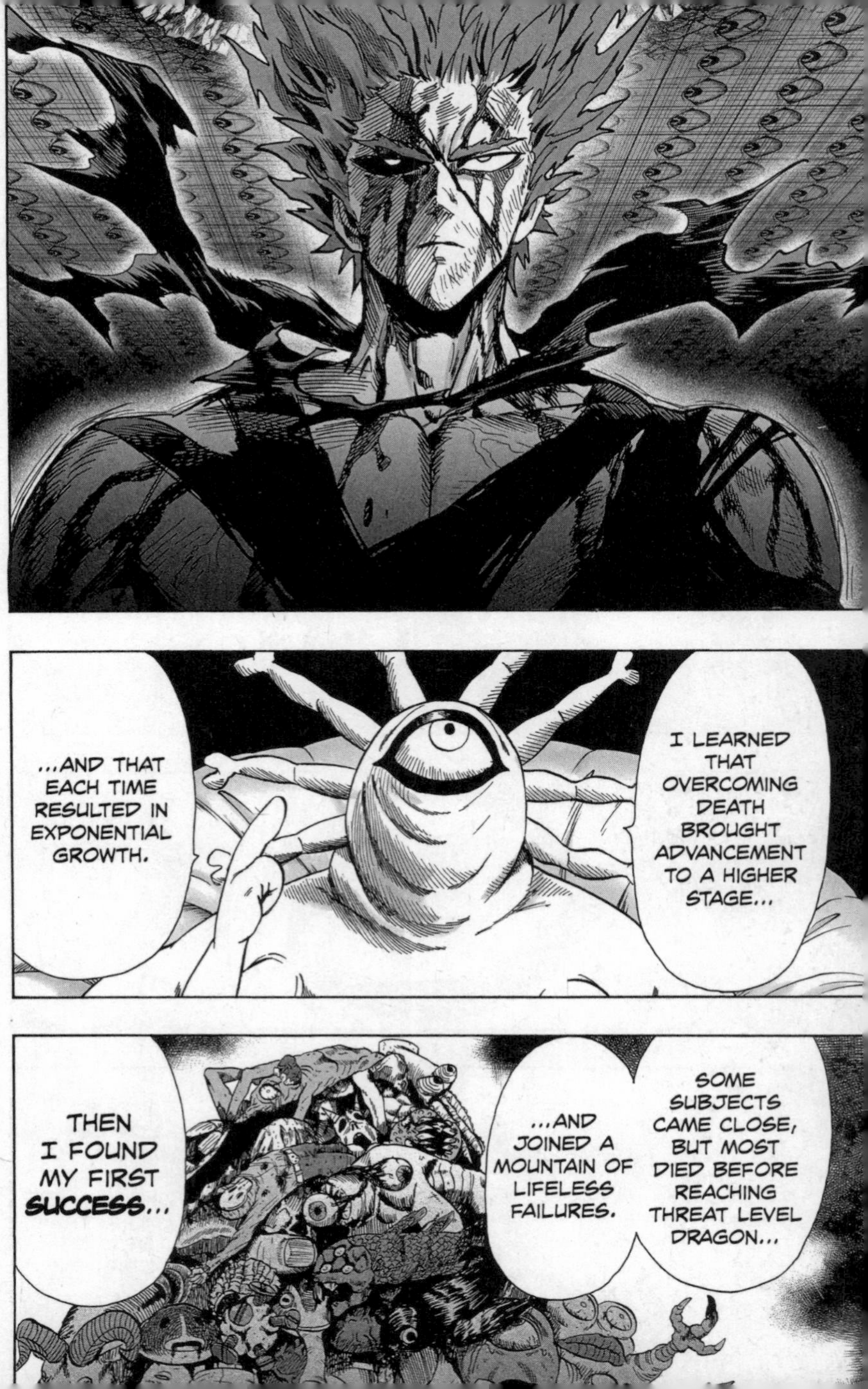
I LEARNED THAT OVERCOMING DEATH BROUGHT ADVANCEMENT TO A HIGHER STAGE...
...AND THAT EACH TIME RESULTED IN EXPONENTIAL GROWTH.
SOME SUBJECTS CAME CLOSE, BUT MOST DIED BEFORE REACHING THREAT LEVEL DRAGON...
...AND JOINED A MOUNTAIN OF LIFELESS FAILURES.
THEN I FOUND MY FIRST **SUCCESS**...

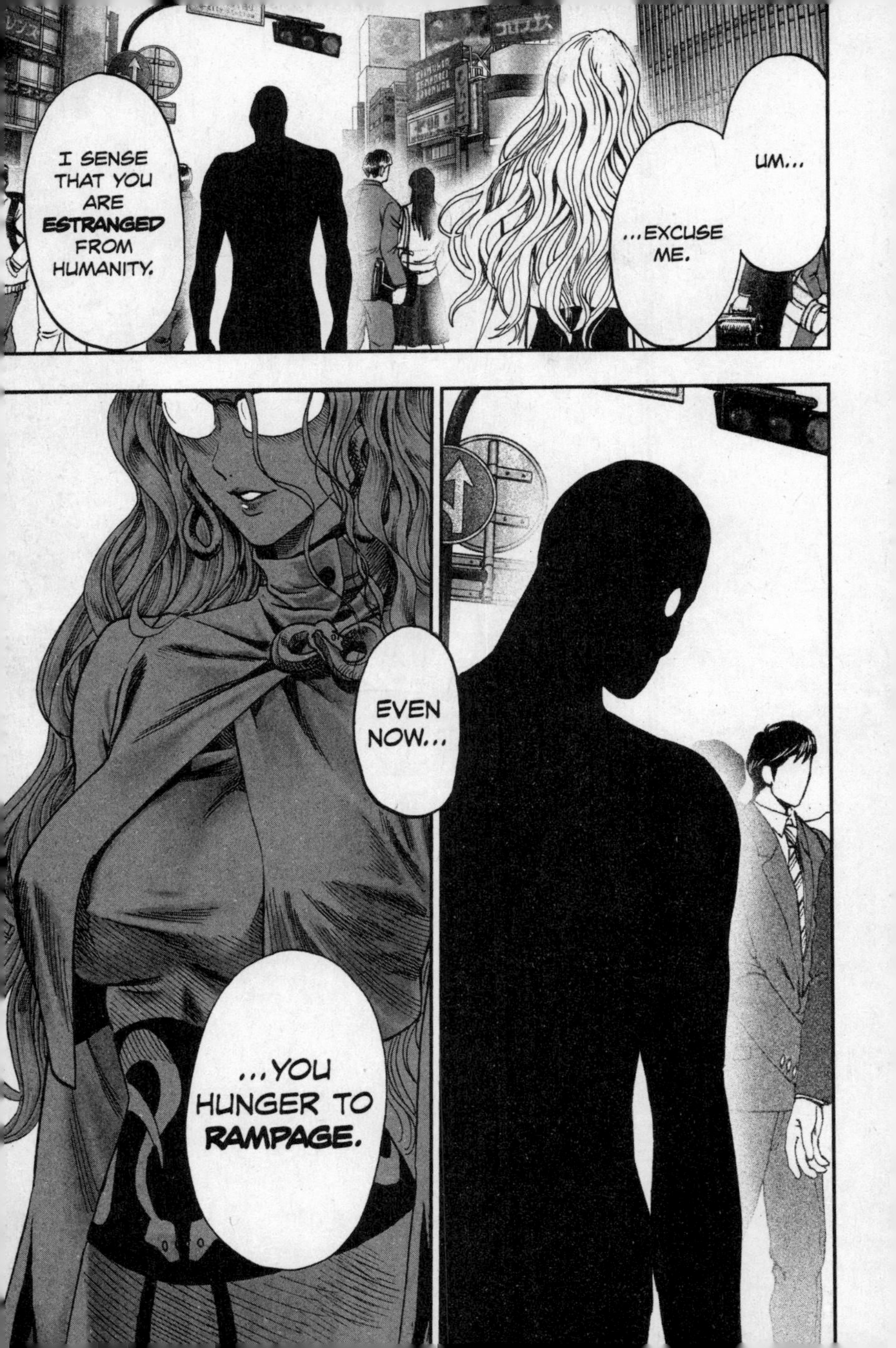
UM...
...EXCUSE ME.
I SENSE THAT YOU ARE ESTRANGED FROM HUMANITY.
EVEN NOW...
...YOU HUNGER TO RAMPAGE.

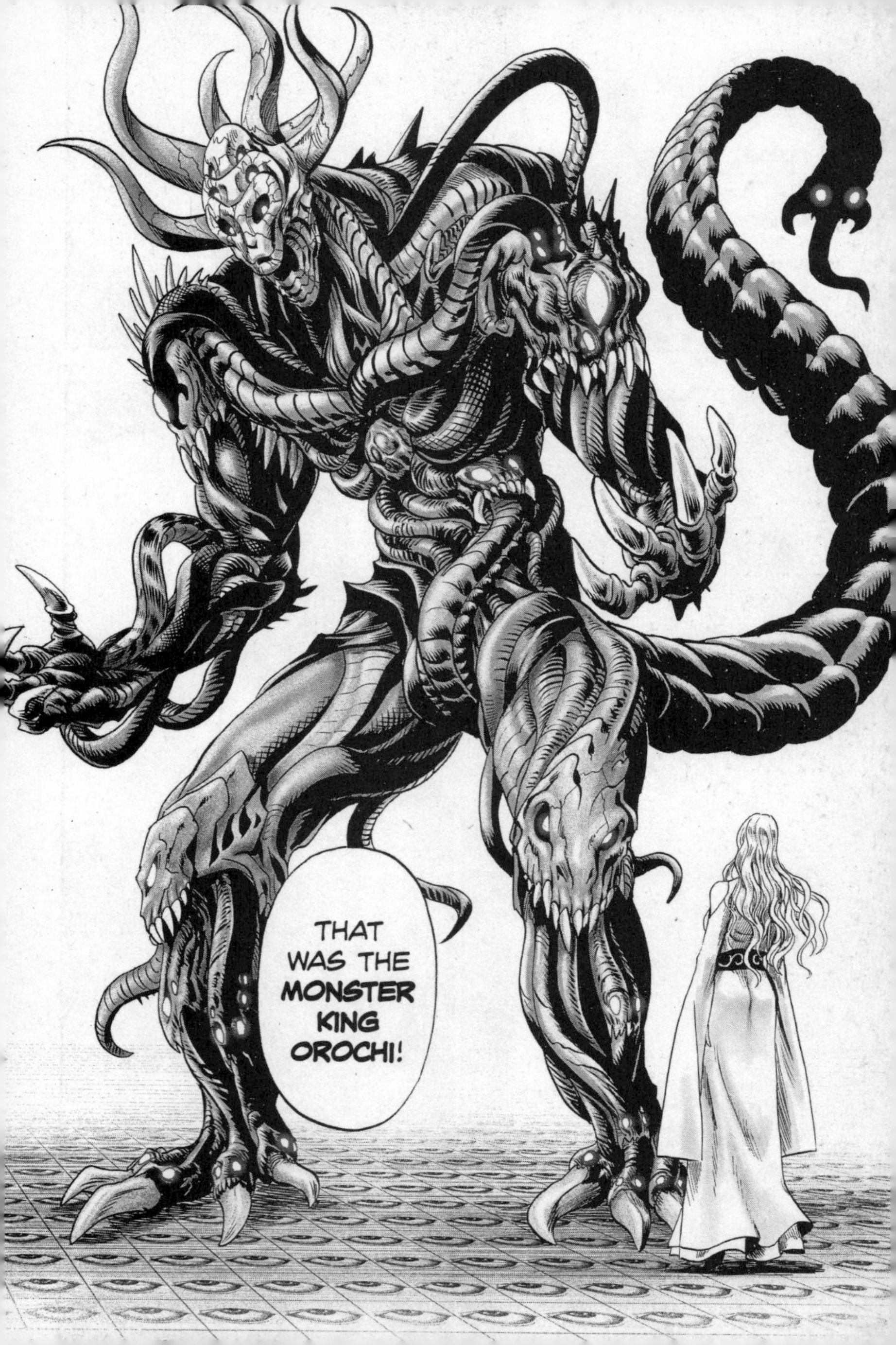
THAT WAS THE MONSTER KING OROCHI!

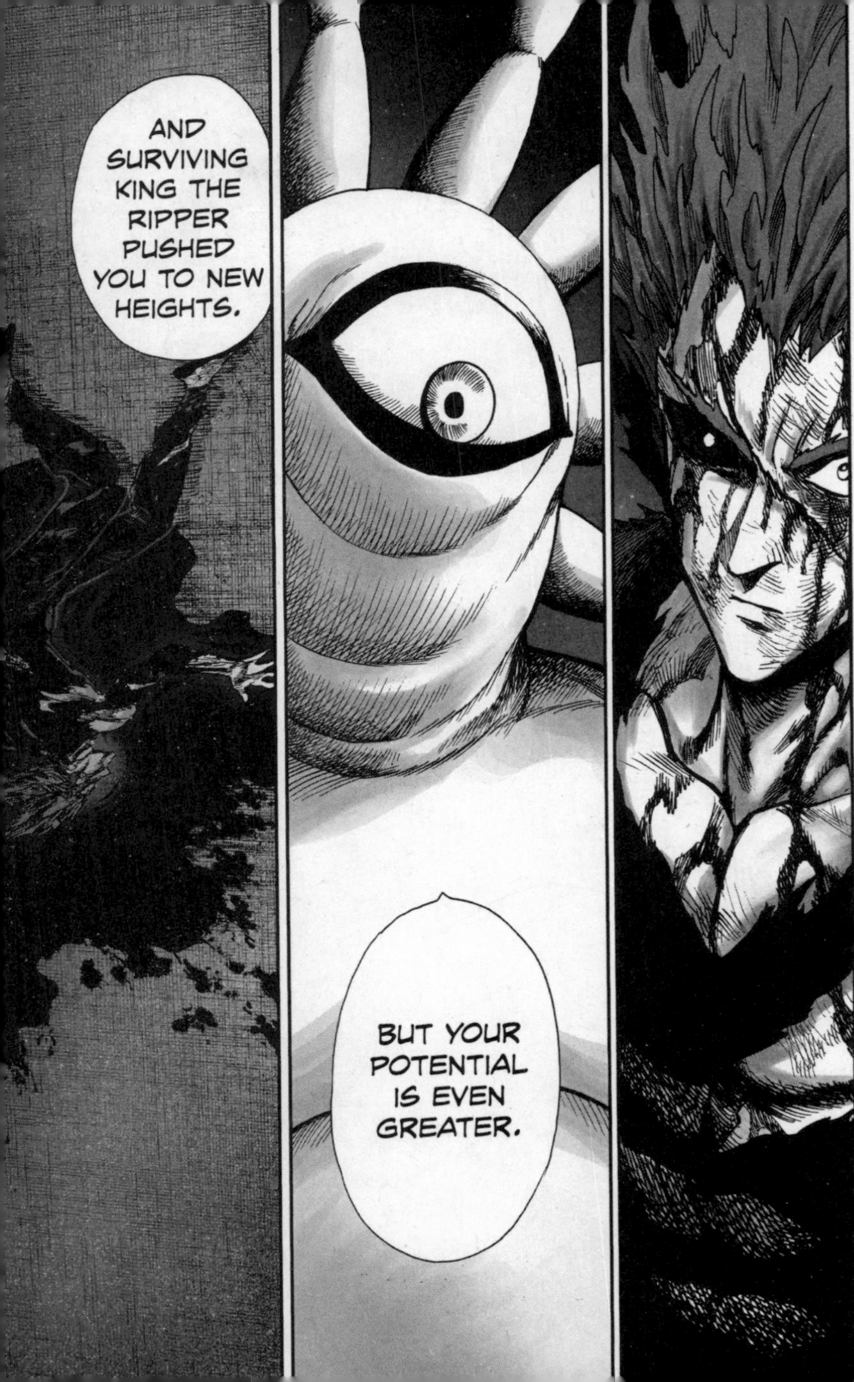
AND SURVIVING KING THE RIPPER PUSHED YOU TO NEW HEIGHTS.
BUT YOUR POTENTIAL IS EVEN GREATER.

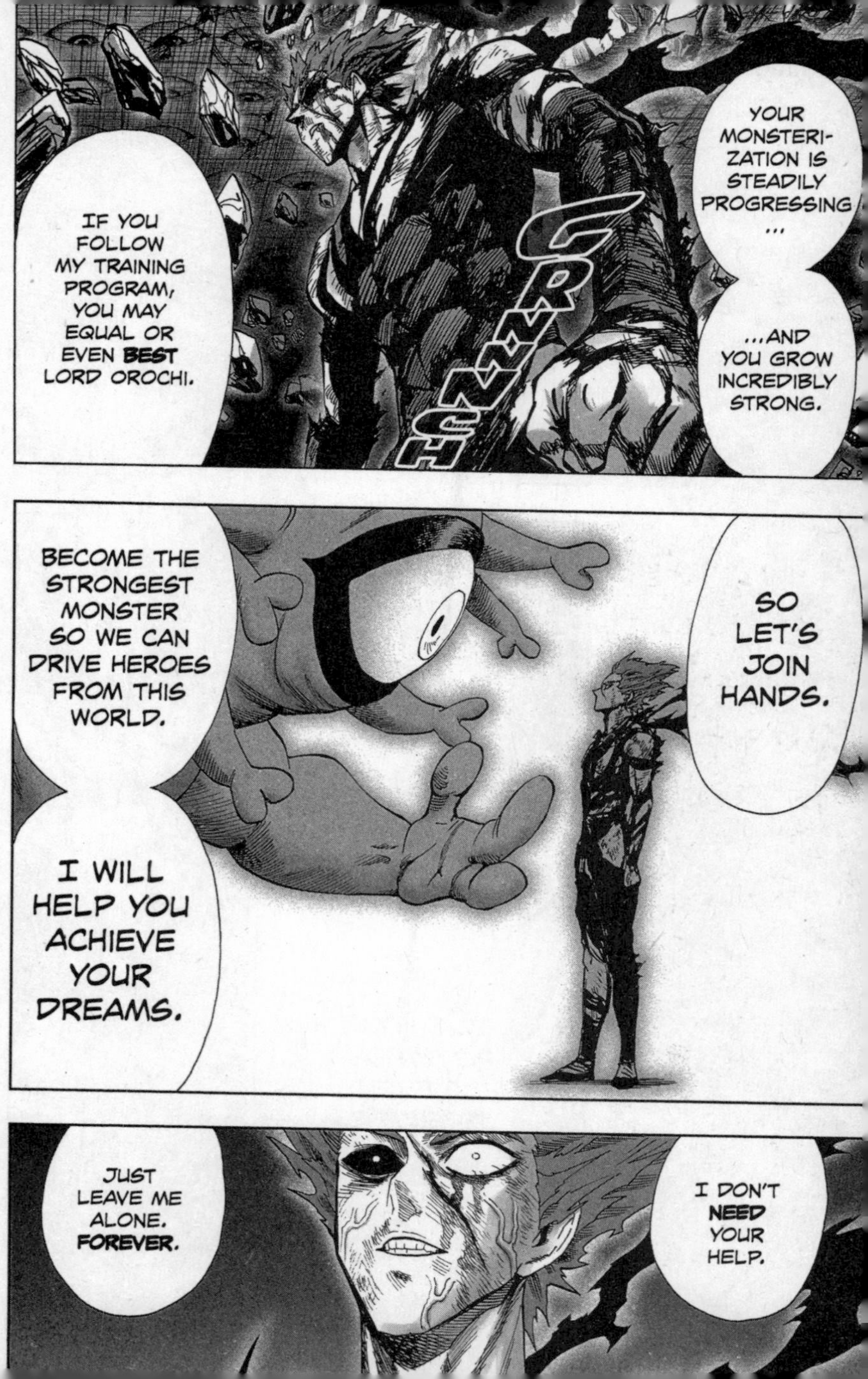
YOUR MONSTERI-ZATION IS STEADILY PROGRESSING ...
...AND YOU GROW INCREDIBLY STRONG.
GRNNNCH
IF YOU FOLLOW MY TRAINING PROGRAM, YOU MAY EQUAL OR EVEN **BEST** LORD OROCHI.
SO LET'S JOIN HANDS.
BECOME THE STRONGEST MONSTER SO WE CAN DRIVE HEROES FROM THIS WORLD.
I WILL HELP YOU ACHIEVE YOUR DREAMS.
I DON'T **NEED** YOUR HELP.
JUST LEAVE ME ALONE. **FOREVER**.

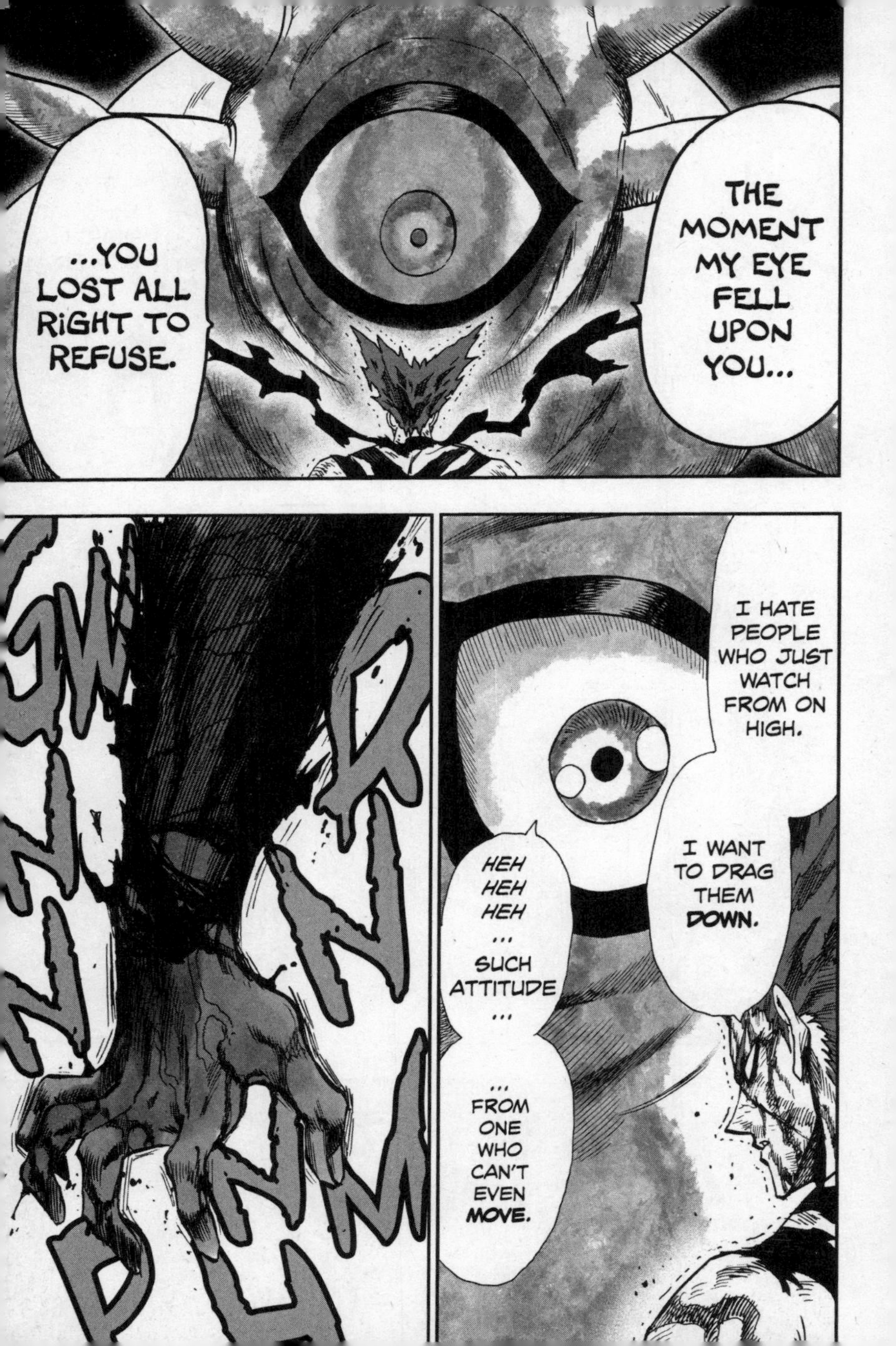
THE MOMENT MY EYE FELL UPON YOU...
...YOU LOST ALL RIGHT TO REFUSE.
I HATE PEOPLE WHO JUST WATCH FROM ON HIGH.
I WANT TO DRAG THEM **DOWN.**
HEH HEH HEH ... SUCH ATTITUDE ...
... FROM ONE WHO CAN'T EVEN **MOVE.**

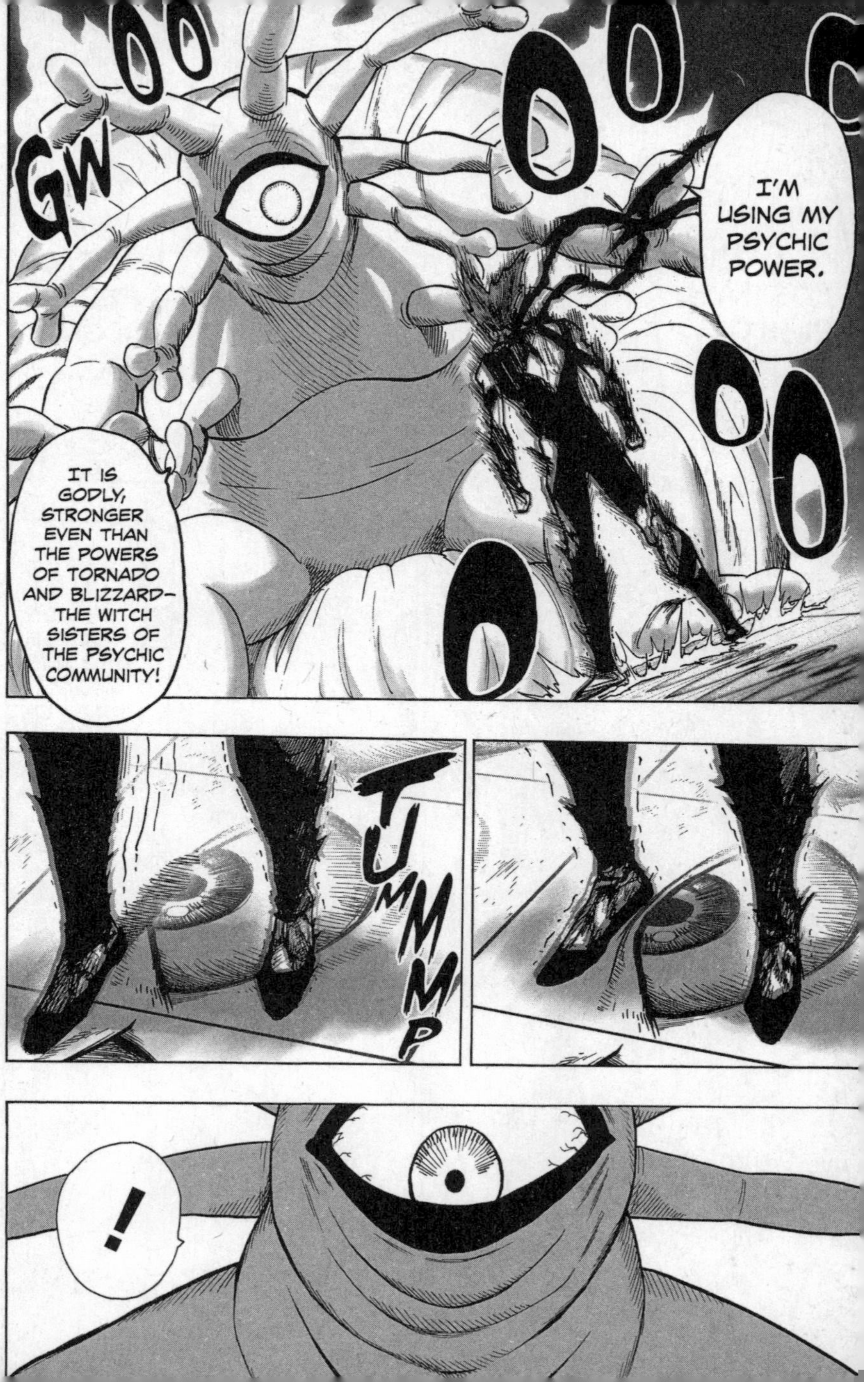
GWOOOOOOOO
I'M USING MY PSYCHIC POWER.
IT IS GODLY, STRONGER EVEN THAN THE POWERS OF TORNADO AND BLIZZARD— THE WITCH SISTERS OF THE PSYCHIC COMMUNITY!
TUMMP
!

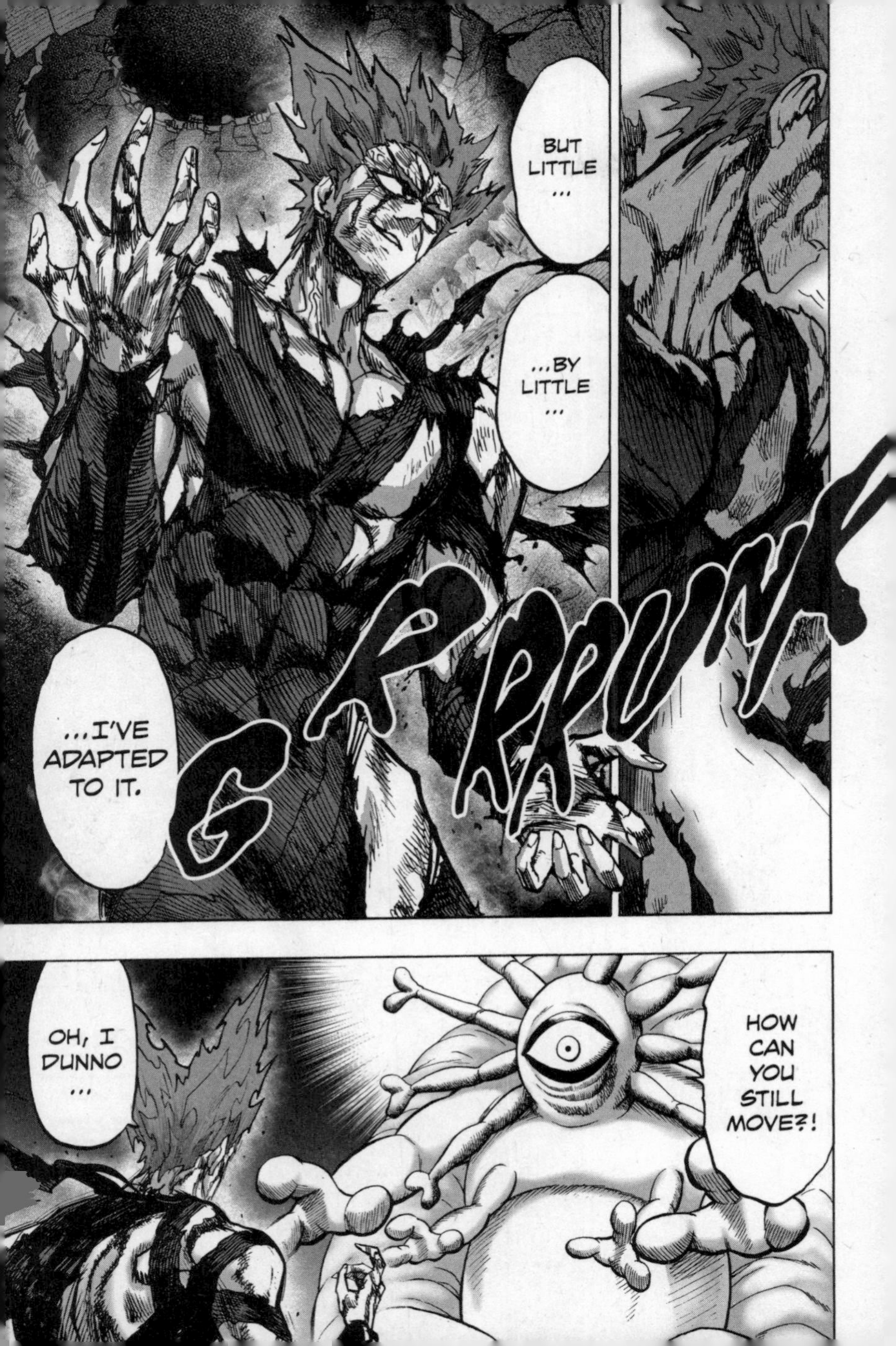
BUT LITTLE ...
...BY LITTLE ...
...I'VE ADAPTED TO IT.
GRRRUNK
HOW CAN YOU STILL MOVE?!
OH, I DUNNO ...

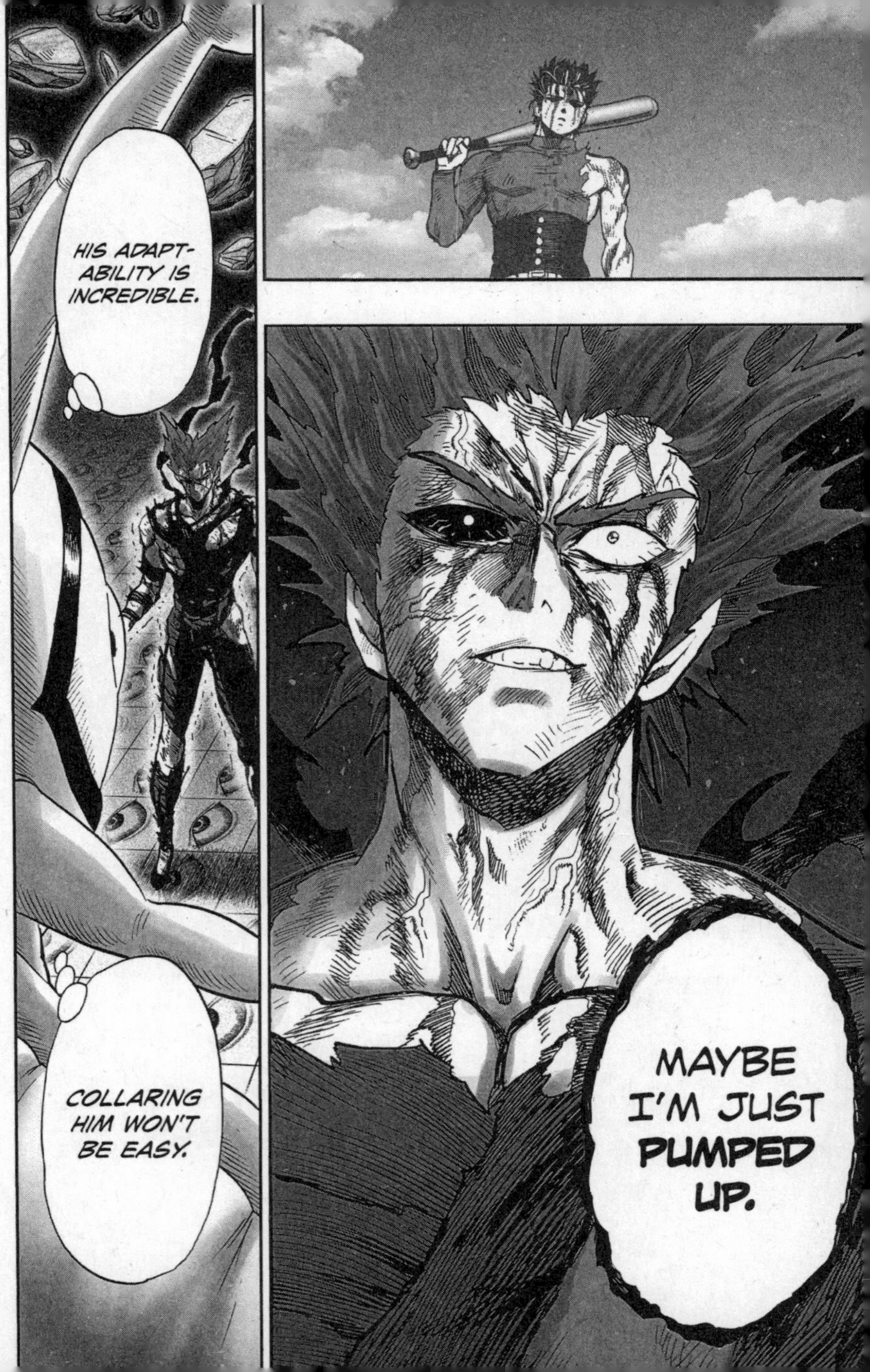
HIS ADAPT-ABILITY IS INCREDIBLE.
MAYBE I'M JUST PUMPED UP.
COLLARING HIM WON'T BE EASY.

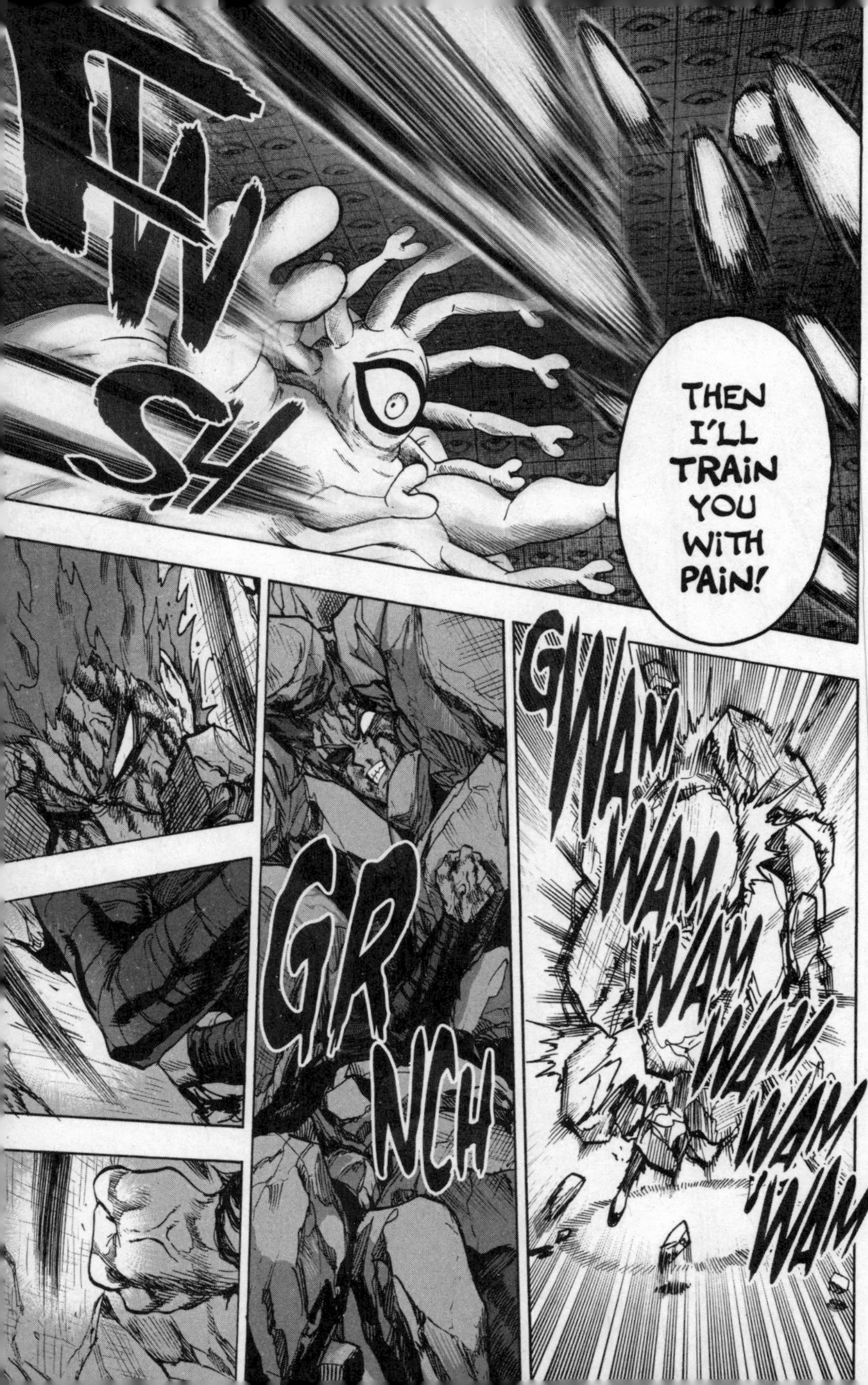
FWSH
THEN I'LL TRAIN YOU WITH PAIN!
GRNCH
GWAM WAM WAM WAM WAM WAM WAM

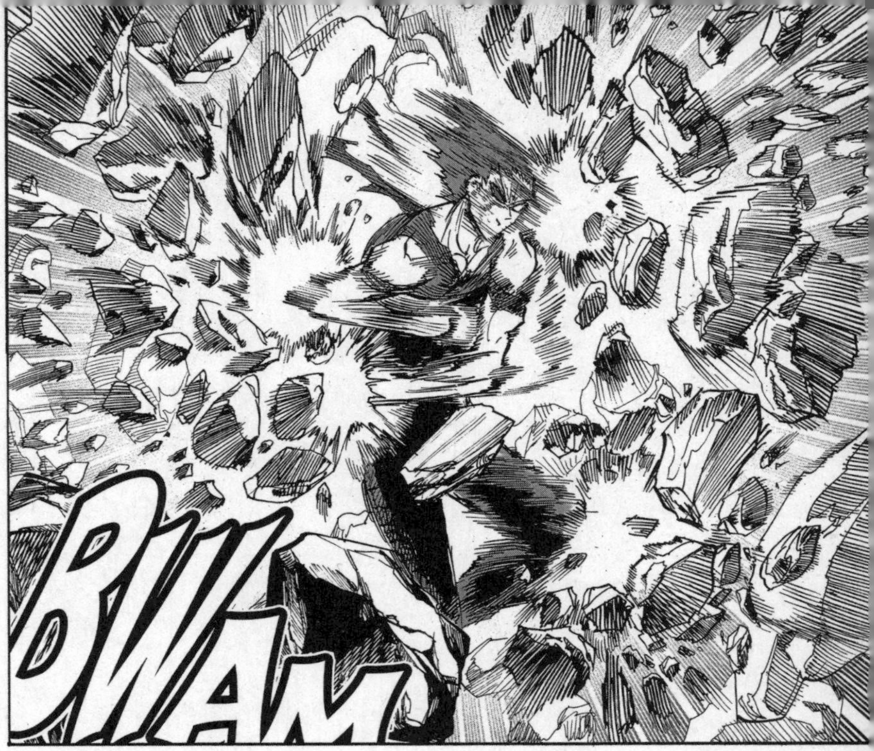
BWAM

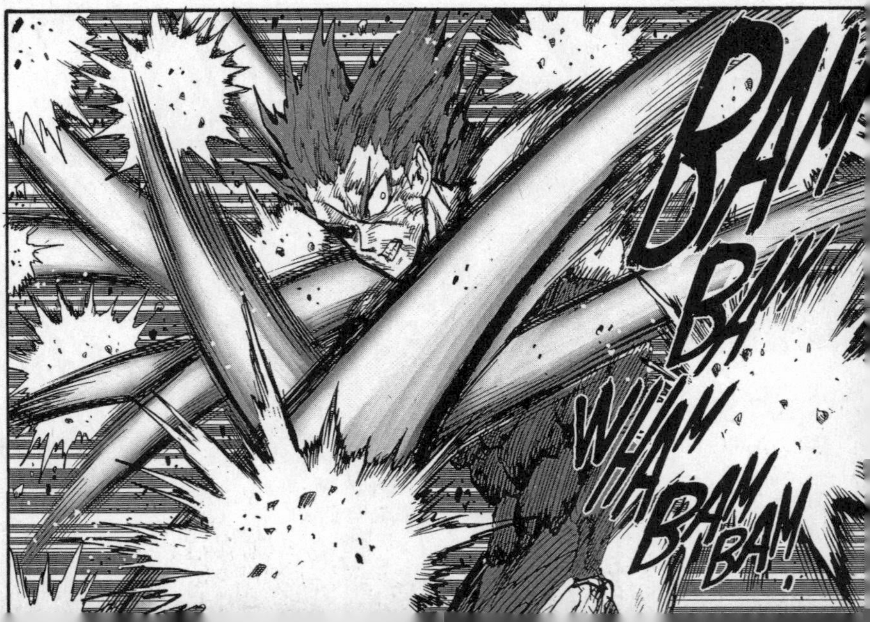
BAM
BAM
WHAM
BAM BAM!

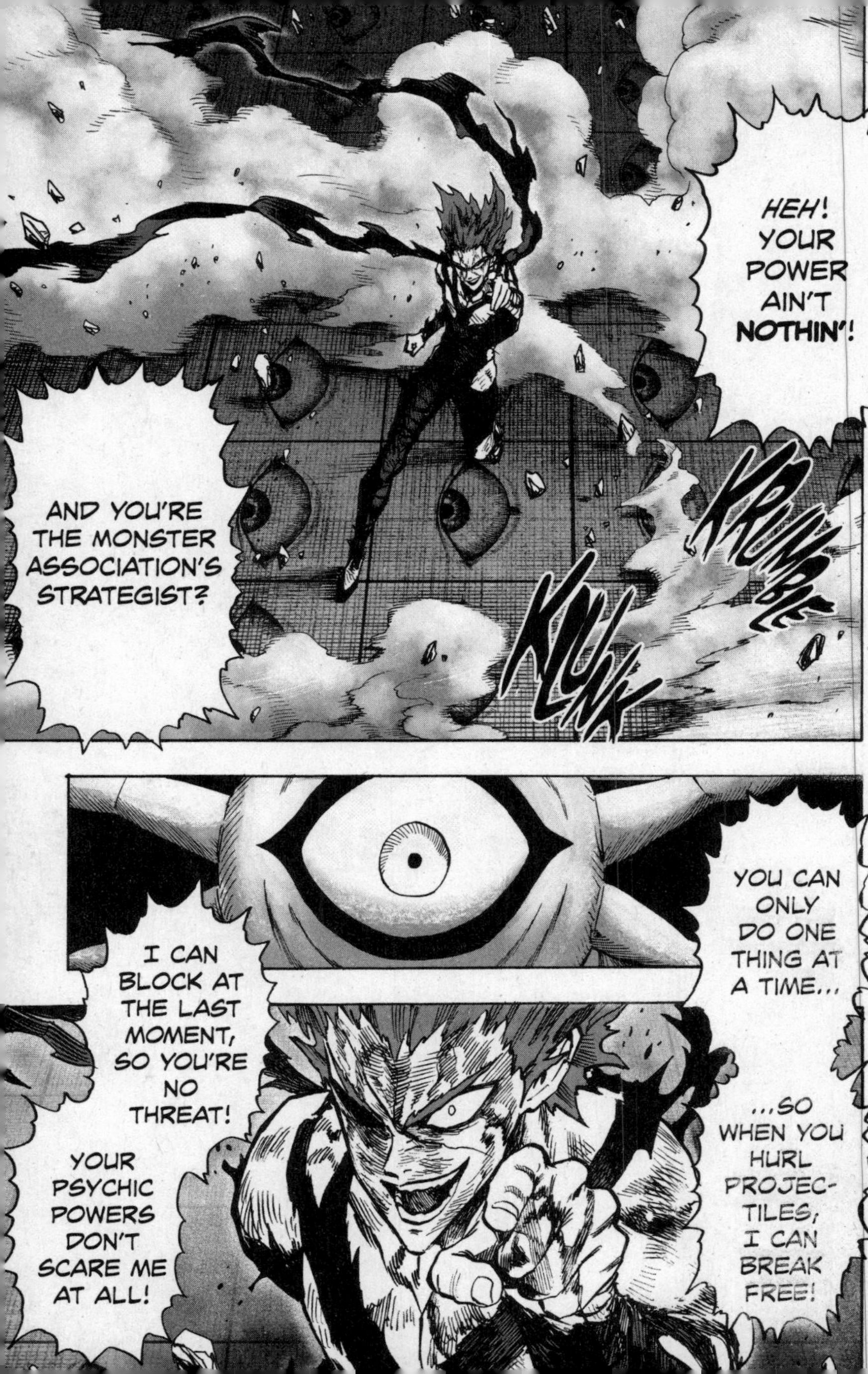
HEH! YOUR POWER AIN'T NOTHIN'!
AND YOU'RE THE MONSTER ASSOCIATION'S STRATEGIST?
KRUMBLE
KLUNK
YOU CAN ONLY DO ONE THING AT A TIME...
I CAN BLOCK AT THE LAST MOMENT, SO YOU'RE NO THREAT!
...SO WHEN YOU HURL PROJECTILES, I CAN BREAK FREE!
YOUR PSYCHIC POWERS DON'T SCARE ME AT ALL!

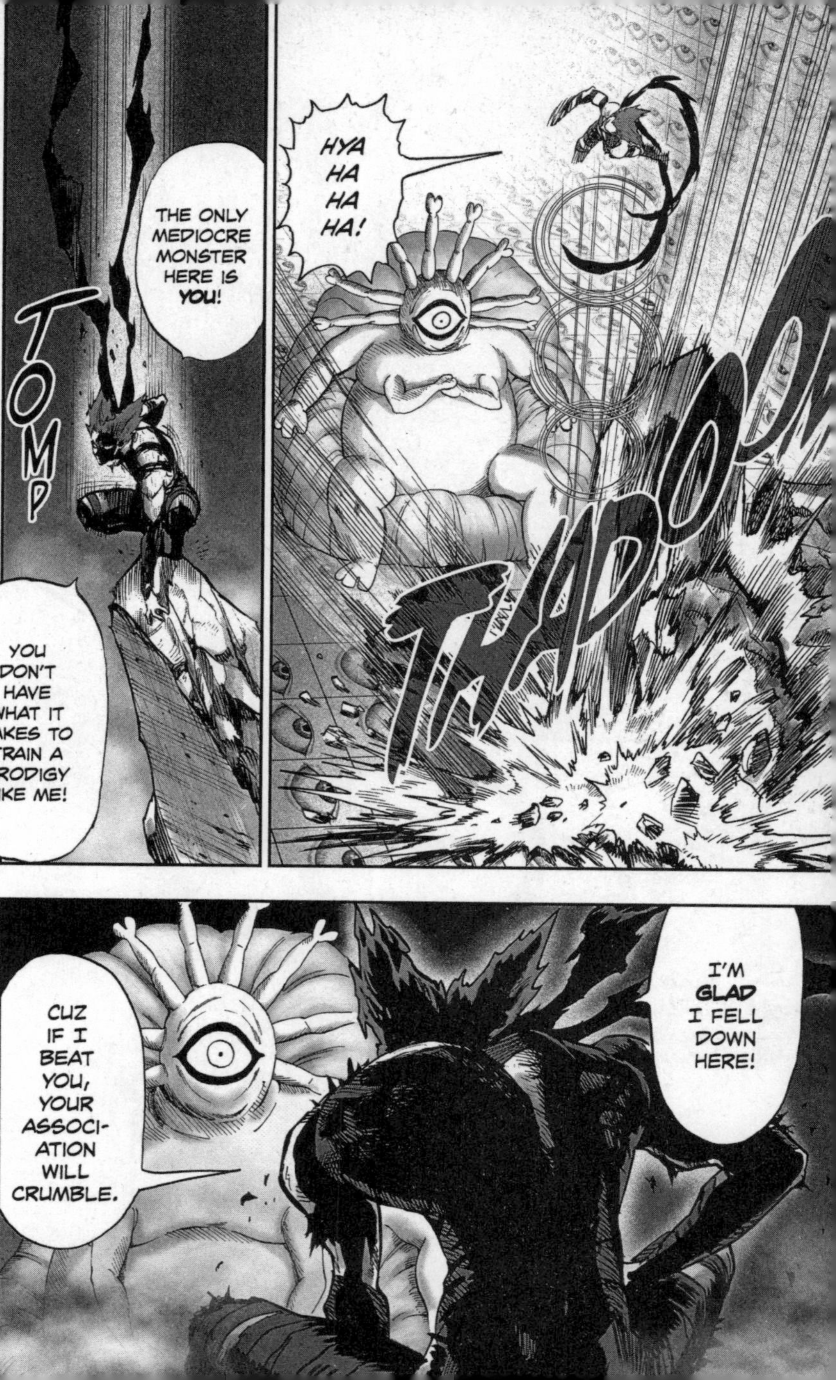
HYA HA HA HA!
THADOOOM
TOMP
THE ONLY MEDIOCRE MONSTER HERE IS **YOU**!
YOU DON'T HAVE WHAT IT TAKES TO TRAIN A PRODIGY LIKE ME!
I'M **GLAD** I FELL DOWN HERE!
CUZ IF I BEAT YOU, YOUR ASSOCI-ATION WILL CRUMBLE.

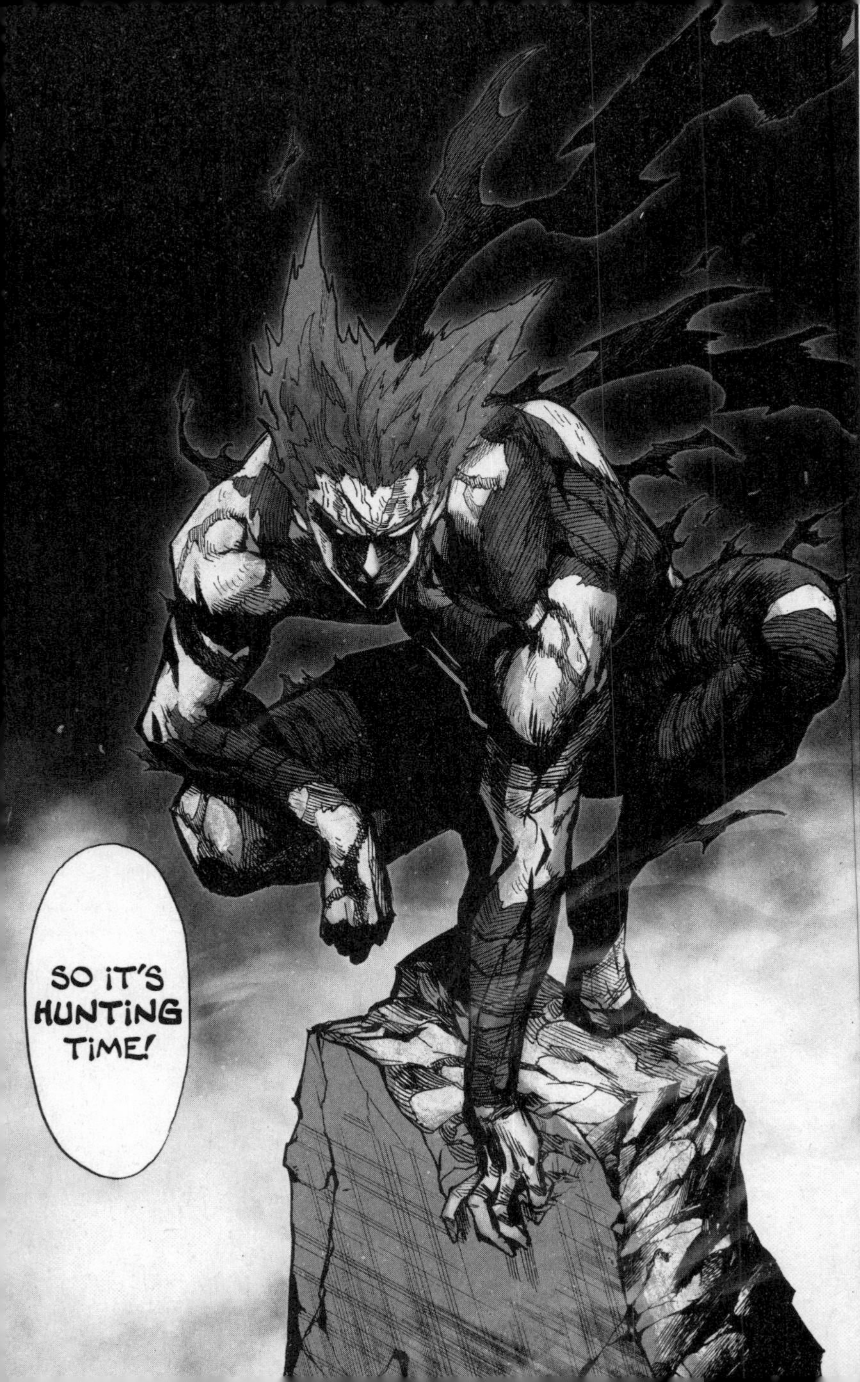
SO IT'S HUNTING TIME!

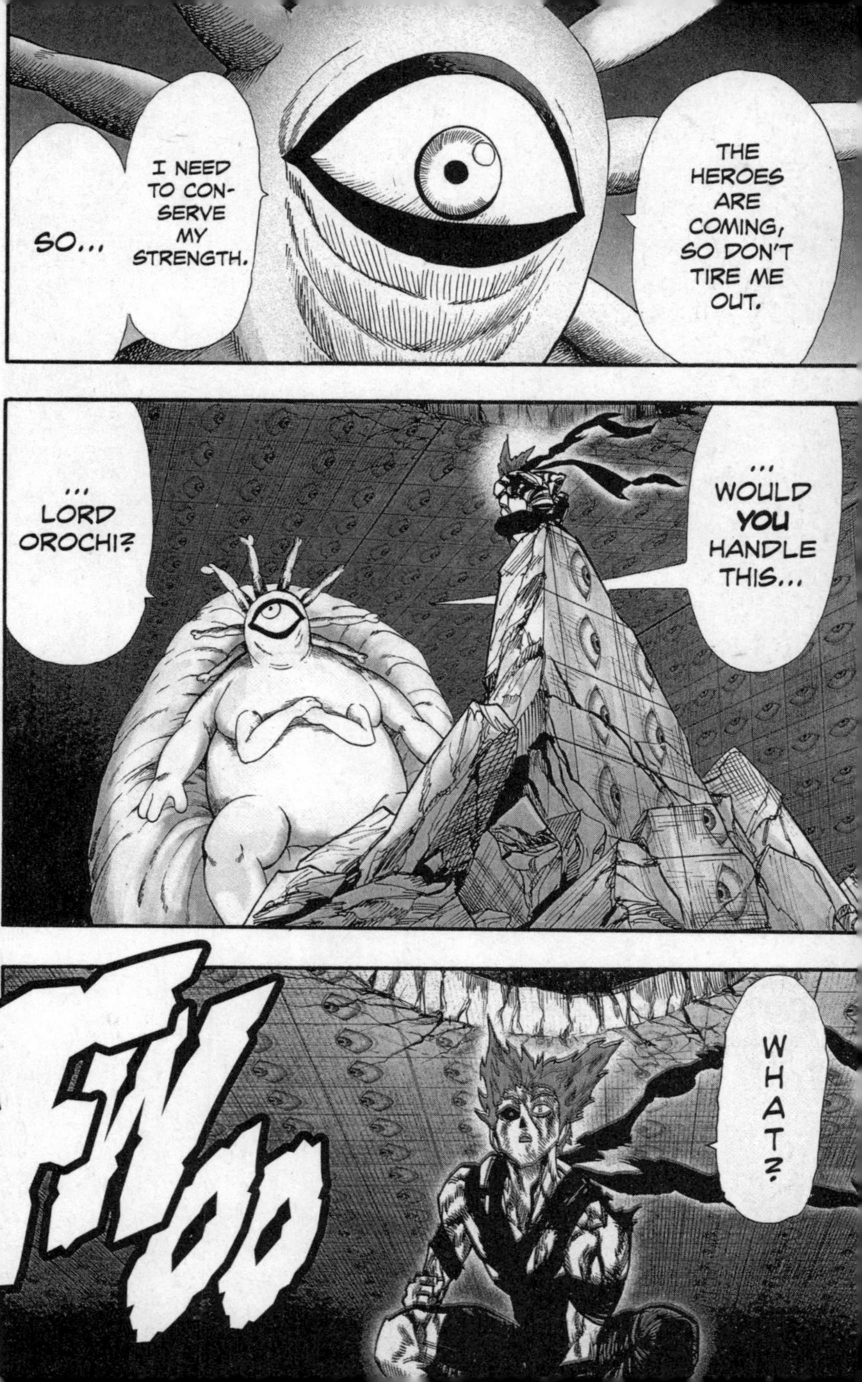
THE HEROES ARE COMING, SO DON'T TIRE ME OUT.
I NEED TO CON-SERVE MY STRENGTH.
SO...
... WOULD **YOU** HANDLE THIS...
... LORD OROCHI?
WHAT?
FWOO

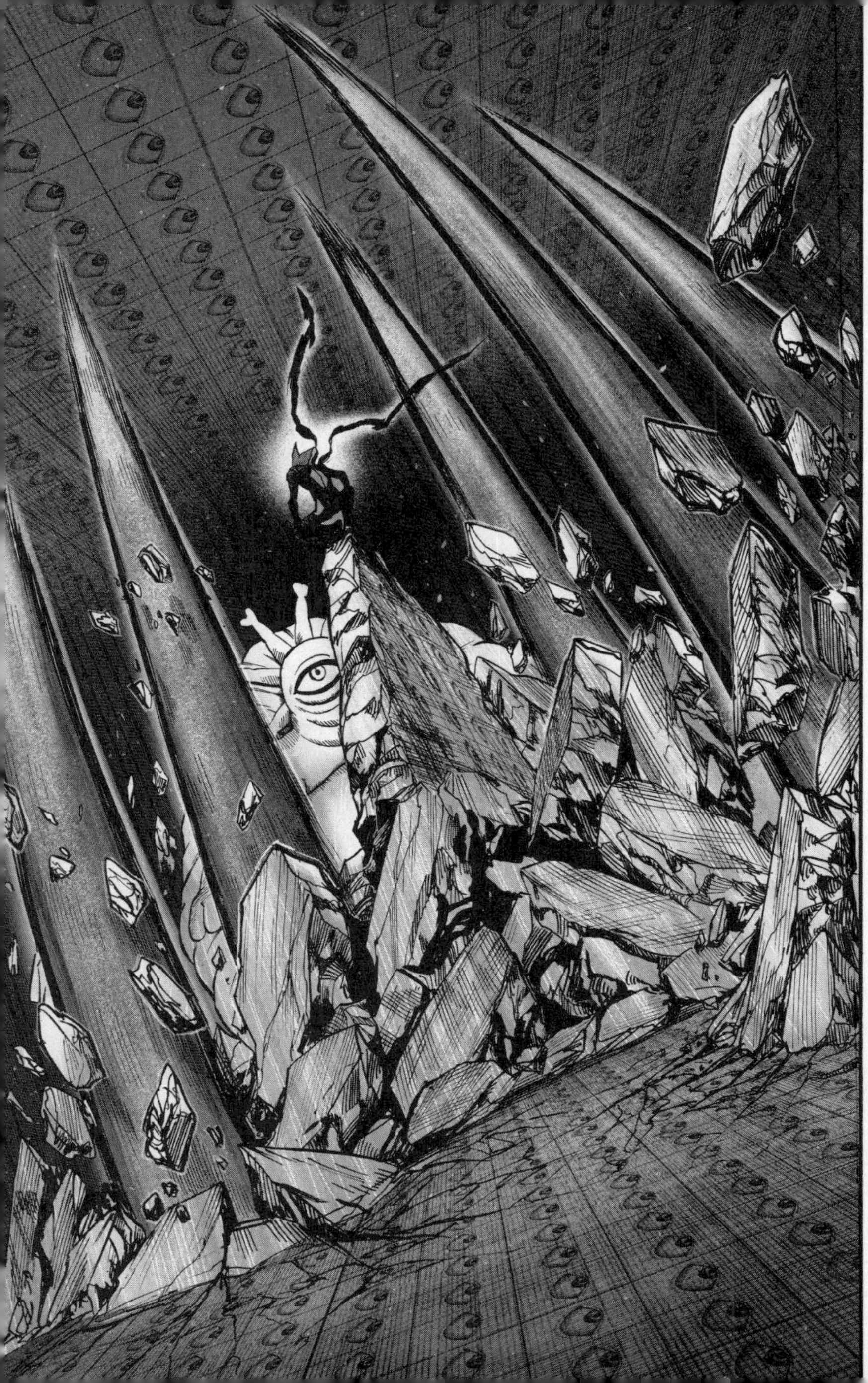

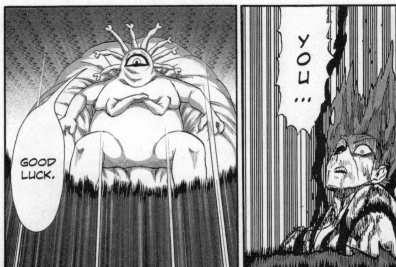

GOOD
LUCK.

YOU
...

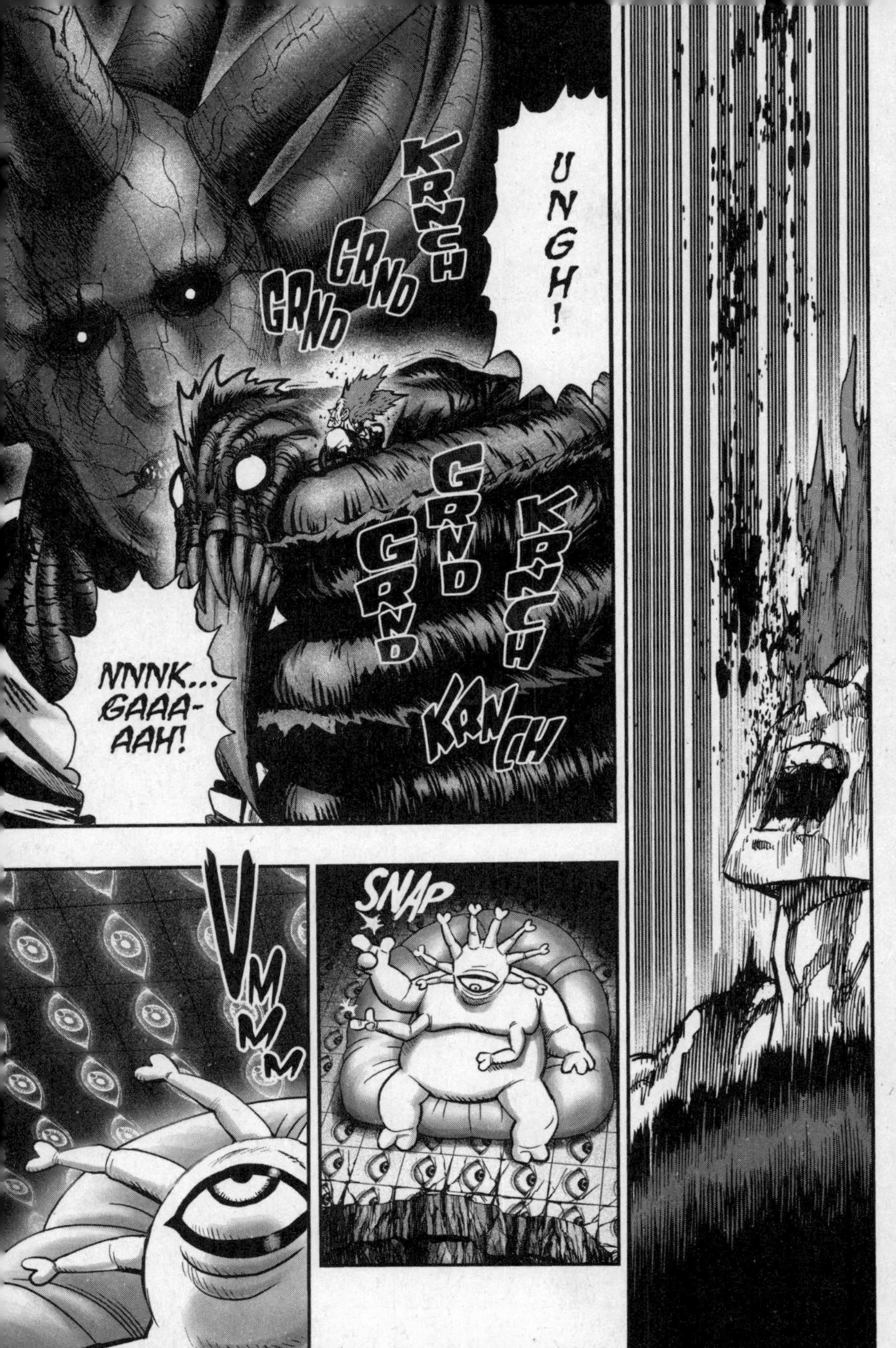
UNGH!
KRNCH
GRND
GRND
KRNCH
GRND
GRND
KRNCH
NNNK... GAAA-AAH!
SNAP
VMMMM

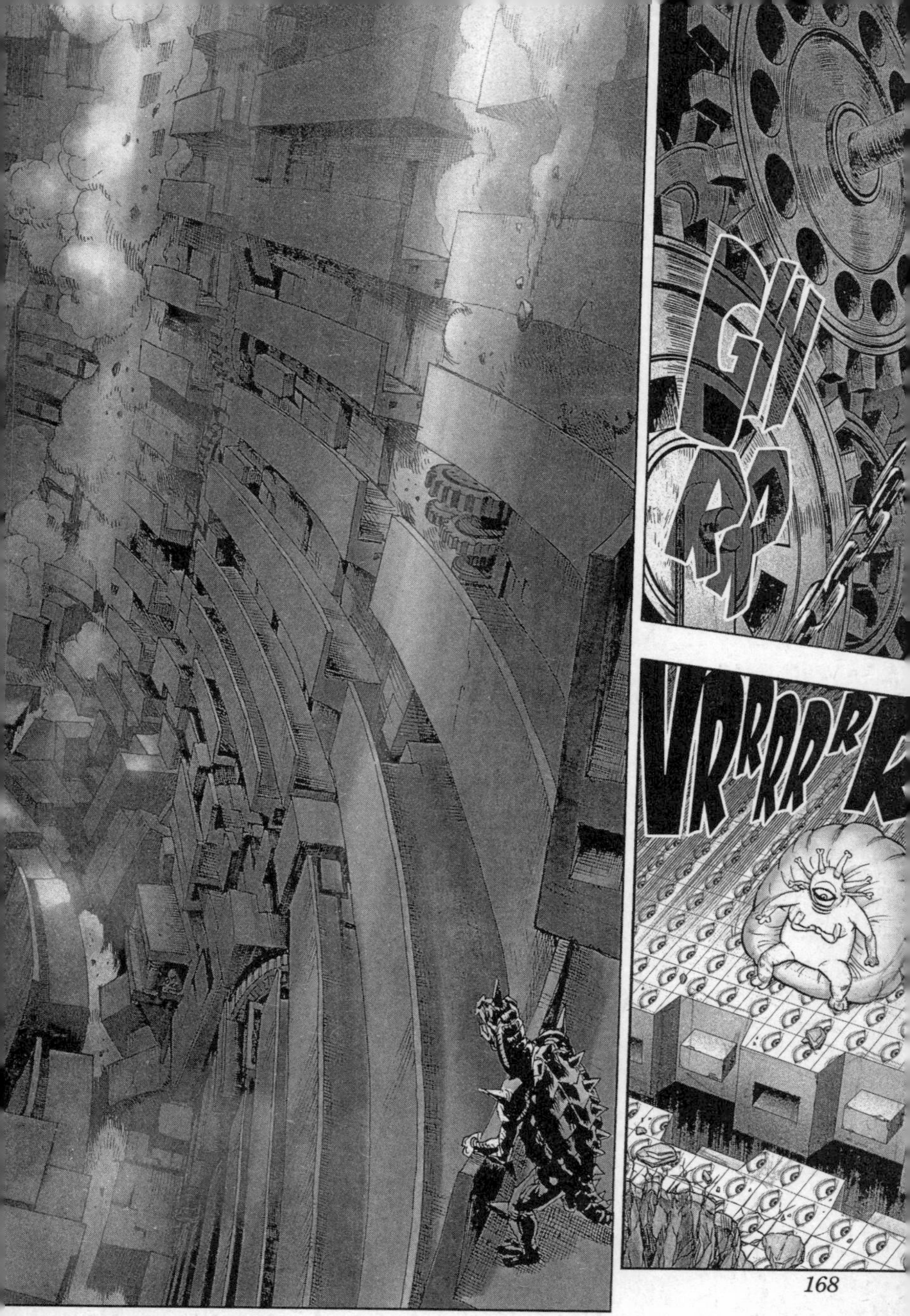
GHRR
VRRRRRR

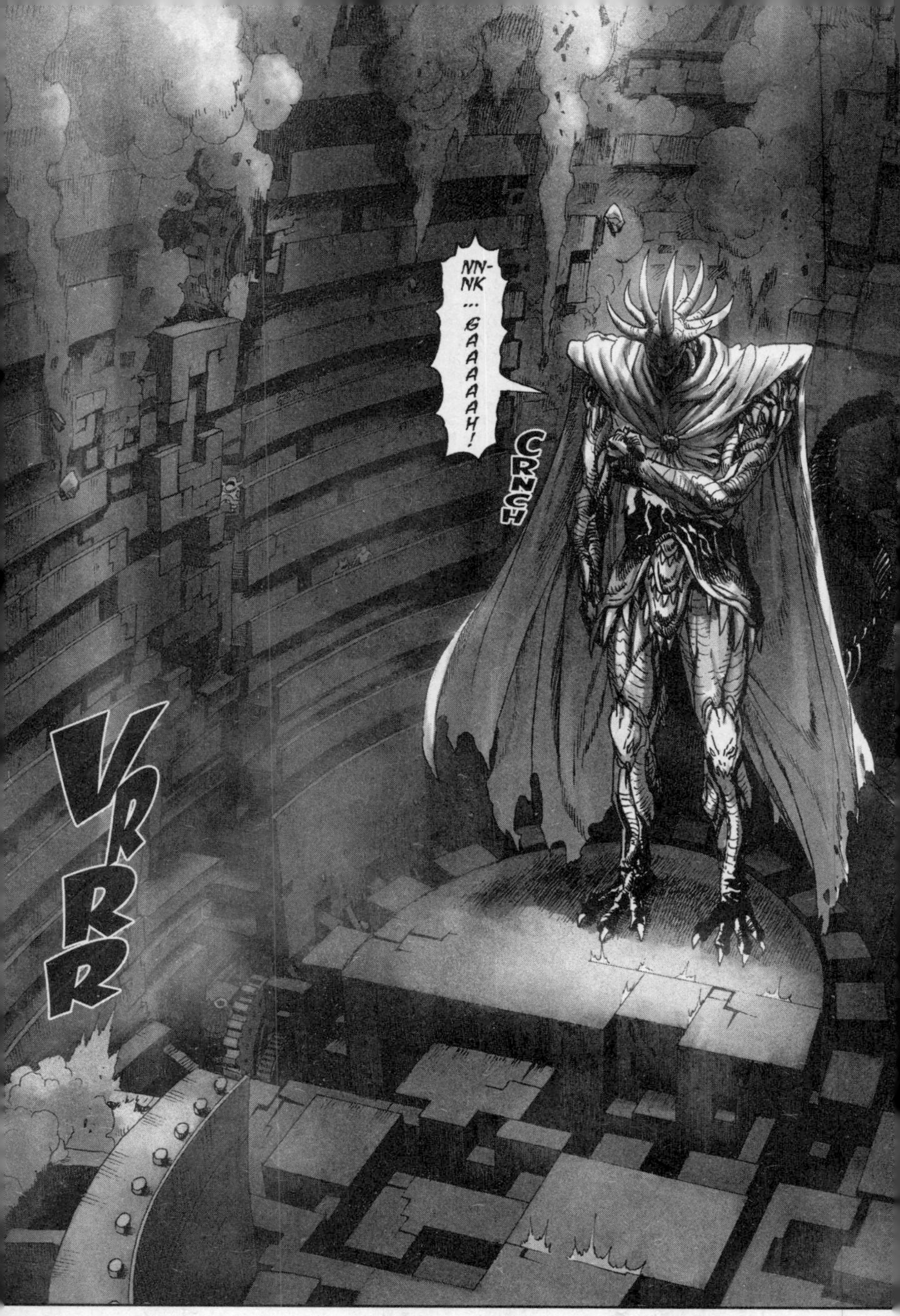
NN-NK... GAAAAAAH!
CRNCH
VRRR

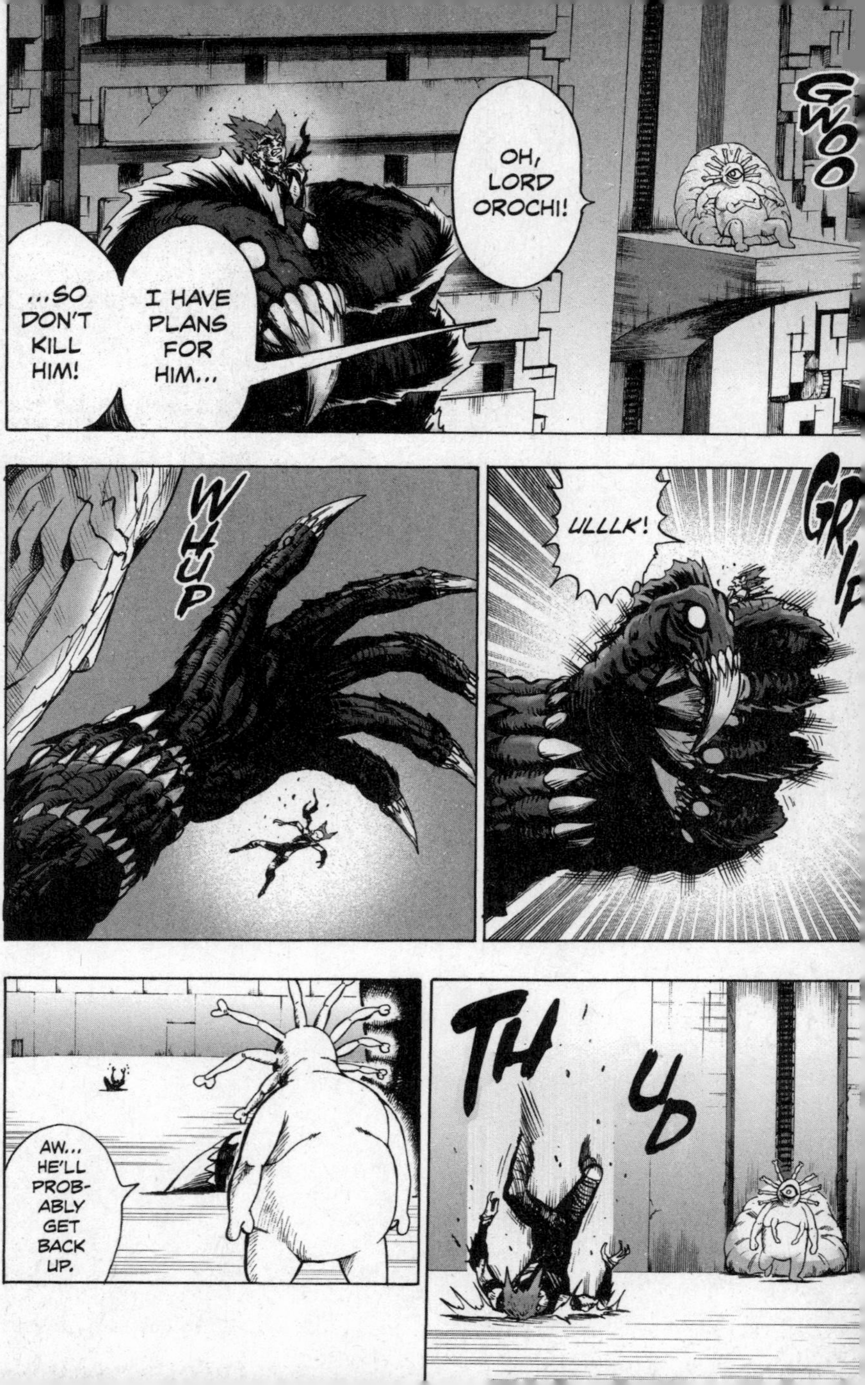
GWOO
OH, LORD OROCHI!
I HAVE PLANS FOR HIM...
...SO DON'T KILL HIM!
WHUP
ULLLK!
GRIP
THUD
AW... HE'LL PROBABLY GET BACK UP.

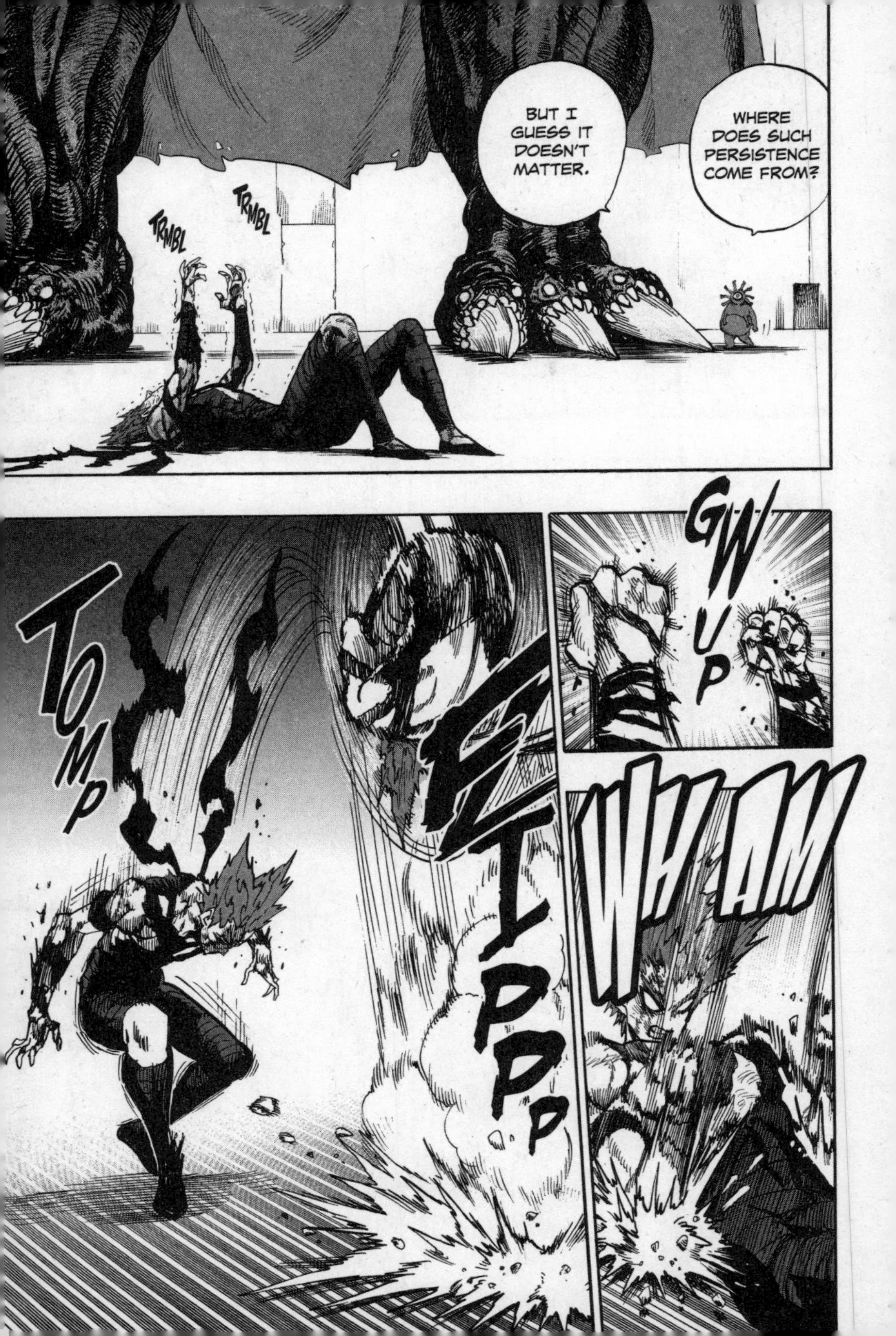
WHERE DOES SUCH PERSISTENCE COME FROM?
BUT I GUESS IT DOESN'T MATTER.
TRMBL
TRMBL
GWUP
WHAM
SZIPPP
TOMP

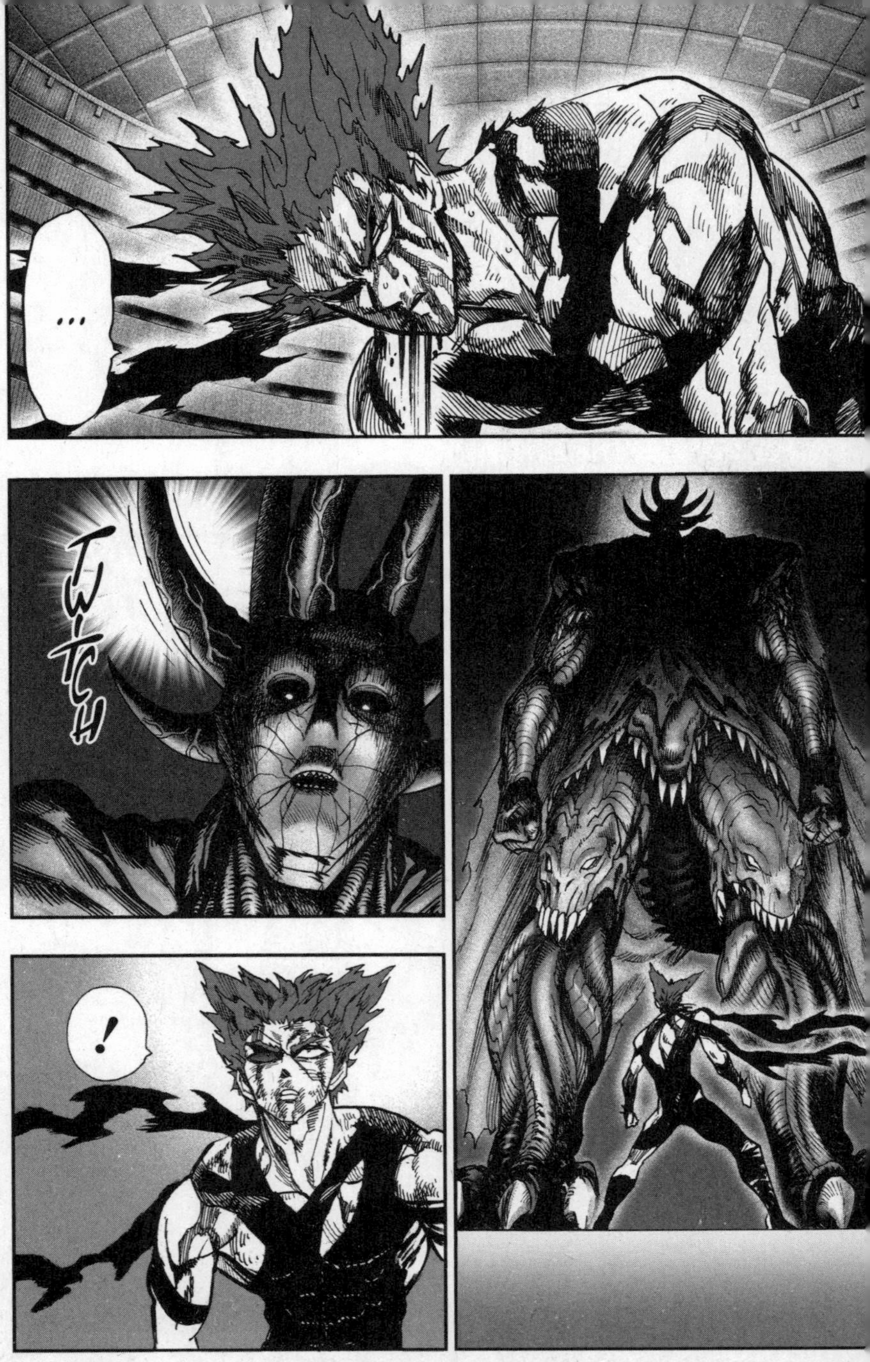
...
TWITCH
!

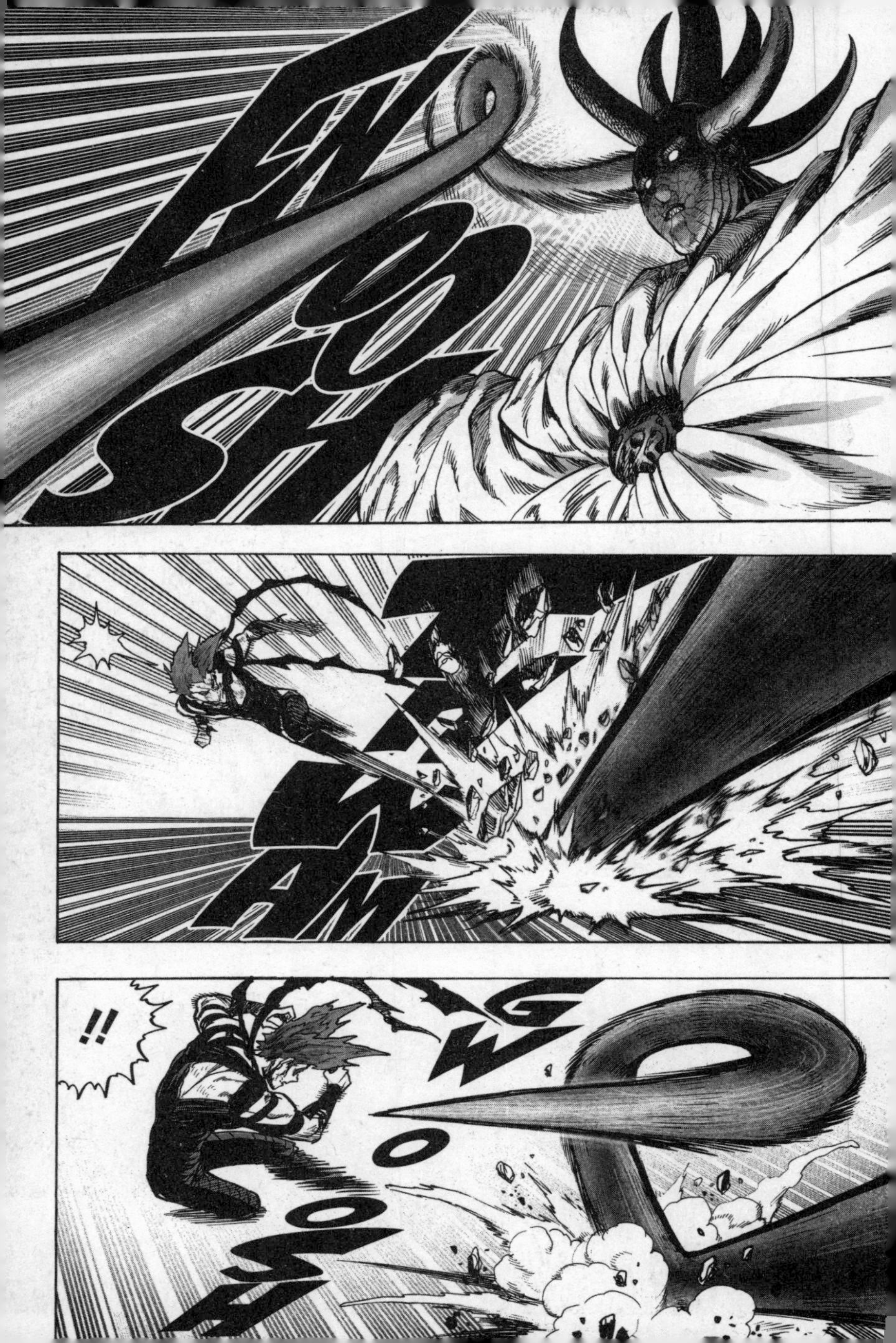
FWOOSH
GWOOSH
!!

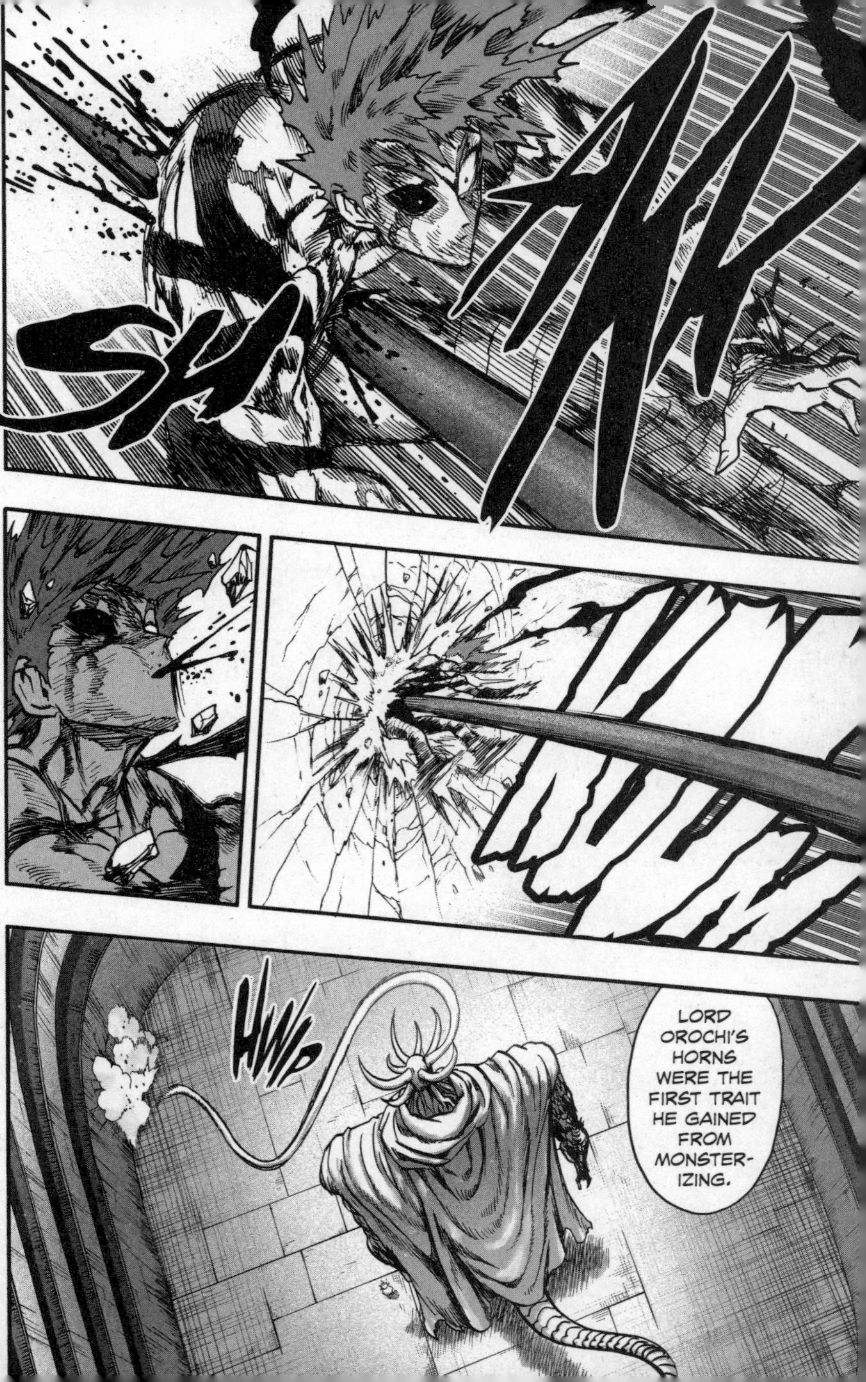
SHNK
THUNK
HWIP
LORD OROCHI'S HORNS WERE THE FIRST TRAIT HE GAINED FROM MONSTER-IZING.

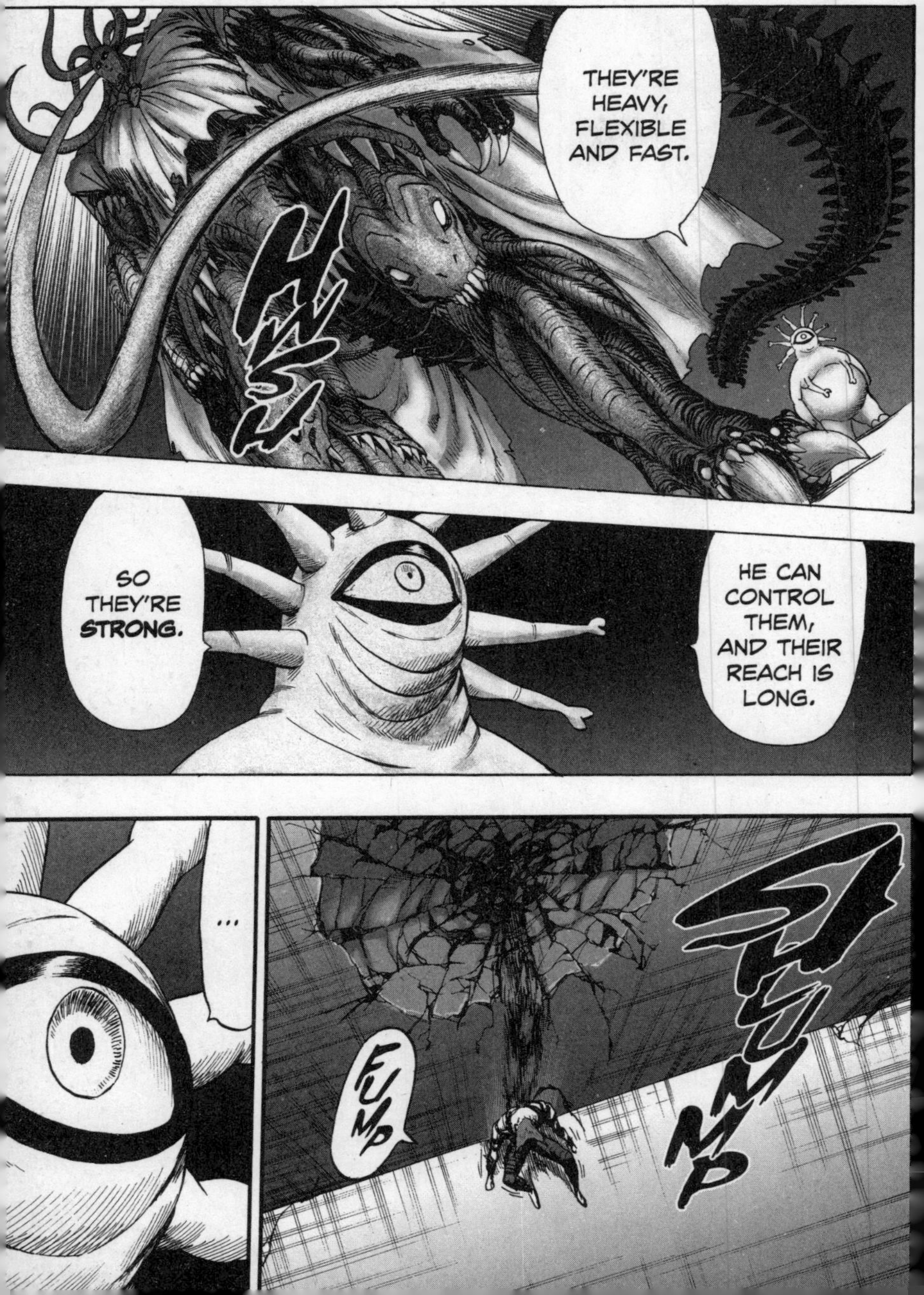
THEY'RE HEAVY, FLEXIBLE AND FAST.
GWSH
HE CAN CONTROL THEM, AND THEIR REACH IS LONG.
SO THEY'RE **STRONG.**
FWUMMP
FUMP
...

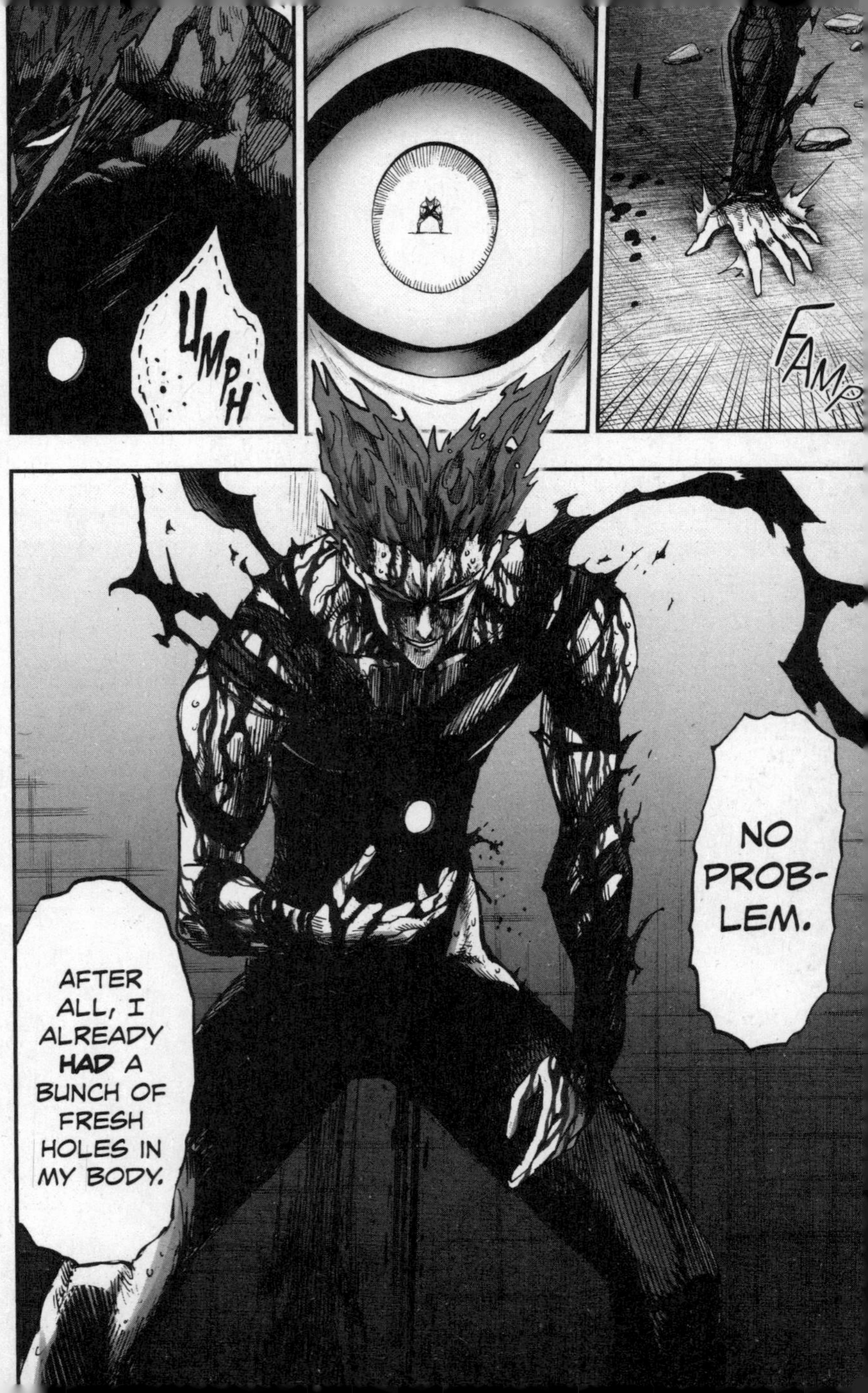
FAMP
UMPH
NO PROB-LEM.
AFTER ALL, I ALREADY **HAD** A BUNCH OF FRESH HOLES IN MY BODY.

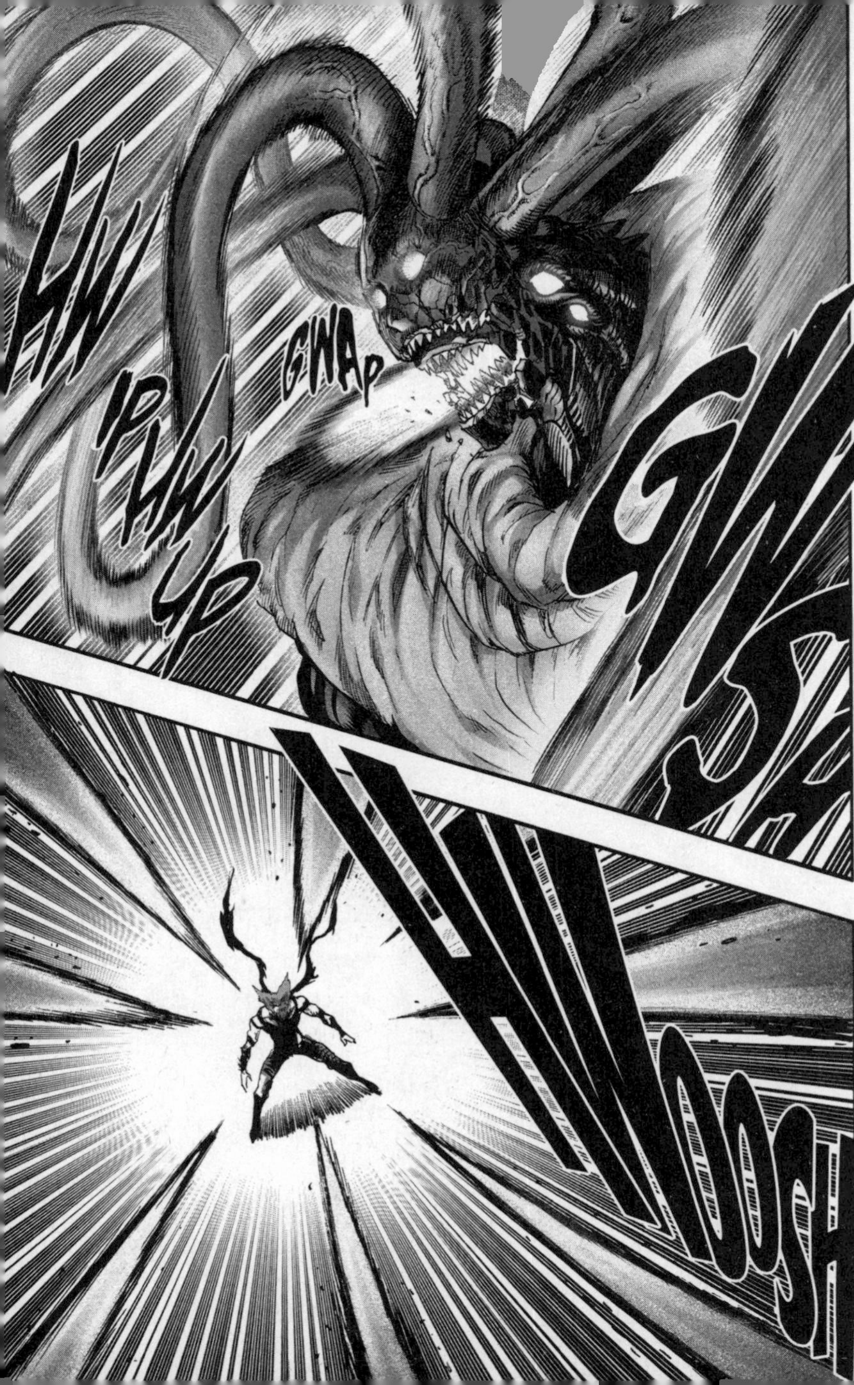
GWASH
GWAP
HWIP
HWUP
WHOOSH

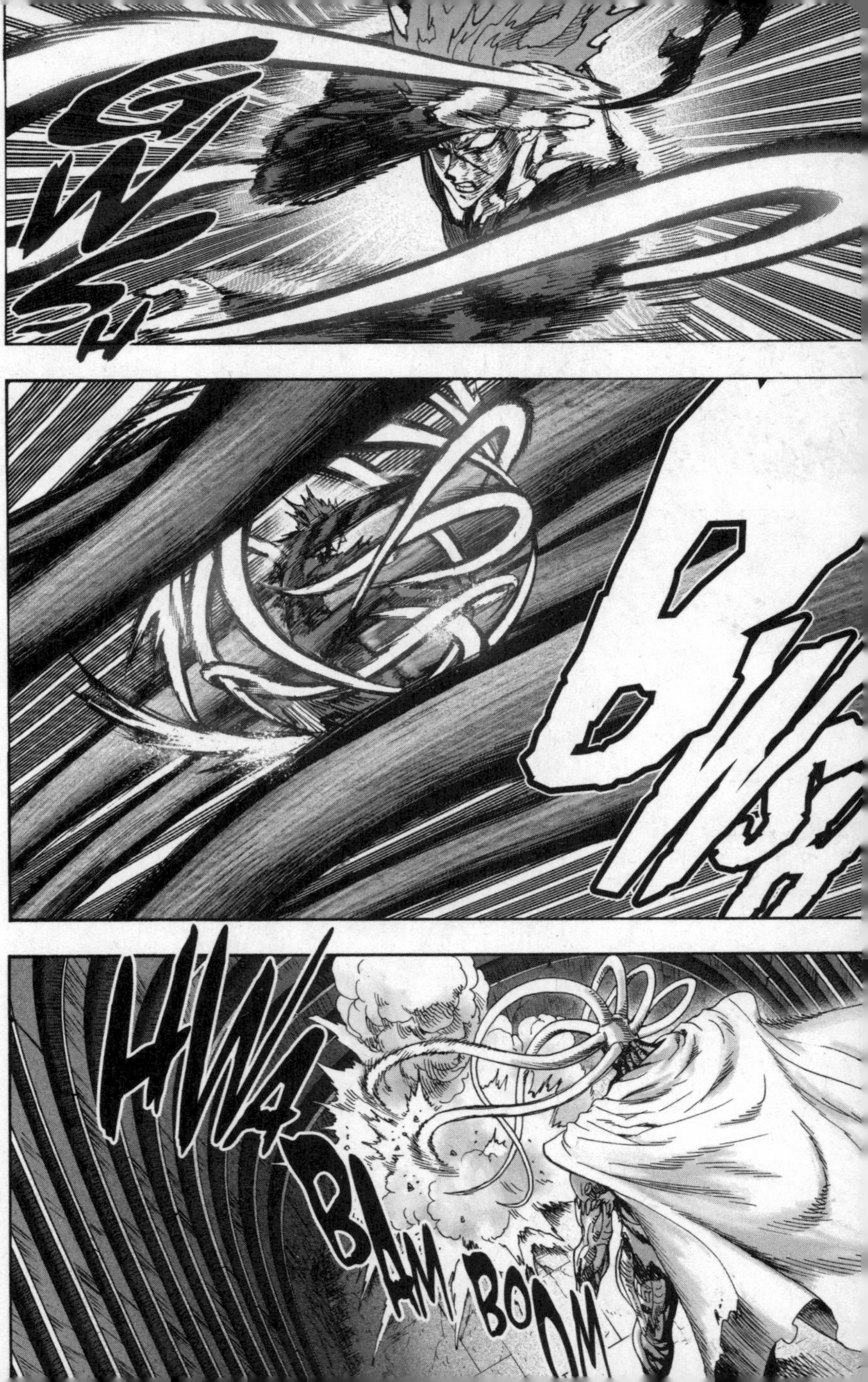
GWSH
HWA
BAM
BOOM

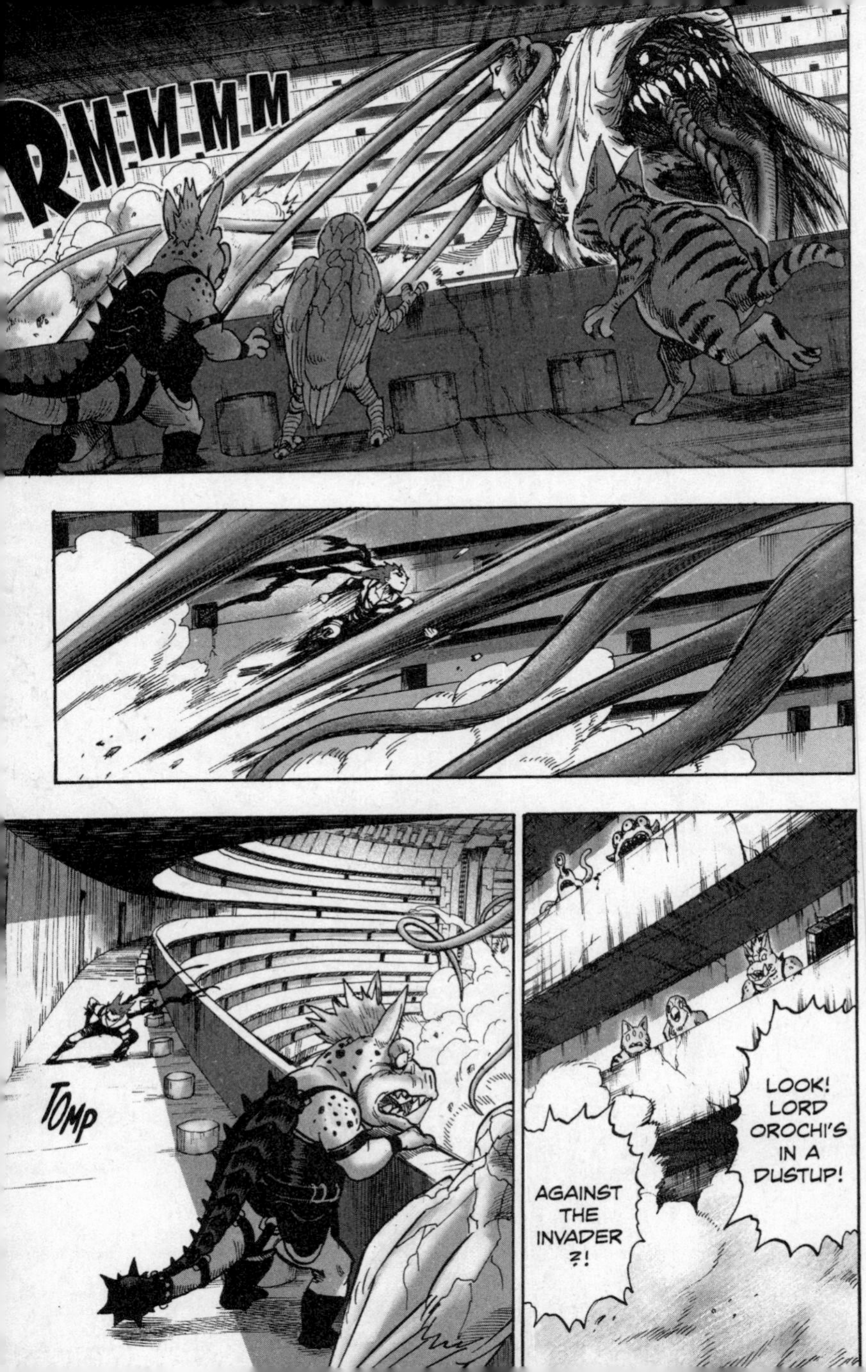
RMMMMM
TOMP
LOOK! LORD OROCHI'S IN A DUSTUP!
AGAINST THE INVADER?!

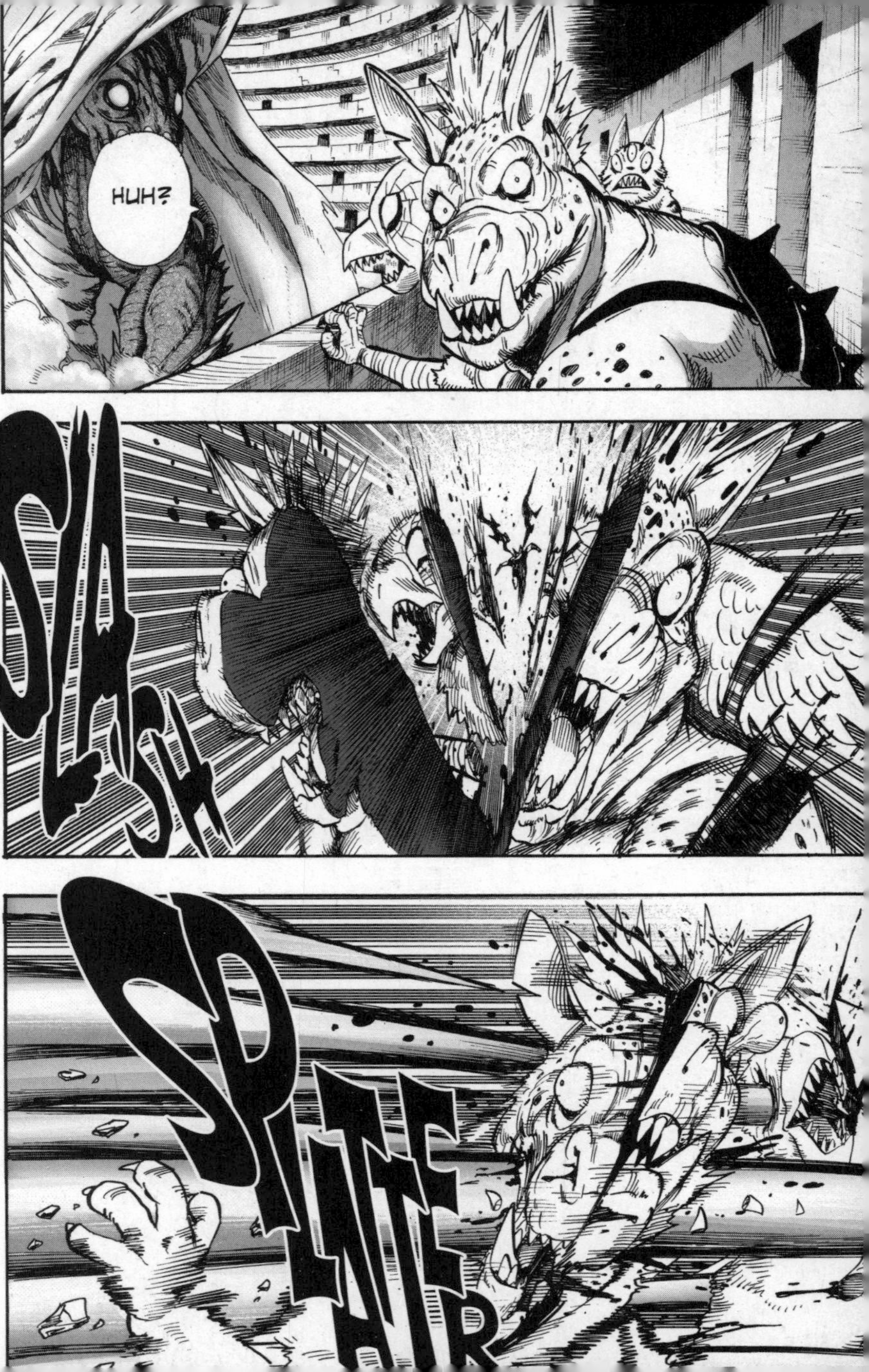
HUH?
SLASH
SPLATTER

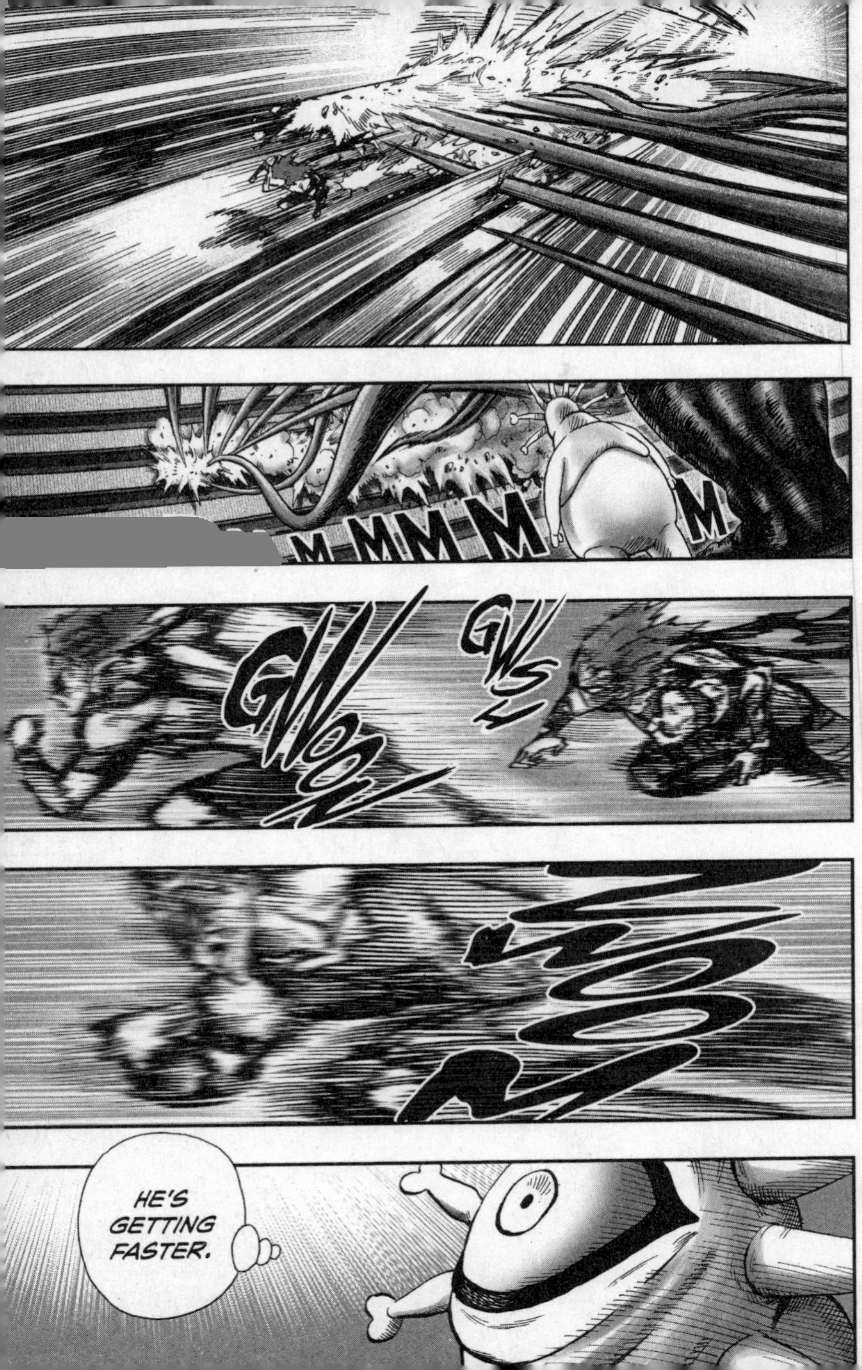
HE'S GETTING FASTER.

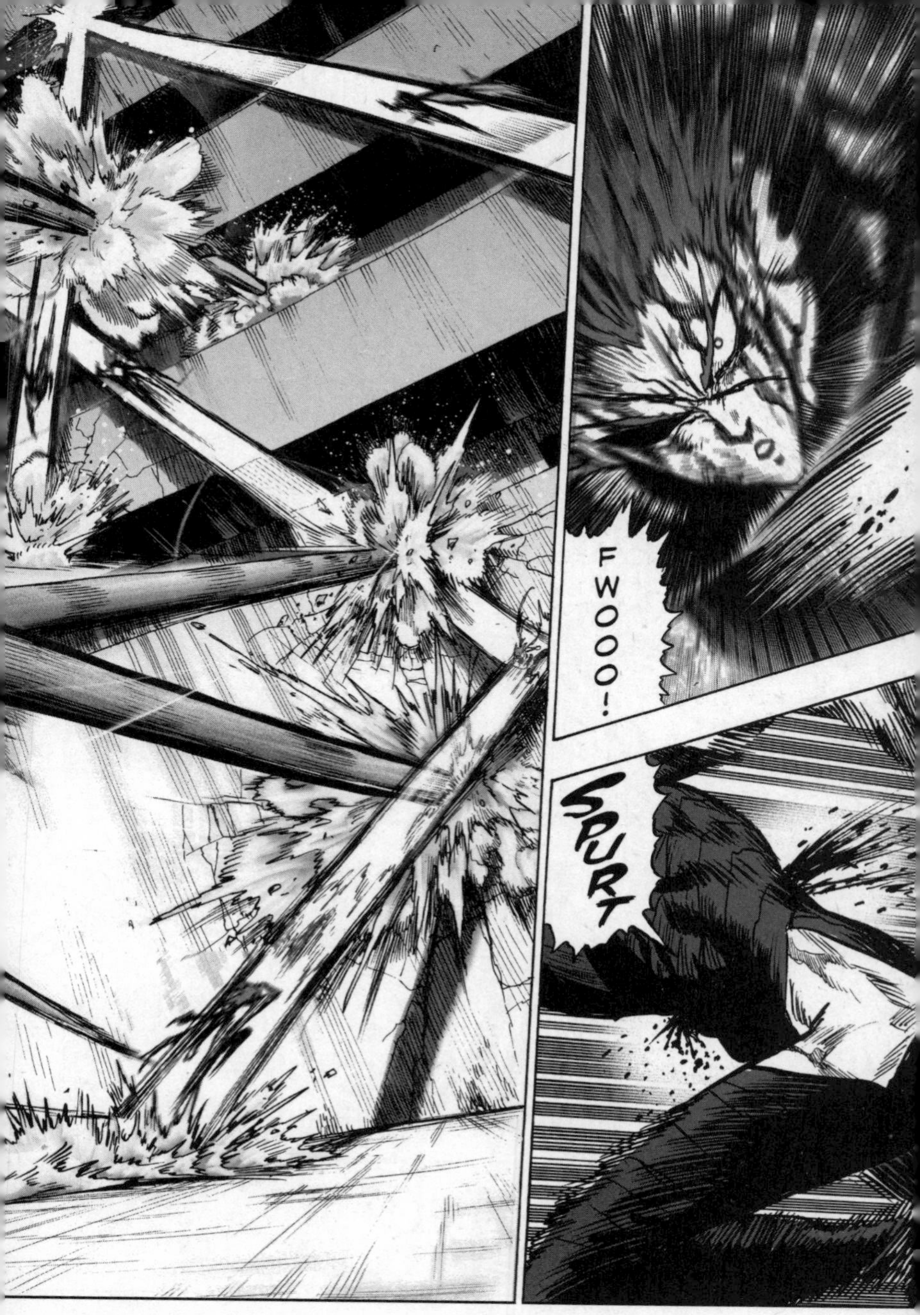
FWOOOO!
SPURT

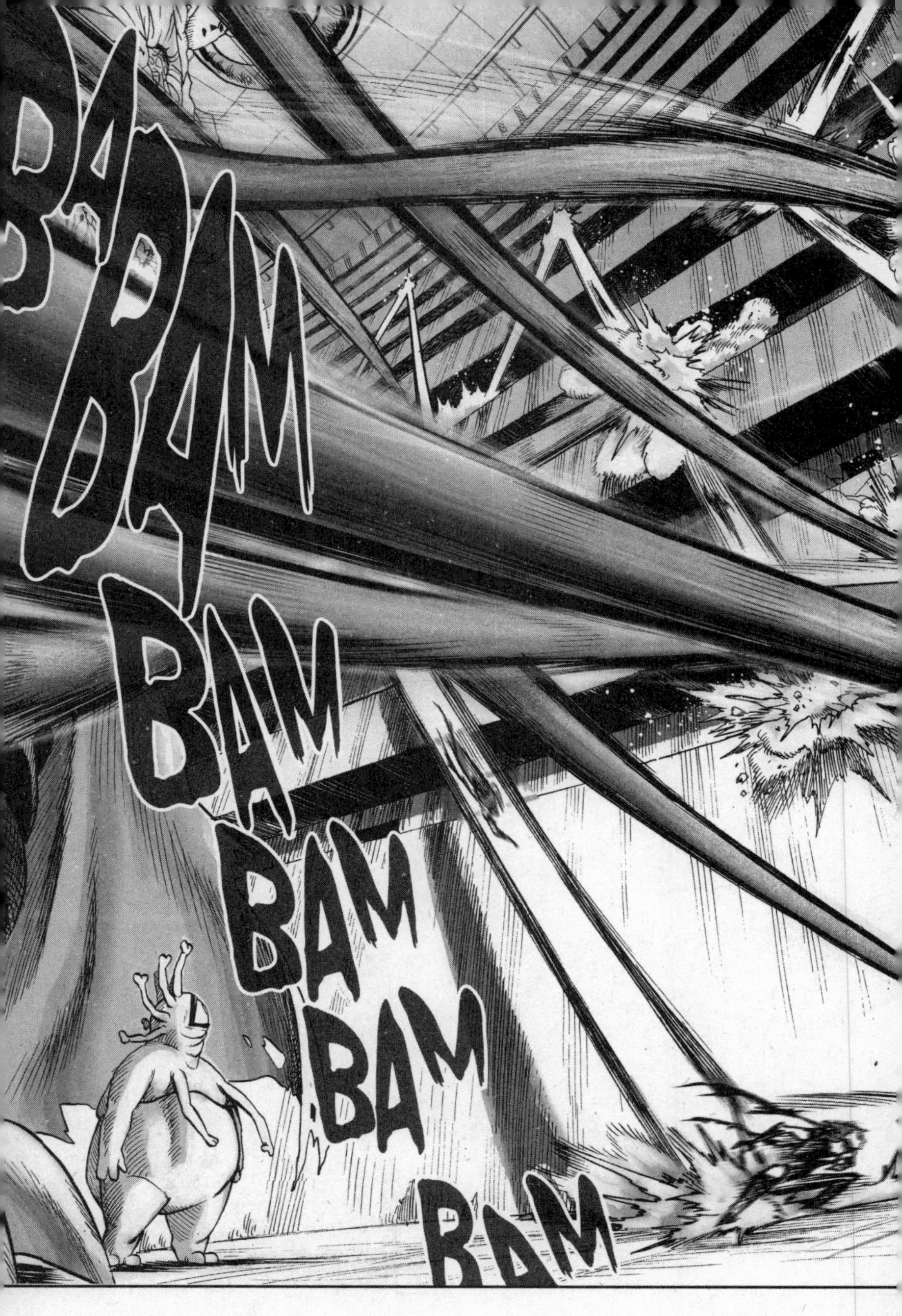
BABAM
BAM
BAM
BAM
BAM

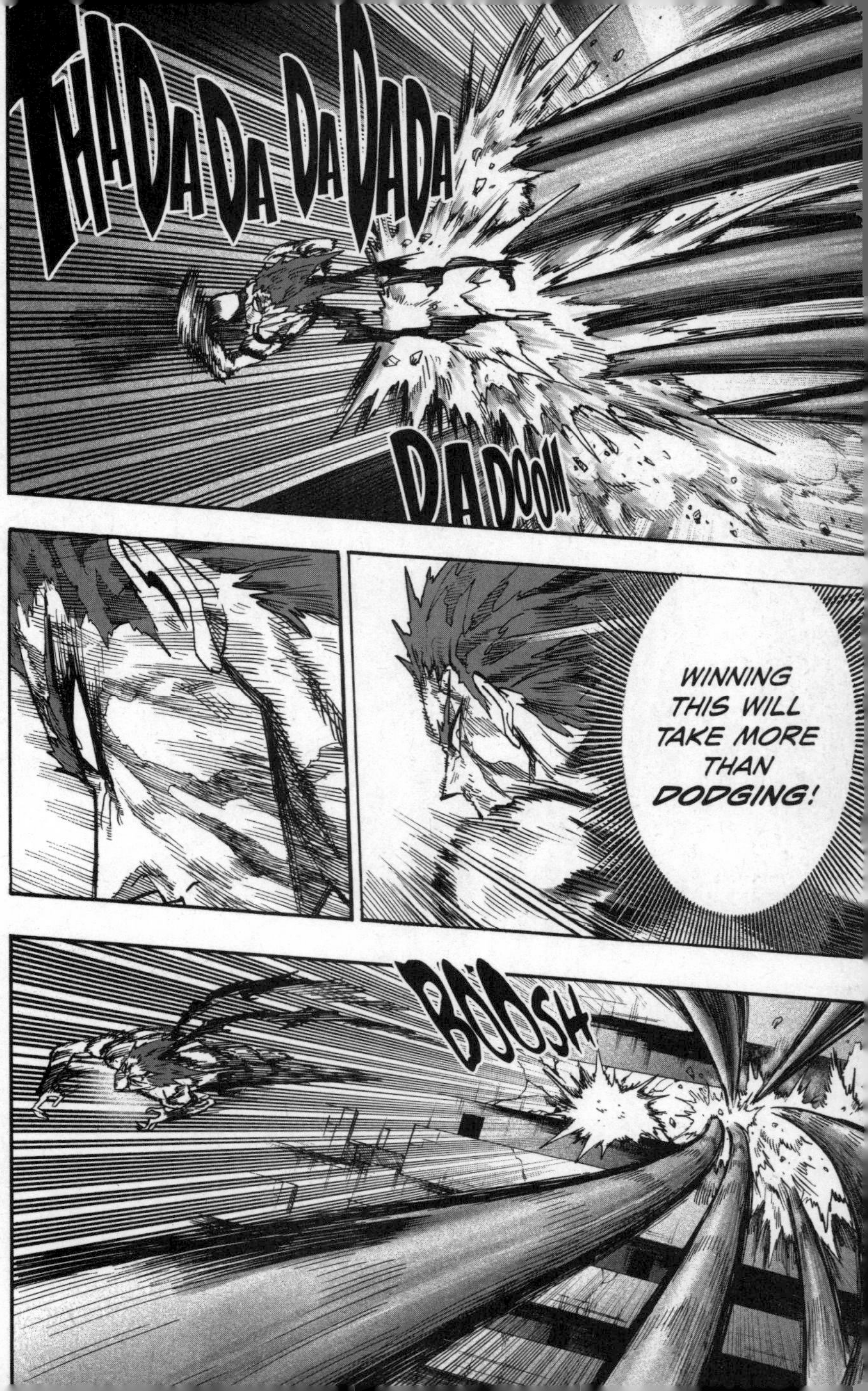
THADADA DA DADA
DADOOM
WINNING THIS WILL TAKE MORE THAN DODGING!
BOOSH

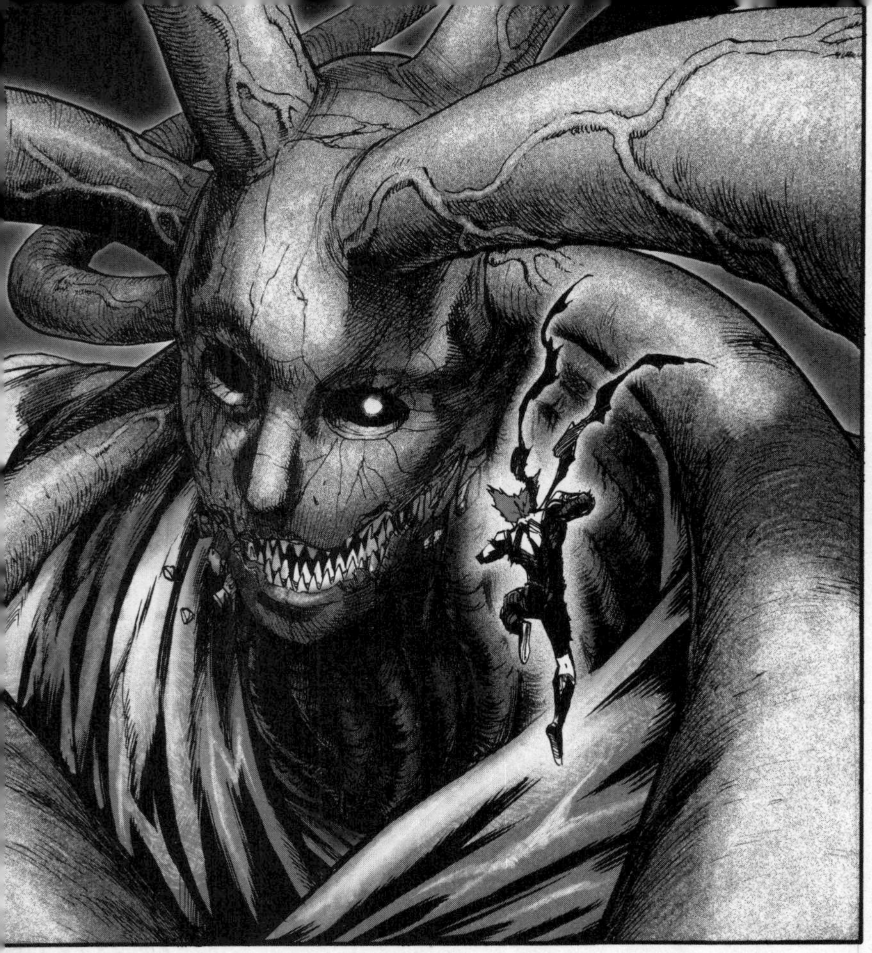

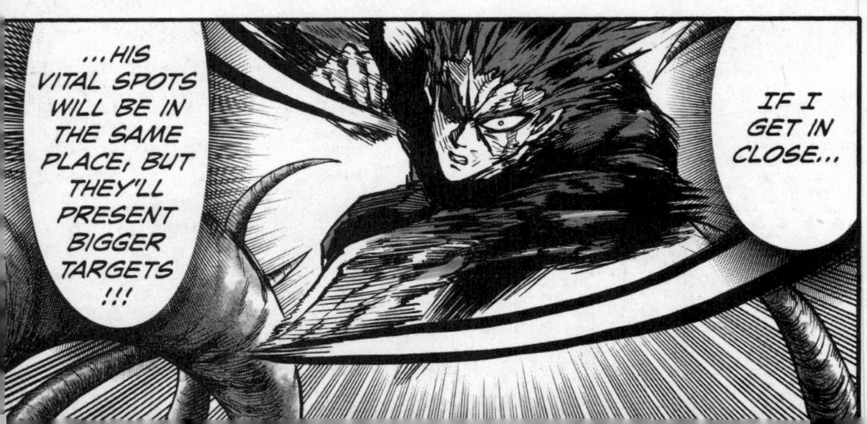
IF I GET IN CLOSE...
...HIS VITAL SPOTS WILL BE IN THE SAME PLACE, BUT THEY'LL PRESENT BIGGER TARGETS !!!

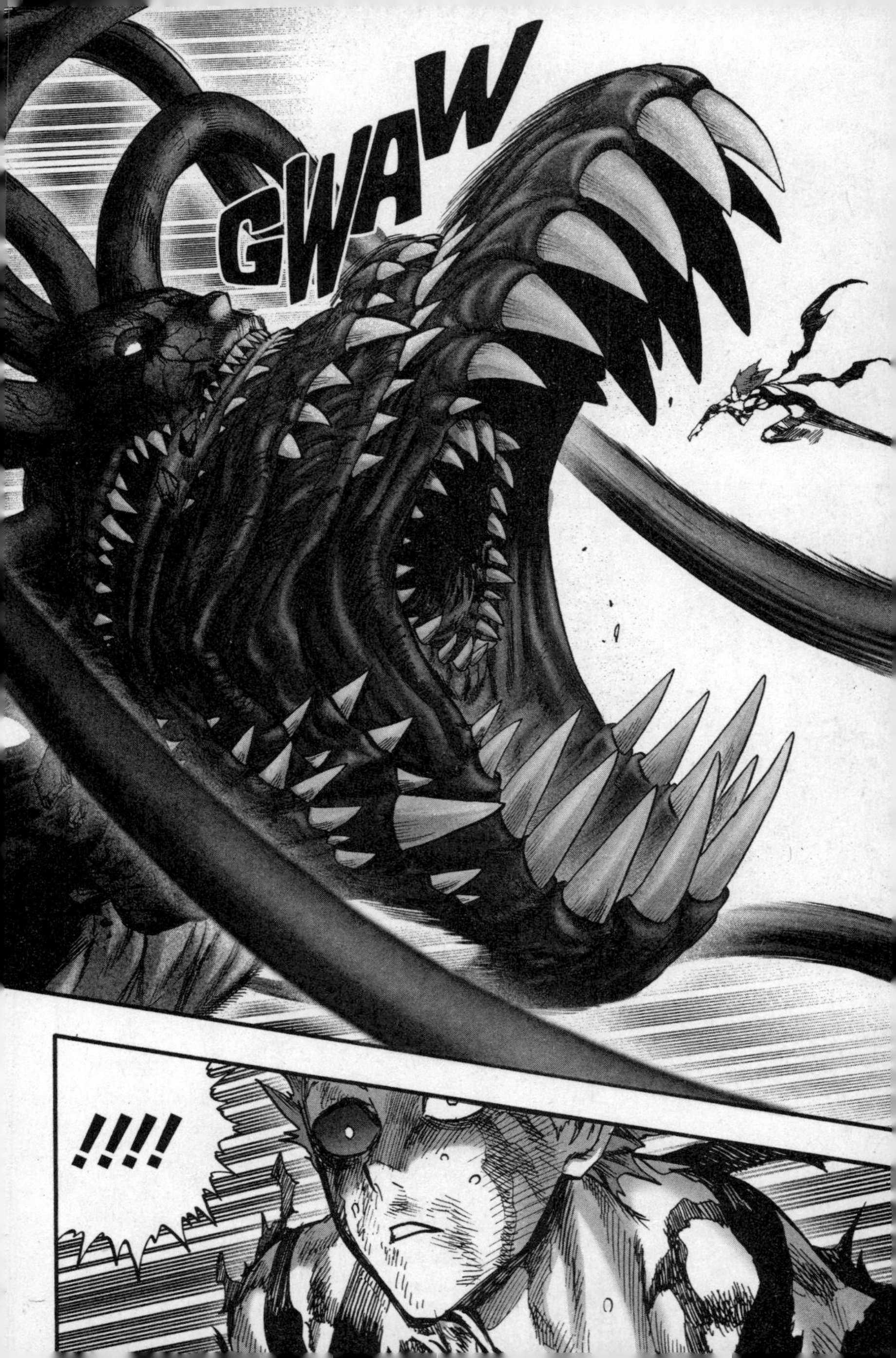
GWAW
!!!!

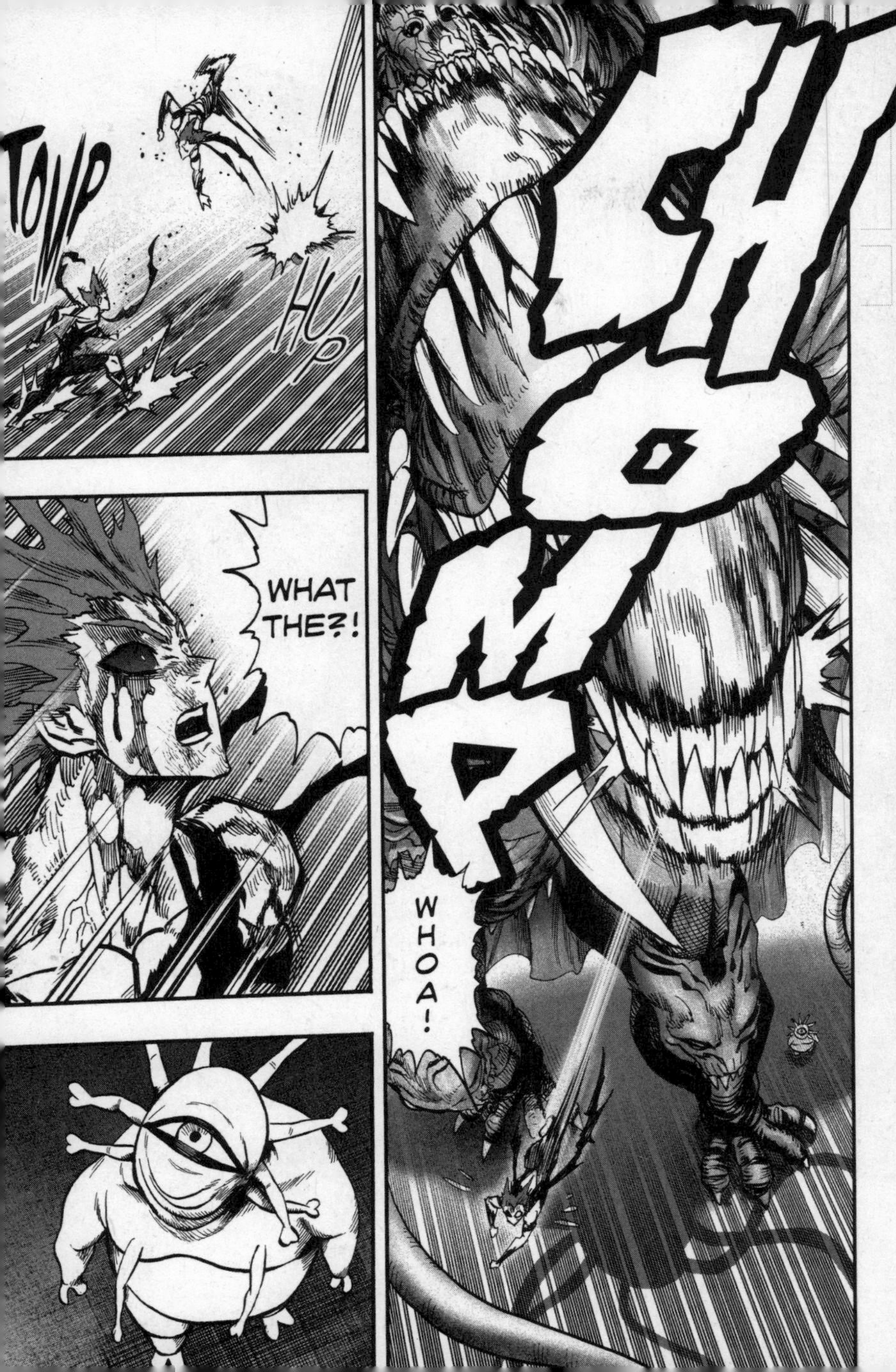
CHOMP
WHOA!
TOMP
HUP
WHAT THE?!

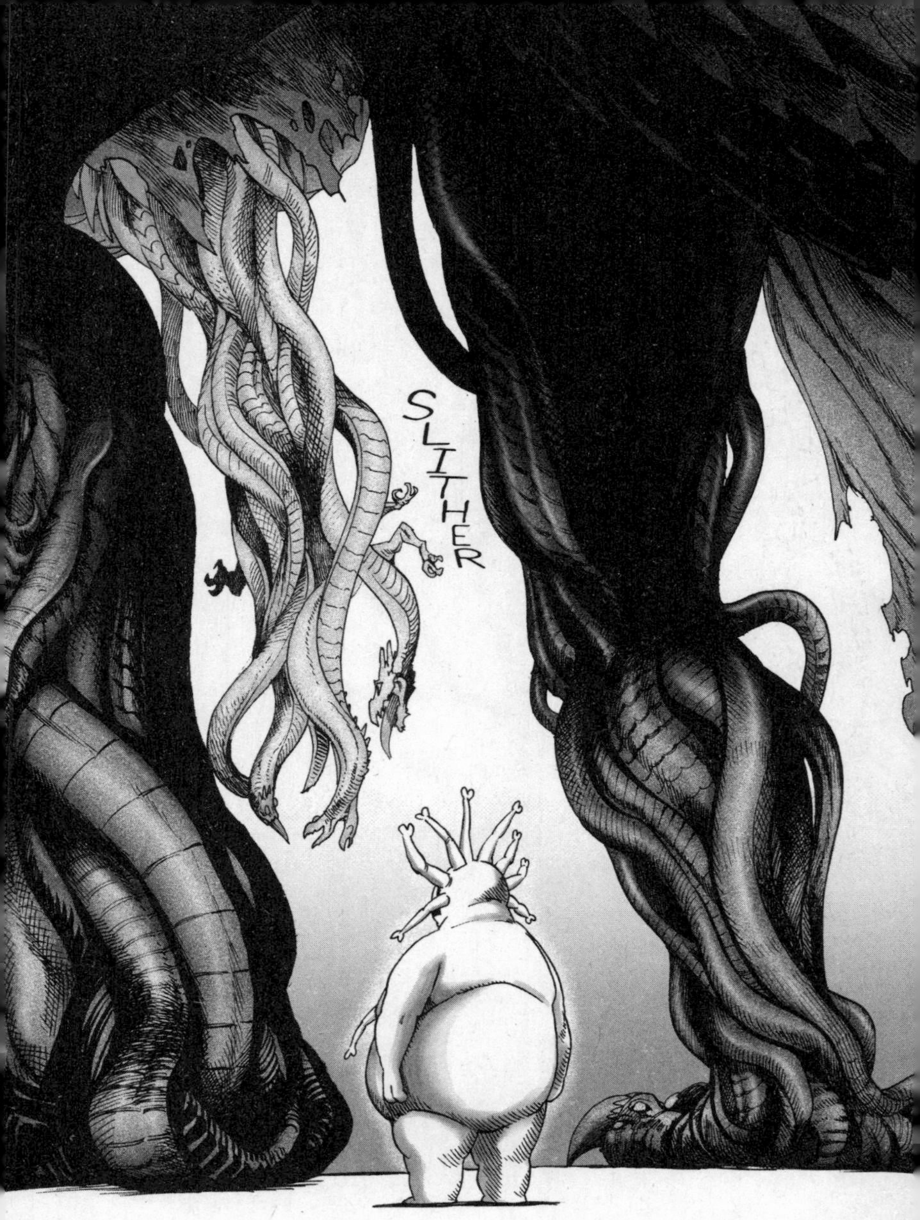
SLITHER

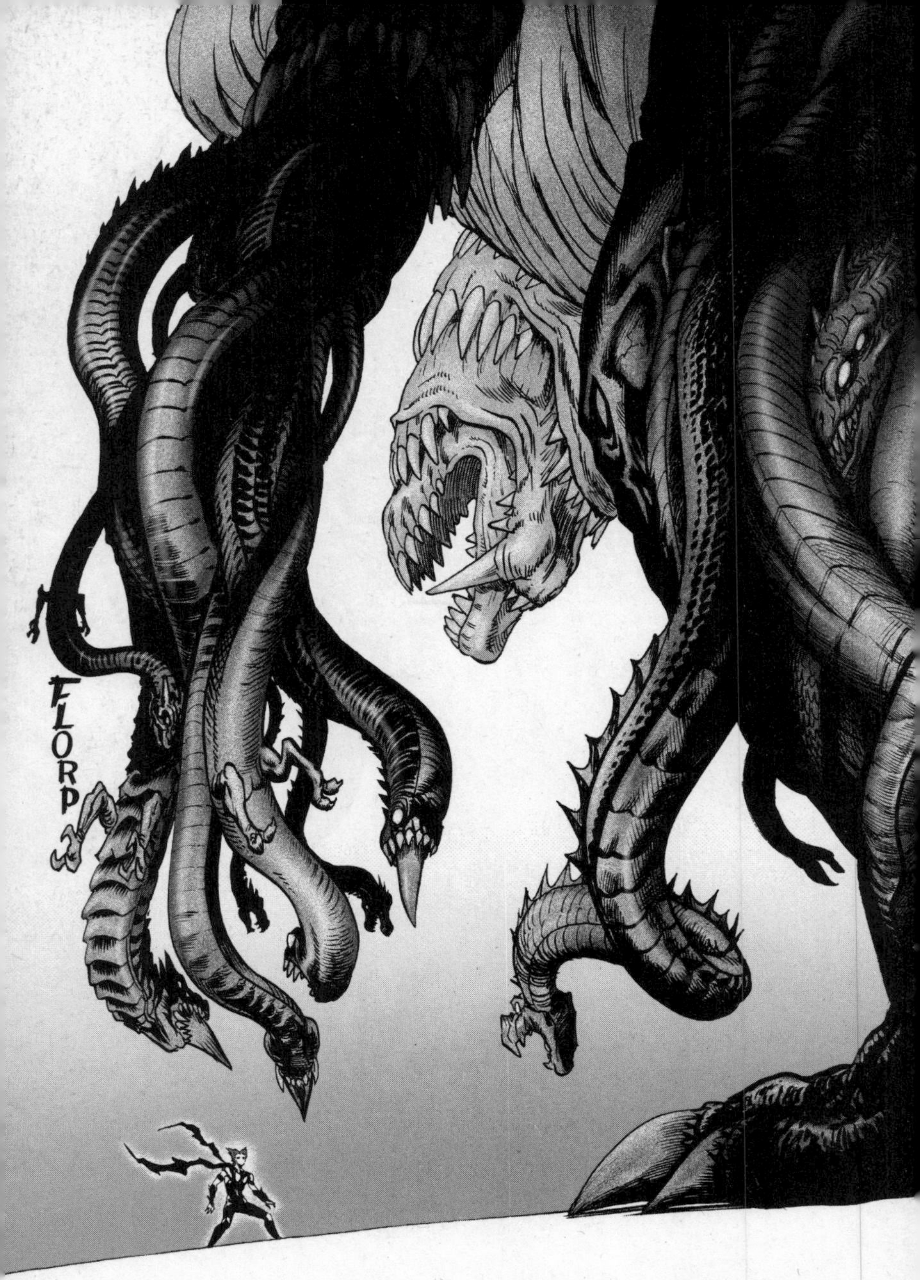
FLORP

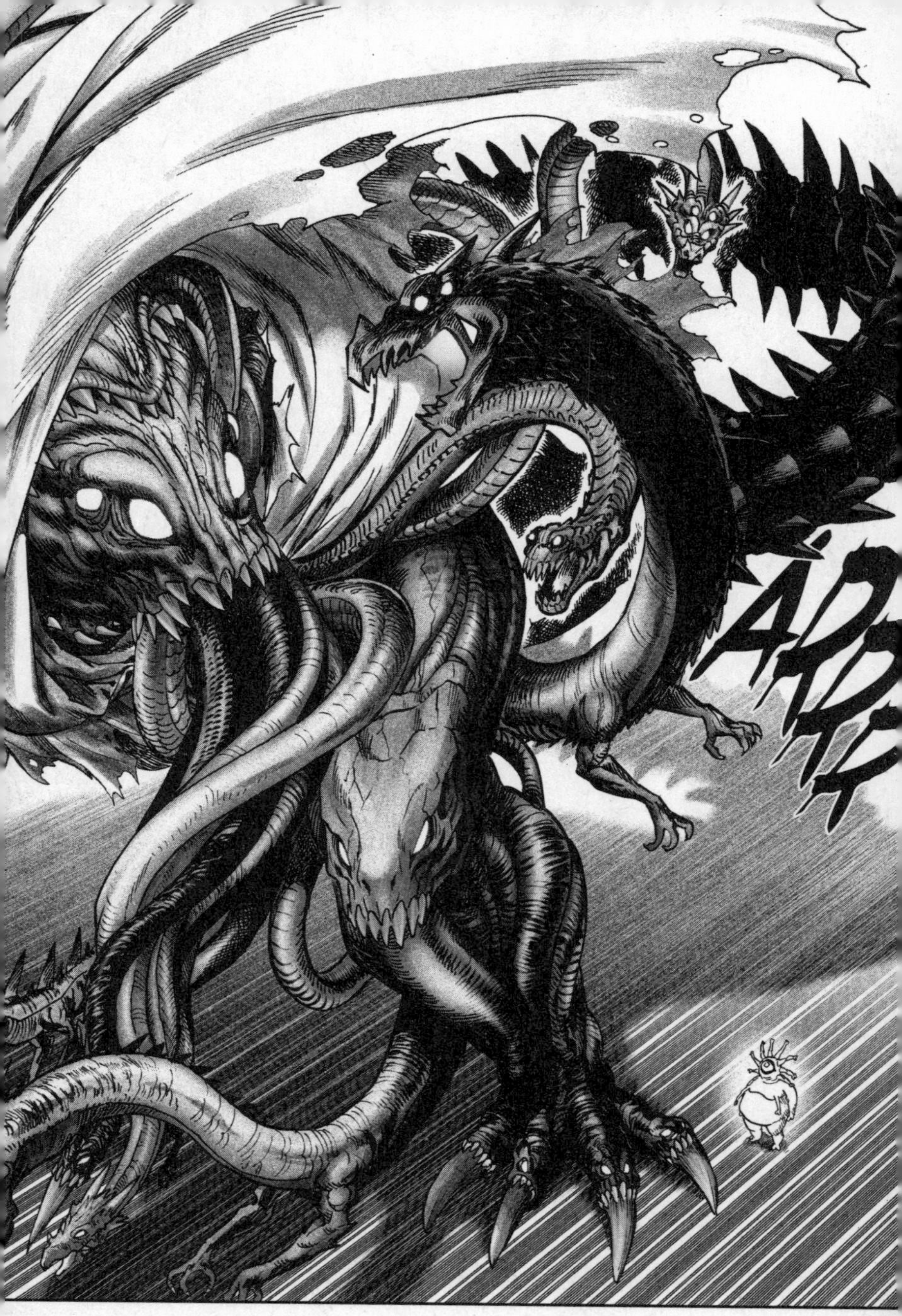
ÁRRR

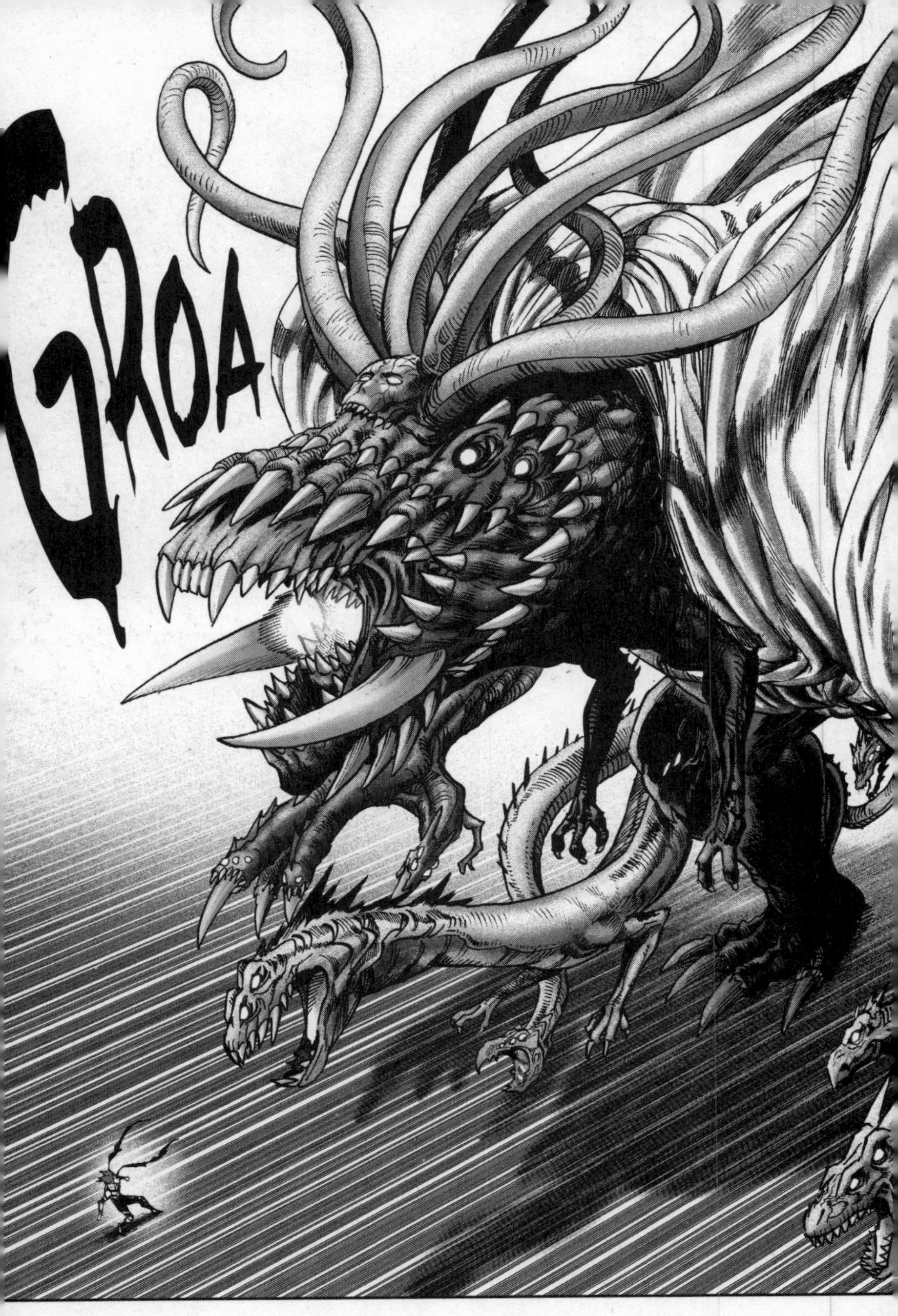
GROA

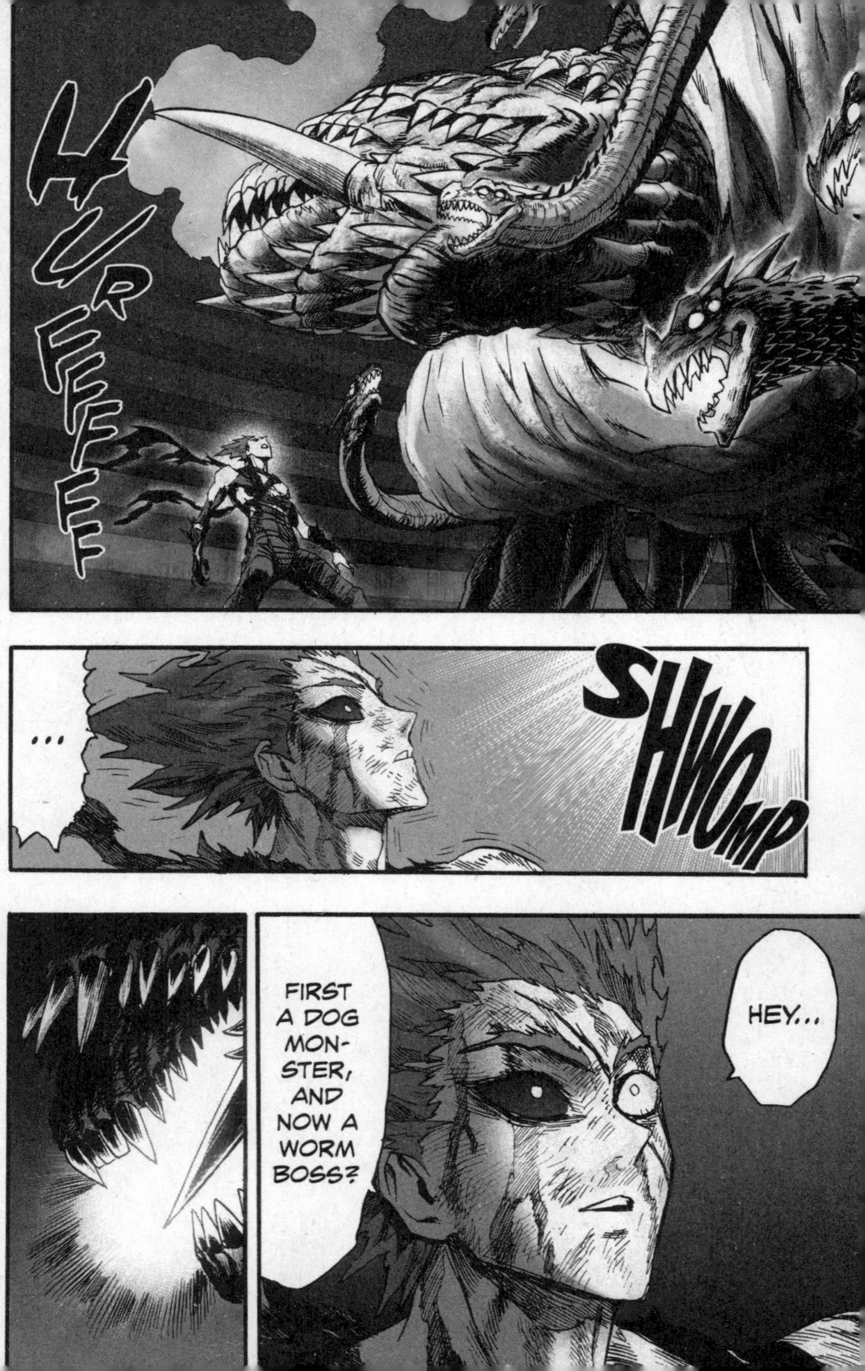
HURFFFFFF
SHWOMP
...
HEY...
FIRST A DOG MONSTER, AND NOW A WORM BOSS?

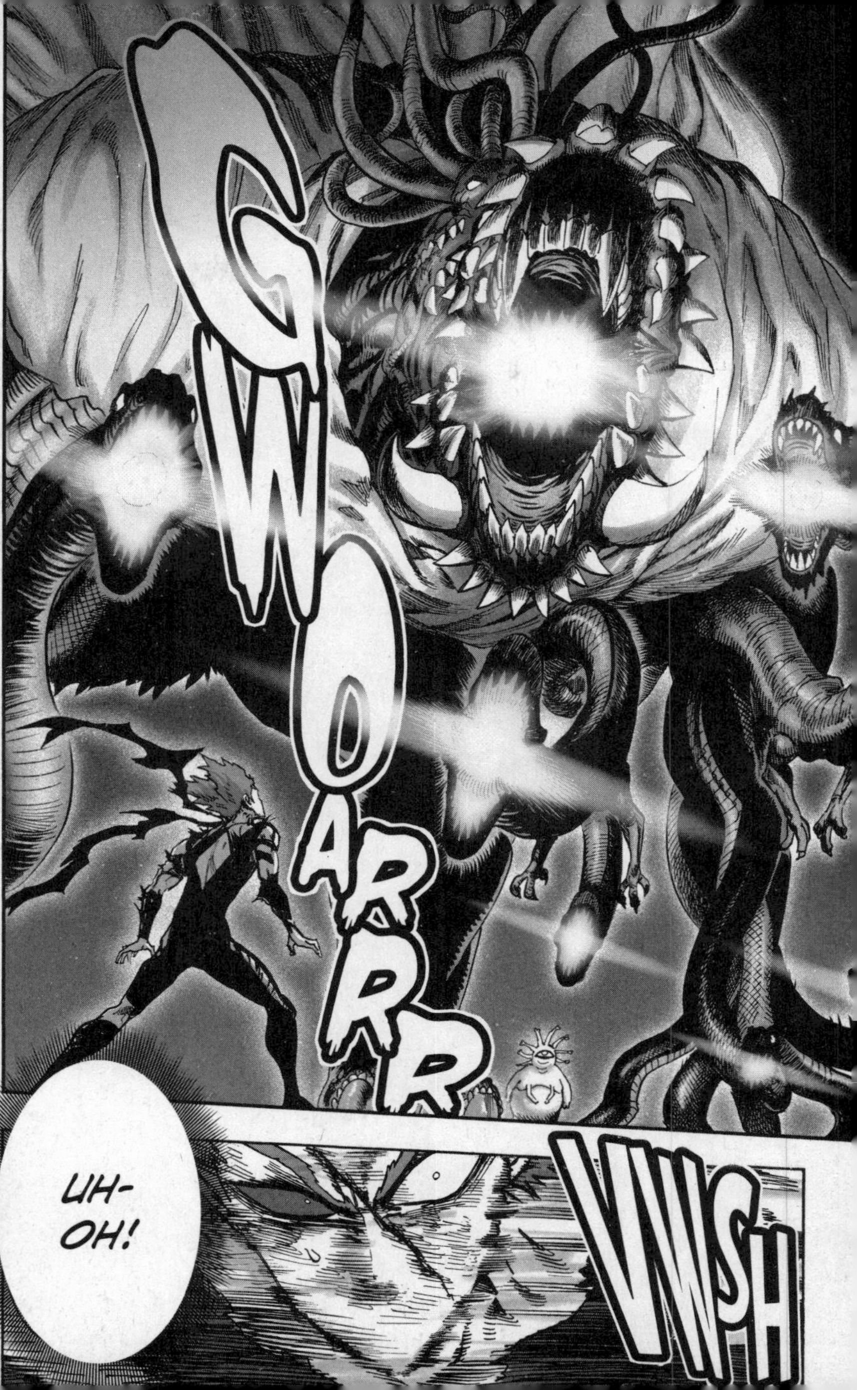
GWOARRR
UH-OH!
VWSH

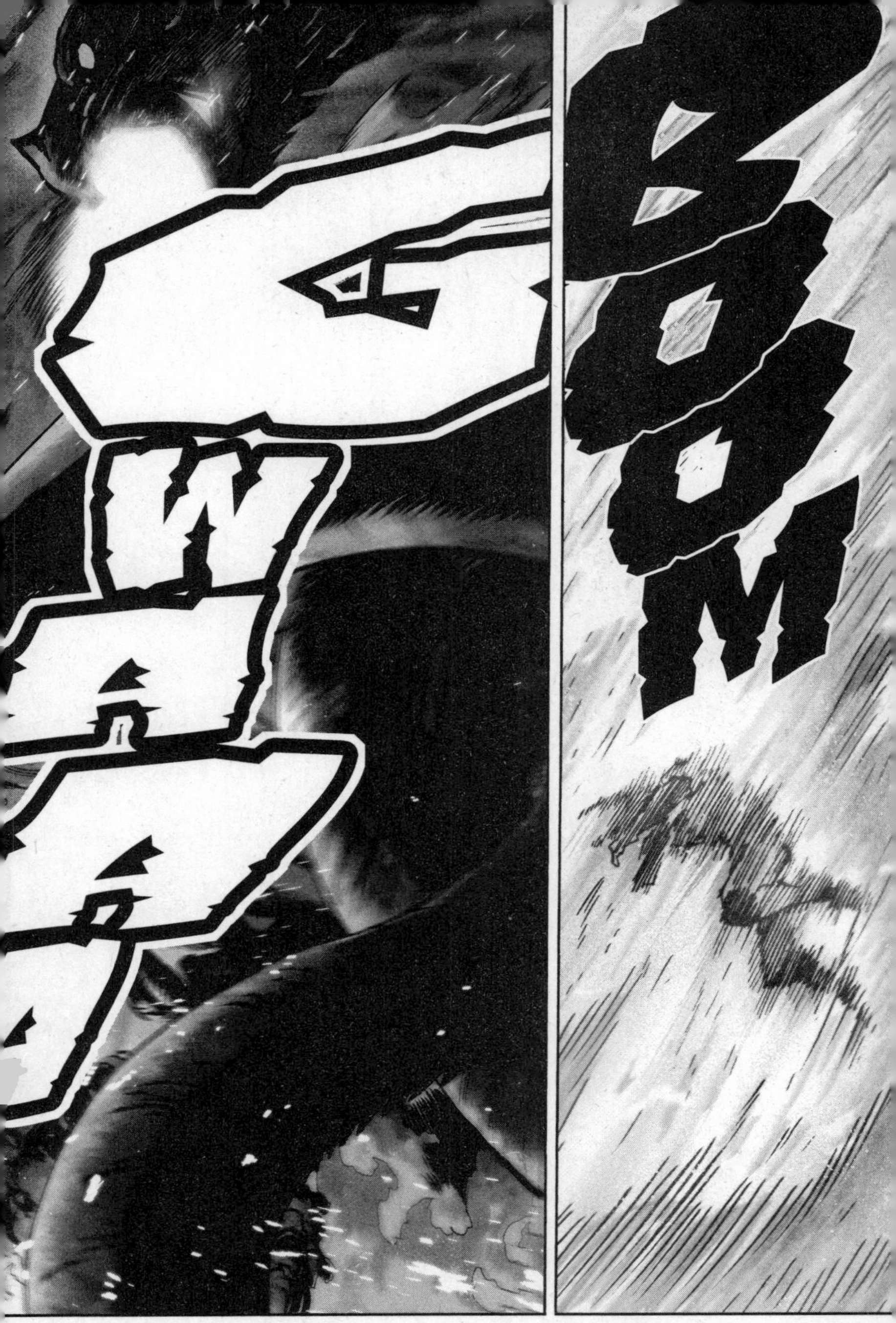
BOOM
GWAAA

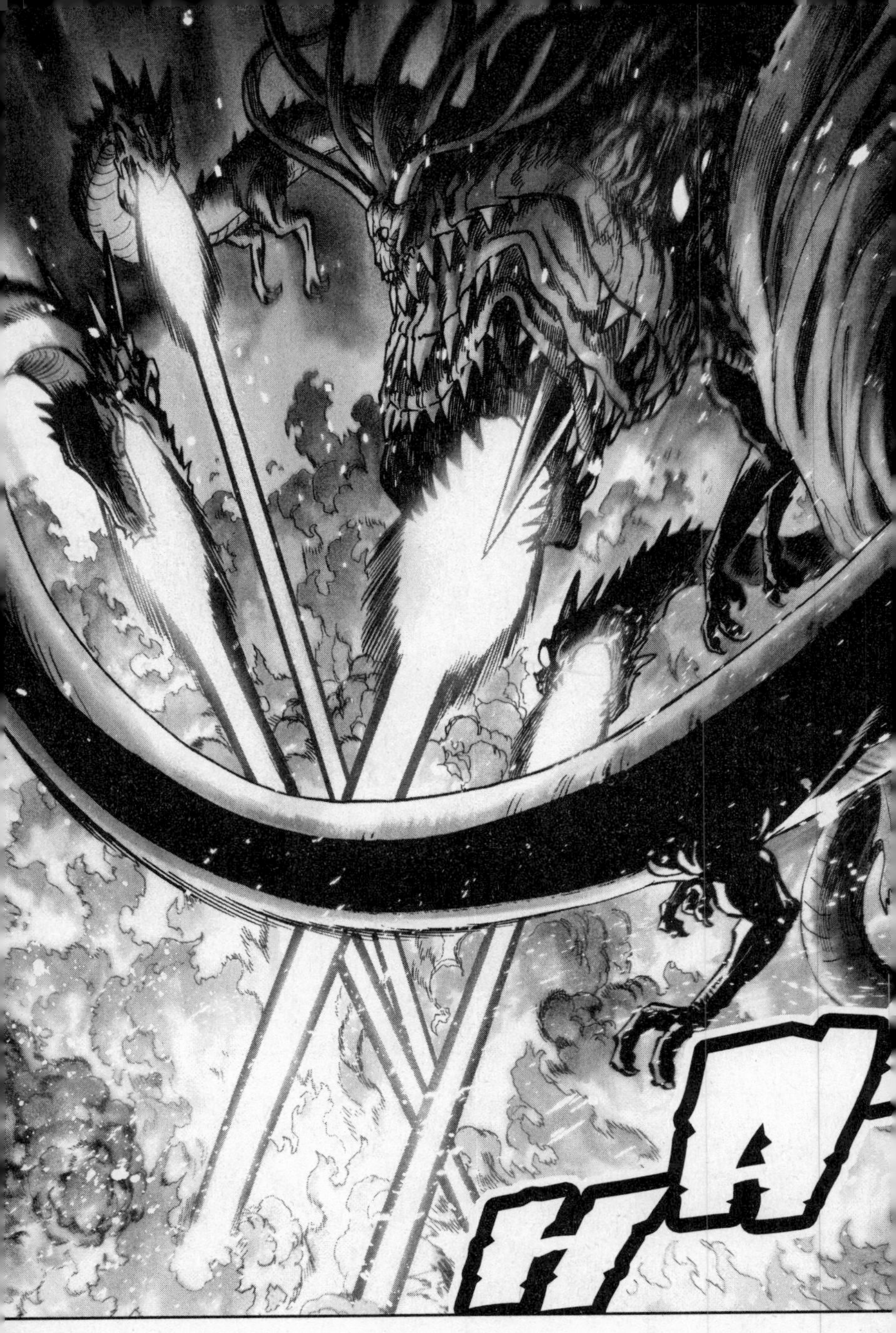
HA

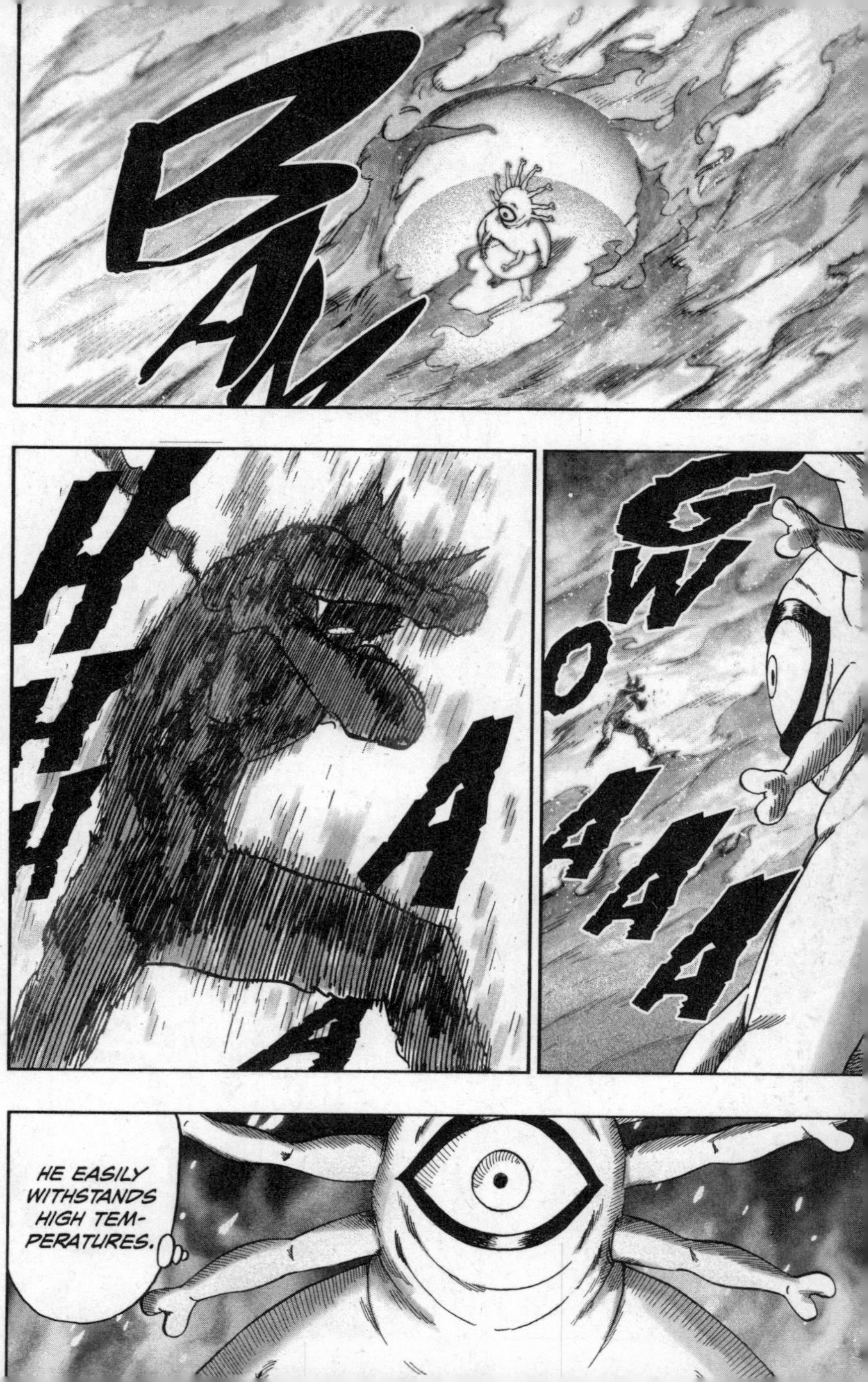
BAM
GWOOAAAAA
HE EASILY WITHSTANDS HIGH TEM-PERATURES.

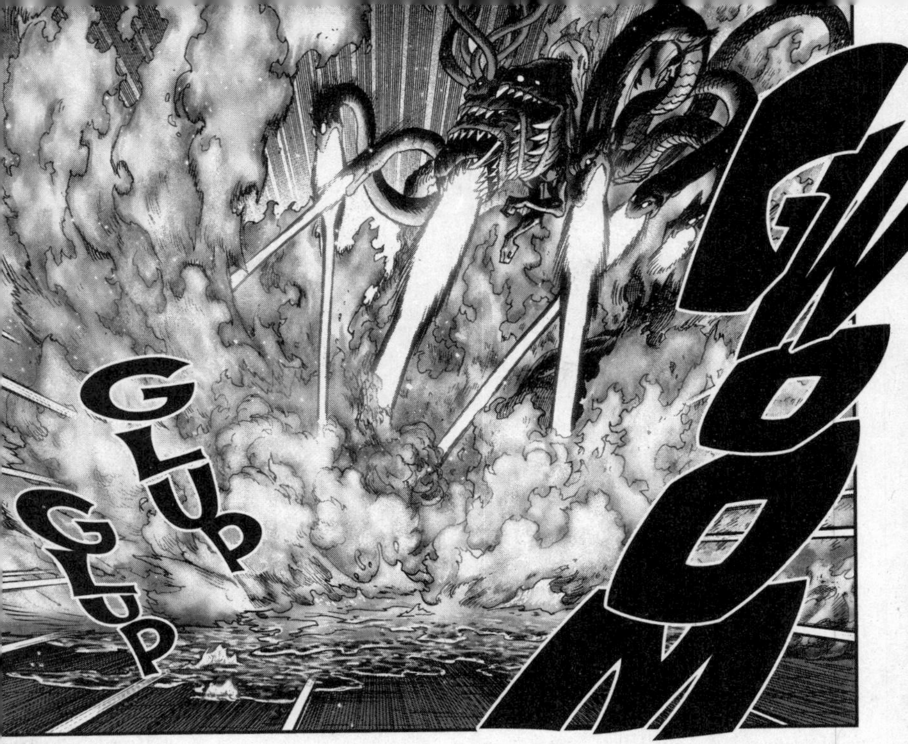
GWOOM
GLUP
GLUP
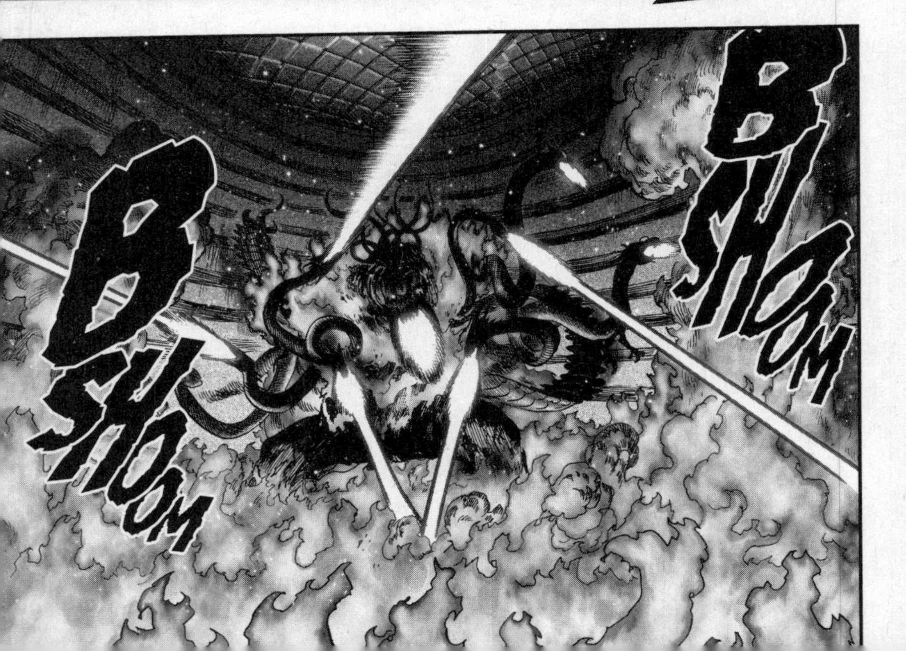
BSHOOM
BSHOOM

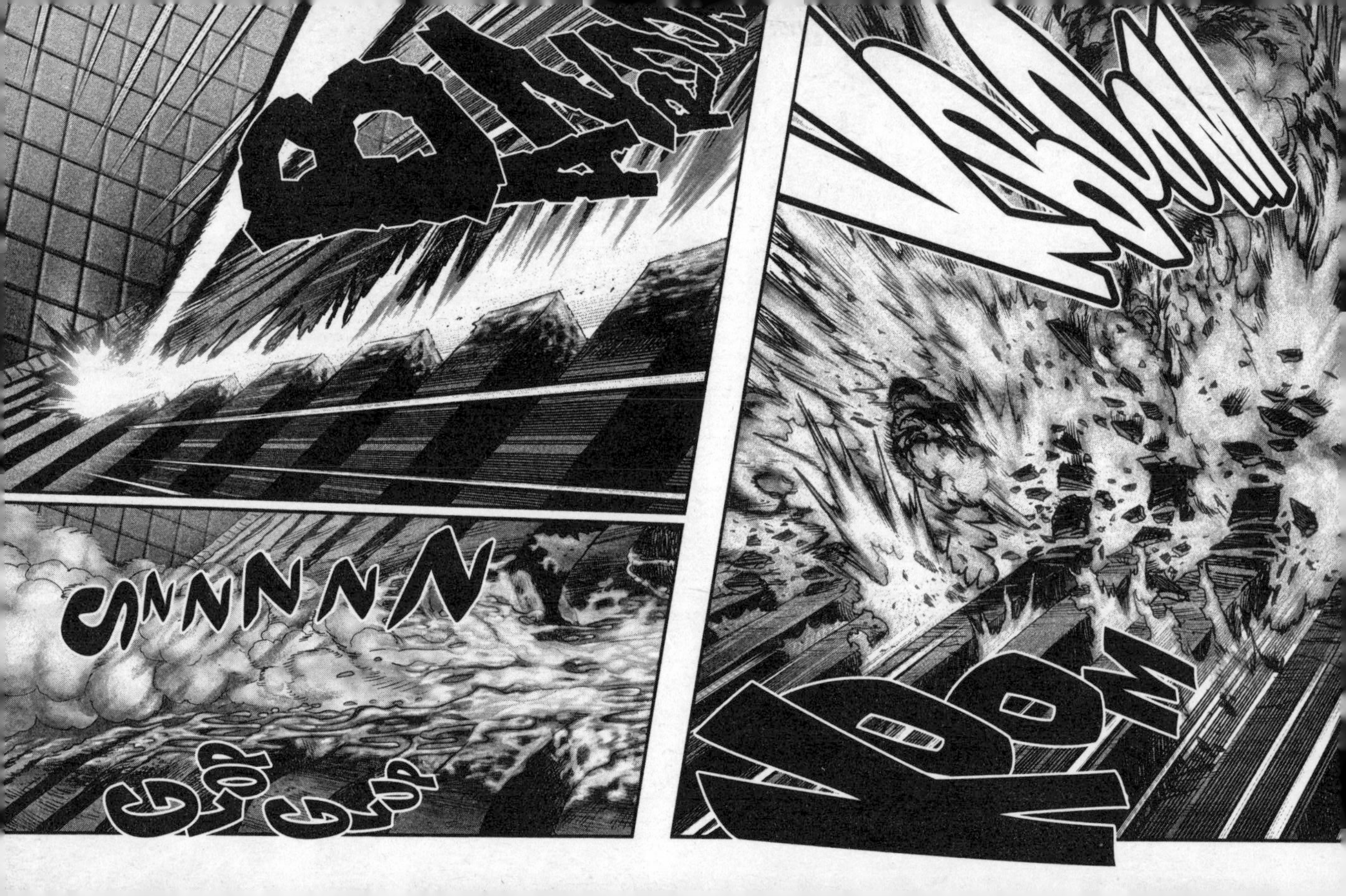
SNNNNN
GLOP
GLUP

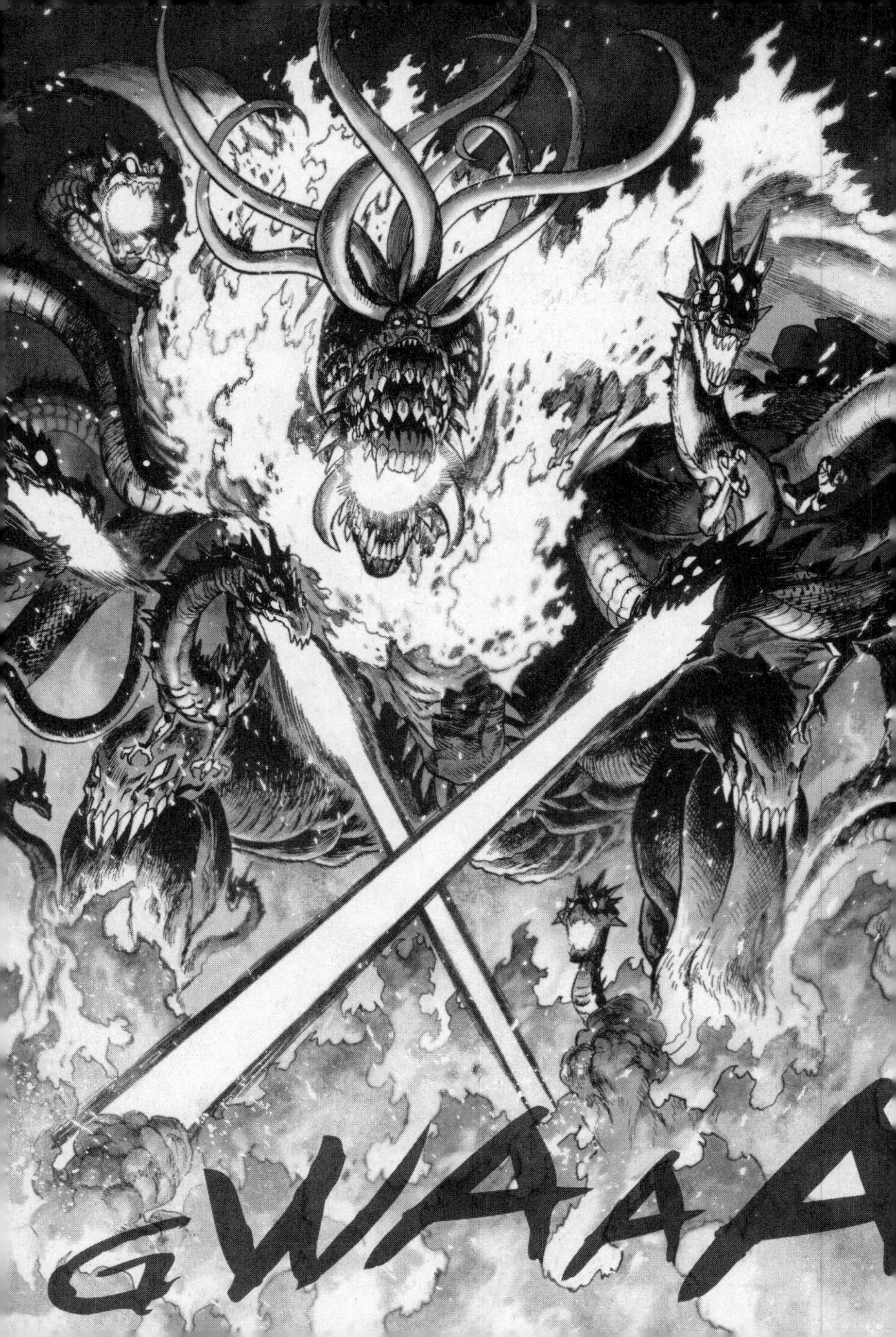
GWAAA

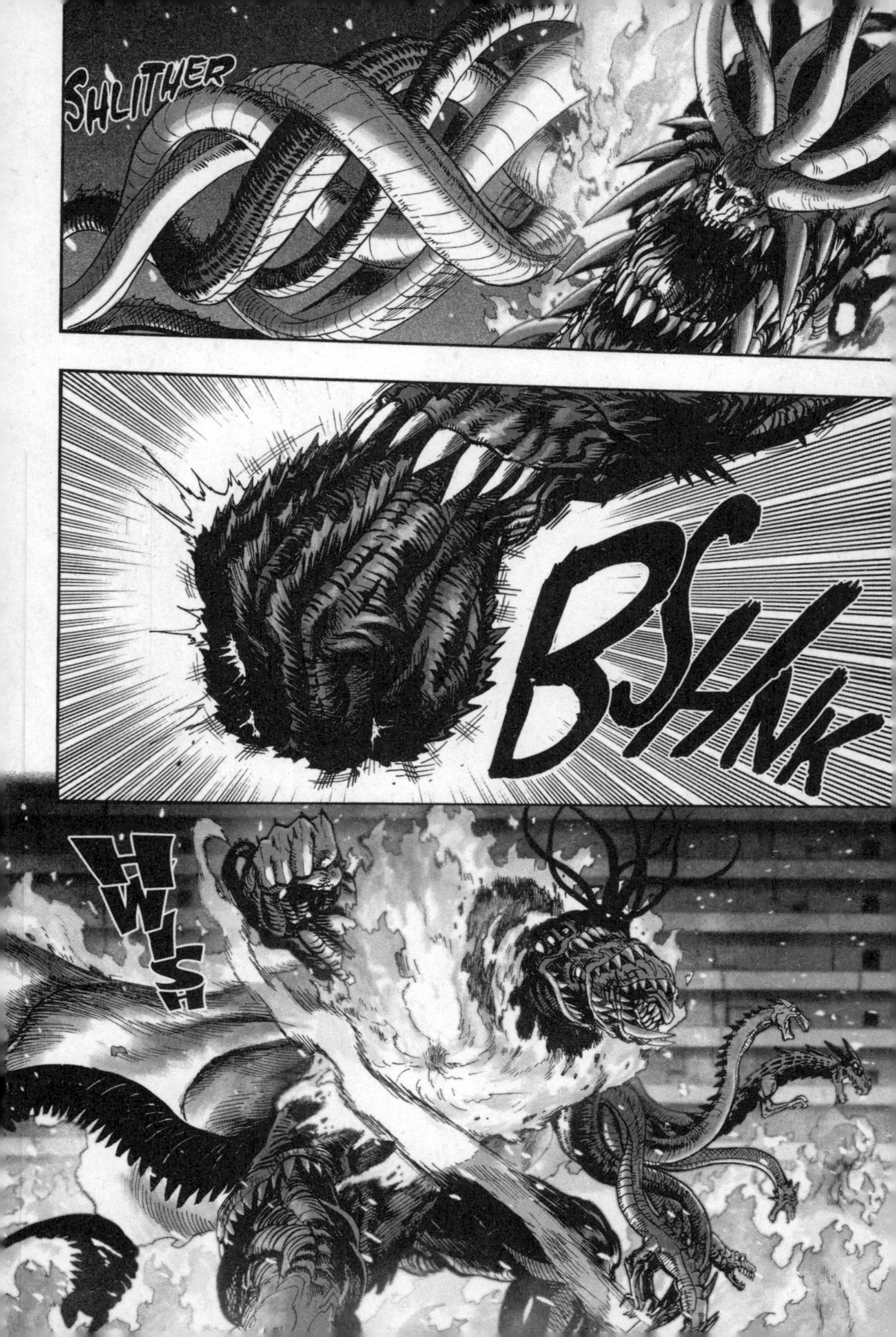
SHLITHER
BSHNK
HWISH

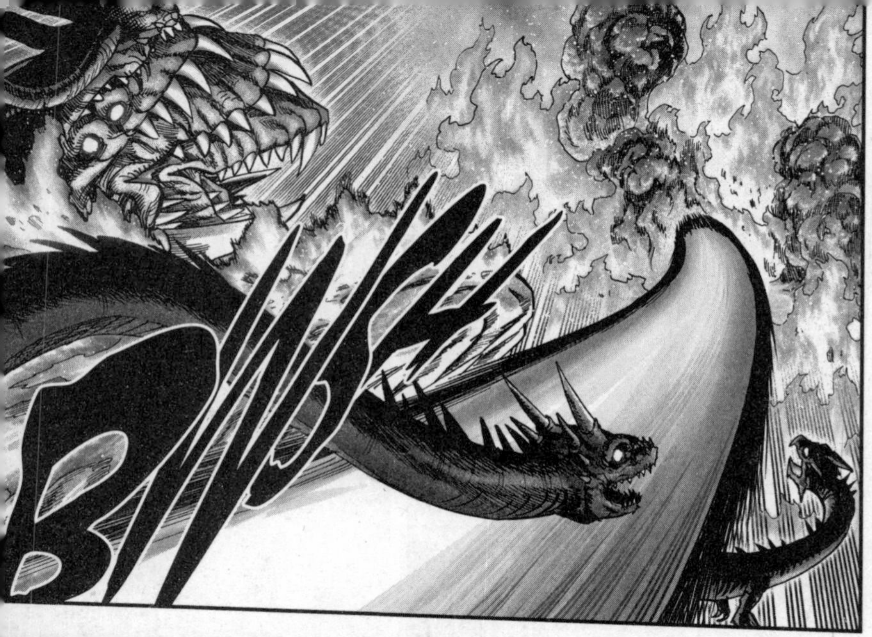

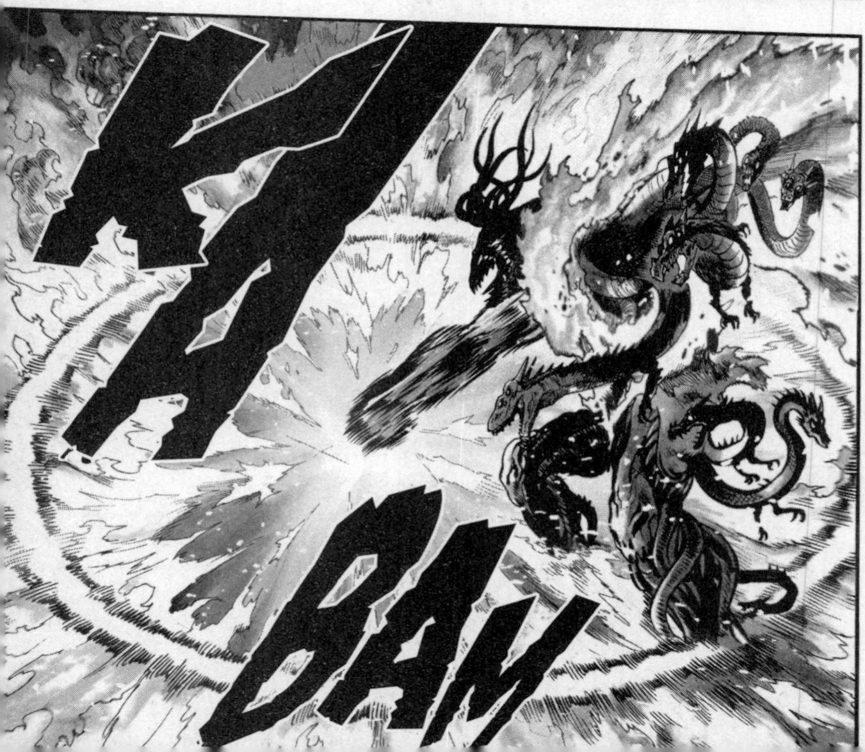
KA
BAM

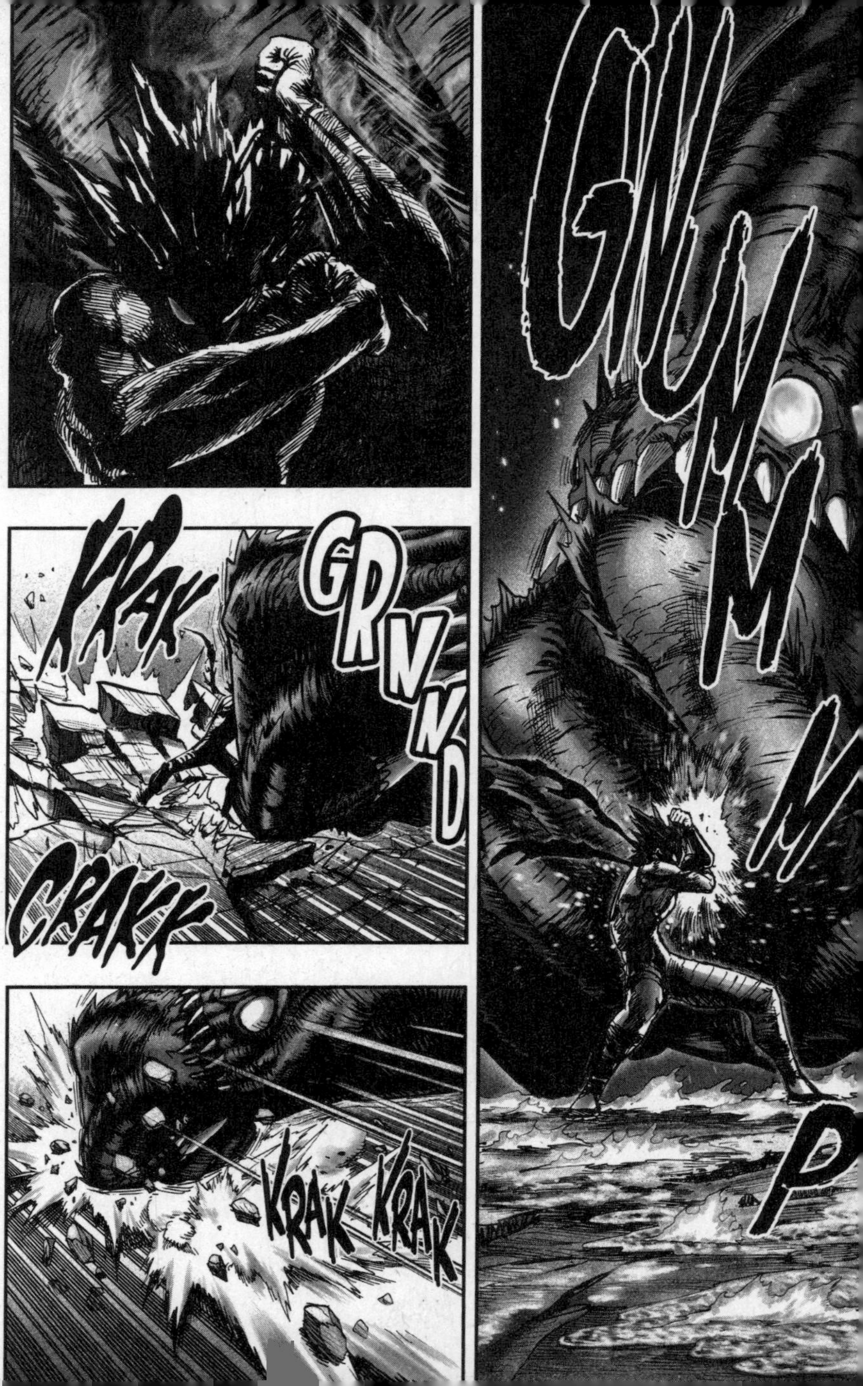
GUMMMMP
GRNNND
KRAK
CRAKK
KRAK KRAK

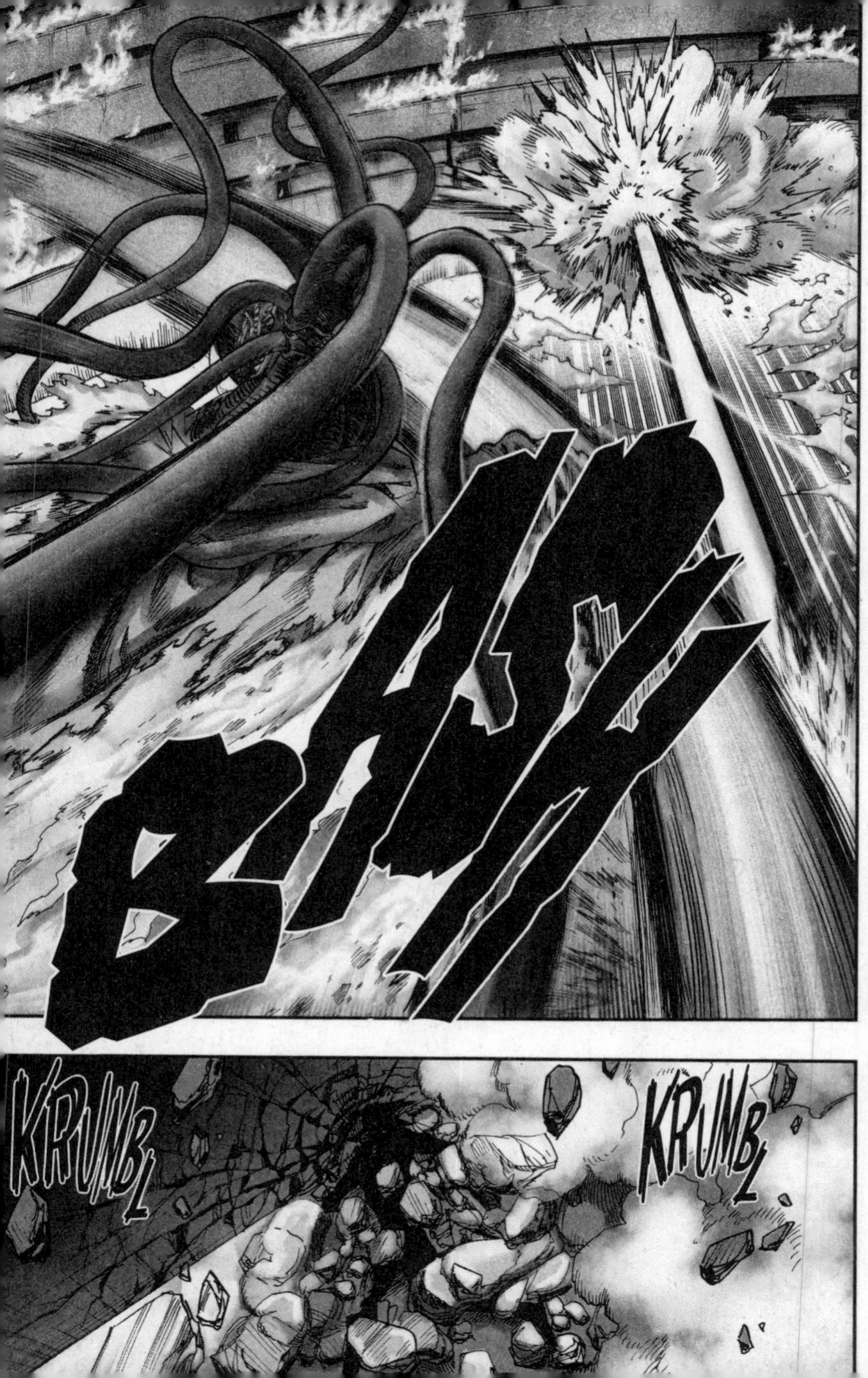
KRUMBL
KRUMBL

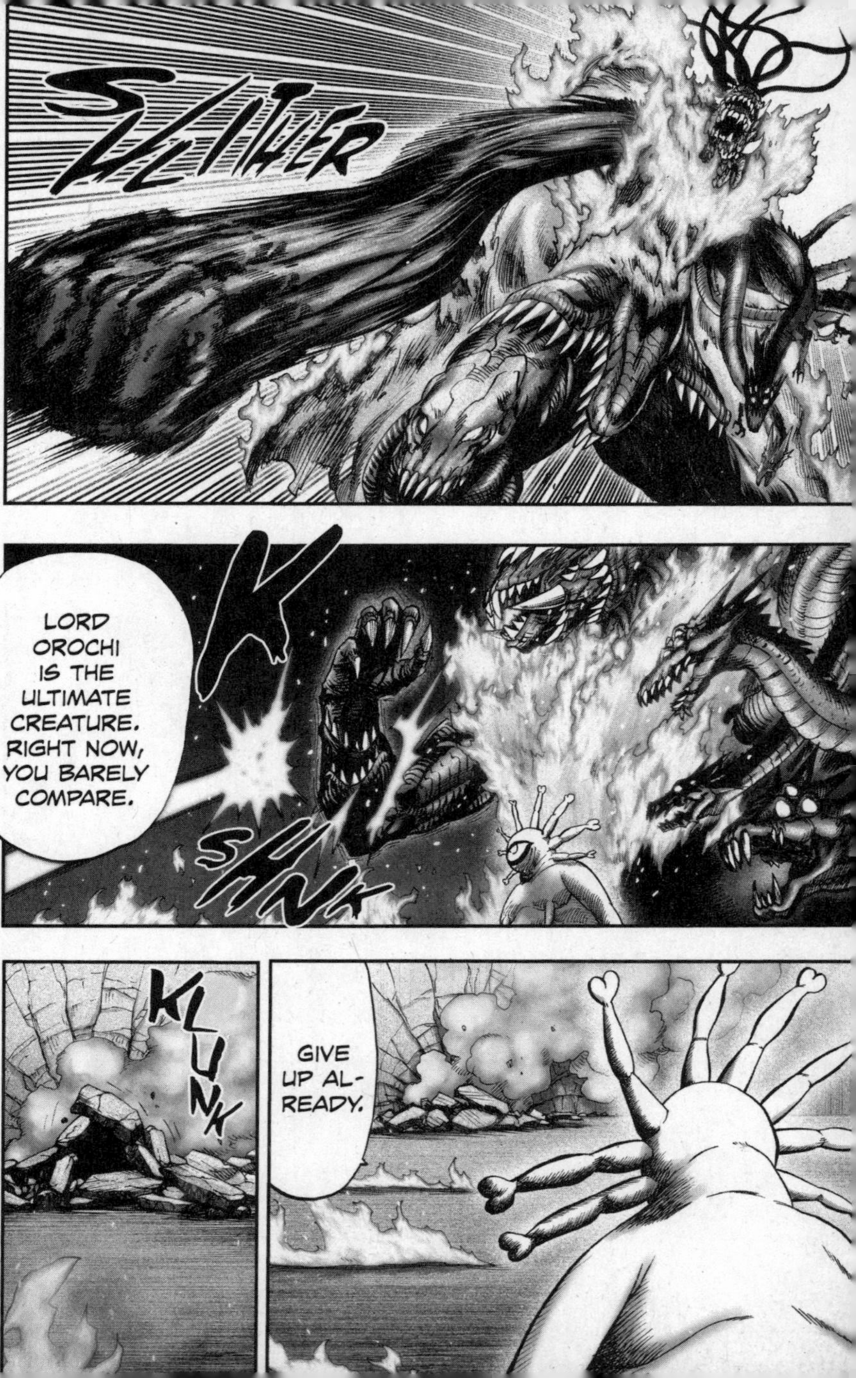
SLITHER
K
LORD OROCHI IS THE ULTIMATE CREATURE. RIGHT NOW, YOU BARELY COMPARE.
SHINK
KLUNK
GIVE UP AL-READY.

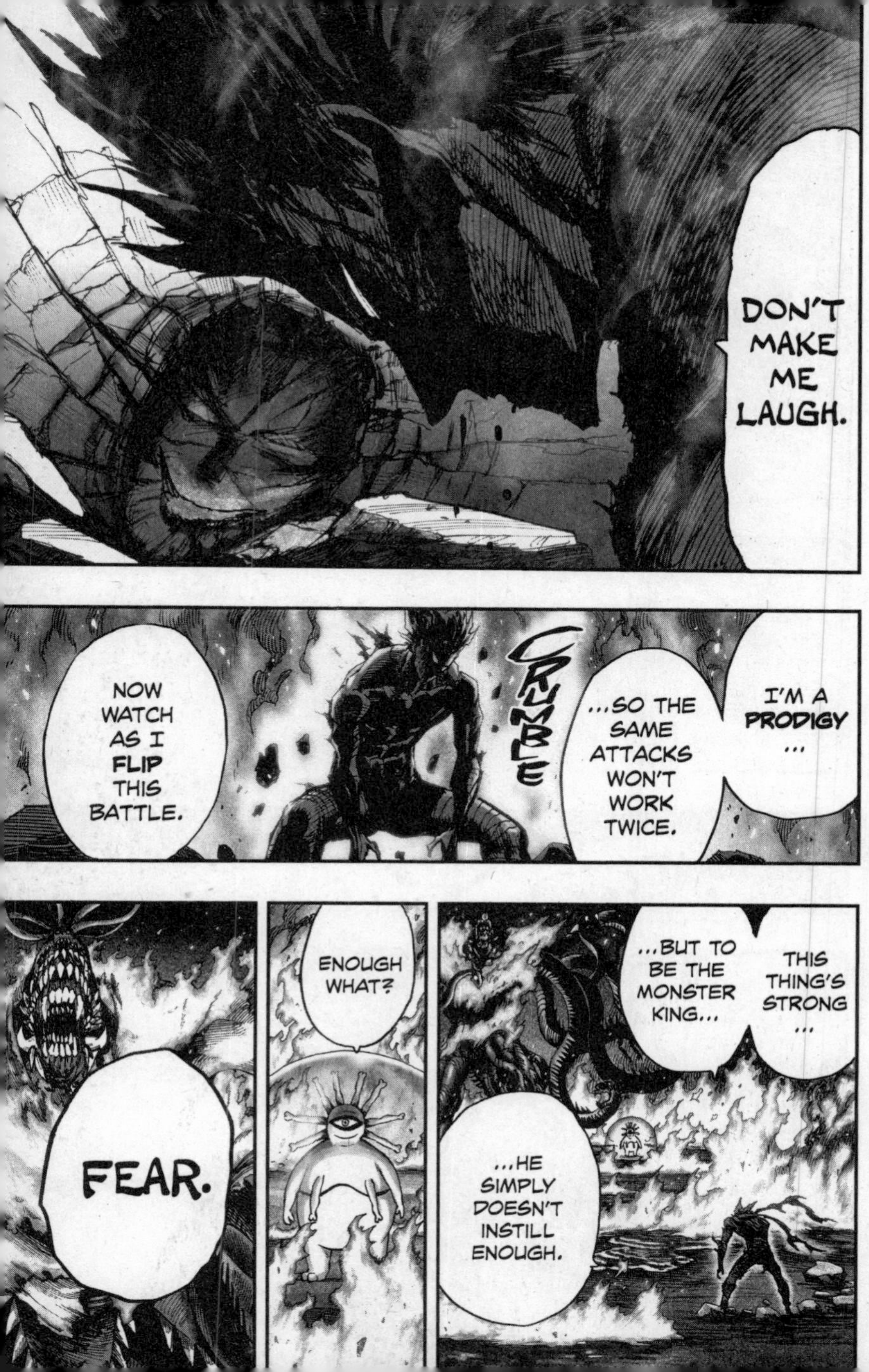
DON'T MAKE ME LAUGH.
I'M A PRODIGY...
...SO THE SAME ATTACKS WON'T WORK TWICE.
CRUMBLE
NOW WATCH AS I FLIP THIS BATTLE.
THIS THING'S STRONG...
...BUT TO BE THE MONSTER KING...
...HE SIMPLY DOESN'T INSTILL ENOUGH.
ENOUGH WHAT?
FEAR.

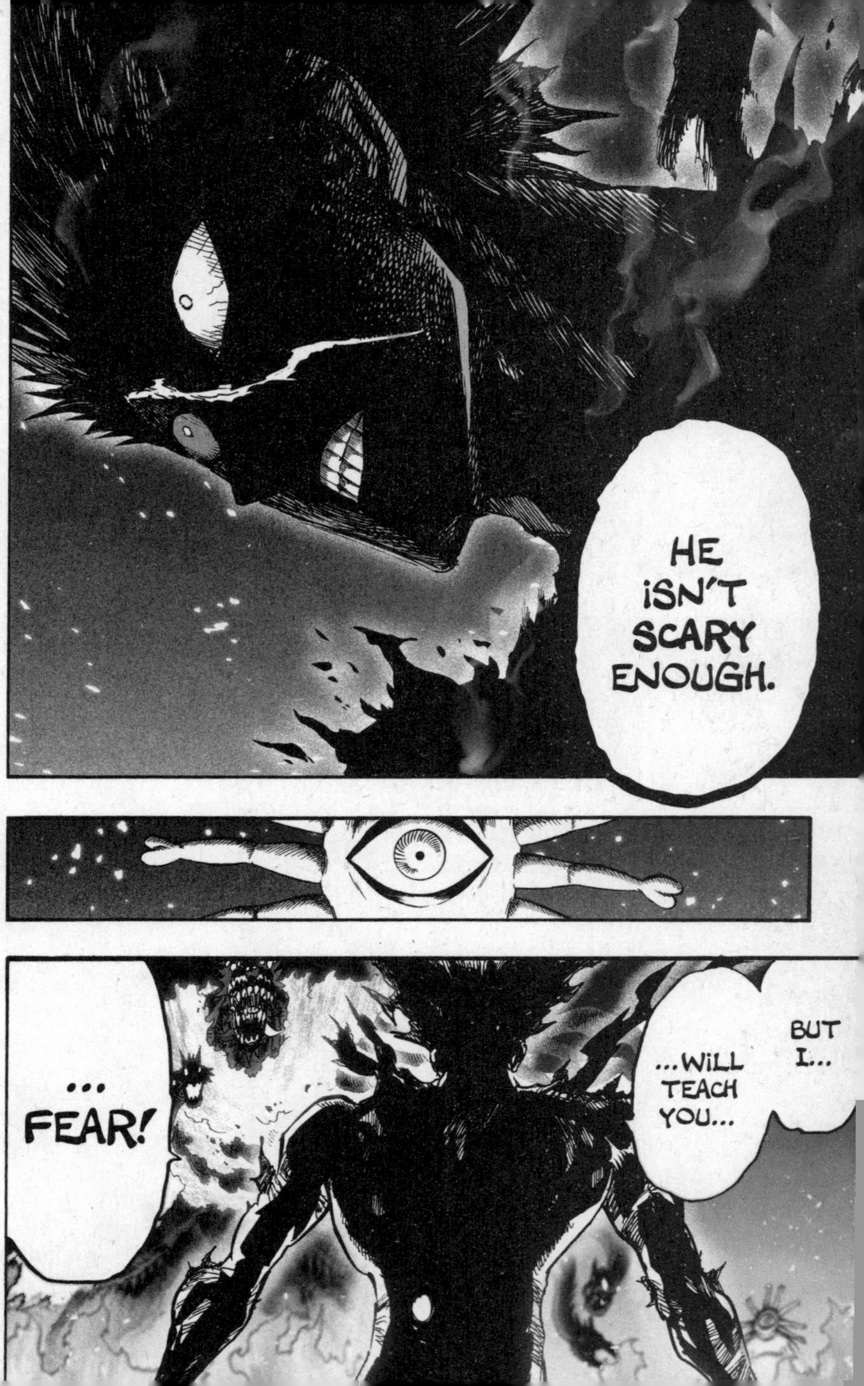
HE ISN'T SCARY ENOUGH.
BUT I...
...WILL TEACH YOU...
... FEAR!

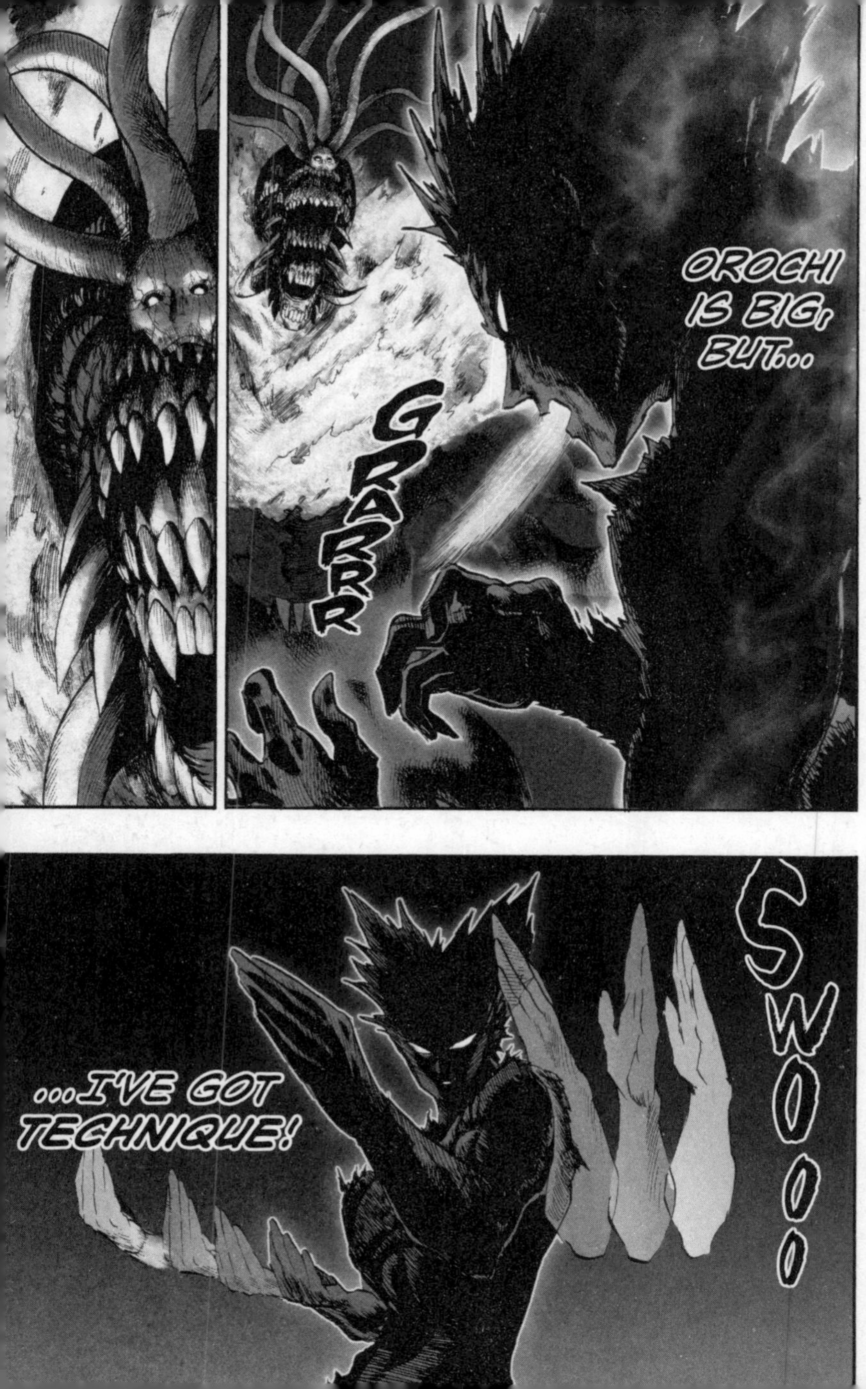
OROCHI IS BIG, BUT...
GRARRR
SWOOO
...I'VE GOT TECHNIQUE!

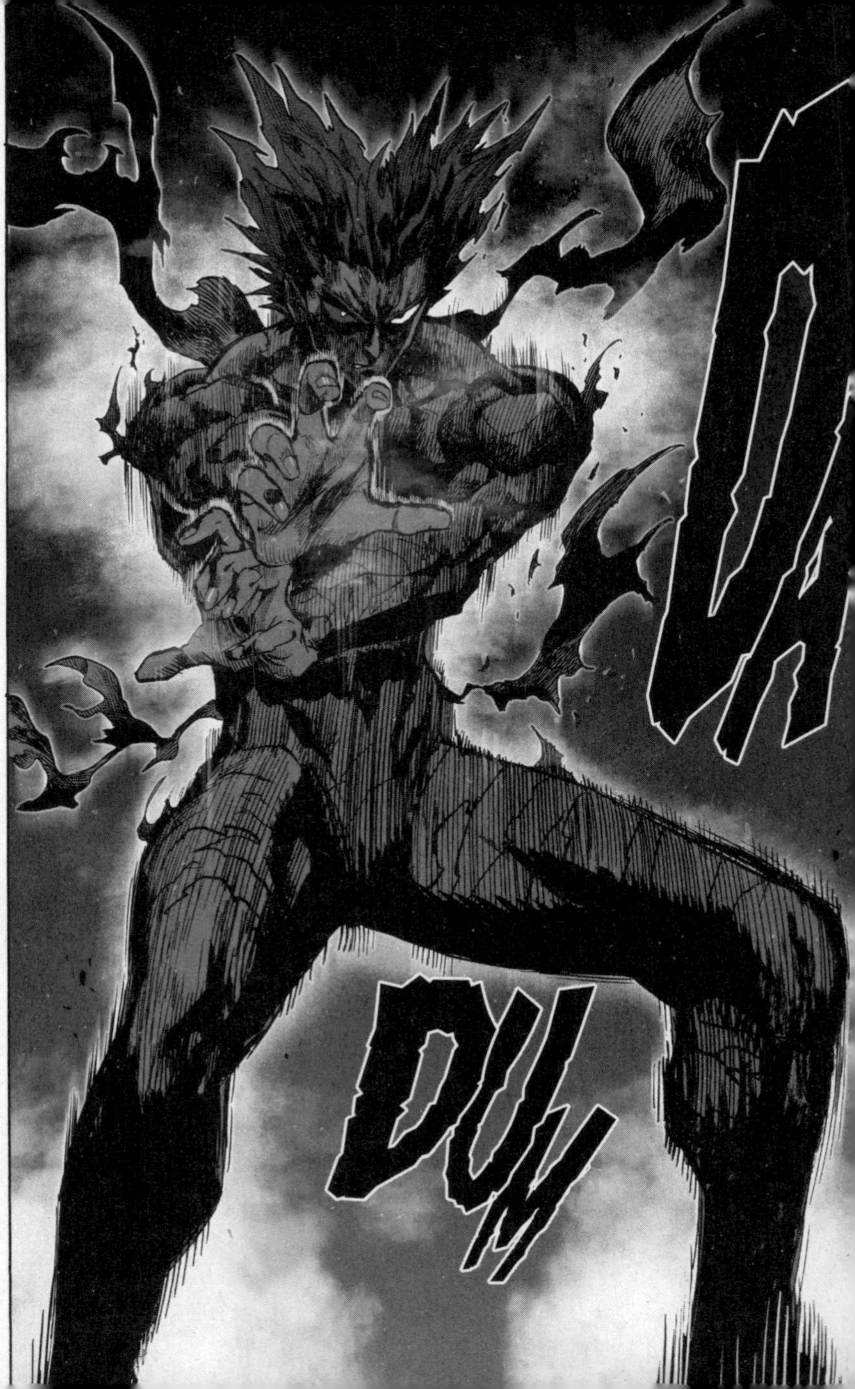
DUN

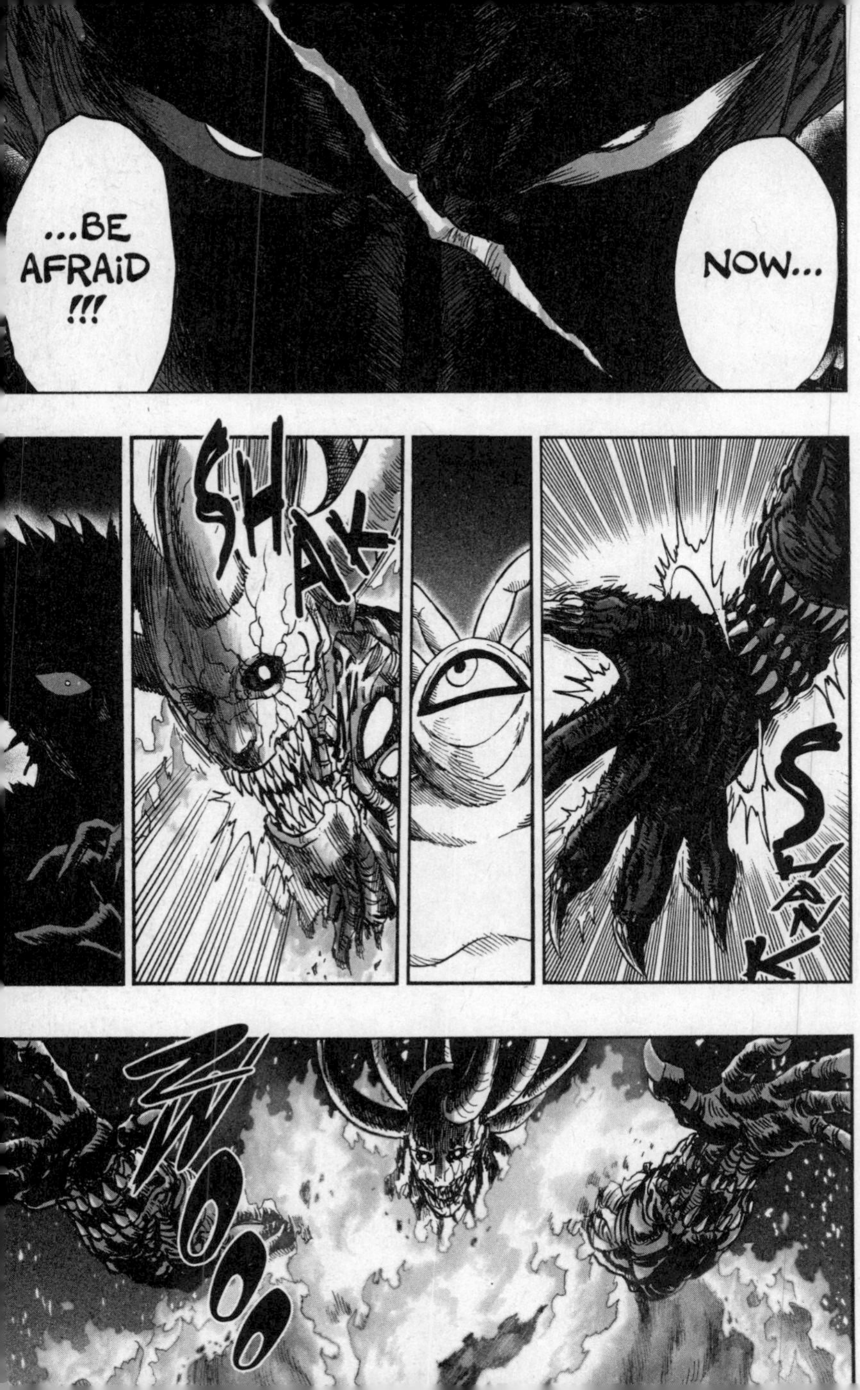
NOW...
...BE AFRAID !!!
SHAK
SWANK
ZWOOO

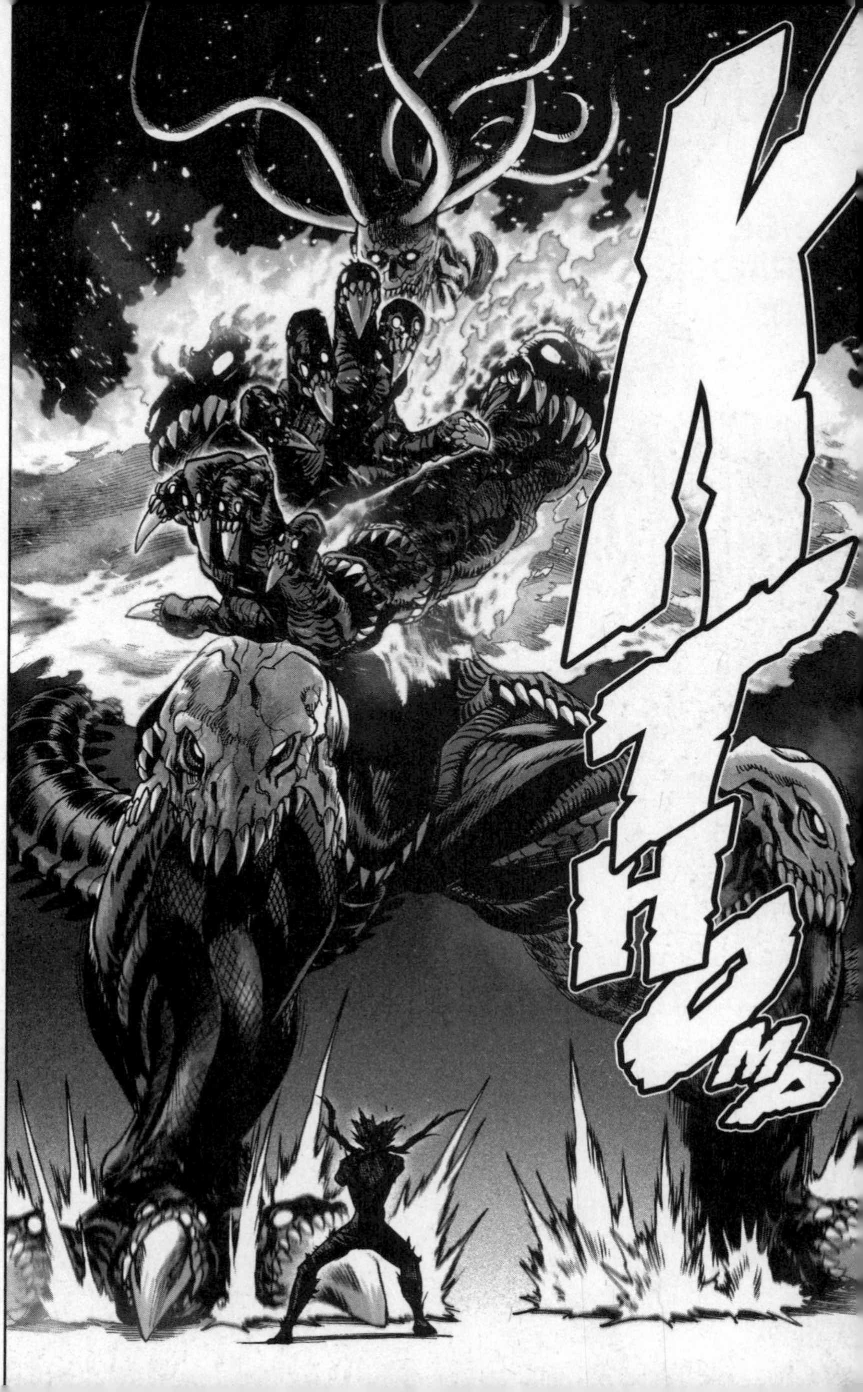

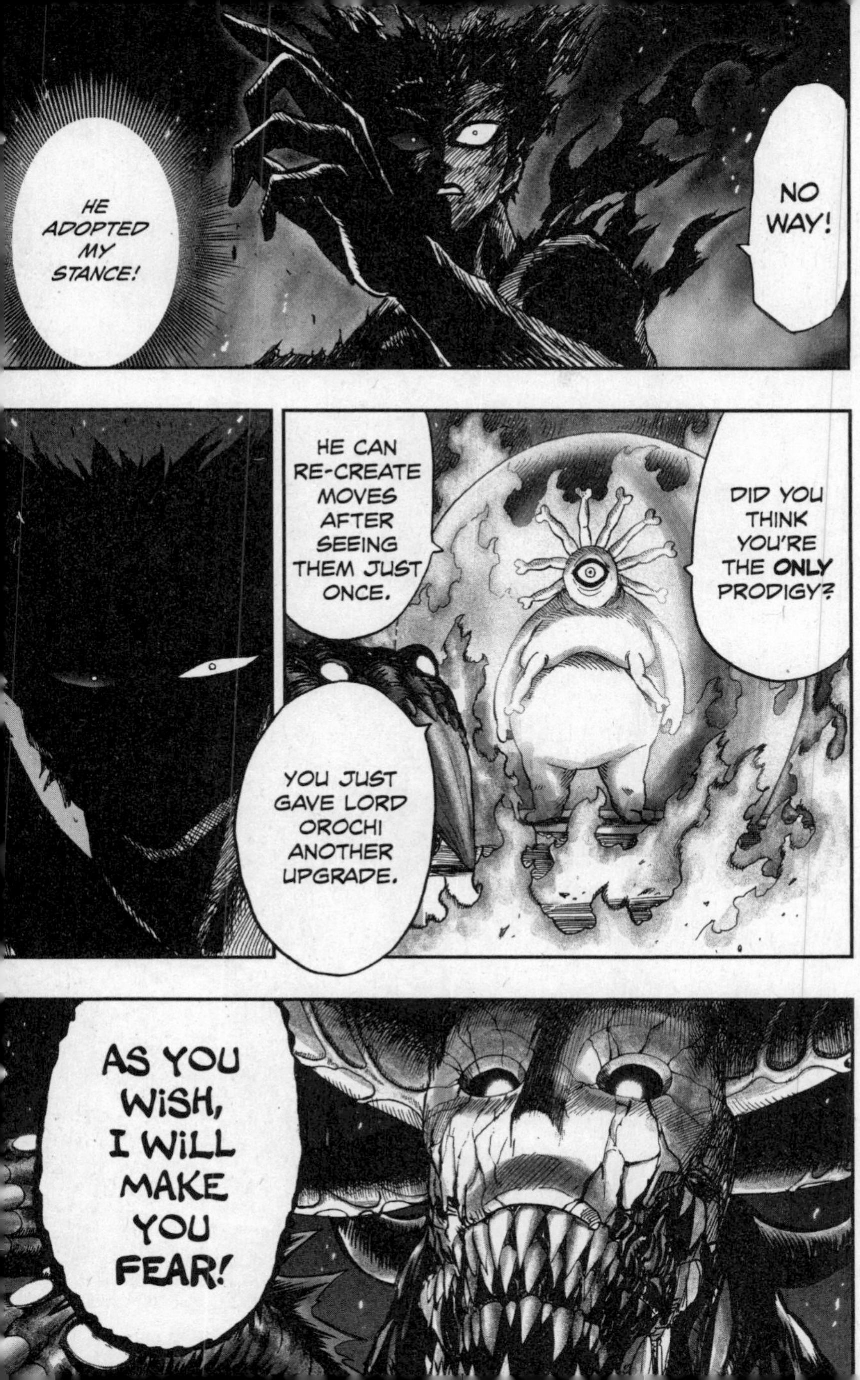
NO WAY!
HE ADOPTED MY STANCE!
DID YOU THINK YOU'RE THE **ONLY** PRODIGY?
HE CAN RE-CREATE MOVES AFTER SEEING THEM JUST ONCE.
YOU JUST GAVE LORD OROCHI ANOTHER UPGRADE.
AS YOU WISH, I WILL MAKE YOU FEAR!

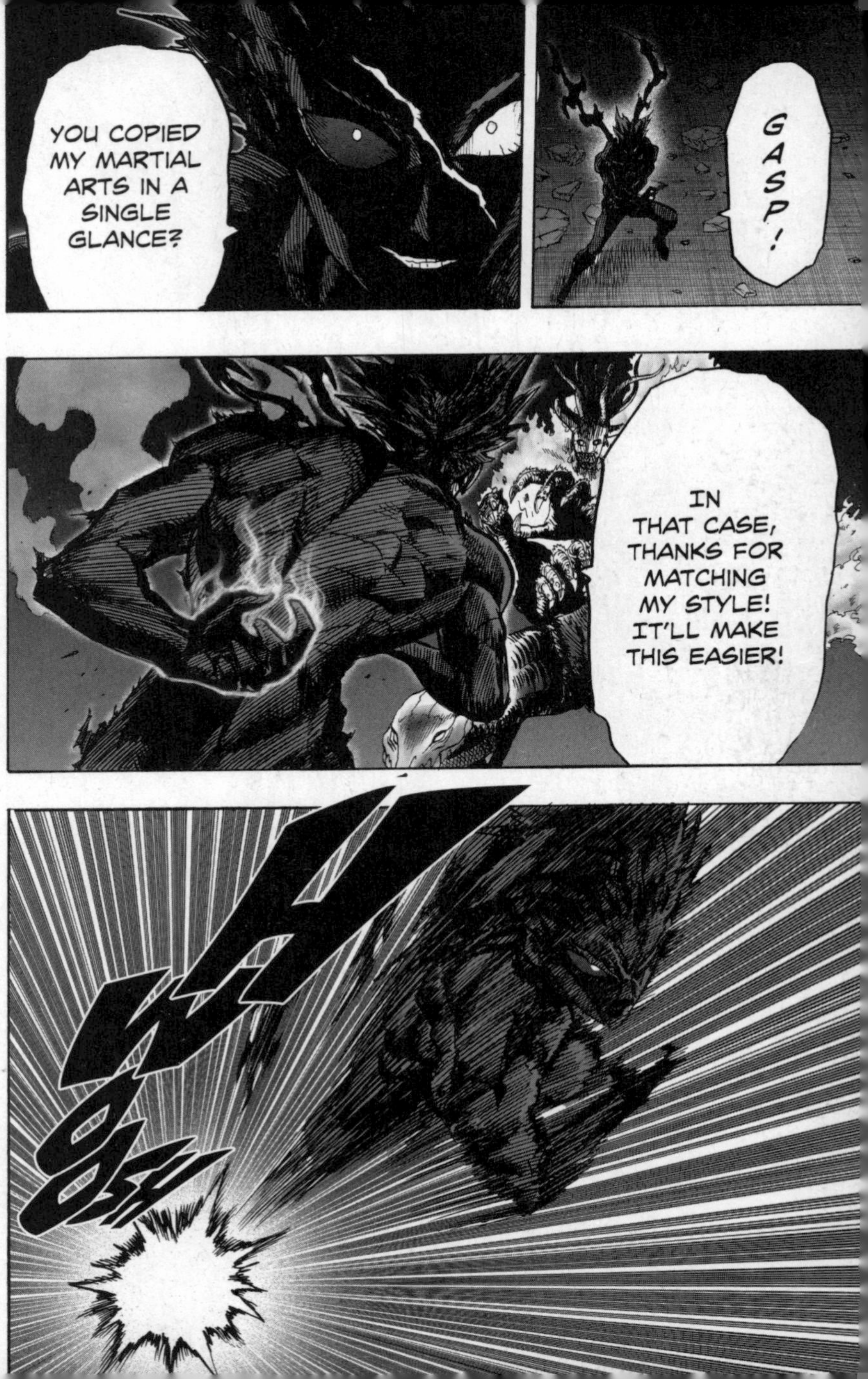
GASP!
YOU COPIED MY MARTIAL ARTS IN A SINGLE GLANCE?
IN THAT CASE, THANKS FOR MATCHING MY STYLE! IT'LL MAKE THIS EASIER!

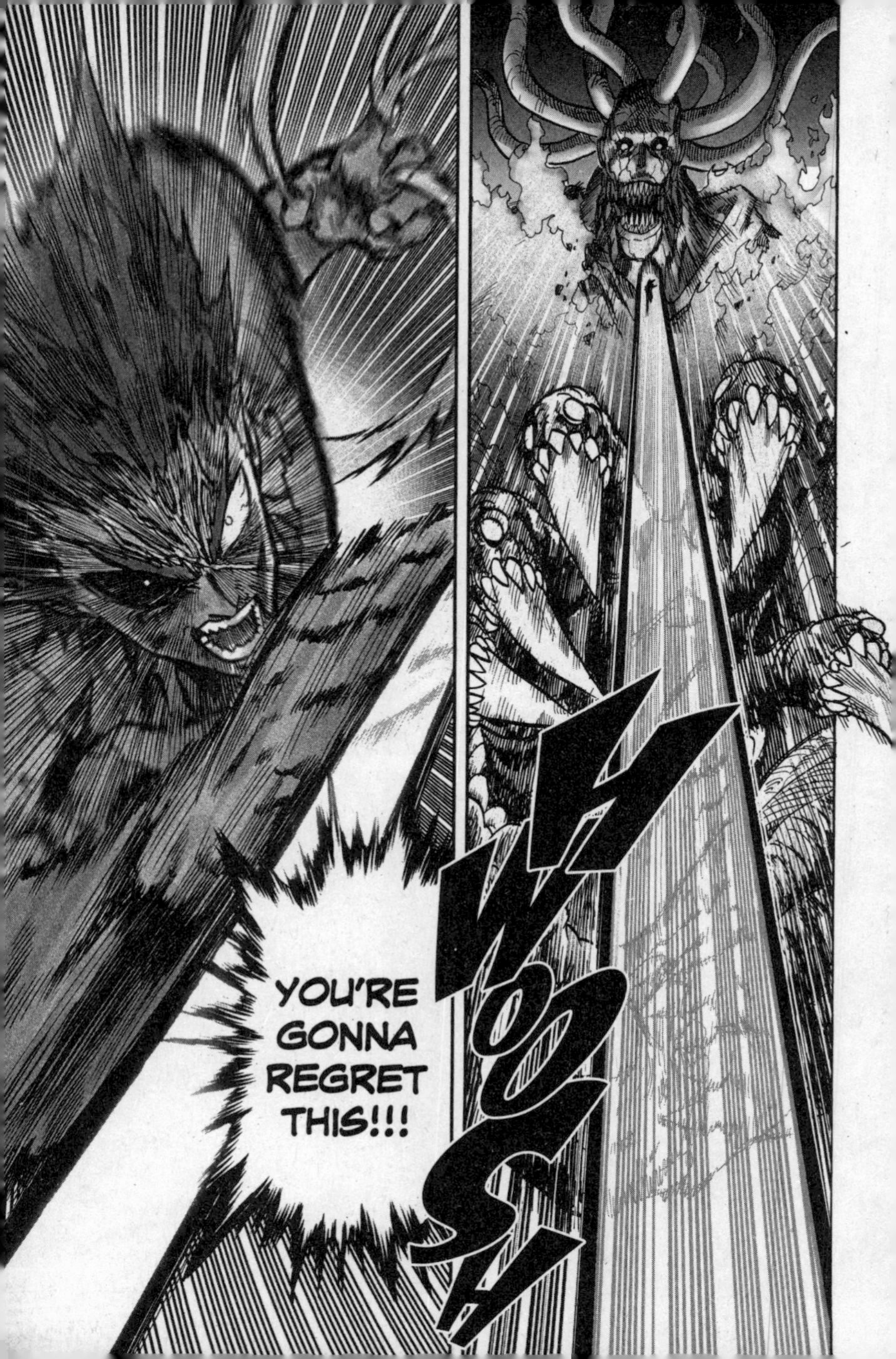
FWOOSH
YOU'RE GONNA REGRET THIS!!!

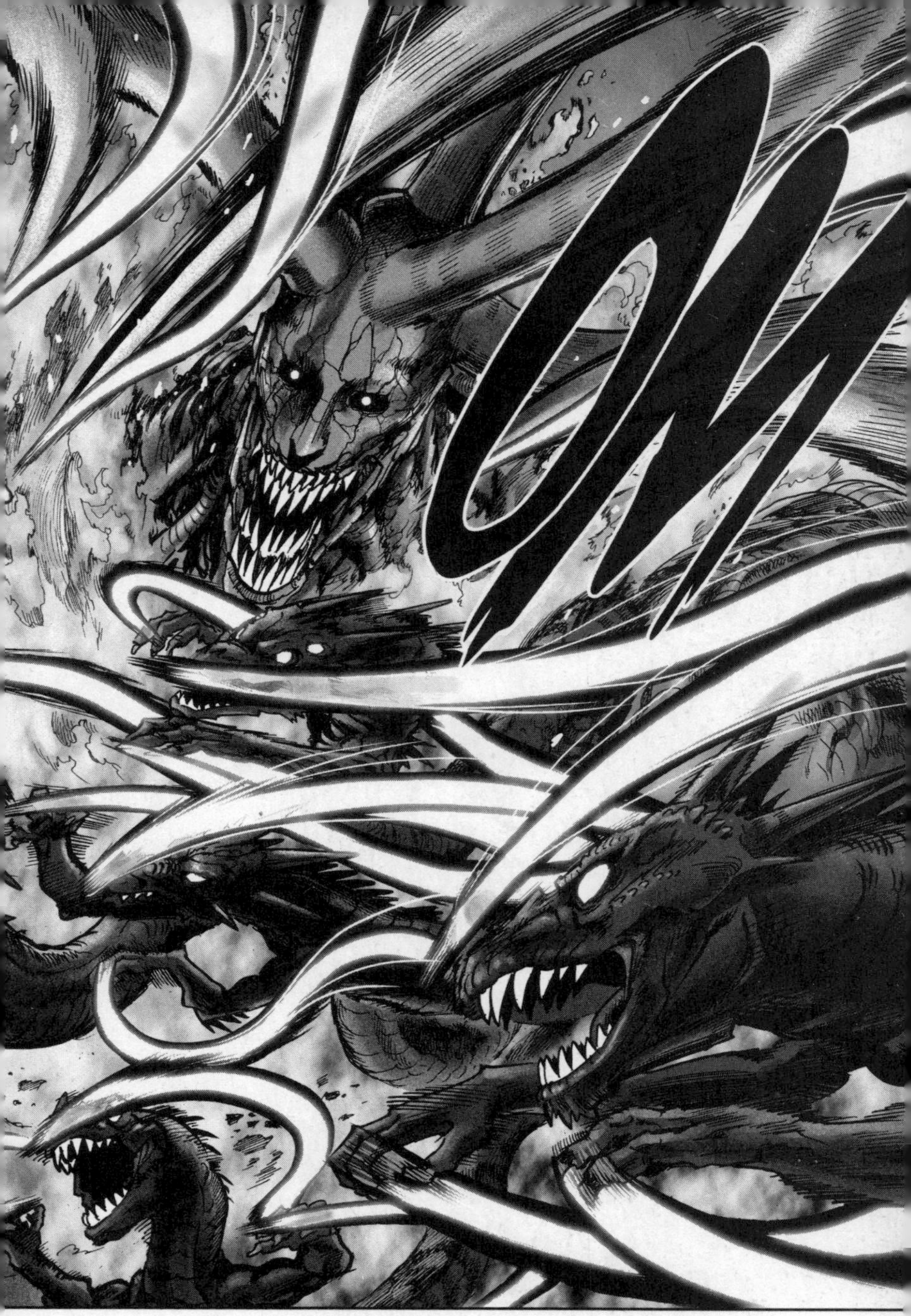

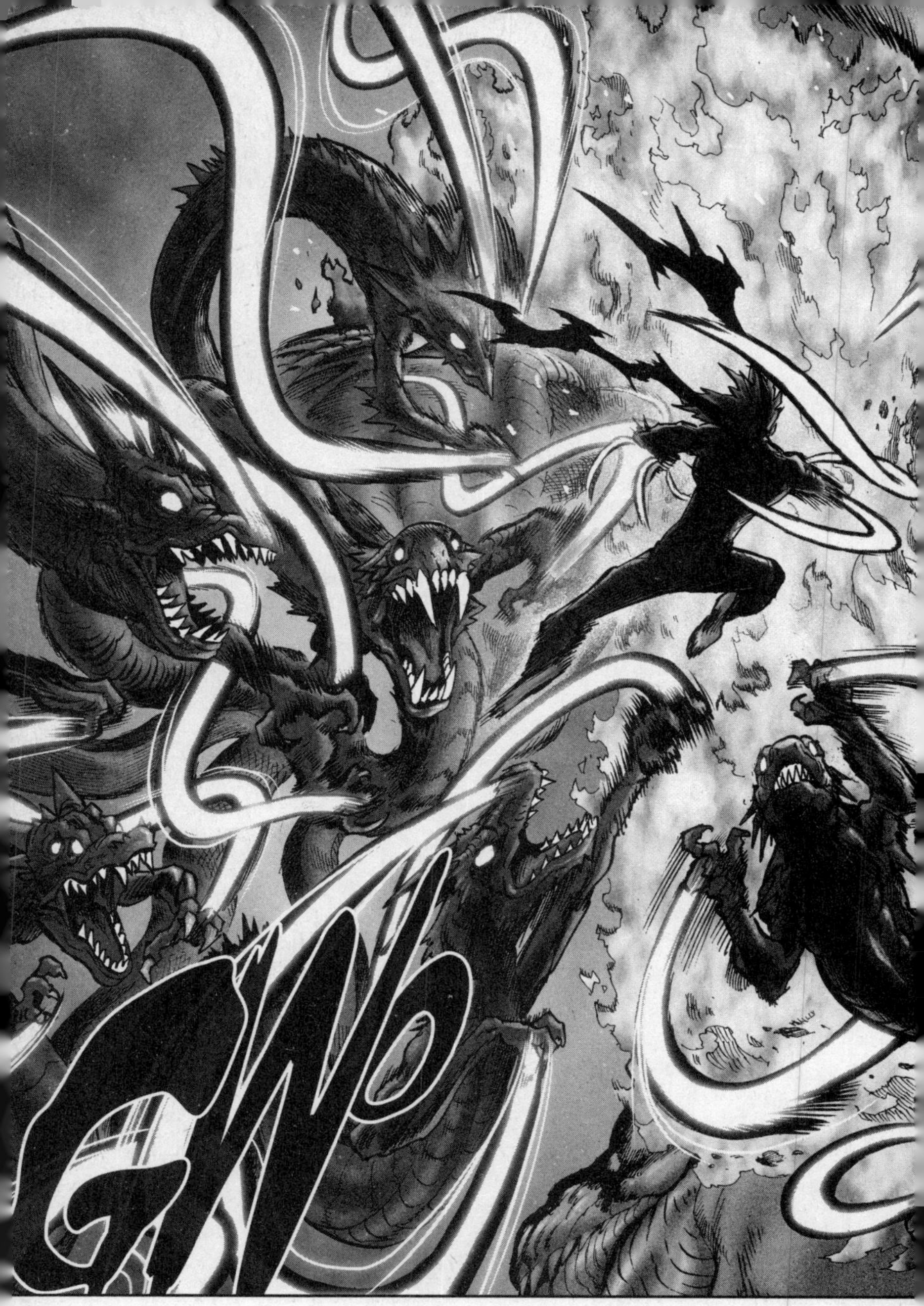

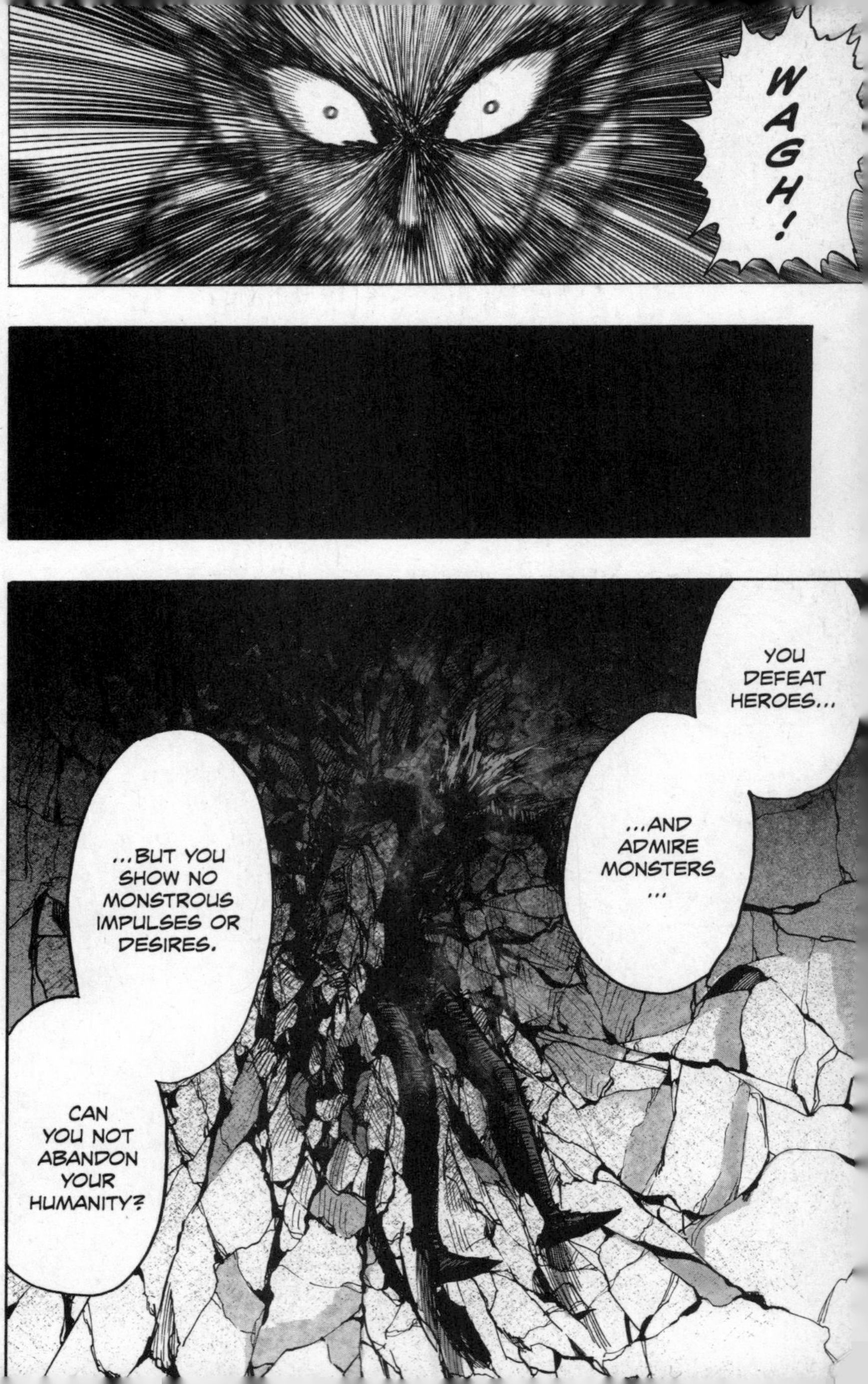
WAGH!
YOU DEFEAT HEROES...
...AND ADMIRE MONSTERS ...
...BUT YOU SHOW NO MONSTROUS IMPULSES OR DESIRES.
CAN YOU NOT ABANDON YOUR HUMANITY?

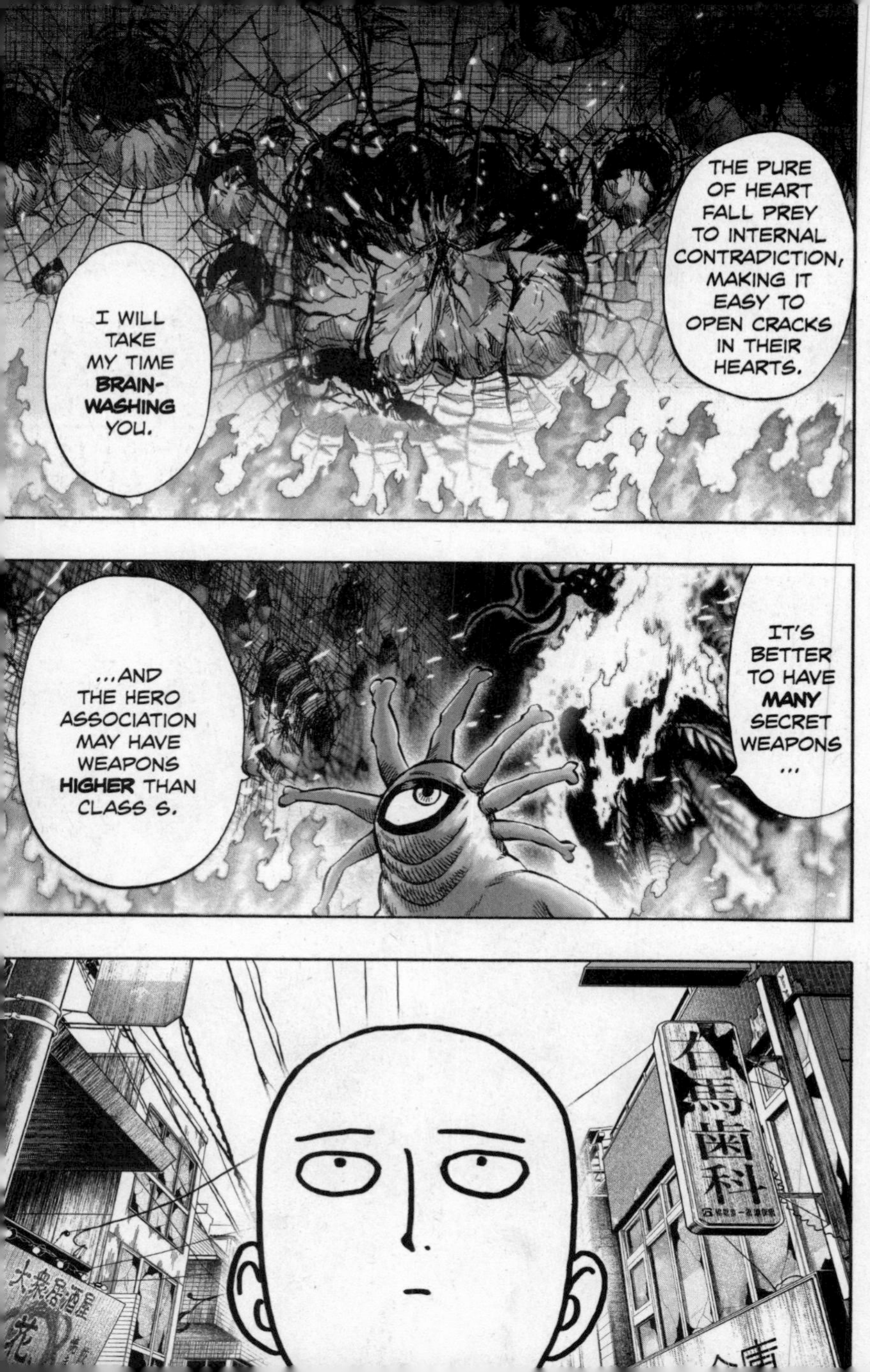
THE PURE OF HEART FALL PREY TO INTERNAL CONTRADICTION, MAKING IT EASY TO OPEN CRACKS IN THEIR HEARTS.
I WILL TAKE MY TIME BRAIN-WASHING YOU.
IT'S BETTER TO HAVE MANY SECRET WEAPONS ...
...AND THE HERO ASSOCIATION MAY HAVE WEAPONS HIGHER THAN CLASS S.
大衆居酒屋
花

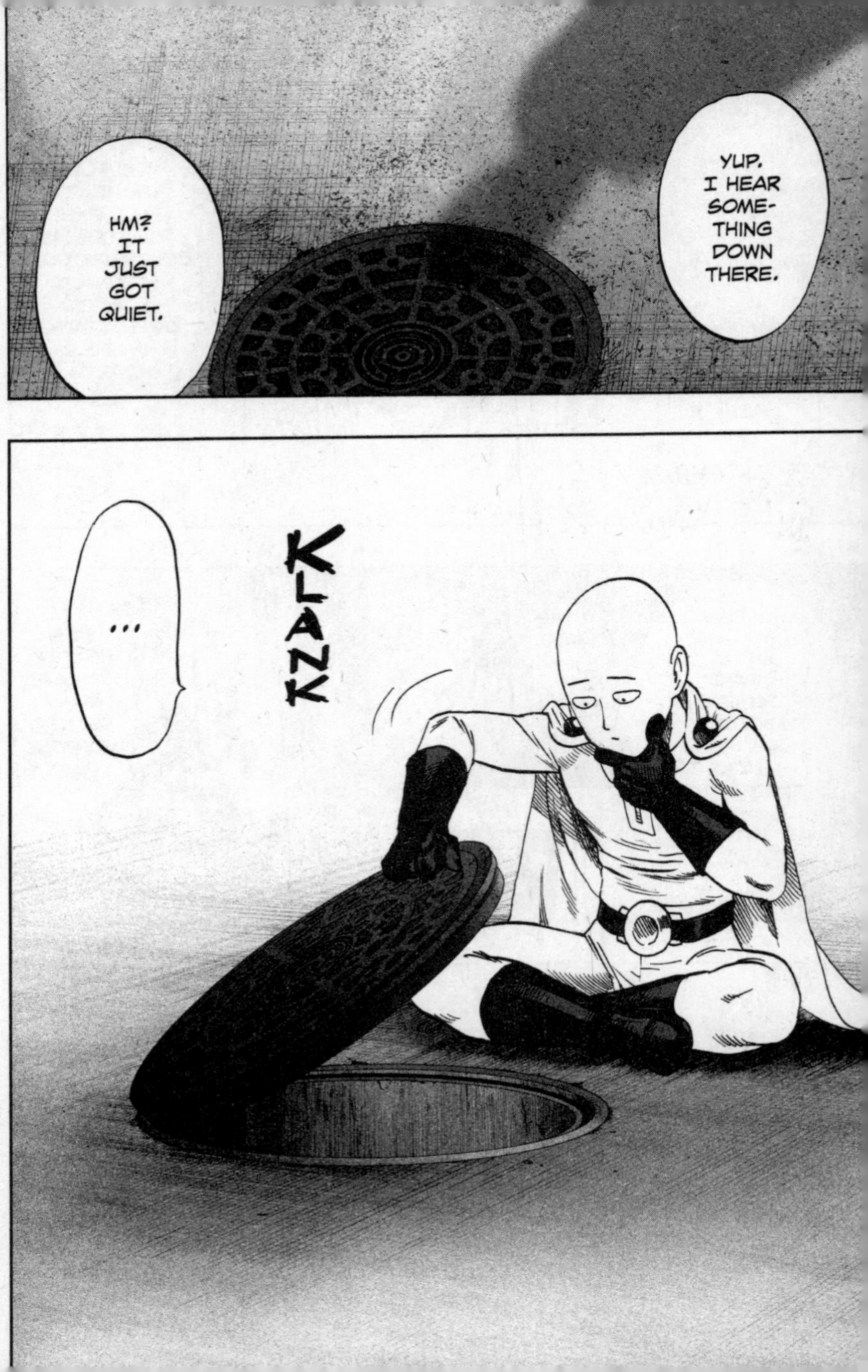
YUP. I HEAR SOME- THING DOWN THERE.
HM? IT JUST GOT QUIET.
KLANK
...

BONUS MANGA: REALITY PUNCH

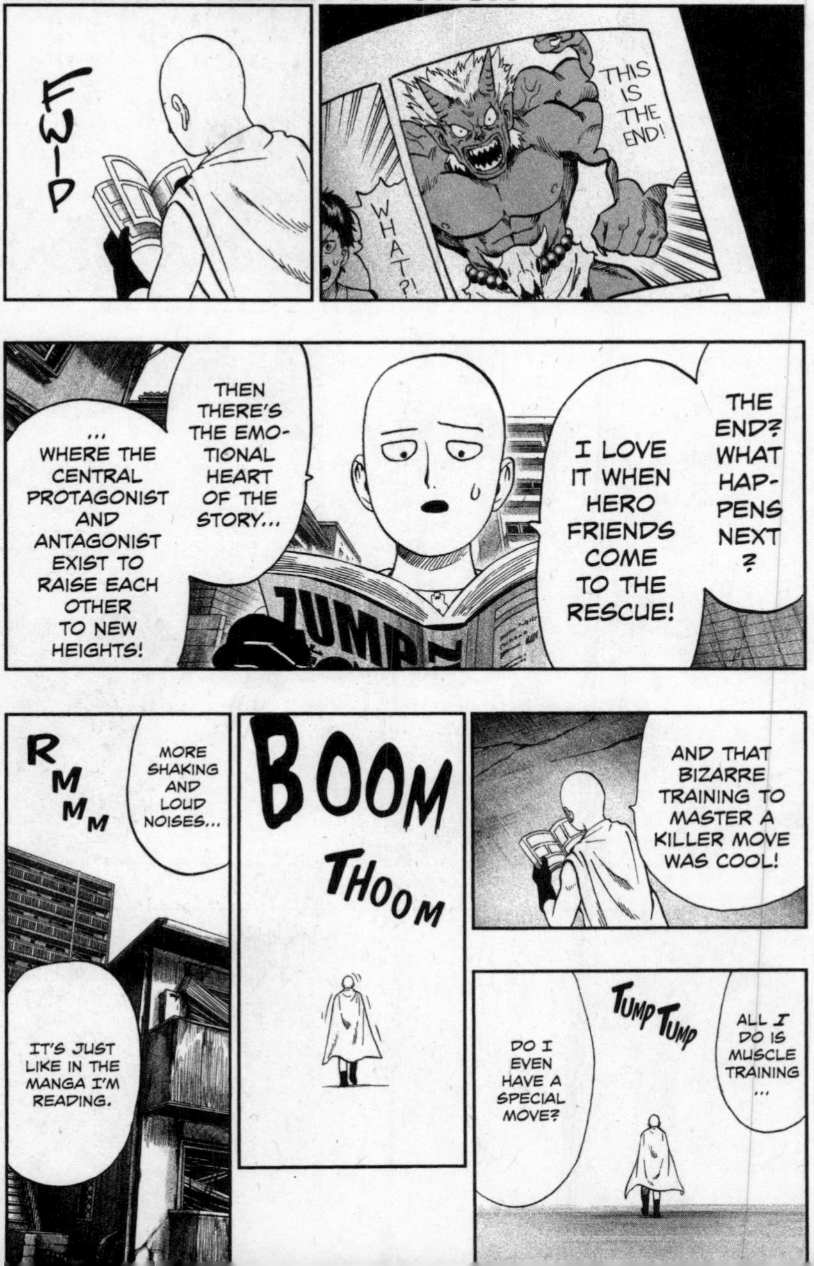
THIS IS THE END!
WHAT?!
FWIP
THE END? WHAT HAPPENS NEXT?
I LOVE IT WHEN HERO FRIENDS COME TO THE RESCUE!
THEN THERE'S THE EMOTIONAL HEART OF THE STORY...
...WHERE THE CENTRAL PROTAGONIST AND ANTAGONIST EXIST TO RAISE EACH OTHER TO NEW HEIGHTS!
AND THAT BIZARRE TRAINING TO MASTER A KILLER MOVE WAS COOL!
ALL I DO IS MUSCLE TRAINING...
TUMP TUMP
DO I EVEN HAVE A SPECIAL MOVE?
BOOM
THOOM
RMMM
MORE SHAKING AND LOUD NOISES...
IT'S JUST LIKE IN THE MANGA I'M READING.

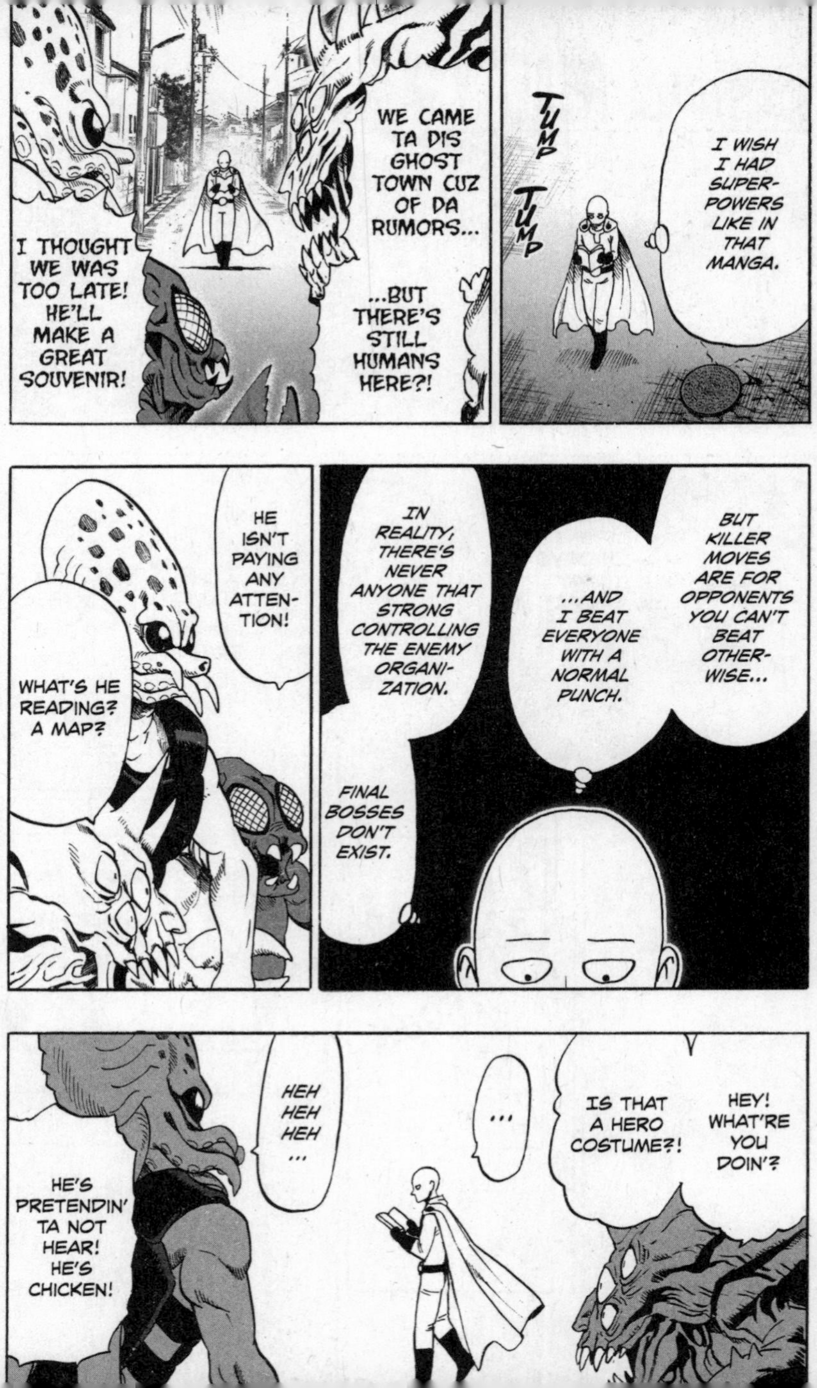
TUMP
TUMP
I WISH I HAD SUPER-POWERS LIKE IN THAT MANGA.
WE CAME TA DIS GHOST TOWN CUZ OF DA RUMORS...
...BUT THERE'S STILL HUMANS HERE?!
I THOUGHT WE WAS TOO LATE! HE'LL MAKE A GREAT SOUVENIR!
BUT KILLER MOVES ARE FOR OPPONENTS YOU CAN'T BEAT OTHER-WISE...
...AND I BEAT EVERYONE WITH A NORMAL PUNCH.
IN REALITY, THERE'S NEVER ANYONE THAT STRONG CONTROLLING THE ENEMY ORGANI-ZATION.
FINAL BOSSES DON'T EXIST.
HE ISN'T PAYING ANY ATTEN-TION!
WHAT'S HE READING? A MAP?
HEY! WHAT'RE YOU DOIN'?
IS THAT A HERO COSTUME?!
...
HEH HEH HEH ...
HE'S PRETENDIN' TA NOT HEAR! HE'S CHICKEN!

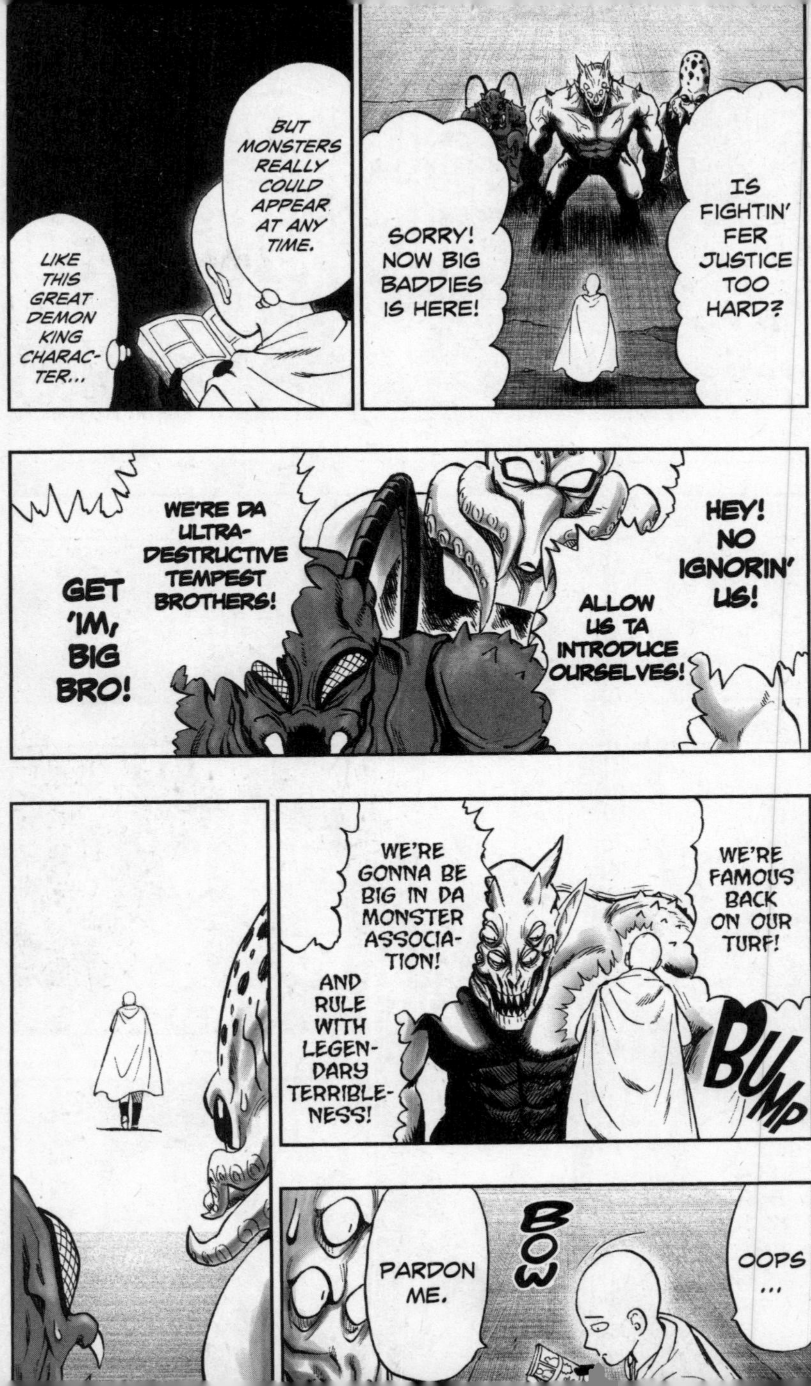
IS FIGHTIN' FER JUSTICE TOO HARD?
SORRY! NOW BIG BADDIES IS HERE!
BUT MONSTERS REALLY COULD APPEAR AT ANY TIME.
LIKE THIS GREAT DEMON KING CHARACTER...
HEY! NO IGNORIN' US!
ALLOW US TA INTRODUCE OURSELVES!
WE'RE DA ULTRA-DESTRUCTIVE TEMPEST BROTHERS!
GET 'IM, BIG BRO!
WE'RE FAMOUS BACK ON OUR TURF!
WE'RE GONNA BE BIG IN DA MONSTER ASSOCIATION!
AND RULE WITH LEGENDARY TERRIBLENESS!
BUMP
OOPS...
BOW
PARDON ME.

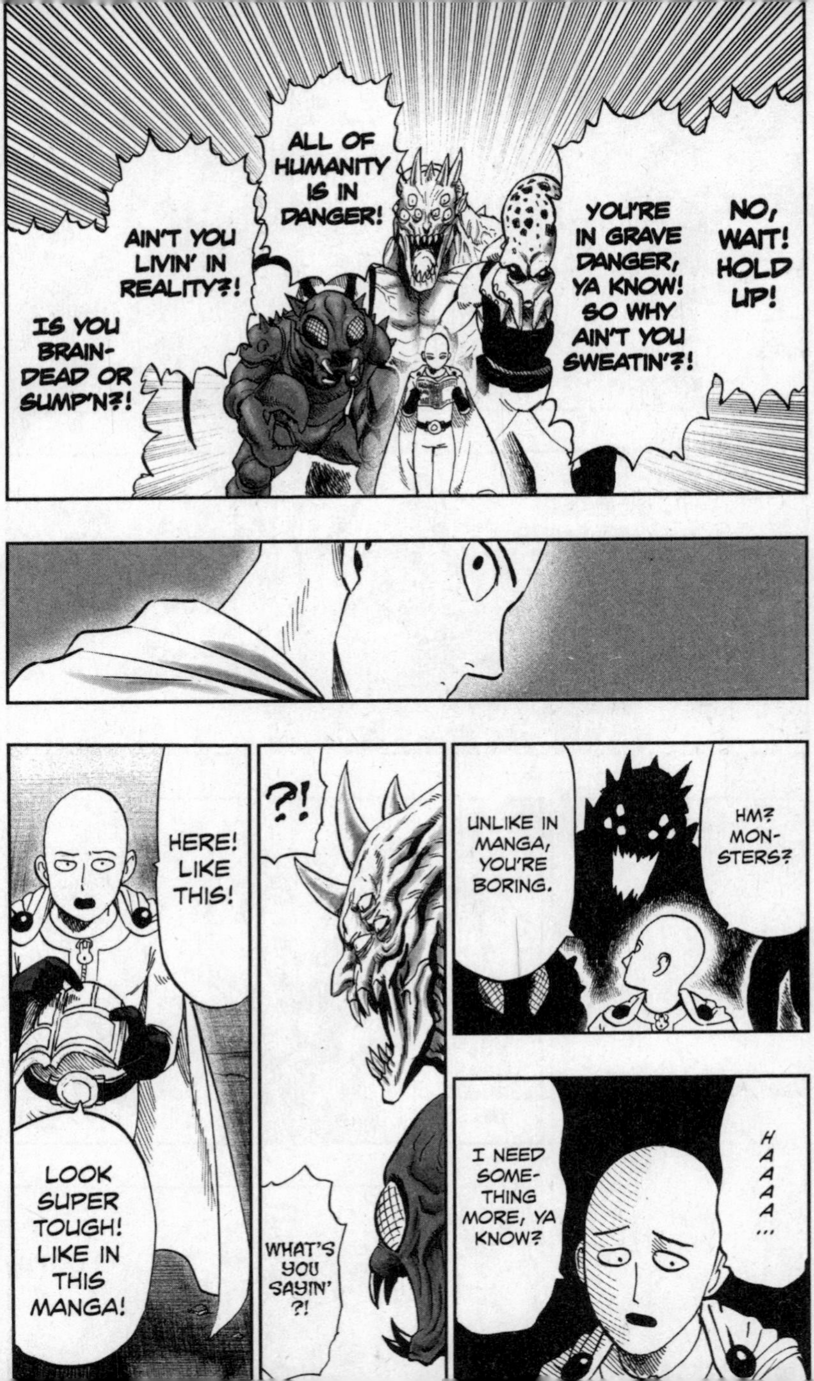
NO, WAIT! HOLD UP!
YOU'RE IN GRAVE DANGER, YA KNOW! SO WHY AIN'T YOU SWEATIN'?!
ALL OF HUMANITY IS IN DANGER!
AIN'T YOU LIVIN' IN REALITY?!
IS YOU BRAIN-DEAD OR SUMP'N?!
HM? MON-STERS?
UNLIKE IN MANGA, YOU'RE BORING.
HAAAA...
I NEED SOME-THING MORE, YA KNOW?
?!
WHAT'S YOU SAYIN' ?!
HERE! LIKE THIS!
LOOK SUPER TOUGH! LIKE IN THIS MANGA!

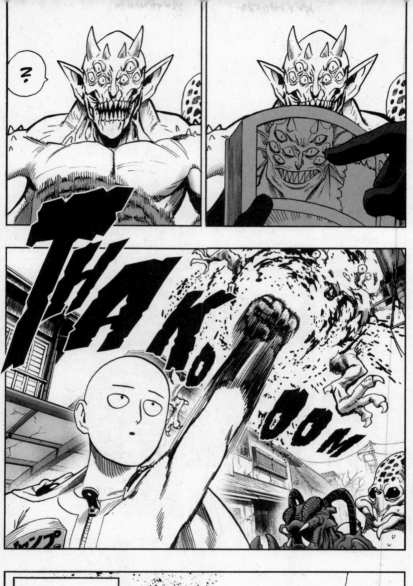

The other
two went
back to
their turf.

I
KNEW IT.
HAAA...

19 All My Cabbage (End)

END NOTES

PAGE 41, PANEL 3:
The character on King's hat means "king."

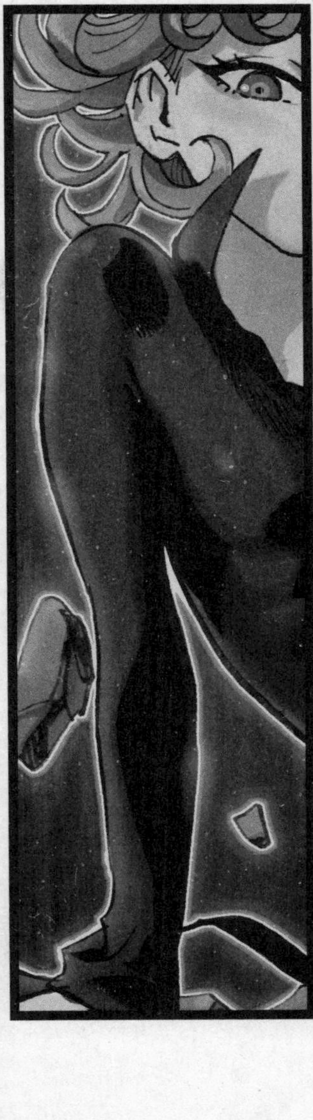

ONE-PUNCH MAN
VOLUME 19
SHONEN JUMP MANGA EDITION

STORY BY | ONE
ART BY | YUSUKE MURATA

TRANSLATION | JOHN WERRY
TOUCH-UP ART AND LETTERING | JAMES GAUBATZ
DESIGN | SHAWN CARRICO
SHONEN JUMP SERIES EDITOR | JOHN BAE
GRAPHIC NOVEL EDITOR | JENNIFER LEBLANC

Printed in the U.S.A.

Published by VIZ Media, LLC
P.O. Box 77010
San Francisco, CA 94107

10 9 8 7 6 5 4 3 2 1
First printing, March 2020

VIZ MEDIA
viz.com

SHONEN JUMP
shonenjump.com

RATED T TEEN ratings.viz.com

PARENTAL ADVISORY
ONE-PUNCH MAN is rated T for Teen and is recommended for ages 13 and up. This volume contains realistic and fantasy violence.

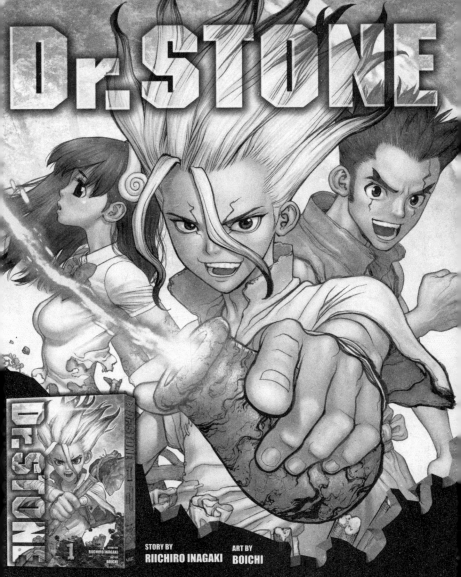

Dr.STONE

STORY BY
RIICHIRO INAGAKI

ART BY
BOICHI

One fateful day, all of humanity turned to stone. Many millennia later, Taiju frees himself from petrification and finds himself surrounded by statues. The situation looks grim—until he runs into his science-loving friend Senku! Together they plan to restart

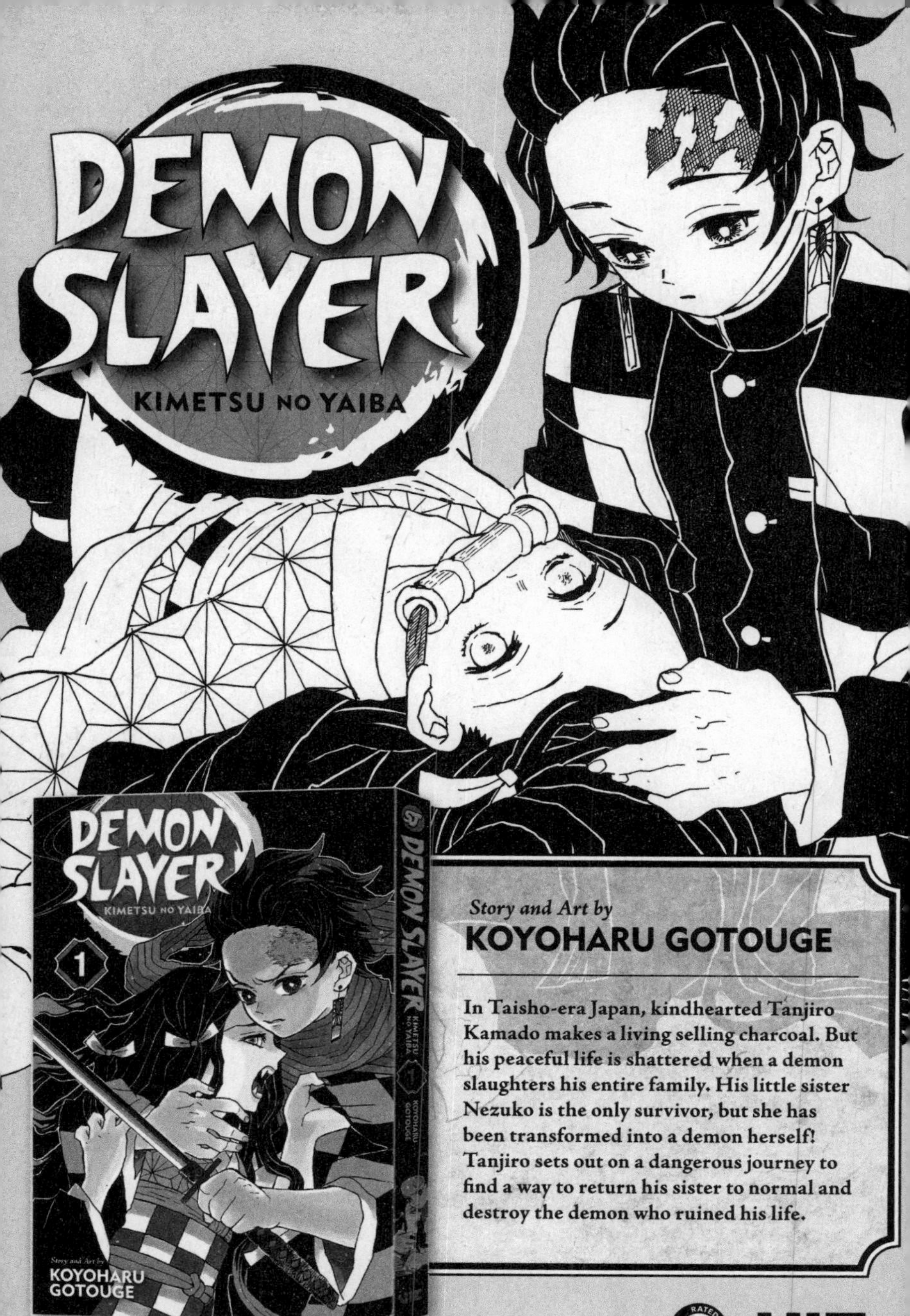
DEMON SLAYER
KIMETSU NO YAIBA
DEMON SLAYER
KIMETSU NO YAIBA
1
Story and Art by
KOYOHARU GOTOUGE
Story and Art by
KOYOHARU GOTOUGE
In Taisho-era Japan, kindhearted Tanjiro Kamado makes a living selling charcoal. But his peaceful life is shattered when a demon slaughters his entire family. His little sister Nezuko is the only survivor, but she has been transformed into a demon herself! Tanjiro sets out on a dangerous journey to find a way to return his sister to normal and destroy the demon who ruined his life.
RATED T TEEN
VIZ

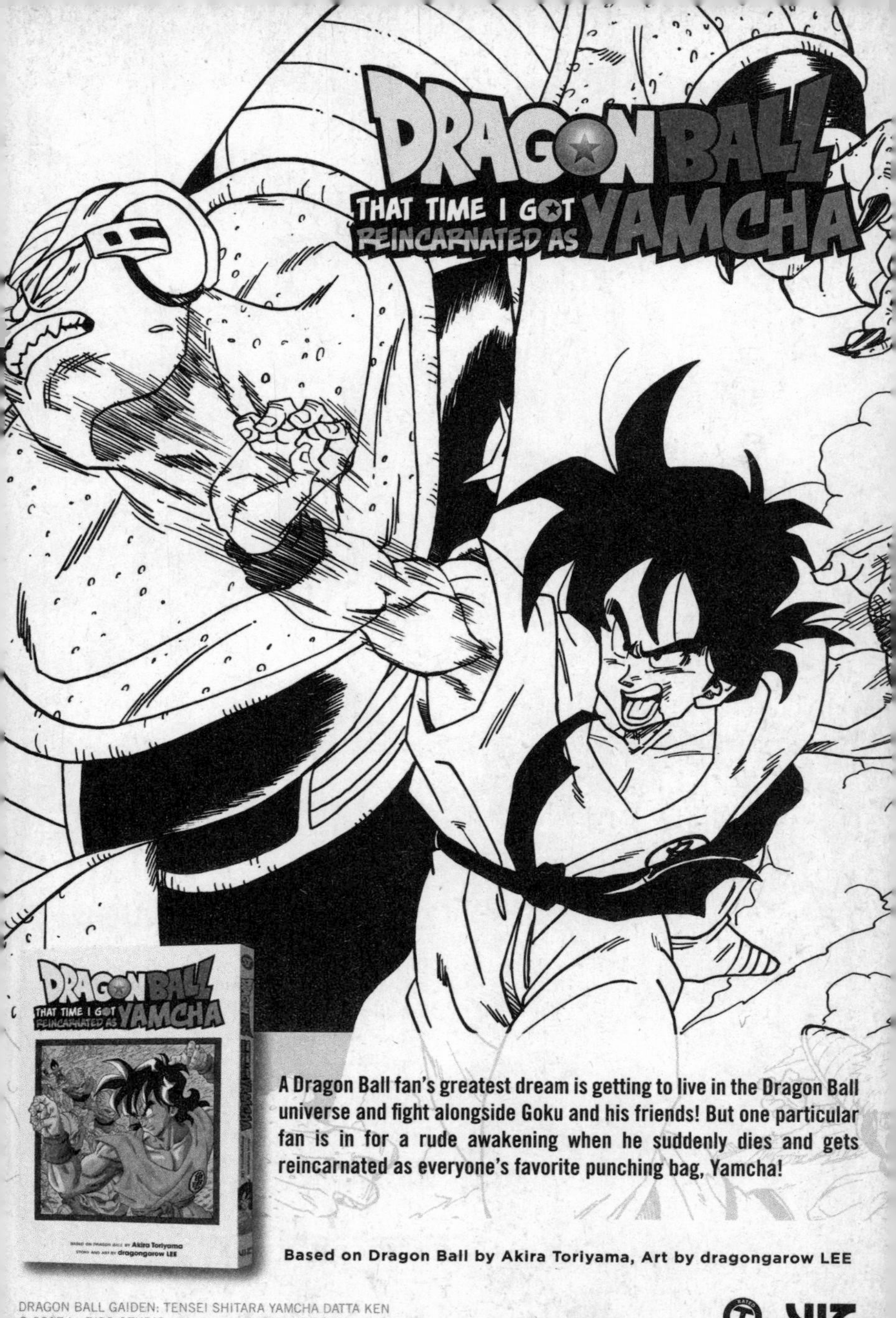
DRAGON BALL
THAT TIME I GOT REINCARNATED AS YAMCHA
DRAGON BALL
THAT TIME I GOT REINCARNATED AS YAMCHA
A Dragon Ball fan's greatest dream is getting to live in the Dragon Ball universe and fight alongside Goku and his friends! But one particular fan is in for a rude awakening when he suddenly dies and gets reincarnated as everyone's favorite punching bag, Yamcha!
Based on Dragon Ball by Akira Toriyama, Art by dragongarow LEE
RATED T TEEN
VIZ

Black ✳ Clover

STORY & ART BY YŪKI TABATA

Asta is a young boy who dreams of becoming the greatest mage in the kingdom. Only one problem—he can't use any magic! Luckily for Asta, he receives the incredibly rare five-leaf clover grimoire that gives him the power of anti-magic. Can someone who can't use magic really become the Wizard King? One thing's for sure—Asta will never give up!

viz media
www.viz.com

ASTRA
LOST IN SPACE

CAN EIGHT TEENAGERS FIND THEIR WAY HOME FROM 5,000 LIGHT-YEARS AWAY?

It's the year 2063, and interstellar space travel has become the norm. Eight students from Caird High School and one child set out on a routine planet camp excursion. While there, the students are mysteriously transported 5,000 light-years away to the middle of nowhere! Will they ever make it back home?!

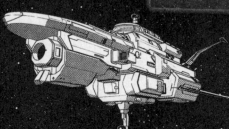

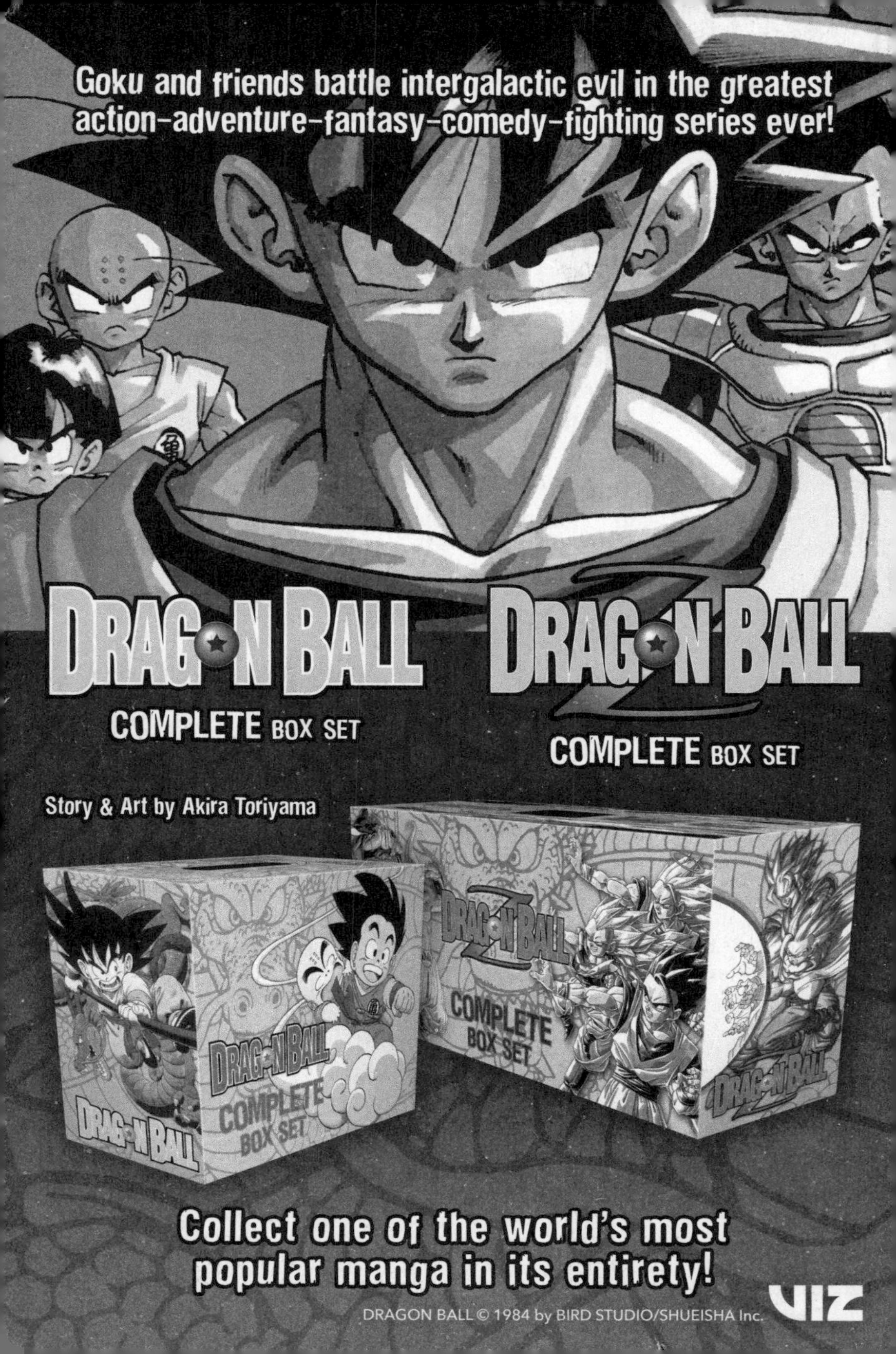
Goku and friends battle intergalactic evil in the greatest action-adventure-fantasy-comedy-fighting series ever!
DRAGON BALL
COMPLETE BOX SET
DRAGON BALL Z
COMPLETE BOX SET
Story & Art by Akira Toriyama
DRAGON BALL
COMPLETE BOX SET
DRAGON BALL
DRAGON BALL Z
COMPLETE BOX SET
DRAGON BALL Z
Collect one of the world's most popular manga in its entirety!
VIZ
DRAGON BALL © 1984 by BIRD STUDIO/SHUEISHA Inc.

STOP!
YOU'RE READING THE WRONG WAY!
★ ONE-PUNCH MAN READS FROM RIGHT TO LEFT, STARTING IN THE UPPER-RIGHT CORNER. JAPANESE IS READ FROM RIGHT TO LEFT, MEANING THAT ACTION, SOUND EFFECTS, AND WORD-BALLOON ORDER ARE COMPLETELY REVERSED FROM ENGLISH ORDER.

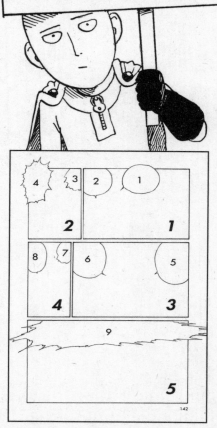